THE PERSISTENCE OF EVIL

A Cultural, Literary and Theological Analysis

Fintan Lyons O.S.B.

t&tclark
LONDON • NEW YORK • OXFORD • NEW DELHI • SYDNEY

T&T CLARK
Bloomsbury Publishing Plc
50 Bedford Square, London, WC1B 3DP, UK
1385 Broadway, New York, NY 10018, USA
29 Earlsfort Terrace, Dublin 2, Ireland

BLOOMSBURY, T&T CLARK and the T&T Clark logo are trademarks
of Bloomsbury Publishing Plc

First published in Great Britain 2023

Copyright © Fintan Lyons O.S.B., 2023

Fintan Lyons O.S.B. has asserted his right under the Copyright, Designs and Patents
Act, 1988, to be identified as Author of this work.

For legal purposes the Acknowledgements on p. ix constitute an extension
of this copyright page.

Cover image: *Faust and Mephistopheles on the Blocksberg*, 1826, Eugene Delacroix.
Thunderstruck/Alamy Stock Photo

All rights reserved. No part of this publication may be reproduced or transmitted
in any form or by any means, electronic or mechanical, including photocopying,
recording, or any information storage or retrieval system, without prior
permission in writing from the publishers.

Bloomsbury Publishing Plc does not have any control over, or responsibility for,
any third-party websites referred to or in this book. All internet addresses given in this
book were correct at the time of going to press. The author and publisher regret any
inconvenience caused if addresses have changed or sites have ceased to exist,
but can accept no responsibility for any such changes.

A catalogue record for this book is available from the British Library.

Library of Congress Control Number: 2023939078

ISBN: HB: 978-0-5677-1012-3
PB: 978-0-5677-1011-6
ePDF: 978-0-5677-1014-7
ePUB: 978-0-5677-1013-0

Typeset by Newgen KnowledgeWorks Pvt. Ltd., Chennai, India
Printed and bound in Great Britain

To find out more about our authors and books visit www.bloomsbury.com
and sign up for our newsletters.

CONTENTS

Acknowledgements ix

INTRODUCTION 1

Part I
THEODICY

Chapter 1
GOD OR EVIL? 9
  Irenaeus (+202) 11
  Augustine (354–430) 15
  Thomas Aquinas (1225–74) 19
  John Hick (1922–2012) 23
  Alvin Plantinga (1932–) 30

Chapter 2
GOD AND EVIL 35
  Friedrich Nietzsche (1844–1900) 35
  Richard Dawkins (1941–) 36
  Divine Hiddenness 37
  Rudolf Otto (1869–1937) 38
  The *Kabbalah* 40
  Karl Barth (1886–1968) 42
  Karl Rahner (1904–84) 51
  Empirical science 54

Part II
A CULTURAL, HISTORICAL AND LITERARY SURVEY

Chapter 3
DOES THE DEVIL EXIST? A PERSISTENT BELIEF 61
  Satan in the Old Testament 62
  The devil in the New Testament and New Testament times 64
  The devil in the life of the early Christian community 70
  The devil in the Patristic Era 76

Chapter 4
STEPPING STONES TO EUROPE   87
  Christian spirituality in Western Europe   87
  Temptation as internal struggle   95

Chapter 5
DEMONOLOGY IN MEDIEVAL LITERARY CULTURE   108
  The plastic and other arts of the Middle Ages and beyond   108
  The evolving culture and the devil's continuing presence evidenced in
      literature   118
  The Mystery Plays   119
  The rise of mysticism   123

Chapter 6
THE REFORMATION: TWO MAGISTERIAL REFORMERS   126
  Martin Luther (1483–1546)   126
  John Calvin (1509–64)   137
  De-sacralisation   148

Chapter 7
THE CATHOLIC REFORM: THREE OUTSTANDING REFORMERS AND
CONFLICT WITH THE DEVIL   151
  Saint Ignatius Loyola (1491–1556)   152
  Saint Teresa of Ávila (1515–82)   161
  Saint John of the Cross (1542–91)   175

Chapter 8
THE DEVIL IN THE ERA OF MODERNITY: POETRY AND LITERATURE
IN A NEW AGE   184
  Christopher Marlowe (1564–93)   184
  Society's acceptance of the devil's existence   189
  The preternatural   190
  Seventeenth-century demonology   191
  Puritanism and de-sacralisation of the culture   191
  John Milton (1608–74)   192
  Satan's dismissal   197
  Johann Wolfgang Goethe (1749–1832)   197
  The Romantic Movement   199
  The Romantic Movement in the United States   201
  The decline of Romanticism   205

Chapter 9
TWENTIETH-CENTURY CHRONICLES OF EVIL   212
  The First World War   212

The War Poets	213
Realignment of forces and regional conflicts	224

Part III
EXORCISM: A HISTORICAL AND THEOLOGICAL ANALYSIS

Chapter 10
EXORCISM: THE HISTORICAL CONTEXT ... 247
  Exorcism in the early centuries ... 247
  From charismatic to official exorcism ... 250
  The Reformation churches and exorcism ... 255
  History of the Catholic *Rite of Exorcism* ... 257
  Anglicanism ... 267
  Contemporary theological perspectives and exorcism ... 269
  Ecumenical perspectives ... 274
  The current growth of exorcisms ... 275

Chapter 11
TOWARDS A THEOLOGICAL ASSESSMENT OF EXORCISM ... 279
  The current Catholic *Rite of Exorcism* ... 279
  Possession, its extent and theological meaning ... 280
  Personal relations in theological perspective ... 281
  Relationships in exorcism: Theological perspective ... 286
  Jesus' exorcisms ... 286
  The Church's exorcism today ... 287
  Current pastoral practice ... 290
  The relevance of free will ... 301
  Christian reassurance ... 304

Chapter 12
CONCLUSION ... 306
  Evil: Polarised views ... 306
  Fundamental theology ... 307
  The devil: Contrasting conclusions ... 308
  Social sin ... 310
  Paul Tillich (1886–1965) ... 311
  Moltmann circles ... 313
  Psychological considerations ... 322
  C. G. Jung (1875–1961) ... 324

Appendix: Towards a psychological analysis of possession and exorcism ... 327
  Possession understood psychologically ... 327
  Relationships in exorcism: A hybrid perspective incorporating the
    psychological ... 329

Human acts of evil and the enablers for such behaviour 329
Attempting to merge the psychological with the theological 330

Bibliography 333
Index of Names 353
Index of Subjects 359

ACKNOWLEDGEMENTS

I'm deeply grateful for the support and active assistance I have received in completing this book from my editors at Bloomsbury, Anna Turton and Sophie Beardsworth; Dr James Dixon of the NHS for his psychological observations; the Librarians of Glenstal Abbey and MIC University of Limerick; Dr Anna Gannon; Dr John O'Callaghan.

The Scripture quotations contained herein are from the New Revised Standard Version Bible: Catholic Edition copyright © 1993 and 1989 by the Division of Christian Education of the National Council of the Churches of Christ in the USA. Used by permission. All rights reserved.

INTRODUCTION

It is a commonplace that what the news media convey is more likely to be bad news than good. All the possible ways in which things go wrong are daily reported – natural disasters as well as suffering arising from human motives. The word 'evil' applies to many instances of unacceptable happenings varying in depth and complexity, from the bearable to the most horrific, and is a conveniently comprehensive term to indicate that all is not well with the world. To use the word in relation to an act is to use it as an adjective, to use it as a noun is to go a step further and attribute existence to some kind of force with continuous existence, something that persists. This situation is often articulated as 'the problem of evil', as it is natural for the human mind to ponder on what can make life so difficult for many, generating a sense of injustice done, making people ask why the evil goes on so long, and wish for an explanation as to why things are as they are.

> The problem consists … in the fact that instead of serving a constructive purpose pain and misery seem to be distributed in random and meaningless ways, with the result that suffering is often undeserved and often falls upon people in amounts exceeding anything that could be rationally intended.[1]

There is a problem here not only for those who believe in God but also for those who do not, but it is particularly pressing for those who do, as believers generally start from the standpoint of God as all-good and loving, who created and sustains all creatures in an outflow of goodness and love. 'Where is God in this?', they will ask. Experience of evil in so many people's lives, along with the widespread observation of its persistence by others who are fortunate not to be noticeably affected by it, these facts raise questions not only about evil's origins but also about the existence of God.

In the centuries when it was 'virtually impossible not to believe in God',[2] a central question for Christian, Jewish and Islamic thinkers was why had God permitted evil to exist in a world created out of the divine beneficence. The early Christian apologist Lactantius (240–320) in his tract *On the Wrath of God*, written against

---

1. John Hick, *Evil and the God of Love* (Glasgow: Collins Fount Paperbacks, 1979), 369.
2. Charles Taylor, *A Secular Age* (Cambridge, MA: Harvard University Press, 2007), 25.

the Epicureans, held that 'if there were no evil, no danger, nothing, in short, that could harm man, the whole matter of wisdom would be removed. ... Thus that argument of Epicurus is dissolved where he says':

> God either wishes to take away evils and is unable; or he is able, and is unwilling; or he is neither willing nor able, or he is both willing and able. If he is willing and is unable, he is feeble – which is not in accordance with the character of God. If he is able and unwilling, he is envious, which is equally at variance with God; if he is neither willing nor able, he is both envious and feeble, and therefore not God; if he is both willing and able, which alone is suitable to God, from what source then are evils? Or why does he not remove them?[3]

For Lactantius, the problem was solved in light of the important human need for wisdom. Many centuries later the philosopher David Hume (1711–76), in his posthumous *Dialogues Concerning Natural Religion* (1779), drew, as Lactantius did, on the Greek philosopher Epicurus. He posed the problem again:

> Is he willing to prevent evil, but not able? Then he is impotent. Is he able but not willing, then he is malevolent. Is he both able and willing? Whence then is evil?[4]

The approach of Hume and his supposed fellow conversationalists was to search for rational arguments from a deistic perspective in favour of the existence of a god, and the problem of evil arose in the discussion.

Thus stated, the dilemma appears to leave the problem of evil insoluble. But over many centuries it was not couched in such blunt terms by Christian philosophical theologians; they chose rather to deal with the acceptance of the persistence of evil in a way that vindicated the justice and goodness of God, a theorising to which the

---

3. Lactantius, *On the Anger of God c.* 13 in *Lactantius. The Minor Works*, Mary Francis McDonald O.P., trans. (Washington, DC: Catholic University of Washington Press, 1965), 92–3. The work was in the form of an argument against the Epicurean assertion about evil, and Lactantius made no reference to the devil as source of evil, but in his *Firmiani Lactantii Epitome Institionum Divinarum (Epitome of the Divine Institutes)* he devoted chapter 28 to daemons and their machinations in the world, in a blanket condemnation of what was classically considered sources or daemons of inspiration (London: S.P.C.K., 1950, 77): 'By their deceits they have plunged the human race into darkness, in order that by suppression of the truth, the name of the great and only God may be forgotten.'

4. David Hume, *Dialogues Concerning Natural Religion* (Buffalo, NY: Prometheus Books, 1989), 84; David Applebaum, *The Vision of Hume* (Rockport, MA: Element Books, 1996), 7–8: 'He had begun in dialogue form, around 1750, a work that dealt directly with spiritual insincerity and other questions of religion, but he did not want the work to appear during his lifetime.'

philosopher G. W. Leibniz (1646–1716) gave the name theodicy, from the Greek for God, *theos*, and justice, *diké*.[5]

But the history of theodicy studies shows that in light of the manifest existence of evil, the existence and nature of God also became part of such investigations and was the dominant issue from the late twentieth century. As a result, various subdivisions emerged within the category of theodicy broadly construed. Among them, misotheism, from the Greek, *misos*, meaning hatred, describes those who do not deny God's existence but because of evil feel hatred towards an unjust God. Anti-theodicy goes a step further by rejecting all attempts to justify God given the evil in the world; it rejects the whole theodicy project, though it does not necessarily reject belief in God.[6]

The approach of this work will in the main be to proceed on the basis of both the existence of God and the problem of evil, while taking account in succeeding chapters of the Christian tradition that associates evil with the existence of a malevolent being called the devil. In that regard, it is worth noting that a declaration by John Hick, whose theodicy theory is well known, takes little account of demonic forces when discussing humanly motivated evil:

> I have argued that we ought to reject ... the theory that the world is in the grip of evil powers, so that the dysteleological surplus of human misery is an achievement of demonic malevolence.[7]

The Anglican theologian Austin Farrer (1904–68) was prominent in English scriptural and theological studies in the first half of the twentieth century and accepted Scripture's teaching on the existence of the devil, but he also held it was not necessary to invoke the figure of Satan in discussing the mystery of evil; evil was clearly endemic to human nature, whatever its origin.

> It is difficult to admit that Satan helps an inch towards explaining the origin of moral evil or of spiritual perversity. Real mysteries should not be talked away or glibly rationalised; but the mystery of iniquity is not Satan, it is the sinful human will.[8]

---

5. G. W. Leibniz, *Theodicy: Essays on the Goodness of God, the Freedom of Man and the Origin of Evil*, E. M. Huggard, trans. (London: Routledge and Kegan Paul, 1951). He was noted for his statement, p. 253: 'God is bound by moral necessity to make things in such a manner that there can be nothing better.'

6. See N. N. Trakakis, 'Anti-Theodicy', in *The Cambridge Companion to the Problem of Evil*, Chad Meister and Paul K. Moser, ed. (Cambridge: Cambridge University Press, 2017), 124–43; Chad Meister, *Evil: A Guide for the Perplexed* (New York: Bloomsbury Academic, 2018²), 84

7. Hick, *Evil and the God of Love*, 369.

8. Austin Farrer, *Love Almighty and Ills Unlimited* (London: Collins, 1962), 139. Farrer also stated: 'Whether there are fallen spirits may be open to doubt. We have not met any.

Theodicy in the twentieth century and on into the twenty-first could and did exist as a theological discipline with only God and evil regarded as the two relevant poles in the discussion.

The range of theodicy studies will be briefly surveyed (Chapters 1 and 2), but attention will subsequently be devoted to the persistence of evil as Christianity has understood it: that a malign force exists to which the name Satan or the devil has traditionally been given. It will be noted that the ultimate origin of this force remains a mystery. Evil will be discussed in its historical context – how it has been perceived by spokespeople of the culture, by philosophers and theologians and in literature, for example. It will include contributions from a clinical psychologist, particularly in relation to the crucial phenomenon of the participation of the various parties in the Catholic Church's *Rite of Exorcism*.

While it is true, as indicated above, that without reference to God evil can be discussed from a scientific perspective, behavioural studies coming within the scope of the psychological sciences can also have a useful role in helping believers to make some sense of the persistence of evil, rather than endlessly seeking theoretical answers to the conundrum of the reconciliation of God's existence or goodness with the persistence of evil. In the existential situation of extreme suffering, theoretical considerations on their own may be of little help or perceived relevance, yet a comprehensive discernment is needed. Here, commonality between the theological and psychological perspectives will be availed of in the interests of discernment in Chapters 11 and 12. Discernment has always been important in spiritual experience; here it will be given added significance through the contribution of psychological assessment of human experience to the mutual exchange of insights between the two disciplines. There must be coherence between theory and practice, with joint pastoral care as an outcome.[9]

It is the issue of the perennial nature of evil's existence that calls particularly for an investigation when God's existence as creator is taken into account. The significance of referring to evil as perennial is that despite the Christian belief that with the coming of Christ – the entire Christ event – Satan was defeated, scripture asserts that there was a 'present but not yet' dimension to Christ's victory:

> For he (Christ) must reign until he has put all his enemies under his feet. …
> When all things are subjected to him, then the Son himself will also be subjected
> to the one who put all things in subjection under him, so that God may be all in
> all. (1 Cor. 15.25, 28)

But we can conceive the bare idea, by borrowing from our notion of fallen mankind. Here at least we are up against facts.' Ibid., 149.

9. Alvin Plantinga, *God, Freedom and Evil* (Grand Rapids, MI: Eerdmans, 1977), 64.

The Christian belief

Among the various ways in which the early Christian belief described Christ's salvific work, combat with Satan was a favoured metaphor.[10] This approach was inspired by the fact that the Gospels present his life as a constant struggle against the evils of his time, often identified with Satan, whether manifested in the lives of those who opposed him – and whom he will on occasion describe as evil (Lk. 11.13) – or in encounters with evil spirits that assume the form of a verbal battle. It is clear that the struggle continued to the end and that the first fruits of his victory were realised in his Resurrection, but the war was not over.

Historically, the first and later generations of the Christian community lived in anticipation of the imminent return of Christ, while in the meantime their struggle was 'not against enemies of blood and flesh, but against the rulers, the authorities, against the cosmic powers of the present darkness, against the spiritual forces of evil in the heavenly places' (Eph. 6.12).[11] Though there were occasional expressions of belief that by baptism Christians had 'dominion over the devils', as Hilary of Poitier (315–367) claimed,[12] writers such as Augustine and others, as will be seen in Chapter 3, took the existence and activity of the devil very seriously, while endeavouring also to understand from a philosophical perspective the very nature of evil.

For the Christian, Jesus' ministry, his life, death and resurrection are key to the resolution of the issue of evil, its ultimate defeat. He said he had overcome the world (Jn 16.33) and when lifted up would draw all people to himself (Jn 12.32), but his 'Paschal Mystery', the working out of the plan of salvation, has many aspects which remain mysterious. How does it extend beyond humanity to all of creation? What does it mean to say that the Resurrection of Christ inaugurated a new creation, given that from an empirical perspective the universe forms part of an entropic process of which the outcome seems to be some form of extinction, the ultimate evil? Such a question is beyond the scope of this work, though in Chapter 2 entropy will be presented as a metaphor for evil.

The witness of the Scriptures regarding the nature of evil can be more easily established by considering the emerging theology of the Pauline and other letters

---

10. See, for example, Irenaeus, *Against the Heresies* 5.1.1, in *Five Books of S. Irenaeus, Bishop of Lyons, Against Heresies*, John Keble M. A., trans. (Oxford: James Parker, 1872).

11. In Col. 1.16, 'thrones or dominions or rulers or powers' are simply all the visible and invisible world created through Christ and for him. Proponents of false teachings in the community may have believed that these beings were Christ's rivals, or more likely, that they could be invoked in order to receive extra spiritual benefits, according to Margaret McDonald, *Sacra Pagina. Colossians, Ephesians* (Collegeville, PA: Liturgical Press, 2000), 60; 'In Eph. 3.10 and 6.12. the heavenly places are viewed as subject to the influence of evil spiritual powers. It is evident that according to the cosmology of Ephesians malevolent forces inhabit all spaces from the earth to the upper reaches of the universe' (ibid., 229). There is, therefore a contrast between the views of Colossians and Ephesians regarding the inhabitants of the air, the intermediate realm between the earthly and the heavenly.

12. Hilary of Poitier, *Discourse on Ps 64:15*.

of the New Testament than by focusing on the poetical style of the Psalms or prophetical writings of the Old Testament, or the phenomena described in the Gospels or even the sayings of Jesus himself. The sayings attributed to him about Satan and hell in the Gospels arose within the prevailing culture and employed rhetoric in the narrative, a special quality of discourse which a speaker or writer utilises to accomplish his purposes. Rhetorical sayings can have diverse purposes and need interpretation in context and in light of present-day exegetical studies as well as the theological insights of the writers in the first and subsequent generations of Christianity, and including theologians of today.[13]

In both Testaments, a disembodied being present in the world clearly occupies a place in God's relationship with the world. It can be that of a prosecuting counsel in God's court as in the case of Job (2.1-6) or Zechariah (3.1-2) and not God's enemy. But in 1 Samuel (19.9) 'an evil spirit from the Lord' came upon Saul and he endeavoured to kill David, so the character or role of Satan has undergone a change. In the Book of Wisdom (2.24), he appears as the adversary against God's plan for humankind because of envy, only to be finally defeated by Michael and his angels in the Apocalypse (12.7).

Relying on the Gospels, the Vatican Council's *Constitution on the Church in the Modern World* speaks of Christ 'who was crucified and rose again to break the strangle hold of personified evil, so that the world might be fashioned anew according to God's design and reach its fulfilment'.[14] But the document continues to regard all of human life, whether individual or collective, as a dramatic struggle between good and evil, between light and darkness.[15]

The document's reference in no. 13 to the 'Evil One' (*Maligni* in the Latin text), needs clarification. The Latin and English texts' use of capital letters implies personification of Satan, an issue to be discussed in Chapter 11 of this work, 'Towards a Theological Assessment of Exorcism'. It is an important one in that the Catholic Church's *Rite of Exorcism* seems to assume an encounter with Satan is possible, while the attitude commonly held in psychiatric medicine circles would tend to regard cases of alleged diabolic possession simply as pathological states of the persons concerned. In the end, the persistence of evil manifests itself for the most part in human activity, though there remain the natural disasters, which have to be described as evils, and even the puzzling phenomenon of paranormal destructive forces, not clearly attributable to human influence.

At the heart of this work is the issue of how to reconcile the understanding of the persistence of evil as a constant threatening fact in the world with the concept of what in the universal Christian tradition has been described as a personal devil, whose existence today's culture finds too bizarre to be credible.

---

13. See, for example, Julian Hills, 'Who Saw Satan Fall? Luke 10:18', *Journal for the Study of the New Testament* (Sage Publications, 1992), 22, which discusses the issue of whether it is a saying of Jesus or a statement concerning the experience of the returning disciples.

14. *Gaudium et Spes*, no. 2.

15. Ibid., no. 13.

PART I

Theodicy

Chapter 1

GOD OR EVIL?

Many of the writings concerned in some way with theodicy make awkward bedfellows and are difficult to bring together within the scope of that term, especially when the debates of recent decades are included. As Kenneth Surin commented in a 1993 article:

> (As) the long and involuted history of theodicy shows, this project has never been a unitary and homogeneous undertaking. For this history reveals that theodicy is better seen as a designation which covers a number of diverse and even incompatible undertakings.[1]

Incompatibility implies that much recent writing is not in fact about theodicy as defined by Leibniz; in fact it often consists of attempts to disprove the very basis of traditional theodicies, namely, the existence of God. There is considerable diversity therefore among theories that are reckoned theodicies. As the project is concerned with the problem of evil, two approaches have been used, one dealing with the logical problem and the other the evidential problem. In the literature, what is described as an account of the 'logical problem' often amounts to an attempt to show that the existence of evil implies inconsistency in claims about the nature of God or even God's existence, while the 'evidential problem' may amount to denial of the evidence advanced in favour of God's justice, or existence.

Within the category of theodicy as traditionally understood, two versions of the logical approach can be identified, the first having two subdivisions, one based on an unquestioning acceptance of the doctrine of God with consequent need to find ways of understanding evil – Augustine's and Aquinas' theodicies, for example. The alternative is an attempt to show that God's existence is not incompatible with the manifest existence of evil – with Plantinga's theory the best-known.

The other version starts from the possibility that the understanding of God could in some way be adapted to the sheer awfulness of the experience of evil, Jürgen Moltmann (*The Crucified God*, 1974) being prominent in this regard,

---

1. Kenneth Surin, 'Evil, Problem Of', in *The Blackwell Encyclopedia of Modern Christian Thought*, ed. Alister E. McGrath (Oxford: Blackwell Publishing, 1993), 192.

though Charles Hartshorne (*Divine Relativity. A Social Conception of God* (1948), originally a disciple of Whiteheadian process theology, had already laid the foundation for a new approach to theism with his critique of both the logical and evidentiary arguments and his thesis that God is 'both transcendent and yet inseparable from temporal processes'.[2] The theories of Irenaeus and Hick on the other hand imply that the issue is the nature of the person.

There is in the end no completely satisfactory theoretical solution to the problem of evil, a common stratagem being to consider evil as the absence of good, and thus in some way lacking 'reality'. That solution is not very satisfactory when one considers how real the devastating effects of a tsunami can be or how horrifically physical the phenomenon of the 'Final Solution' was. Kenneth Surin said in a 1983 article that attempts to formulate a theodicy are 'fraught with the likelihood of failure'.[3]

Today's secularised culture makes questioning the existence of God almost unavoidable, thus posing the problem of evil in a different way from the dilemma of Lactantius. The issues of God's and evil's existence are related in that if God does not exist, it is difficult to give a rational account of evil. While evil is real, its profile, so to speak, at a conceptual level, is somewhat vague in the absence of conviction that there is a God to whom it is in some sense opposed. In any culture, there will still be the need to apply the resources of reason to the evils the world actually experiences.

The position of Walter Sundberg of Luther Theology Seminary, Minnesota, is worth noting:

> I must confess that theodicy has always left me cold; the preoccupation with theodicy that has been characteristic of Western theology since the beginning of the eighteenth-century seems to me to have served largely to sanitize God.[4]

What this comment implies is that the perception of God that emerges from theodicy studies is one that obscures rather than illuminates both the mystery of God and the mystery of evil.

---

2. Donald Wayne Viney and George W. Shields, 'Charles Hartshorne: Dipolar Theism', in *Internet Encyclopedia of Philosophy* ISSN 2161-0002, https://iep.utm.edu/29/01/22.

3. Kenneth Surin, 'Theodicy?', *Harvard Theological Review*, vol. 76, no. 2 (April 1983): 225–47, at 226; Paul Ricoeur, in 'Evil, a Challenge to Philosophy and Theology' in Paul Ricoeur, *Figuring the Sacred: Religion, Narrative and Imagination*, trans. David Pellauer (Minneapolis, MN: Fortress Press, 1995), 249–61, expressed a similar view.

4. Walter Sundberg, 'A Primer on the Devil', *First Things*, January 1993. See also Samuel A. Meier, 'Evil', in *The Oxford Companion to the Bible*, ed. Bruce M. Metzger and Michael D. Coogan (Oxford: Oxford University Press, 1993), 209: 'Evil as a philosophical problem is never really addressed in biblical literature. Attempts in Judaism and Christianity to resolve the logical problem of the existence of evil in a world created by a compassionate, just, omnipotent, and omniscient God belong to postbiblical reflection on the text.'

Classically, a theodicy theory required that the evident existence of widespread and serious evil in the world be reconciled with the accepted existence of an omnipotent, omniscient, morally perfect and loving divinity, that of Irenaeus (+202) being considered prototypical. With the decline in belief in God in recent centuries, the process was reversed and God's existence needed to be vindicated in light of undeniable evil.

A survey by Michael Peterson of theodicy studies broadly understood over the period from John Hick's *Evil and the God of Love* in 1966 until publication of that study in 1983, named over forty single or joint authored works, very many in reaction to the work of Hick and of Alvin Plantinga (*God, Freedom and Evil*, 1977).[5] In 2017, Peterson edited *The Problem of Evil: Selected Readings. Second Edition*, a survey in thirty-two chapters of virtually all contributions to the issue of theodicy from the classical to the most modern, from Augustine to Peter Van Inwagen, including atheists such as Mackie.[6]

Below only samples will be given of the various categories.

Irenaeus (+202)

One of the earliest Christian thinkers, Irenaeus, developed his theodicy on the basis of humanity's imperfection and use or misuse of free will in the course of his writing against the Gnostics, especially those who were followers of Valentinian in Rome.[7] He focused particularly on those among them who were considered, and considered themselves, the 'perfect'.

> For as gold deposited in mud does not lose its beauty but preserves its own nature because mud cannot harm gold, so they themselves, they say, no matter what material acts they experience, cannot be harmed or lose their spiritual substance. Therefore the perfect among them fearlessly perform all the forbidden acts, of which scripture affirms that those who perform them will not inherit the kingdom of God. (Gal 5.21). (*Adv. Hereses* I.vi.2-3)[8]

Against this and other deviations from scriptural orthodoxy, Irenaeus developed his theology of creation and redemption, including theological anthropology: in

---

5. Michael L. Peterson, 'Recent Work on the Problem of Evil', *American Philosophical Quarterly*, vol. 20, no. 4 (1983): 321–39.

6. *The Problem of Evil: Selected Readings. Second Edition*, Michael L. Peterson, ed. (Notre Dame: Notre Dame Press, 2017²).

7. Robert M. Grant, *Irenaeus of Lyons* (London: Routledge, 1997), 21: 'He seems to have been concerned with the Valentinians because they were taking his own route westward from Asia.'

8. All quotations from *Adversus Hereses* are taken from *Five Books of S. Irenaeus against Heresies*, John Keble, trans. (Oxford: James Parker, 1872).

what condition was humankind created and what was its path to fulfilment. To an extent, the formulation of his ideas depended on the fact that he was answering the teaching of the Gnostics, such as their assertion that God could have made humankind perfect from the beginning (IV.xxviii.1). His response to this was

> Let him know, that although unto God, who is always just and wise and Unoriginated, in respect of himself all things are possible; yet the things that were made by him, so far as that, coming afterwards, they have each its own beginning of generation, so far they must also fall short of him who made them. (IV.xxviii.1)

The positive foundation of his argument was his understanding of the vocation of humankind, following 2 Pet. 1.4, to share in God's life in such a way as to be partakers in divinity:

> For to this end the Word of God was made man, and he who is the Son of God, made Son of Man: that man, blended (*commixtus*) with God's Word, and receiving the adoption, might become a son of God. (III.xix.1)

He quoted Paul's saying to the Corinthians that he had fed them with milk rather than meat because of the imperfection[9] and weakness of their conversation; they 'had the organs of their soul's sensation as yet weak and unpractised in divine exercise: so also at the beginning, God was indeed able to give perfection unto man, but he having been just begun to be, was unable to receive it' (III.xix.1).

But man was destined to receive perfection through the indwelling of the Spirit:

> Man being originated and formed comes to be in the image and likeness of the Unoriginated God: the Father approving and commanding, the Son performing and creating, the Spirit giving nourishment and growth, and man for his part silently advancing and going onward to perfection; that is, coming near the Unoriginate. For the Unoriginate is perfect; and this is God. (IV.xxviii.3)

For this progress to take place, it was necessary that man exercise free will.[10] But 'disobedience to God and loss of what is good is indeed in a man's power, but it brings no ordinary harm and loss'. Life on earth is then a testing time for

---

9. Ἀκατάρτιστος: the basic meaning is 'ignorance'.

10. Irenaeus' thought received indirect support from a twentieth-century Orthodox theologian, Vladimir Lossky, *Orthodox Theology. An Introduction*, Ian and Ihita Kesarcodi-Watson, trans. (Crestwood, NY; St Vladimir's Seminary, 1978), 73: 'God created man like an animal that has received the order to become God, says a deep saying of St Basil, reported by St Gregory of Nazianzus. To execute this order one must be able to refuse it. God becomes *powerless* before human freedom.'

humankind on the way to perfection.[11] The world will come to an end in the number of thousands of the days of its creation, which Irenaeus reckoned as six. Humankind was being made in the image and likeness of God 'by the casting away of the chaff', by which he meant the heretics, and by gathering into the garner of the wheat, that is such as bear fruit unto God' (V.xxviii.4).

> And therefore is tribulation necessary for such as are saved, that being in a manner bruised, and beaten small, and by patience kneaded up with the Word of God, and put into the fire, they may be meet for the King's banquet. (V.xxviii.4)

His argument here was based on the opposition the faithful encountered from the Gnostics, but the chaff and the wheat language implied it was not simply a case of opposition; it emphasised suffering on the part of the faithful. It had the endorsement of Scripture and reflected the situation of the first centuries of Christianity, when persecution and martyrdom were widespread forms of evil. In this way Irenaeus presented a theodicy suited to his time; Christians could be enabled to grasp that what they encountered was part of God's plan for creation. Despite the presence of evil God's justice was vindicated.

It would be more difficult to maintain that his theodicy was timeless, that in all ages the lives of Christians needed to encounter evil on a large scale in order to attain perfection. Yet, his argument was articulated at a time when Gnostics claimed perfection despite immoral or amoral lives; his theory of gradual perfection remains appropriate for generations of Christians who have lived lives of manifest goodness while aware of their weaknesses.

As John Hick, who developed a theodicy along similar lines, pointed out, there is in Irenaeus an approach to the problem of evil that stands in contrast with Augustine's theodicy (which will be discussed below):

> Instead of the doctrine that man was created finitely perfect and then incomprehensively destroyed his own perfection and plunged into sin and misery, Irenaeus suggests that man was created as an imperfect, immature

---

11. His idea of the gradual process of perfection for humankind found an echo in the teachings of his Alexandrian contemporary, Origen (*c.* 185–*c.* 253), who also taught humanity's free will and the gradual evolution of the cosmos, its recapitulation to a primeval order, though for him this could include successive cycles of worlds and the possible conversion of devils: 'Iam vero si aliquis ex his ordinibus qui sub principatu diaboli agunt ac malitiae ejus obtemperant, poterunt aliquando in futuris saculis converti ad bonitatem, pro eo quod est in ipsis libri facultates arbitrarii.' Origen, *De principiis* 1.6.3, trans. Rudolf Redepenning (Leipzig: Bibliopolio Dypiano, 1836), 146. See J. N. D. Kelly, *Early Christian Doctrines* (London: A. & C. Black, 1977⁵), 474: 'When Origen was taken to task on this point, he indignantly protested, according to his later champion, Rufinus, that he held no such theory.'

creature who was to undergo moral development and growth and finally be brought to the perfection intended for him by his maker.[12]

Irenaeus saw creation as an environment incorporating a mixture of good and evil, but one necessary for humankind's growth to perfection through the exercise of free will. Humanity is to be brought to maturity at some future time and thus enabled to see and comprehend God. But in holding that humanity was created imperfect, faced with a journey through life to perfection, and burdened with evil, Irenaeus seemed to make God the source of evil – a state of things Aquinas will confront successfully – and gave no other explanation of its origin.

> Irenaean theodicy appears to place the ultimate responsibility for much of the world's evil on the shoulders of the creator. But at the same time it seeks to show that it was for a good reason that he created a world where evil is built in.[13]

One saving feature of it came from the idea of recapitulation introduced by Irenaeus. The incarnation of the Second Adam recapitulated the history of the first by the obedience he showed to the Father, in contrast with the disobedience of Adam. The disobedience of Adam was an important theme for Irenaeus; the image and likeness of God had been lost in Adam (III.xviii.1) – though, according to V.vi.1, he lost the likeness but not the image. 'Christ, the creative Word, restored one or both to human beings by the gift of the Spirit and made them immortal.'[14]

> He for his part was made 'in the likeness of sinful flesh' that he might condemn sin and so cast it out, as a condemned thing, from the flesh; and might provoke man to resemble himself, appointing him to be an imitator of God, and

---

12. John Hick, *Evil and the God of Love* (Glasgow: Fontana Paperbacks, 1979), 220–1.
13. Aidan Nichols O.P., *The Shape of Catholic Theology* (Edinburgh: T&T Clark, 1991), 69.
14. Grant, *Irenaeus of Lyons*, 52. In 'Naturalism, Evil and God', in *The Cambridge Companion to the Problem of Evil*, Chad Meister and Paul K. Moser, eds (Cambridge: Cambridge University Press, 2017), Michael Ruse, writing from the perspective of metaphysical naturalism interpreted Irenaeus' theology of the imperfect nature of humankind by relativising, rather than emphasising, the story of Adam's disobedience as the reason for the incarnation and redemption. 'Would it not be better to have the story of Jesus and his sacrifice be intended from the beginning? Humans were created imperfect and the Christian story is one of God helping us on our way until we are ready for eternal life. Adam and Eve are purely symbolic', 262–3. Irenaeus of course did not de-emphasise Adam's disobedience, but made it central to his theory of recapitulation. Nevertheless, from the point of view of biological evolutionary theory, Ruse's suggestion as to how to interpret Irenaeus is attractive.

inserting him in the father's List, that he might see God, and granting unto him to comprehend the Father – he the Word of God, which dwelt in man, and was made Son of Man, that he might inure (*accustom*) man to receive God, and God to dwell in man – according to the good pleasure of the Father. (III.20.2)

Augustine (354–430)

Augustine's treatment of the subject of Satan and his activities belongs to the period after his conversion to Christianity, when he had become a theologian and commentator on the Scriptures. But in his younger days, as a rhetorician, he had been drawn to philosophy and concentrated on a search for wisdom. The Christian scriptures he encountered, translated some centuries previously by 'humble, nameless writers' seemed to his educated taste full of jargon and slang and he turned instead to a sophisticated group of 'new' Christians who despised the traditional church; they were called the Manichees after their founder, Mani, in the late third century. At that stage, the spiritual seemed to Augustine only a finely structured version of the material, as the Ptolemaic world view could suggest. He was by disposition firmly rooted in the material, and conscious of a struggle within himself between evil and good. The dualistic Manichean doctrine of separation of matter and spirit identified matter as an evil power eternally at war with good, with the spirit. The Manichees identified their mind or soul as part of the divine substance.

> Their religion was directed to ensuring that this, the good part of themselves, would remain essentially untouched and unaffected by their baser nature.[15]

That went some way to accounting for the observable ills of humankind consisting of soul and body and for Augustine's own inner struggles. It enabled him to hold the view that it was not he that sinned, but some other nature sinning within him. It pleased his pride, he was to say later, to be beyond fault and when he had done any evil not to confess that he done it.[16]

The Manichees had a select inner group, the Perfect or Elect, who had special powers to transmute matter into spirit. They surrounded themselves with disciples whose service 'helped the cause of good in the universe'.[17] Augustine became a disciple as a 'Hearer', a status in which he remained for nine years. But he suffered from disquiet. In his *Confessions*, he would come to recognise this period as one of loss:

---

15. Peter Brown, *Augustine of Hippo: A Biography* (London: Faber and Faber, 1969), 50.
16. Augustine, *Confessions* V. x. 18 (London: Sheed and Ward, 1944), 74.
17. G. R. Evans, 'Evil', in *Augustine through the Ages: An Encyclopedia*, Allan D. Fitzgerald OSA, ed. (Grand Rapids, MI: Eerdmans, 1999), 341.

> But what did all this profit me while I held that you, Lord God of truth, were a luminous immeasurable body and I a kind of particle broken from that body? It was an extreme of perverseness, but so I then was.[18]

His disquiet was intellectual and spiritual and caused him to disengage from the Manichees when the leader, Faustus, came to North Africa and Augustine discovered that he was a man less educated and less intelligent than he.[19] Disenchanted by the encounter, he left the Manichees, but still did not recognise that he was divided within himself and thought of God as a bodily mass, and of evil as 'possessed of its own foul and misshapen mass'.[20] In an uncertain state of mind, he left Africa and came to Milan, where he was impressed by Ambrose's preaching, but was frustrated in his desire to speak to him by the crowds that always gathered round him. It was in Milan that he heard the voice of a child singing 'take and read' and was prompted to take up the Letter to the Romans. He became a Christian and now had to rethink his understanding of evil, not simply in philosophy but in effect philosophical theology; evil could not exist, as its existence would be incompatible with that of a God who was wholly good.

But in his search for the origin of evil, his cosmology was still a pantheistic one which identified God and creation, making the problem more intractable.

> I ranged before the eyes of my mind the whole of creation, both what we are able to see – earth and sea and air and stars and trees and mortal creatures; and what we cannot see – like the firmament of heaven above, and all its angels and spiritual powers: though even these I imagined as if they were bodies disposed in its own place. And I made one great mass of God's creation, distinguished according to the kinds of bodies in it, whether they were really bodies, or only such bodies as I imagined spirits to be. ... And I saw you, Lord, in every part containing and penetrating it, yourself altogether infinite, as if your being were a sea, infinite and immeasurable everywhere. ... Thus I conceived your creation as finite and filled utterly by yourself, and you were infinite.[21]

Convinced, then, that of his goodness God created all things good and that he 'contained' them, he wondered where evil could be, what was its source and how had it crept into creation, how could it be that it was wholly without being. Here his residual Manichean leanings seemed, at least, to be showing their influence – some students of Augustine, though not the authoritative Peter Brown, would say that he never completely freed himself from Manicheism; at the start of his days as a bishop he was in fact regarded by a senior bishop as a crypto-Manichean.[22] As one present-day commentator remarked,

18. Augustine, *Confessions* IV. xvi. 61.
19. Ibid., V. vii. 12. 92.
20. Ibid., V. x. 20. 75.
21. Ibid., VII. v. 7. 105.
22. Brown, *Augustine of Hippo*, 203–4.

The Christian Augustine was never quite able to free himself of certain legacies in his own account of the problem of evil: a sense of the dichotomy between, and indeed eternal incompatibility of, body and soul; of the recognition that that there is eternal warfare in human beings; of a mistrust of material things, although in the profundity of his faith he found Christian ways of addressing these dilemmas.[23]

He asked how it could be that evil was 'wholly without being' – rather than 'being' something that infected creation – but he accepted in faith that this was the case. He had, he said, in his pre-Christian days been taken in by those who implied that God was 'bounded by a bodily shape'; he did not know then that 'evil has no being of its own, but is only an absence of good'.[24]

He had always been convinced that God who was good made all things good and the goodness of creation came from the goodness of God.[25] But created things were necessarily less than their creator as he said in *Confessions* VII.xii:

> I thought about those other things that are less than you, and I saw that they neither necessarily are, nor yet totally are not; they are in as much as they are from you: they are not, in as much as they are not what you are. ... And it became clear to me that corruptible things are good: if they were supremely good they could not be corrupted; ... If they were in no way good there would be nothing in them that might corrupt.[26]

He dealt with aspects of corruption elsewhere, asserting that even when corrupted, some things are better than others that remain uncorrupted.

The idea that corruptible things are good could be the basis for a theology of natural evil, and Augustine begins to lay the foundations in the next chapter:

> To you, then, evil utterly is not – and not only to you, but to your whole creation likewise, evil is not, because there is nothing above your creation that could break in or derange the order you imposed upon it. But in certain of its parts there are some things which we call evil because they do not harmonise with other things; yet these same things do harmonise with still others and thus are good. ... All these things which do not harmonise with one another, do suit well with that lower part of creation which we call the earth, which has its cloudy and windy sky in some way apt to it. God forbid that I should say: 'I wish that these things were not.'[27]

---

23. Evans, 'Evil', 341.
24. Augustine, *Confessions*, III. vii. 12. 37.
25. Augustine, *City of God*, XI, 22 (New York: Image Books, 1958), 228.
26. Augustine, *Confessions*, VII. 12. 114.
27. Ibid., VII. 13. 115.

In *De Civitate Dei* XI. 22, he was critical of 'certain heretics' who held that many things in creation were unsuitable to humans, 'such as fire, cold, wild beasts, and things like that, without considering how wonderful such things are in themselves'. He had not sufficient knowledge, presumably, of environmental phenomena, such as the tectonic plates covering the earth's surface, or their movement that causes earthquakes and permits volcanoes to erupt, but these phenomena would fall into the category of things that do not harmonise with some things but do with others; they are necessary for the earth's overall stability, while causing disruption to human society and great suffering and death. Underlying Augustine's concept of corruptible nature and harmonisation or its alternative was the belief that there were laws governing all processes in the material world and that these brought about a stable order reflecting God's plan for creation; otherwise chaos would have returned.

> Corruption is seen in the arrangement of changeable things which give way to one another according to laws eminently designed for the governance of the universe according to the natural capacity of each part. If the sun's brightness should injure someone whose eyes are weak by nature to withstand its light, we should not imagine that the sun causes this alteration in the eyes to supply a deficiency in its own light or through any vice on its part.[28]

Augustine did not delay over a possible theology of natural evil but proceeded, like Irenaeus, to the evil that arises from free will, moral evil. This he did in detail in his *De natura boni*. The basic principle was that sin was not a desire for naturally evil things, since evil as such did not exist, but the desertion of the better (*desertio melioris*). He admitted elsewhere (*De Genesi ad Litteram* 1) that the desertion of the better for the good was not necessarily sinful; what was desired must be a forbidden good. Sin was evil, not the nature that was used evilly. For evil is to make bad use of the good. He referred to Rom. 1.25, where the ungodly 'exchanged the truth about God for a lie and worshiped and served the creature rather than the Creator'.[29]

In *De libero arbitrio*, he dealt with the question of where the movement of the will originates when it turns from an immutable good to a mutable good. The movement is actually evil even though free will must be reckoned as a good, 'since it is impossible to live rightly without it'. If the turning away of the will from the Lord is undoubtedly sinful, God cannot be said to be the source of the evil. But if this movement of the will does not come from God, the question arises of where it comes from. He had to reply that he did not know, but this was because 'what is nothing cannot be known'.[30]

---

28. Augustine, *De libero arbitrio* III. xiv. 40, The Fathers of the Church 59 (Washington, DC: Catholic University of America, 1968), 203.

29. Augustine, *De natura boni* XXXVI, *S. Augustini Opera Omnia* 29 (Paris: Paul Mellier, 1842), 267.

30. Augustine, *De libero arbitrio* II. 162x. 54.

The issue of evil had occupied Augustine in his youth. In his maturity, he held that evil existed in the form of self-initiated corruption on the part of created beings, whether spirits or humans; there was no outside influence on acts of free will. In this assertion he was dependent on the faulty text of the Vulgate for Rom. 5.12 – on sin entering the world – and arrived at the idea of inherited sinfulness. His theodicy, however, was that God cannot be the source of evil, and while natural evil has to be seen as a result of the laws of creation, moral evil is a mystery.

As Augustine's theology was dominant in Western Christianity from his time until the development of scholastic theology in the Middle Ages by Peter Lombard and others, especially Thomas Aquinas (1225–74), so also his theodicy had considerable influence on the medieval understanding of evil.

Thomas Aquinas (1225–74)

The views of Aquinas on evil were broadly Augustinian, but they were formulated in his own theology, which utilised philosophical concepts derived from the thought of Aristotle and were more abstract as a result. John Hick commented:

> Aquinas writes about the problem of evil in an abstract and detached manner that seems well suited to the somewhat impersonal aesthetic principle that governs his theodicy.[31]

This is the beginning of a critique by Hick, which, ironically, will in turn lead to a critique on Aquinas' behalf, so to speak, of Hick's own theodicy by a current Thomist, as will be seen below.

Aquinas depended to an extent also for his treatment of evil on Pseudo-Dionysius. He turned to Boethius for an articulation of the problem of evil, saying in the *Summa Contra Gentiles* III.lxxi.10 that Boethius had introduced a philosopher who asked: 'If God exists, whence comes evil?' He disposed summarily at this point of the error of those who, because they noticed that evils occur in the world, said that there is no God.

> But it could be argued to the contrary: 'If evil exists, God exists.' For, there would be no evil if the order of good were taken away, since its privation is evil. But this order would not exist if there were no God.[32]

This was in his treatment of Providence. He discussed evil early in the *Summa Theologiae* Ia, where the basic issue was the existence of God. He began with the classic syllogism formulated in terms of contradictions: If God exists, there can be no evil, but evil does exist. His first response was to adduce the

---

31. Hick, *Evil and the God of Love*, 99–100.
32. Aquinas, *Summa Contra Gentiles*, III. lxxi. 10.

famous five arguments indicating the existence of God (q2, a3). In q2. a1 ad2, he disagreed with the ontological argument of St Anselm that the existence of God is self- evident.

In q48 of the *Summa Theologiae* (*S.T.*) Ia, he turned to an argument made by Pseudo-Dionysius (*Div. Nom.* iv. 4) that evil does not exist, nor is it in that which exists. He quoted Augustine (*Enchiridion* 14), who said that evil exists only in good. He responded:

> Evil imports the absence of good. But not every absence of good is evil. For absence of good can be taken in a privative and in a negative sense. Absence of good, taken negatively, is not evil, otherwise it would follow that what does not exist is evil, and also that everything would be evil, through not having the good belonging to something else; for instance man would be evil who had not the swiftness of a roe, or the strength of a lion. But the absence of good, taken in a privative sense, is an evil; as, for instance, the privation of sight is called blindness. Now the subject of privation and of form is one and the same, namely, being in potentiality (whether absolute of relative potentiality). ... It is manifest that the form which makes a thing actual is a perfection and a good; and thus every actual being is a good, and likewise every potential being, as such, is a good as having relation to a good. ... Therefore the subject of evil is a good. (Ia. q48. a3)[33]

Pursuing the issue of the existence of evil, he asked in q48 aa2–3, a5[34] whether evil could be found in things, as Pseudo Dionysius had said that evil was distant from existence and even more distant from non-existence, so it seemed evil could not be found in things. But, on the contrary, if that were so, prohibitions and penalties would cease for they exist only for evils! His principal response was that the perfection of the universe required that there should be inequality in things, grades of goodness. While everything is good in itself, there must be things that are incorruptible and things corruptible. One grade of goodness is that of the good that cannot be corrupted, cannot fail, another that which can. It is in this that evil consists, a failure of goodness. God does not interfere in this, as many good things would be taken away if God permitted no evil to exist; for example, fire would not be generated if air were not corrupted.

---

33. Brian Davies, *The Thought of Thomas Aquinas* (Oxford: Clarendon Press, 1992), 90: 'It is important to notice that Aquinas is not here asserting that evil simply 'does not exist. He is not, for example, telling us that evil is an illusion, as Mary Baker Eddy taught in her claim that "all inharmony of mortal mind and body is an illusion, possessing neither reality nor identity, though seeming to be real and identical".' (Mary Baker Eddy, *Science and Health with Key to the Scriptures* (Boston, 1971)).

34. Aquinas, *Summa Theologiae* Ia. q48. aa2–3, a5 (London: Burns, Oates & Washbourne, 1912), 266–73.

The order of the universe requires that there should be some things that can, and sometimes do, fail. And thus God, by causing in all things the good of the order of the universe, consequently, and as it were by accident, causes the corruption of things.

His two final discussions concern the division into pain and fault (natural and moral evil) and whether there be one supreme evil, the cause of every evil. In a complex statement, he dealt with both pain and fault. Briefly, he held that

> because good in itself is the object of the will, evil, which is the privation of good, is found in a special way in rational creatures which have a will. Therefore, the evil which comes from the withdrawal of the form and integrity of the thing has the nature of a pain, especially so on the supposition that all things are subject to divine providence. (a5)

That is to say that rational creatures will the good, but when in act rather than potency (but not operation) the form and integrity of the thing willed is deficient, the evil of pain (*malum poenae*) results, for example, the evil of blindness. However, there is the further dimension, what is today called moral evil.

> But the evil which consists in the subtraction of the due operation in voluntary things has the nature of a fault (*malum culpae*); for it is imputed to anyone as a fault to fail as regards perfect action, of which he is the master by the will. (a5)

He expanded on this succinct statement in article 6:

> The evil of fault is properly opposed to uncreated good; for it is opposed to the fulfilment of the divine will, and to divine love, whereby the divine good is loved for itself, and not only as shared by the creature.

The Thomist theologian, Herbert McCabe O.P., commented on this opposition:

> The opposition here is not between the created goods of this life, which are lost by *malum poenae* and the uncreated good of the next life, which is lost by *malum culpae*, for in St Thomas's view beatitude is a created good – the vision of God is not itself God. ... The opposition is between two goods considered as objects of human desire; one is a created thing that participates in the divine goodness; the other is the *bonum universale*, the uncreated good itself. Someone may lose the former in *malum poenae*, a person turns from the latter in *malum culpae*.[35]

---

35. Herbert McCabe O.P., *God and Evil in the Theology of St Thomas Aquinas* (London: Continuum, 2010), 119.

McCabe continued by considering the question of the responsibility of the person who does evil, since it could appear that God is the final cause of the evil.

> We can say, first of all, that while God could not have created a world of things with lifetimes that was of its nature incorruptible, ... he could have created a world without sin. This is implied by my assertion that sin plays no part in the perfection of anything. We are then tempted to say that if God could have made a world without sin but did not do so, he is responsible for sin. We may grant that this does not remove the responsibility from the sinners, but we might still want to attach it to God. ... But here we must remember (that) although God could certainly prevent sin from occurring without any interference with human freedom, he does not *do* an evil when he permits evil to happen.[36]

McCabe pointed out that, for Aquinas, although *to do evil* and its negation *not to do evil* are contradictory opposites, it is not the case that 'X wishes evil to be done' is the contradictory opposite of 'X wishes evil not to be done', since both are affirmatives. Hence the denial of the latter (i.e. the denial of that God *wishes evil not to be done*) does not entail the affirmation of the former (that God *wishes evil to be done*).

Towards the end of his treatment of evil in the *Summa*, Question 49, Aquinas took account of the part the Manichean heresy had played in the history of the problem of evil, by dealing with the question of whether there was one supreme evil that was the cause of every evil or many contrary principles, one of good, the other of evil. He had of course said elsewhere that there were many fallen angels, sources of evil, but this discussion was important in the context of the Manichean belief in one supreme evil principle. He pointed out that those 'ancients' failed to consider the universal cause of all being and considered only the particular cases of particular effects. They did not know that evil can only be an accidental and not a first cause.

> For on that account, if they found a thing hurtful by its own nature, they thought that the very nature of the thing was evil, as, for instance, if one should say that the nature of fire was evil if it burnt the house of a poor man. The judgment of the goodness of anything does not depend on its order to any particular thing but on what the thing is in itself and its order to the whole universe. (q49, a3)

In summary, Aquinas dealt with evil by accepting, like Augustine and others, that evil is a privation of good. His main points in relation to the whole issue of natural and moral evil can be summarised thus: (1) Absence of good can be taken either as a privation or a negation; absence of good as something negative does not imply

---

36. Ibid., 125–6.

evil, as otherwise everything that did not have perfections that others have would be evil, but absence of good in a privative sense is an evil, whether natural or moral. (2) Many good things would be taken away if God permitted no evil to exist; for example, fire would not be generated if air were not corrupted. Fire is a good thing but entails evil for others. God, then, permits natural evils in the interests of the overall good of creation. (3) Moral evil exists for it is imputed to anyone as a fault to fail as regards perfect action, of which he is the master by the will. This is because it is opposed to the fulfilment of the divine will, and to divine love, whereby the divine good is loved for itself. (4)There is not one supreme source of evil.

John Hick (1922–2012)

John Hick had a fundamental problem with Aquinas' theodicy. Following Jacques Maritain (*St Thomas and the Problem of Evil*) and Charles Journet (*Le Mal*), he turned from what he considered Aquinas' aesthetic vision of the universe, with its orderly balancing of good and evil, to his teaching regarding grace and redemption, the economy of salvation. He asked, in what he considered a hypothetical but crucial question for theodicy,

> Could God, had he wished, have exerted the irresistible influence of his grace within men's souls in such a way as to bring all mankind freely to salvation? [37]

For Journet, the unanswerable question was 'Why does God sometimes do what he is not bound to do, and why does he do it for one person, rather than another?'[38]

Hick concluded that this was the way that Catholic theodicy must strike the agnostic, and this was the way it struck him as a Christian not committed to the speculative Augustinian and Thomistic doctrines.[39] It is interesting that the putative judgement of the agnostic was in fact that made by Cornman and Lehrer on Plantinga's theodicy (see below), resulting in their conclusion against the existence of God.

The starting point for Hick was that there is an implicit theodicy, a vindication of God's justice, in the Scriptures.[40] This biblical approach differs significantly from many modern theodicies (and obviously anti-theodicies). But Hick was selective in his attribution of significance to biblical texts.

---

37. Ibid., 118.
38. Ibid., 118–19.
39. Ibid., 120.
40. The foundation for Hick's theodicy was laid in his account of an eschatological verification of theism in his article 'Religious Statements as Factually Significant', in *The Existence of God: Readings Selected, Edited and Furnished with an Introductory Essay*, John Hick (New York: Macmillan, 1964), 252–74.

> Whether or not the traditional doctrine of an historical fall (i.e. the fall of man as an event that took place on this earth some definite, though not necessarily ascertainable, number of years ago) is true, considered as a contribution to the solution to the problem of evil it only explains *obscurum per obscurum*.[41]

A fundamental problem for him was how beings, whether angels or humans, could rebel against God; it was absurd that creatures living face to face with limitless power and goodness should even be tempted to rebel.[42] He was not going to depend on the traditional doctrine of the fall of angels or men for his theodicy; in fact he considered this tradition to be an unhelpful drawing of conclusions of fact from what was clearly a myth.[43]

Every kind of evil was chronicled in the Old Testament, both evils inflicted on God's chosen people and those they inflicted on their enemies, yet the prophets assured them that God's promise of a Messiah to liberate them from all evil would be fulfilled. The New Testament Gospels recount the combat with evil in the form of the devil or demons on the part of Jesus, the Son of God in the flesh. His victory, realised in the Resurrection, was the ultimate proof of God's justice. For Hick, it was sufficient to point to the existence of evil, without considering its ultimate origin.

> The aim of a Christian theodicy must thus be the relatively modest and defensive one of showing that the mystery of evil, largely incomprehensible though it remains, does not render irrational a faith that has arisen ... from participation in a stream of religious experience which is continuous with that recorded in the Bible.[44]

Hick took account of modern anthropological knowledge in order to assert that 'some form of two-stage conception of the creation of man has become an almost

---

41. Ibid., 180–1: 'Only a drastic compartmentalization of the mind could enable one to believe in a literal historical fall of man from paradisal perfection taking place in the year x BC.'

42. Ibid., 314. Among those upholding the Augustinian-Thomistic doctrine of the Fall, against Hick's new theodicy were Illytd Trethowan, 'Dr Hick and the Problem of Evil', *Journal of Theological Studies*, vol. 18 (1967): 407–16.

43. He published this book in 1968. In 1979 he elaborated on his thesis in an essay 'Incarnation and Atonement. Evil and the Incarnation', in *Incarnation and Myth. The Debate Continued*, Michael Goulder, ed. (Grand Rapids, MI: Eerdmans, 1979), 76–84. Ibid., 80: 'The main alternative, of course, of the traditional Christian myth of the fall of man from grace, and then his salvation by the atoning blood of Christ, is a theology (suggested by the thought of the early Hellenistic Fathers) in which one does not separate creation and redemption, but sees our present human existence as a phase in the gradual creation of finite beings who are to live in conscious filial relationship to him.'

44. Hick, *Evil and the God of Love*, 281.

unavoidable Christian tenet'.[45] The first stage he believed could be the emergence from the evolutionary process of a creature with a degree of human autonomy. Only an epistemic distance between God and man would allow this: 'The reality and presence of God must not be borne in on men in the coercive way in which their natural environment forces itself upon their attention'.[46] God must be a hidden deity, veiled by his creation. The apparently atheous character of the human environment may be expected to require 'religious faith if man is ever to know God and yet also by its fitness to mediate the divine presence and its activity, to be such as to make faith possible'.[47]

> On the one hand, then, we should expect the reality of God to be other than automatically and undeniably evident to us; it will, on the contrary be possible, for our minds to rest in the world itself without passing beyond it to its maker.[48]

For Hick, this was the actual world in which people live. The second stage of evolution of the relationship with God he saw as a different kind that could not be performed by omnipotent power as such, but one essentially free and self-directing. He emphasised that this process of becoming was not by a natural and inevitable evolution 'but through a hazardous adventure in individual freedom'. Because it is an individual pilgrimage, it does not imply an overall improvement in the moral state of the world. In imagining what kind of world God would create to achieve this purpose for humankind, Hick drew on the idea of parental relationship inspired by Christ's teaching about God as father. While parents seek pleasure for their children, they do not desire for them unalloyed pleasure at the expense of their growth in even greater values such as moral integrity, and especially the capacity for love.

---

45. Ibid., 291.
46. Ibid., 317. Peterson, 'Recent Work on the Problem of Evil', 328:

> Against Hick, G. Stanley Kane argues that the maintenance of man's epistemic distance from God does not logically require the existence of severe moral and physical evils, since there are other ways God can conceal his presence. Furthermore, Kane argues that epistemic distance actually makes intelligent moral choice impossible, since one's duty is not discernible. Hick replied, first, that he had never asserted that evil is logically necessary to epistemic distance, but that it is contingently true that evil reinforces our separateness from God. Second, Hick responded that the concept of epistemic distance implies not that moral obligations are hidden, but that God's existence is.

See G. Stanley Kane, 'The Failure of Soul-Making Theodicy', *International Journal for Philosophy of Religion*, vol. 6 (1975): 1–22.
47. Hick, *Evil and the God of Love*, 317–18.
48. Ibid., 318.

If then there is any true analogy between God's purpose for his human creatures and the purpose of loving and wise parents for their children, we have to recognise that the presence of pleasure and the absence of pain cannot be the supreme and over-riding end for which the world exists. Rather this world must be a place of soul-making.[49]

As noted earlier, Hick saw an implicit theodicy in the Scriptures and wrote from the perspective of a believer, convinced of the possibility of a real relationship with God. His two interlocutors (Flew and Mackie, see below) wrote from an atheistic or at most a deistic perspective and his concluding summary brought out that divergence of position.

Hick died in 2012. In a book published in 2013, *Aquinas and the Cry of Rachel*, a Thomist John F. X. Knasas took issue with Hick's theodicy on the basis of Hick's non-acceptance of the Thomistic (and Augustinian) doctrine of the Fall. This meant that Hick could not 'appeal to an antecedent good to explain evil'.[50] This does follow from Hick's existential starting point. He had said that his theodicy must centre on the soul-making process he believed to be taking place within human life, so that the starting point for him was to relate the realities of sin and suffering to the perfect love of an omnipotent creator. Ultimately, this must result in an eschatological theodicy.[51]

It should be noted here that Knasas's metaphysics of causation centred on 'explanation', while Hick talked of 'a clue to a mystery' and his perspective was eschatological rather than aetiological. In his analysis of moral evil, he stated that the ethical concepts of wrong moral action and bad moral character, when seen in a theological context, indicate a wrong relationship with God. The wrong relationship with God could be investigated by considering what a right relationship with him would be, 'even though this latter represents an ideal that has not (with one exception) been exemplified in human history'.[52] He recounted in detail what the right relationship would be, regarding Jesus as one who represented a higher purpose in conflict with the prevailing dynamics of human society. While he acknowledged that man's story is illumined by heroism, self-sacrifice, love and compassion, 'these gleams of light only throw into darker relief the surrounding, and chronic, human self-centredness from which have flowed so many forms of man-made evil'. This led him to discuss sin as a disorientation at the very centre

---

49. Ibid., 295.

50. John F. X. Knasas, *Aquinas and the Cry of Rachel: Thomistic Reflections on the Problem of Evil* (Washington, DC: Catholic University Press, 2013), 164. Had he lived, Hick could have countered with an argument which in fact he developed in his book: 'When the latter theory (the standard account of the Fall) goes on to explain that Satan had fallen through a sin of pride it comes no nearer to offering an explanation of evil's origin, since the question now arises as to the origin of this sinful pride' (p. 320).

51. Hick, *Evil and the God of Love*, 297.

52. Ibid., 298.

of human existence, in the relationship with the Source and Lord of life and the Determiner of human destiny. This makes sin the heart of the problem of evil.[53]

His approach was, as in both the Augustinian and Irenaean tradition, to assert the freedom of the will on the part of a finite personal being. His reliance on free will met opposition in philosophical articles by other writers, in particular Anthony Flew and J. L. Mackie on the basis that God could have made humans so that they would always do what is right.[54]

In addition to his objection that Hick could not appeal to an antecedent good to explain evil, Knasas also asserted that without the traditional account's reduction to the natural state, the Fall, Hick could not distinguish types of evil; only the moral evil stemming from human motivation and activity was within the scope of his enquiry. To it Hick did devote a complete chapter, noting that 'violence, treachery and bestial cruelty have left their blood-stained marks on recent history'.[55] It is true that he broadened the concept of moral evil to include what might at first glance appear to be natural evil, diseases which the population is liable to contract, for example. But in these cases he asserted: 'We cannot at present set a limit to the extent to which mental and emotional factors, both individual and collective, enter into our liability to both disease and physical accident.'[56] Though obviously valid in these cases, his argument obviously could not cover natural evils such as a volcano, or indeed the physical incident that caused the extinction of dinosaurs many millions of years before the emergence of humans. Aquinas' understanding of incorruptible and corruptible things required by the perfection of the universe was beyond his ken:

> The perfection of the universe requires that there should be inequality in things, so that every grade of goodness can be realised. Now one grade of goodness is that of the good than cannot fail. Another grade of goodness of that of the good that can fail in goodness. (*S.T.*, 1a. 48. 2c)

Knasas's more fundamental critique concerns Hick's discussion of God's responsibility for evil. In his final chapter, 'On the Kingdom of God and the Will of God', Hick addressed the question, returning to earlier discussion of the evils of the Holocaust.

> What does the ultimate context of divine purpose and activity mean for Auschwitz and Belsen …? Was this in any sense willed by God? The answer is obviously no. These events were utterly wicked, devilish and, as far as the human

---

53. Ibid., 299–301.
54. Anthony Flew, 'Divine Omnipotence and Human Freedom', *Hibbert Journal*, vol. 53, no. 135 (1954); J. L. Mackie, 'Evil and Omnipotence', *Mind* LXIV, 200–12.
55. Ibid., 324.
56. Ibid., 300.

mind can reach, unforgivable. Most certainly God did not want those who committed these fearful crimes against humanity to act as they did.[57]

Knasas commented:

> There is the perspective of the universe (or the world), and there is the perspective of the 'ultimate context of the divine purpose'. I have noted Hick to extend soul-making beyond death. Hence the second perspective is different from the first as something much larger. But it is in the perspective of the world or universe that Hick says the Holocaust is not willed by God and is called utterly evil. What is the case from the perspective of the divine purpose?[58]

It is true that in opting for a futurist theodicy rather than looking to the past, an evidentiary rather than logical approach, Hick did not have the solution to the problem of evil availed of by Aquinas and subtly dissected by the Thomist McCabe in his text above, in terms of 'permitting' evil. The difficulty often mentioned in relation to Ireneaus' theodicy, with which Hick identified, is the possible lack of proportion between the suffering of the individual who needed to be 'bruised, beaten and small' in order to reach perfection. The horrors of the Holocaust could be regarded as disproportionate to the soul-making process.

Towards the end of his work, however, Hick returned to the evidentiary offerings of the scriptures, which was his starting point, the implicit theodicy of both testaments. Referring to the paradox that God himself is ultimately responsible for the existence of evil and yet that evil is truly evil and truly subject to his condemnation and rejection, Hick stated that the two conceptions of evil run as intertwined threads through the entire Bible. He pointed to the fact that in the Old Testament there are passages in which evil is directly related to the will of God.[59] He quoted texts such as 'Does evil befall a city, unless the Lord has done it?' (Amos 3.6) and 'Is it not from the mouth of the Most High that good and evil come?'(Lam. 3.38). On the other hand, he indicated that there were innumerable passages expressing, through the prophets, God's abhorrence of evil. In the New Testament, the dualistic strain of thought, he averred, was most evident in the Gospels. Evil in the form of sin and suffering is depicted there as the enemy of God and man.

> But the other and contrasting strand of biblical thought, in which evil is more positively related to the will of God, is also abundantly present in the New Testament. Christ faces the cross as a sacrifice that his Heavenly Father desires him to make. … A divine purpose overshadows all the events of Passion Week.[60]

---

57. Ibid., 397.
58. Knasas, *Aquinas and the Cry of Rachel*, 171–2.
59. Hick, *Evil and the God of Love*, 390.
60. Ibid., 391.

There is an answer in that passage to Knasas's inference that, in the context of ultimate purpose, 'for Hick, God in some fashion causes and is responsible for evil'. According to Heb. 12.3, the sufferings of Christ, the evils inflicted on him, were part of God's plan for the salvation of humanity. Aquinas is in fact quite clear on this; he held that though the Incarnation was in itself salvific, there were certain obstacles that prevented us from enjoying Christ's previously acquired merits and so it was necessary for him to suffer.[61] Further, he devoted *S.T.* III. 48. 3 to the question of whether God gave up Christ to his passion. He responded that Christ suffered voluntarily out of obedience to the Father, and the Father gave him up under three headings: he pre-ordained it by his eternal will; he inspired in Christ the will to suffer, filling him with love; he did not protect him from his persecutors. In support, he quoted Rom. 8.32, 'He gave him up for us all'. To objection 2 in his text, he said that Christ as God gave himself up with the same will and action as those of the Father. To 3, he replied that both were to be praised for the one action.[62] In III. 46. a5, he listed the details of Christ's sufferings, as they affected all his senses, adding that the least suffering of Christ would have sufficed to liberate the human race from all its sins.[63] That last point is very significant; it was the will of the Father that the human race be redeemed in the way it was, by the immense sufferings of Christ, the evils inflicted upon him. Aquinas in effect supported Hick's contention that 'the mystery of evil, largely incomprehensible though it remains, does not render irrational a faith that has arisen ... from participation in a stream of religious experience which is continuous with that recorded in the Bible'.[64] Yet, in taking the approach he did – of avoiding the theology of the Fall – Hick seemed ambiguous on the issue of Christ's death being an atoning sacrifice, one in which the Father and the Son collaborated, as Aquinas would have it, but he did seem to accommodate this idea when he spoke of God sharing in the painful process of human suffering.[65]

Hick's theodicy was characterised by the need, implied by the not very happy term, soul-making, to posit an intermediate state of human existence in which

---

61. *S. T.* III, 48. 1 ad 2: '*Christus a principio suae conceptionis meruit nobis salutem aeternam: sed ex parte nostra erant impedimenta quaedam, quibus impediebamur consequi effectum praecedentium meritorum. Unde ad removendum illa impedimenta oportuit Christum pati, ut supra dictum est.*' This refers to III, 46. 3, where the human race was said to be in servitude to the devil.

62. Thomas F. O'Meara, O.P., *Thomas Aquinas Theologian* (Notre Dame: Notre Dame Press, 1997), 135: 'In the last analysis, it is God's countering moves of love which save humanity, for Calvary is an example and climax of the divine activity struggling with evil in history.'

63. This evokes the verse of his hymn, *Adoro te*, in which he pleads with Christ: *Pie pelicane, Jesu Domine, me immundum munda tuo sanguine, cuius una stilla salvum facere totum mundun quit ab omni scelere.*

64. Hick, *Evil and the God of Love*, 281.

65. Hick, 'Incarnation and Atonement', 81.

through sharing in the sufferings of Christ, union with the risen Christ would bring all humanity to share in his glory. A question arises, however, regarding the course of salvation history: how corporate is this process, is the church a necessary part of it? In his treatment of 'soul-making', there was no mention of the role of baptism or of the church.[66] Like his predecessor, Irenaeus, he did not deal with the issue of apocatastasis and avoided the issue of Predestination, which both Augustine and Aquinas dealt with. He saw in Calvin and Calvinism the failure to think of God and his attitudes to mankind in fully personal and agapeistic terms which he considered the basic defect of theodicies of the Augustinian kind.[67] It is significant that the title of his best-known work is *Evil and the God of Love*, rather than one simply linking 'God' with 'the problem of evil'.

Alvin Plantinga (1932–)

Like John Hick, Plantinga wrote from the perspective of Christian belief and has been described as the 'most redoubtable' upholder of the free will defence.[68] His argument in *God, Freedom and Evil* (1977), is a logical one, showing that God's existence is compatible with the existence of evil, rather than a theodicy establishing that this is factually the case. See note below for structure of his argument.[69]

His free will argument was countered by the self-professed atheist, J. L. Mackie, in *The Miracle of Theism: Arguments for and against the Existence of God* (1982).

---

66. Hick, *Evil and the God of Love*, 289–97. Jack Mahoney, *Christianity in Evolution: An Exploration* (Washington, DC: Georgetown University Press, 2011), followed Hick's approach of disregarding the myth of the Fall, and endeavoured to explain away the idea of Christ's death being an atoning sacrifice. His fundamental principle was that of the divine altruism of which Christ is the prime image, and in evolutionary terms a cosmic achievement for humanity, so that human altruism becomes a 'breakout' from evolutionary self-obsession, and can become a reflection of, and participation in, the creative altruism of God. 'Baptism remains the sacrament of initiation into God's people, the church. ... The idea of being washed clean from the stain of original sin loses its relevance, although the theme of immersion and emergence, that is of death and rebirth in Christ and in the womb of the church, can take on a new evolutionary cosmic and eschatological symbolism' (147).

67. Hick, *Evil and the God of Love*, 132.

68. Surin, 'Problem of Evil', 193.

69. Alvin Plantinga, *God, Freedom and Evil* (Grand Rapids, MI: William B. Eerdmans, 1977). His argument was summarised on p. 54:

The task is to show that

(1) God is omnipotent, omniscient and wholly good is consistent with

(2) There is evil.

(3) It was not within God's power to create a world containing moral good but no moral evil. (*Already proven in previous pages, by the use of the technical apparatus of possible worlds.*)

Mackie, who also critiqued Plantinga's version of the Anselmian ontological argument, concluded his treatment of the free will argument with the assertion:

> No concept of the free will argument has yet been proposed that both requires that free choices should be isolated from the antecedent nature (or essence) of the agent and from the possibility of divine foreknowledge, and at the same time shows this freedom to be … a good so great that it outweighs the certainty of all unabsorbed evils that occur, or the risk of all those that might occur. … All forms of free will defence fail, and since this defence alone had any chance of success, there is no plausible theodicy on offer.[70]

Mackie did acknowledge the possibility of revised religious views, but believed that each of the changes that would make theism more coherent would also do away with some of its attractions.

Plantinga's argument was also challenged the year he retired, 2010, by Kenneth Einar Himma in an essay 'Plantinga's version of the free-will argument: the good and evil that free beings do', on the basis of a denial by Himma that free beings do more good than evil. For Himma, the logical argument may hold but not an evidential argument.[71] He correctly acknowledged that the gist of the Free Will argument was that 'the existence of free beings by itself is a moral good outweighing the evil that cannot be achieved without allowing such evil'.[72] Himma made an

---

Is possible and consistent with God's omniscience and omnipotence. But then it is clearly consistent with (1). So we can use it to show that (1) is consistent with (3) For consider

(1) God is omnipotent, omniscient and wholly good

(3) It was not within God's power to create a world containing moral good without containing moral evil

and

(4) God created a world containing moral good.

These propositions are evidently consistent, that is, their conjunction is a possible proposition. But taken together they entail

(3) There is evil

For (4) says that God created a world containing moral good, this along with (3) entails that he created moral evil. But if it contains moral evil it contains evil. So (1), (3) and (4) are jointly consistent and entail (3), hence (1) is consistent with (3).

70. J. L. Mackie, *The Miracle of Theism: Arguments for and against the Existence of God* (Oxford: Oxford University Press, 1982), 176.

71. *Religious Studies*, vol. 46, no. 1 (March 2010): 21–39. Himma's argument was similar in form to that of John Stuart Mill, *Nature and Utility of Religion and Theism* (London: Longmans, Green, Reader and Dyer, 1874), 34: '(If) good frequently comes out of evil, the converse fact, evil coming out of good, is equally common.'

72. Kenneth Himma, 'Plantinga's Version of the Free-Will Argument', 39 n1.

empirical study of the practice of good and evil in the real world, in a very rigorous assessment of what presents as altruistic behaviour, but for him is questionable.

> Fallen incorrigible sinners, try as we might to reform and repent, will inevitably fail in our attempt to follow the path of Christ and do his will as expressed in the first and second laws.[73]

It is interesting that Plantinga was reared in a Calvinist environment, but it would appear that his intellectual (and perhaps spiritual) development was influenced by familiarity with medieval theologians such as Anselm and Aquinas, making him less restricted – more positive – in his theological anthropology than Himma.[74] Though Himma apparently freed himself from Christian exclusivist beliefs,[75] his assessment of humanity prevented him from seeing how good might prevail in the present world.

The evidential argument is open to the risk of subjectivity on both sides, and this was evident in the 1968 work of J. W. Cornman and Keith Lehrer (*Philosophical Problems and Arguments: An Introduction*). In a section on 'Evil as Evidence against the Existence of God', the authors invited the reader to do a thought experiment:

> If you were all-good, all-knowing and powerful and were going to create a universe in which there were sentient beings – beings that are happy and sad, enjoy pleasure; feel pain; express love, anger, pity, hatred – what kind of world would you create?[76]

The expected answer was the best kind of world one could imagine, one in which sentient beings would suffer least. It is not likely that a person would choose to create a world such as this one, so it is easy to understand why the evil that is suffering and pain in this one is such a problem for anyone who thinks God created the world. The authors concluded:

> This does not seem to be the kind of world God would create and certainly not the world he would sustain. Given this world then, it seems we should conclude that it is improbable that it was created by anything we could call God. ... Consequently, the belief that God does not exist rather than the belief that he does exist would seem to be justified by the evidence we find in this world.

---

73. Ibid., 38.
74. In relation to Plantinga's ontological argument, see William Lane Craig, 'In Defense of Theistic Arguments', in *The Future of Atheism: Alister McGrath and Daniel Dennett in Dialogue*, Robert B. Stewart, ed. (London: SPCK, 2008), 67–96, especially 92–3.
75. Kenneth Himma, 'I Can't Help What I Believe: The Moral Case against Religious Exclusivist Doctrines', *Think: Philosophy for Everyone*, vol. 17, no. 48 (Spring 2018): 51–65.
76. J. W. Cornman and Keith Lehrer, *Philosophical Problems and Arguments: An Introduction* (New York: Macmillan, 1968), 340–1.

They considered various objections but concluded:

> Though the evidence provided by the existence of evil relative to evidence unavailable to us may be quite paltry it is sufficient, nevertheless, to tip the scale of total evidence available in favour of the hypothesis that God does not exist.[77]

In a 1979 article, Plantinga responded to this criticism:

> This appears to be an argument for the dual conclusion that G (God's existence) is improbable on E[78] and is improbable also on the relevant total evidence. And while its exact structure may not be totally clear, it is clear that the argument is vitiated by its reliance on 'Leibniz's Lapse' – the idea that if God is omnipotent, it follows that He could have actualised just any possible world. And in any event is there really more, here, than the simple assertion that G is indeed improbable on E – and on the relevant total evidence?[79]

His argument centred on the idea of noetic structure, 'the set of propositions (a person) believes, together with the various logical and epistemic relations among those propositions';[80] the way prior probabilities are assessed is relative to one's noetic structure. Peterson commented:

> Since the overall noetic structures of an atheist and a theist are going to differ, and there is no reason why the atheist's noetic structure should have preference over the theist's, Plantinga concludes that we need not accept the low probability which the atheist assigns to theism in light of the facts of evil.[81]

It is clear that for quite a long time, possibly since Hume, what was originally a study of theodicy has become a debate between theists and atheists, giving rise even to the term atheology. A recent essay by Graham Oppy, a naturalist/atheist, sets out to summarise the logical arguments from evil against the existence of God. He holds that while the argument of Mackie (mentioned above) was killed off by Plantinga, 'it is obvious that there are other logical arguments from evil that are not killed by considerations about free will.'

> Moreover, it is equally obvious that we have not examined all logical arguments from evil and that we have no neutral – non-question begging – grounds for

---

77. Ibid., 349.
78. E = 10^{13} units of evil, all the evil past, present and future the actual world holds.
79. Alvin Plantinga, 'The Probabilistic Argument from Evil', *Philosophical Studies: An International Journal for Philosophy in the Analytic Tradition*, vol. 35, no. 1 (January 1979): 6.
80. Ibid., 44.
81. Peterson, 'Recent Work on the Problem of Evil', 326.

claiming that these logical arguments from evil that we have not yet examined can be 'killed'.[82]

His own 2017 conclusion in what seems to be a modification of his own atheistic stance was:

> While we currently have no good reason for thinking that there are successful *logical* arguments – or successful logical arguments from data – on either side of the dispute between naturalists and theists, we also currently have no good reason for thinking that it is *impossible* that we will some day come into possession of successful logical arguments – or successful logical arguments from data – on one side in this dispute.[83]

The conclusion reached by Peterson in his 1983 survey was:

> Although salient points have been made on both sides of the debate, each side has failed to pursue some important aspects of the overall issue. For example, non-theists have not thoroughly challenged the greater-good criteria for deciding whether an evil is justified and theists have not sufficiently pressed the point that theism probably explains evil in the world better than other views do.[84]

When all the following are taken into account – the various attitudes to the concept of the Fall of humankind, its literal interpretation of the Biblical account or some more nuanced interpretations that stress the truth behind it, its effective ignoring by Ireneaus, or simple denial by Hick (and by biological evolutionary theory) – when all of these are taken into account – it becomes clear that evil remains unexplained. It is interesting that Aquinas and Augustine appear content with the idea of evil as the absence of good, without endeavouring to explain how this might be consistent with the presence of the devil, a being whose existence they affirmed.

---

82. Graham Oppy, 'Logical Arguments from Evil and Free-Will Defences', in *The Cambridge Companion to the Problem of Evil*, Chad Meister and Paul K. Moser, eds (New York: Cambridge University Press, 2017), 45.
83. Ibid., 63.
84. Peterson, 'Recent Work on the Problem of Evil', 335.

Chapter 2

GOD AND EVIL

Non-theists have expended a great deal of energy debating with theists on logical and evidentiary grounds, thus getting involved unwittingly or unwillingly in theodicy. The result can be more favourable to theism, a deadlock, or appeals to future possibilities, as in the case of Graham Oppy.

Chad Meister, in his *Evil: A Guide for the Perplexed*, lists five ways in which atheists can account for evil while subscribing to the idea of morality – that there is in some sense good and evil.[1] Briefly, these are, first, by introducing the idea of moral relativism, which may be personal or cultural – each individual having a personal moral code or, alternatively, moral values being determined by the culture. Given that there will always be a multiplicity of cultures, no one culture would have the right to critique another, and so no objective standards could be upheld, nor could anyone on the basis of personal moral values challenge the cultural norms. Some atheists have themselves pointed out that 'there needs to be some standard that transcends culture, by which to make … a complaint'.[2]

Friedrich Nietzsche (1844–1900)

Meister lists as the second option that proposed by Friedrich Nietzsche (1844–1900). For him, moral language was just language; good and evil as traditionally understood were no longer useful and should be jettisoned. In his Darwinian perspective, destruction, exploitation and domination were not morally objectionable, the will to power was the dominant guide in judging action.[3]

---

1. Chad V. Meister, *Evil: A Guide for the Perplexed* (New York: Bloomsbury Academic, 2018²), 118–28. He makes no reference to devil or demons, and mentions Satan once (p. 45) in relation to Augustine's theology.

2. Ibid., 120.

3. Friedrich Nietzsche, *Beyond Good and Evil*, Helen Zimmern, trans. (New York: Modern Library, 1917), 14: 'Psychologists should bethink themselves before putting down the instinct of self-preservation as the cardinal instinct of an organic being. A living thing seeks above all to discharge its strength – life itself is Will to Power; self-preservation is only one of the indirect and most frequent results thereof.'

Richard Dawkins (1941–)

The third approach is the grounding of morality in biological evolution, as Richard Dawkins claims. For him the universe is the product of the 'Blind Watchmaker';[4] it is utterly without purpose or meaning; 'our moral beliefs are predetermined aspects of our genetic machinery, selfishly programmed to advance the gene pool'.[5] For Dawkins:

> In a universe of blind physical forces and genetic replication, some people are going to get hurt, other people are going to get lucky, and you won't find rhyme or reason in it, or any justice. The universe we observe has precisely the properties we should expect if there is, at bottom, no design, no purpose, no evil and no good, nothing but blind, pitiless indifference.[6]

'Pitiless' seems a slip towards emotion that should have no place in Dawkins's scheme. His position amounts to a denial of the traditional concept of intrinsic evil, one which has come to be both questioned and defended in moral theology circles in recent years.[7]

Nor does he take account of religious experience, a universal phenomenon testified to throughout history, which should not be ignored in the most scientific, in the sense of intellectual, investigation (or indeed by empirical science). As Hugh J. McCann commented,

---

4. *The Blind Watchmaker: Why the Evidence of Evolution Reveals a World without Design* (New York: W.W. Norton, 1986) is the title of one of his books, implying a repudiation of a theory of William Paley (1743–1805) who predicated the necessity of an intelligent designing mind in creation. He famously used the analogy of the workings of a watch with those of the universe. In Dawkins's book, each step in evolution was 'sufficiently simple to have arisen by chance', 43.

5. Meister, *Evil*, 122.

6. Richard Dawkins, *River out of Eden: A Darwinian View of Life* (London: Weidenfeld and Nicholson, 1995), 133. In *Outgrowing God: A Beginner's Guide* (London: Bantam Press, 2019), 131, Dawkins describes moral values as being 'in the air' and changing from century to century and even decade to decade. 'But, in addition to our evolutionary past, where do they actually come from? And why do they change? Partly the changes come from ordinary conversations, in cafés. And in pubs and around the dinner table. We learn from each other.' He then has two people discuss the issue in terms of consequentialism and utilitarianism as he had done in *River out of Eden* (1995) but as in 1995 does not commit to either position.

7. See Nenad Polgar and Joseph A. Selling, eds, *The Concept of Intrinsic Evil and Catholic Theological Ethics* (Lanham, MD: Fortress Academic, 2019). See also John O'Neill, 'Intrinsic Evil, Truth and Authority', *Religious Studies*, vol. 31, no. 2 (June 1995): 209–19. O'Neill, a self-confessed atheist, defends the concept of intrinsic evil. 'To assert that some acts are intrinsically evil is to affirm the Pauline principle that it is not permissible to do evil so that good might come of it (Rom. 3.8). To affirm that principle is to deny consequentialism'.

One way or another, the testimony of people who report religious experience suggests that they are compelling enough in their content and the way in which they occur that they breed conviction. I think that that conviction is in the end what holds religion together and its institutions in place – so that to the extent it outreaches the scientifically empirical, it is simply another *kind* of phenomenon.[8] (italics in the original)

A fourth position goes further than Dawkins by asserting that 'moral beliefs' are an illusion 'fobbed off on us by our genes to get us to cooperate'.[9]

The fifth atheistic approach described by Meister is the utilitarian approach, summarised as the view

that we ought always to do what will produce the greatest good –with 'good' defined in terms of happiness or pleasure: the greatest happiness (or pleasure) for the greatest number.[10]

These theories held by atheists are not theodicies, as that term implies God's existence, though they do attempt to give a rational account of evil. But it has to be acknowledged that 'the existence of evil remains a mystery',[11] and humility as well as resourcefulness is needed in the approach to providing a rational account of it.

Divine Hiddenness

In recent years, there has been a shift to the other pole of the debate about evil and God, possibly a result of the repeated assertion of atheism by Dawkins and others; it has taken the form of a return to the question of God under the heading of 'hiddenness'. The topic has roots going back to the Reformation in Luther's treatment of the *Deus absconditus* and Calvin's *Institutes* on 'The knowledge of God'. It has paralleled the theodicy debate in the controversies of the recent decades. A comprehensive study, *Divine Hiddenness: New Essays*, appeared in 2002, largely as a result of the publication of J. L. Schellenberg's *Divine Hiddenness and Human*

---

8. Hugh J. McCann, 'Getting Scientific about Religion', in *The Future of Atheism: Alister McGrath and Daniel Dennett in Dialogue*, Robert B. Stewart, ed. (London: SPCK, 2008), 113–25, at 125.

9. Michael Ruse and Edward O. Wilson, 'The Evolution of Ethics', in *Philosophy of Biology*, Michael Ruse, ed. (New York: Macmillan, 1986), 316, cited in Meister, *Evil*, 125.

10. Meister, *Evil*, 127.

11. Kevin J. Vanhoozer, *Remythologizing Theology Divine Action, Passion and Authorship* (Cambridge: Cambridge University Press, 2010), 503; Emil Brunner, *The Christian Doctrine of Creation and Redemption*, Dogmatics, Vol. 2, Olive Wyon, trans. (Eugene, OR: Wipf and Stock, 2014), 142: 'Immanuel Kant threw up the sponge when confronted with the problem of the origin of evil.'

Reason of 1993.[12] The core argument of that book was the syllogism: if there were a perfectly loving, personal God he would see to it that each person capable of relationship with him reasonably believes he exists – unless a person culpably lacks such belief. But there are capable, inculpable, non-believers. Therefore, there is no perfectly loving God.[13] But Schellenberg, in an essay in dialogue form in *Divine Hiddenness: New Essays*, conceded that if God is not understood as loving and personal in their usual meanings,

> God may exist for all we know, leaving us free to pursue religious enquiry in the spirit in which it ought to be pursued. It's fascinating to consider, isn't it, that God may be hidden even more from believers of certain kinds than from agnostics? [14]

He could not speculate about what that understanding might be, and that is understandable from the Christian perspective, because of the sense of mystery the serious searcher for God encounters.

Rudolf Otto (1869–1937)

The theodicist has traditionally been intent on vindicating the presence and justice of a God who has knowable characteristics of power, and knowledge and goodness, and has had to accept that these qualities exceed the limits of human understanding. The prefix 'omni-' after the characteristics of God serves to express this. Schellenberg's suggestion of an understanding of God that does not include the usual meanings of love and person hardly appeals. It is worth recalling the thesis of Rudolf Otto (1869–1937) in *The Idea of the Holy*, 1923:

> All language in so far as it consists of words, purports to convey ideas or concepts – that is what language means; – and the more clearly and unequivocally it does so, the better the language. And hence, expositions of religious truth in language inevitably tend to stress the 'rational' attributes of God. But though the above mistake is a natural one enough, it is nonetheless seriously misleading.[15]

---

12. J. L. Schelling, *Divine Hiddenness and Human Reason* (Ithaca, NY: Cornell University Press, 1993).

13. Schellenberg's argument is summed up in this way in the introduction to Daniel Howard-Snyder and Paul K. Moser, eds, *Divine Hiddennness: New Essays* (Cambridge: Cambridge University Press, 2002), 4.

14. J. L. Schellenbeg, 'What the Hiddenness of God Reveals', in ibid., 61.

15. Rudolf Otto, *The Idea of the Holy: An Inquiry into the Non-rational Factor in the Idea of the Divine and Its Relation to the Rational*, John W. Harvey, trans. (Oxford: Oxford University Press, 1958), 2.

In a series of chapters on the numinous, the mysterious, the holy, Otto considered the elements of religion 'not exclusively contained and exhaustively comprised in any series of "rational" assertions'. These elements were not simply hidden, however, but expressed themselves directly and indirectly, in the 'solemn devotional assembly of a congregation at prayer',[16] in the Old and New Testaments, and even in the imagery associated with the non-Christian religions.

Divine hiddenness from the perspective of experience is then not an impossible problem for the religious person, even if it remains a difficult one for the theodicy project. As the introduction to *Divine Hiddenness: New Essays* put it,

> Proponents of the argument from divine hiddenness against theism tend to pose the argument as 'an epistemic problem' for theistic belief. That is, they tend to regard divine hiddenness as having sufficient evidential force to move a rational person from theism to agnosticism or from agnosticism to atheism.[17]

Those proponents do not distinguish between epistemic problems and the epistemic distance John Hick considered an important obstacle to be overcome in formulating an eschatological theodicy. In an approach similar to Hick's, Paul Moser, in 'Cognitive Idolatry and Divine Hiding', recognised the importance of experience and narrative when he stated that divine hiddenness was no argument against Jewish-Christian theism. For him, 'the epistemology of Jewish-Christian theism disallows that God's being can be trivialised as an undemanding object of knowledge for convenient examination or speculation'. Rather, 'it calls for filial knowledge of God as the Lord, who is the supreme *personal* guide and gift giver for human life.'[18] In so doing he recognised the point Otto made about 'rational' assertions. He considered the issue of Divine hiding from the contrasting perspective of God's self-revelation, because ideally 'evidence and assurance regarding God's call come first-hand, from God's direct communication rather than from just our own reasoning.'[19] In relation to theodicy, this would indicate an evidential approach and Moser stated that Jesus brought the Hebrew prophetic tradition to its unique climax when he remarked that the pure in heart will see God.

> [Jesus] also suggested, in keeping with the Hebrew Scriptures, that God 'hides' his ways from ungrateful holdouts and reveals himself to those humbly open to God's program of morally serious living community (see Lk. 10.21-22; Mt. 11.25-27).[20]

---

16. Ibid., 60.
17. Daniel Howard-Snyder and Paul K. Moser, eds, *Divine Hiddennness: New Essays* (Cambridge: Cambridge University Press, 2001), 17.
18. Paul K. Moser, 'Cognitive idolatry and Divine Hiding', in ibid., 127.
19. Ibid., 131.
20. Ibid., 132.

There are important passages in the New Testament letters making it clear that what is described as God's hiddenness really refers to God's existence, a mystery in the sense of exceeding human understanding, but in fact revealed: '[God] has made known to us the mystery of his will, according to his good pleasure that he has set forth in Christ, as a plan for the fullness of time' (Eph. 1.9). Similarly, in Colossians, Paul says, 'we have not ceased praying for you and asking that you may be filled with the knowledge of God's will in all spiritual wisdom and understanding' (Col. 1.9).

The mystery of evil, for which theodicy endeavours to account, needs to be approached by Christians in light of God's self-revelation in the Scriptures, culminating in God speaking 'to us by a son' (Heb. 1.2). As the Second Vatican Council's Constitution on Revelation put it, Christ 'is himself the mediator and the sum total of revelation' (*Dei Verbum* no. 2). In his person, Jesus revealed God's justice and love precisely through the combat with evil in which he ultimately triumphed.

A contemporary writer, Kevin J. Vanhoozer, treats the issue of suffering from a Trinitarian perspective, relying on what he calls divine communicative action:

> What then is evil? To confess that the Son sits on the right hand of the Father is to shift the perspective from which to address the problem. Christ may not suffer in session, but he is far from indifferent. The Mediator intercedes for us with the Father and ministers to us via the Spirit. ... While the existence of evil remains a mystery, the triune God is not hapless before it. Nothing can separate us from the love of Christ, because God's love stands fast, enduring forever.[21]

The Kabbalah

The Jewish mystical tradition has its own approach to the mystery of evil. The medieval Jewish Kabbalist movement, especially in the form expounded by Rabbi Isaak Lauria (1534–72), addressed the issue of evil in a unique way. A fundamental principle, *Tzimtzum,* meaning contraction or concealment, gives rise to a doctrine of creation in which the universe is a result of a cosmic negation. The universe is not so much a something that has been created from nothing, 'but rather a genre of nothingness resulting from a contraction or concealment of the one true reality, which is God'.[22] From this arises the notion of evil; 'evil is to creation as the

---

21. Kevin J. Vanhoozer, *Remythologizing Theology: Divine Action, Passion and Authorship* (Cambridge: Cambridge University Press, 2010), 502–3.

22. Sanford L. Drob, *Symbols of the Kabbalah: Philosophical and Psychological Perspectives* (Northvale, NJ: Jason Aronson, 2000), 120.

outside of a container is to the space it contains'.[23] David S. Ariel explained in his *Kabbalah: The Mystic Quest in Judaism*:

> The Kabbalists introduced a distinction between the hidden and revealed aspects of God. The hidden, infinite aspect of God is called *Eyn Sof* (The Infinite). … The name suggests only that God exists without implying anything about his character. … Because of the great sublimity and transcendence of God, no name at all can be applied to The Infinite. … The Infinite has no relationship with his creation.[24]

Nonetheless God's existence pervades all creation because of ten aspects or instruments of activity of God's revealed Being, or, more simply, ten emanations, echoing Plato.[25] The odd conjunction of hiddenness and creation is expressed by the terminology employed:

> The Hebrew word for 'universe' and 'eternity', *olam*, comes from the root '–l-m, which also means 'hiding' or 'concealment'. Only when God is hidden can the universe exist.[26]

The task for the Kabbalists was how to give a rational account of this polar situation. It involved the elaboration of the emanation idea in the concept of the *Shevirat ha-kelim*, or 'breaking of the vessels', a catastrophe theory of creation. As Jonathan Sacks explained:

> God, in making the world, could not leave it devoid of his presence. He therefore sent forth rays of his light. … The light was, however, too intense for its containers, which thereby broke, scattering fragments of light throughout the world.[27]

The *Shevirat* is called by other authors the ten *Sefirot* and is an attempt to explain how the infinite God can have a relationship with finite being. 'What appear to

---

23. Ibid., 329: 'Evil is to creation, and the individual finite existence that is creation's very essence, as the outside of a container is to the space it contains. Evil is written into the very idea of creation and is woven into the fabric of the human soul.'

24. David S. Ariel, *Kabbalah: The Mystic Quest in Judaism* (Lanham, MD: Rowman and Littlefield, 2006), 59.

25. See Gerold Necker, 'Circle, Point and Line', in *Creation and Recreation in Jewish Thought: Festschrift in Honor of Joseph Dan*, Rachel Elior and Peter Schäfer, eds (Tübingen: Mohr and Siebeck, 2005), 195; The sixteenth-century kabbalistic scholar Abraham Herera interpreted the Lurianic kabbalah in a Platonic key.

26. Jonathan Sacks, *To Heal a Fractured World: The Ethics of Responsibility* (London: Continuum, 2005), 74.

27. Ibid., 74–5.

be changes are only the various modes by which the *Sefirot* channel, reflect and employ the essence of The Infinite."[28]

The fourth and fifth *Sefirot*, called *Hesed* (mercy) and *Din* (judgement), respectively, represent archetypes of contrary powers that act in the world; *Din* is said to be capable of issuing its own emanation, which takes place outside of the world of the *Sefirot* as the world of demonic forces. The 'left emanation'[29] from *Din* creates a universe of evil that stands locked in permanent and mortal combat with the power of the *Sefirot*. The mythology of *Din* is meant to convey that there is not a great essential difference between good and evil, and that one God has created them both.[30]

So far there is reference to evil, but no account of its overcoming. According to Jonathan Sacks, it is the task of humanity to gather up the scattered fragments of light and restore them to their proper place and this is part of Jewish spirituality, given the name *tikkum olam*, mending or perfecting the world. The importance of this view of spirituality is that involves a gradual healing and in Lauranic kabbalah it avoids the false messianism of a giant leap that would bring exile to an end. '*Tikkum-olam*, as R. Isaac Lauria conceived it, is a mystical and spiritual idea. It is *not* social action.'[31]

From the perspective of Christian theodicy, kabbalistic spirituality acknowledges the existence of evil, even radical evil affecting the material world, but is somehow not attributable to the hidden God. Understandably, it does not envisage a redeemer and is averse to messianic figures, so that the response to evil devolves on the shoulders of humanity through actions that are more hidden than socially manifest. Humanity has engaged in transgression, *averah*, from the start, and is responsible for restoring order to creation. There is something of a parallel between this vision and that of Irenaeus, but the recapitulation, so to speak, of creation does not involve the Incarnation.

Karl Barth (1886–1968)

The reference above to the Vatican Council's *Constitution on Divine Revelation* can serve as an introduction to the theology of Karl Barth (1886–1968) and to what is often referred to be, perhaps not quite accurately, his theodicy.[32] His *Church*

---

28. Ariel, *Kabbalah*, 67.

29. Right and left in this scheme represent masculine and feminine.

30. Ariel, *Kabbalah*, 76–7. There are various conceptions of the *Sefirot*. See Moshe Idel, *Kabbalah: New Perspectives* (New Haven, CT: Yale University Press, 1988), 136–53.

31. Sacks, *To Heal a Fractured World*, 78.

32. The General Index to his works gives many references to 'theodicy', indicating many sections of the *Church Dogmatics* in which in fact the word 'theodicy' does not appear and are simply expositions of his theology of atonement. He himself uses the word in passing in reference to traditional theodicies such as that of Irenaeus or Leibniz.

Dogmatics was completed before theological renewal in the Catholic Church was given official expression in the Second Vatican Council, but before his death, Karl Barth engaged in discussions with theologians in the Vatican and was largely approving of the Council's documents, especially the Constitution on Divine Revelation.[33]

In *Church Dogmatics* II/1 Barth dealt with the knowledge of God using the dialectical method he derived ultimately from Calvin. He emphasised the initiative of God in a revelation that does not take away God's hiddenness. Much later in the *Church Dogmatics*, in IV.iii.1 (Section 70) his exegesis of the Book of Job dealt with the hiddenness of God in terms of the relationship between God and Job. Job's puzzlement at his treatment, and the final understanding he reached, Barth presented in terms of a transition. Job asked 'Why have you made me your target?' (Job 7.20), while saying also: 'Even now, in fact, my witness is in heaven and he that vouches for me is on high' (16.19). But when God answered 'out of the whirlwind' (38.1) Job was eventually reduced to silence and submission, contrasting his two states: 'I had heard of you by the hearing of the ear, but now my eye sees you, therefore I despise myself and repent in dust and ashes' (42.5-6). Barth described Job's dilemma from the outset as:

> In trying to hold fast to God, and actually holding fast to him, as the One who acts in this way, how can he understand and acquiesce in the concealment in which he now encounters him, in his existence as *Deus absconditus*?[34]

The solution proposed by Barth turns on the different ways in which God is revealed in the story of Job, as in the Scriptures generally.

> Yahweh is the ruling Subject in the history of Job. ... As this Subject God is always known to him. ... It is in relation to him that he knows... that what befalls him has to do with God. It is on the basis of this knowledge that he disputes with God. The disputing or problem arises from Yahweh's being as Elohim and Shaddai, from the majestic and almighty operation in relation to him. In this predication and activity, which are undoubtedly intrinsic and proper to Yahweh, he is unknowable to him.[35]

---

33. His death in 1968 foreclosed on what might have been fruitful dialogue with Catholic theology. Unable to accept an invitation to be an official 'observer' at Vatican II, he subsequently visited the Vatican and engaged in discussions on the documents of the Council, especially the *Constitution on Divine Revelation*. He gave an account of these exchanges, including his quite positive reactions in his book, *Ad Limina Apostolorum* (Richmond, VA: John Knox Press, 1968).

34. *Church Dogmatics* IV. 3. 1. 422.

35. Ibid., 428.

The implications of this unknowability or hiddenness were examined by Harold M. Schulweis in an article, 'Karl Barth's Job'.[36]

> The divine Other is Subject personality, not impersonal moral or metaphysical ideals. The divine Person cannot be made perceptible to man, reasonable and amenable to human standards, without reducing his dignity. The true Subject of faith is Yahweh, the unique Personality, who will not be confined to any limits outside himself. ... With Yahweh one must be prepared to live in surprise.[37]

This is in accord with the standard comment that Barth's theology involves, as David Ford said, 'the denial of any continuity or any natural point of contact between God and humanity or between the gospel and culture'.[38] Schulweis drew the conclusion:

> For Barth, the need for theodicy is itself a symptom of man's enslavement to moral and logical criteria and norms irrelevant to the conduct of the divinely unique One. Yahweh neither requires nor asks for Job's 'understanding, agreement or applause'. The very question underlying the alleged need for theodicy is presumptuous.[39]

The reason for this lies in Barth's theology of the Subject and its relations with the multiplicity of divine predicates, as in the case of Elohim and Shaddai. Barth was ever concerned, according to Schulweis, 'lest the predicates of divinity, once assigned meaning independent of the Subject, become the measuring rod of God. Once they are given separate status, characterised unequivocally, the Subject is open to judgment according to the sense of predicates.'[40] God the Subject, in whom all reality dwells, then needs to be justified. In contrast, Barth's analysis suggests the need for an anthropodicy, not a theodicy, for a justification of man's sinfulness not God's justice.[41]

The grand theme of his *Church Dogmatics* was to progress from a doctrine of God, to a doctrine of Creation and Redemption, with Christ as the final self-revelation of God and bringer of the atonement, the destroyer of evil.

---

36. Harold M. Schulweis, 'Karl Barth's Job', *Jewish Quarterly Review*, New Series, vol. 65, no. 3 (January 1975): 156–67.
37. Ibid., 158.
38. David Ford, 'Barth, Karl', in *The Blackwell Encyclopedia of Modern Christian Thought*, Alister E. McGrath, ed. (Oxford: Blackwell Publishing, 1993), 30.
39. Schulweis, 'Karl Barth's Job', 157.
40. Ibid., 159.
41. Ibid., 164.

Das Nichtige

In this scenario, the question arises as to the status of Barth's introduction of the term *das Nichtige* into his theology in the course of his discussion of Creation (in Book III), whether it is to be regarded as integral to his thought, his solution to the problem of evil – even his theodicy? The general context of his work was a return to the pre-eminence of Scripture; 'he recognised the exhaustion of the 'modern' German intellectual projects (Hegel, neo-Kantianism, Harnack) already in the opening of the twentieth-century'.[42] Yet his speculation about 'nothingness' goes beyond the Scriptural framework and for John Hick the speculation in which Barth indulged was mythological rather than rational.[43]

There is the question, therefore, as to whether the introduction of *das Nichtige* as part of the account of creation was in some sense arbitrary, given that he had included also the traditional teaching on the devil as agent of evil. His thought on the issue had developed over time from his early writings on creation to a definitive formulation in the *Church Dogmatics*. In an early work, *The Faith of the Church: A Commentary on the Apostles' Creed*, but effectively on Calvin's *Geneva Catechism* (1545) – which has a question on what is to be said about wicked men and devils – Barth interprets Calvin's position as affirming God's creation as 'the grand Yes, whereto any opposite is No'.[44] In his *Dogmatics in Outline* he described creation as a grace; 'the very existence of the creature alongside God is a great puzzle and miracle'.[45] His reverential view of creation led to the statement: 'Everything outside God is held constant by God over nothingness'.[46] This is clearly a metaphysical comment; the contingent creature is threatened by the possibility of destruction, of nothingness, which is excluded only by God. The consequence of this is that the whole realm that we term evil – death, sin, the devil and hell – is not God's creation, but rather what was excluded by God's creation, that to which God has said 'No'.

He concluded in *Dogma in Outline*:

> And if there is a reality of evil, it can only be the reality of this excluded and repudiated thing, the reality behind God's back, which he passed over when he made the world and made it good. … What is not good God did not make; it has no creaturely existence. But if being is to be ascribed to it at all, and we would rather not say that it is non-existent, then it is only the power of the being that arises out of the weight of the divine No.[47]

---

42. Philip Clayton, 'God and the World', in *The Cambridge Guide to Postmodern Theology*, Kevin J. Vanhoozer, ed. (Cambridge: Cambridge University Press, 2003), 203.
43. John Hick, *Evil and the God of Love* (Glasgow: Collins. Fount Paperbacks, 1968), 142. Hick had other criticisms, which will be considered later.
44. Karl Barth, *The Faith of the Church: A Commentary on the Apostles' Creed* (London: Fontana Books, 1960).
45. Karl Barth, *Dogmatics in Outline* (London: S.C.M., 1966), 54.
46. Ibid., 55.
47. Ibid., 57.

It is noticeable that his reverence for creation as God's grace, as a good, caused him to withhold God's permission from the existence of what is not good, but he felt constrained to admit to some kind of reality. This situation had to be faced in the end and he returned to it in the *Church Dogmatics*.

The *Church Dogmatics* included material written during his earlier years but did show development of the positions already quoted from his early works. In *CD* II.1, On Creation, speaking of God's knowledge, he said that God knows the impossible, 'that which he has rejected, excluded and denied, sin as sin, death as death, the devil as the devil',[48] and in II.2, he said that 'sin, death and the devil do exist within the sphere of *res creatae*, as principles of disobedience, evil and rebellion. But they do not belong to these *res creatae*. They are not themselves created by God. Their being is simply non-being, which disturbs and denies God's creation.'[49] The fact that they are within the sphere of creation must mean that they belong to its shadowside, yet there seems to be little to distinguish them from what he will go on to describes as nothingness, *das Nichtige*. The lack of clarity here must arise from the fact that there was a progress from the earlier writings to the final position to be found in the *Church Dogmatics*. In fact as will be seen below, he devoted a paragraph of *CD* III to 'The Misconception of Nothingness', and will say in *CD* III.3 c.50, 2 that creation praises God 'even on its shadowy side, even in the negative aspect in which it is so near to nothingness'.[50] He will also say that 'the concrete form in which nothingness is active and revealed is the sin of man in his personal act and guilt'.[51] But the question remains: given his treatment of these 'negativities' associated in some way with creation, what purpose could the introduction of a further negative, a nothingness, serve, especially as in his treatment of Reconciliation (*CD* IV c.58, 4) 'the gracious will and act of God in Jesus Christ' is presented as superior to and as overcoming, sin, while nothingness is not mentioned?

His formal treatment of nothingness began in *CD* III.3 with two chapters, ch. 49, 'God the Father as Lord of his Creatures', including a section on Divine Preserving, and ch. 50, devoted to 'God and Nothingness', with a section on the Reality of Nothingness. According to the English-language editors, 'Nothingness' – the usual translation of *das Nichtige* – is not used in the more common or abstract way but in the sense of 'that which is not'.

Creation out of nothing meant that God distinguished what he willed from that which he did not will. The preservation of creation is a matter of its being maintained against overthrow by that which is not. He looked to the Genesis text – 'the earth was a formless void and darkness covered the deep' (1.2) – in support of his assertion that there was here an exclusion from creation, and though he

---

48. Karl Barth, *Church Dogmatics* II.1, *The Dogma of Creation* (Edinburgh: T&T Clark, 1960), 552.
49. Ibid., 560.
50. *Church Dogmatics* III.3 c.50, 2 297.
51. Ibid., III.3 c.50, 3 305.

eschews philosophical terminology, he could be said to be referring to unrealised potency.

In Chapter 50, he considered the issue of nothingness in detail. He made some positive statements:

> There is opposition and resistance to God's world-dominion. There is in world-occurrence an element, indeed an entire sinister system of elements which is not comprehended by God's providence ... and which is not therefore preserved, accompanied, nor ruled by the almighty action of God like creaturely occurrence.[52]

While not comprehended by it, it cannot escape God's providence, yet the manner in which this is done is highly peculiar in accordance with the particular nature of this factor. 'This opposition and resistance, this stubborn element and alien factor, may provisionally be defined as nothingness.'[53]

In an important paragraph, 'The Misconception of Nothingness' (*CD* III, c.50, 2), he returned to the idea of the shadowside of creation:

> Light exists as well as shadow; there is a positive as well as a negative aspect of creation and creaturely existence. ... Viewed from its negative aspect, creation is as it were on the frontier of nothingness and orientated towards it. Creation is continually confronted by this menace. It is continually reminded that as God's creation it has not only a positive side but a negative side.[54]

The shadowside of creation obtrudes on the relationship between God and the creature and renders problematic the relationship summarily described in the text: 'Of him and through him and to him are all things to whom be glory for ever. Amen' (Rom. 11.36). What does 'of him (God), through him and to him' mean? In *CD* III. 1 c.42, 3, he had recognised this.

> [The] witness of the created world itself is not and as such objectively exhausted in the affirmation of its immanent goodness, for it does not offer us only a positive but also a negative aspect, thus placing a negative as well as a positive judgment on our lips. We are not in a position altogether to elude the shadow that is also characteristic of existence.[55]

A fortiori, 'all things', humans first, but through humankind all things are also affected by nothingness, 'being enmeshed in and bound up with it, bearing its marks and in some degree, directly or indirectly, actively or passively, overtly or

---

52. Ibid., c.50 289.
53. Ibid.
54. *Church Dogmatics* III.3, c.50, 2, 295–6.
55. Ibid., III.1 c.42. 3 372.

covertly, being involved in the existence and operation of this alien factor'.[56] Is not the question of God's lordship posed afresh? For Barth this meant that whatever may be said about the relation between the Creator and the creature, 'it also belongs to the existence and activity of the creature to be involved in nothingness and also to be partly determined by it in its present form'.[57]

All of this puts a question mark against the relationship between Creator and creature. There is an alien factor at work that cannot be explained from the side of the Creator or creature but must be reckoned with in all its peculiarity. The truth and power of the doctrine of God's providence must be applied to this factor, but how then to avoid error on one side or the other? For Barth, it would be an error if it were asserted that this element of nothingness derives from the positive will and work of God, so that the Creator is responsible for its nothingness, the creature being exonerated from all responsibility for its existence and activity. It would also be 'an error to maintain that it derives *solely* from the activity of the creature in relation to which the lordship of God can only be a passive permission and observation, an ineffectual foreknowledge and a subsequent attitude'. This use of the word 'solely' is important, as it allows sinful humanity to be accounted for fully in Barth's theory of atonement.

Barth somewhat hesitantly referred to the so-called (as he put it) Parable of the Prodigal Son as containing an analogy for Christ's work of atonement. For him, the parable had no direct Christological content, and he wished to avoid a strained interpretation, but he did recognise an indirect one, 'even though there is not a single word in the parable about Jesus Christ and the atonement accomplished in him'.[58] The way of the son who went into a far country was not in any direct sense the way of the Son of God who is obedient to the Father. (This section nonetheless has the heading The Homecoming of the Son of Man.)

> And yet it cannot be denied that the way of the latter [Christ] is in fact the way into the far country of a lost human existence – the way in which he accepts identity and solidarity with the lost son, unreservedly taking his place, taking to himself his sin and shame.[59]

But it has been pointed out that though the liberation of humankind was real, Barth hesitated to use the word punishment as the mechanism.

> Even though Jesus Christ is our Substitute who stands in our place and bears the full penalty of our sins, Barth is hesitant to call this a real punishment.[60]

56. Ibid., III.3, c.50. 2 291.
57. Ibid., 305.
58. Ibid., IV.2 c.64 22.
59. Ibid., IV. 2 c.64 23.
60. Frank M. Hasel, 'Karl Barth's *Church Dogmatics* on the Atonement: Some Translational Problems', Andrews University Seminary Studies, vol. 29, no. 3 (Autumn 1991): 205–11, at 208.

By giving emphasis to the analogy between Christ's work of atonement and the parable, Barth attributed an objectivity to the destruction of evil, 'the deliverance of sinful man and sin itself to destruction', by Christ 'our Representative and Substitute'.[61] Paul S. Fiddes[62] has raised the question of how humankind's actual sin could be killed in another person, given that Barth acknowledged the continued existence of nothingness in the world: 'the account tips too much towards the objective end of the spectrum'. But Barth did hold that in suffering the punishment humankind deserves Christ freed everyone from the divine judgement – all this he discussed in the section 'The Judge Judged in our place' (IV I, 214–15).

It is odd that at this point (IV.1, c.14) he did not discuss the difference the Resurrection of Christ had made, the new creation announced by St Paul in Gal. 6.15 and 2 Cor. 5.17, giving humanity a new life in Christ. But in IV.2, c.15 he did refer to the various relevant texts in Galatians, Romans, Colossians and Ephesians concerning the community's life in Christ. He described as an understatement one commentator's use of the term *sedes assignata, suo tempore possidenda*. Calvin's comment in a sermon on Eph. 2.6 was a true one: it was impossible that the Head should be separated from his Members.[63]

Nothingness in its relation of opposition and resistance to God's dominion could not assume the form of a monster, which with its demonic qualities would inspire fear and respect instead of awakening Easter joy.

> For Barth, the freedom to laugh in the midst of the barbaric stage-management of evil was a moment of that freedom from sin we experience in faith in Jesus Christ. It was a variation on the Easter laughter of the early church in view of Christ's victory over 'sin, death and the devil'. Whoever lives from this victory cannot finally take nothingness seriously, despite its consequences.[64]

As it is already judged in Jesus Christ, evil can injure but no longer kill or destroy. But there is also the danger of underestimating its power in relation to the creature. Barth asked: 'How can justice be done to the holiness and omnipotence of God

---

61. *Church Dogmatics* IV.I, c.14. 2. 230.

62. Paul S. Fiddes, 'Christianity, Atonement and Evil', in *The Cambridge Companion to the Problem of Evil*, Chad Meister and Paul K. Moser, eds (Cambridge: Cambridge University Press, 2017), 210–29 at 222.

63. Ibid., *Church Dogmatics*, IV.2 c.15 277. Cf. John Calvin, *John Calvin's Sermons on Ephesians* (Edinburgh: Banner of Truth Trust, 1973), 153: 'We must [I say] suffer these things and yet, in the meanwhile, be fully persuaded and fully resolved of this doctrine, that we, for all that, shall not fail to inherit the kingdom, for it is impossible for the head to be separated from the members, and our Lord Jesus Christ has not gone there for his own sake alone'.

64. Wolf Krötke, *Sin and Nothingness in the Theology of Karl Barth*. With a new Foreword by the Author. Philip G. Ziegler and Christina-Maria Bammel, trans. and ed. (Princeton, NJ: Princeton Theological Seminary, 2005), xii.

when we are faced by the problem of nothingness?'[65] In effect, could the project of theodicy really succeed? For him this problem provided a clear demonstration of the necessary brokenness of all theological thought and utterance. Paul Ricoeur recognised this brokenness aspect of theology asserted by Barth when he described his dialectic as 'broken'.

> The famous section of *Church Dogmatics* entitled 'God and Nothingness' ... may be assigned to a "broken" theology, to the extent that it sees in evil a reality that is not commensurate with the goodness of God and creation, and furthermore a reality that is not reducible to the negative side of human experience.[66]

Paul Ricoeur saw that for Barth it was necessary to think of a nothingness hostile to God and not just as a deficiency and privation.

> [We] may say that we 'know' the reality of evil to the extent that we confess that nothingness is what Christ has vanquished by 'nihilating' himself and that God met and struggled with this nothingness in Jesus Christ.[67]

But Ricoeur was not satisfied by the fact that Barth related the reality of nothingness to the left hand of God, the one that rejects when the right hand elects.[68]

> Can this coordination without conciliation between left and right hands make sense? Is it not a covert concession to the failed theodicies of the past and accordingly a weak compromise substituted for a broken dialectic, does it not reopen the way to speculations such as those of Giordano Bruno and Schelling on the demonic aspect of the deity?[69]

Barth's practical conclusion was that the power of nothingness should be rated as low as possible in relation to God and as high as possible in relation to ourselves.[70]

This tendency on Barth's part to move between considerations of nothingness in relation to the Creator and in relation to the creature arises from the recognised dialectical nature of his theology. 'Dialectic is a permanent feature of Barth's theology, not a temporary phase left behind in the 1930s.'[71] While his dialectical

---

65. *Church Dogmatics* III.3 c.49 292.

66. Paul Ricoeur, 'Evil: A Challenge to Philosophy and Theology', in *Figuring the Sacred: Religion, Narrative and Imagination* (Minneapolis, MN: Fortress Press, 1995), 257.

67. Ibid.

68. *Church Dogmatics* III.3. c.50 351: 'He is Lord both on the right hand and the left. It is only on this basis that nothingness "is". But on this basis it really "is".'

69. Ricoeur, 'Evil: A Challenge to Philosophy and Theology', 258.

70. *Church Dogmatics* III.3 c.49 295.

71. John Webster, 'Introducing Barth', in *The Cambridge Companion to Karl Barth*, John Webster, ed. (Cambridge: Cambridge University Press, 2000), 13.

theology was considered a new approach in Reformed circles in the 1920s, it clearly showed signs of the influence of Calvin, to whom Barth devoted much attention as he abandoned an earlier attachment to the Liberal Protestantism of the time.

In adopting this dialectical approach, where his exploration of evil was in the context of a secularised society and abandonment of the enchantment culture of the late Middle Ages was no longer an issue, Barth was not faced with the difficulties theologians over many centuries have encountered in developing theodicies. It should be noted, however, that his use of the term 'devil' in *CD* III.3, c.49 indicates a continuing leaning towards the Scripture's presentation of a world where the devil is personified as a combatant, especially against Christ and defeated by Christ. Whether the difficult concept – or perhaps term – *das Nichtige* can provide a convincing alternative to the biblical narrative when there is need, as will be seen later in this work, for a coherent and consistent framework for clinical investigations of morbid psychological states, does however remain an issue.

Karl Rahner (1904–84)

Karl Rahner (1904–84) devoted a section of *Theological Investigations*, Vol. 19, to discussion of the topic 'Why Does God Allow Us to Suffer?' It took the form of an assessment of the various categories of theodicy, by effectively treating evil as impersonal. His approach was to avoid bringing 'an absolutely firm notion of God' to the question of suffering:

> The possibility remains entirely open that we shall gain a correct idea of God only when we attempt to answer this question.[72]

This was an unusual move, since the traditional starting point for a theodicy, and the source of the project's challenge, would be to predicate characteristics of goodness and omnipotence to God. He was also not discriminating between different real or conceivable possibilities of God's relationship to human suffering and thus avoided the traditional distinction between permitting and causing, in contrast with Aquinas' meticulous discussion of the difference. In fact, for Rahner the distinction was not important because God is the ground and cause of all reality. Because of God's omnipotent freedom, permission and causing come so close together that 'we can ask quite simply why God allows us to suffer without having to distinguish *a priori* in this between permitting and causing'.[73] There was the further issue of the distinction between the suffering that arises from sin and all the incidents that cause suffering but cannot be ascribed to any freely chosen sin; he held that suffering arising from creaturely freedom, which is never absolute,

---

72. Karl Rahner S.J., *Theological Investigations*, Vol. 19 (London: Darton, Longman and Todd, 1984), 195.
73. Ibid., 196.

is interwoven in an indissoluble way with other suffering. For this reason, he felt he could pursue the basic question in its entirety without denying the distinction.

The first attempt to answer the question he surveyed – without mentioning proponents – 'tends to see suffering as a practically unavoidable side effect in a pluralistic and evolving world'. This world consists of many complex realities and there is a struggle for existence that involves the pike swallowing the young whitefish. To interpret biological activity as suffering is 'merely stupid'.

According to this theory, in the last resort moral evil and the suffering that it involves must also be understood in the same way. These too are frictional phenomena which necessarily accompany mind, freedom and moral development. Evil is no more than the good that is not yet perfect or the inescapable tribute the finite mind must make to its material foundation on which it rests and which it has to use.[74]

In the last resort, here evil must be explained entirely as a consequence of heredity, social conditions, psychological environment and bad education. But protest against suffering in this context could be an exaggeration of the demand which a materially conditioned mind can properly make on reality. However, in the end, this answer is in fact unsatisfactory and superficial in view of the limited scope of the question as formulated – why does God allow us to suffer? The realisation of spirit, of freedom and personal decision are materially conditioned – spirit must be regarded as a secondary manifestation of matter.[75]

But it is not sufficient to ascribe suffering to the hardships arising from the material world as such. Freedom itself produce suffering and pain. It has produced immense and indescribable suffering that cannot be blamed on material and biological conditions.

> Responsibility for the march into the gas chambers at Auschwitz cannot be spread over the phenomena leading to the plunge of migratory ants into an abyss.[76]

Rahner next considered the interpretation of suffering that seeks to derive it exclusively from creaturely freedom and explain it in this light. If creaturely freedom is responsible in every respect for suffering, sin and death, it is not absurd to 'take into account a *creaturely* freedom which is not identical with *human* freedom' and has created a history prior to the biological nature of this earth, thus co-determining the history of nature and the history of humanity, and marking it with suffering. In this broad statement Rahner seems not to have been referring to a Manichean theory but to one that centred on fallen angels who had exercised their freedom with deleterious consequences for humanity. He pointed out, however, that a freedom purely and simply absolute and underivable in its decisions cannot

---

74. Ibid., 198.
75. Ibid., 198–9.
76. Ibid., 199.

exist, because all freedom is created freedom, sustained in its existence, its power and decisions by God's providence.

> We may not be able to see how true creaturely freedom can so exist with the inalienability of its decision *and* at the same time with the inescapability from God's sovereignty, in which God sustains this creaturely freedom and places it in its freedom, but for that very reason does not share his sovereignty with the creature's freedom; this in no way alters the fact that our freedom is completely embraced in God's supreme providence.[77] (Italics added)

He concluded that the statement that suffering arises from freedom is not a final and definitive conclusion, but a hint that, important as it may be, disappears into the mystery of the sovereign freedom of God.

> In these circumstances, how far suffering in the world is to be ascribed to man's creaturely freedom and eventually to that of the angels and the devils, and how far suffering exists that is truly man's suffering and yet does not spring from an evil use of freedom, is more or less merely a question of theoretical curiosity, the answer to which in no way alters our existential situation. Whatever form the answer takes, it remains in any case provisional and in the end is lost in God's incomprehensibility and in his freedom.[78]

Rahner considered briefly the theodicy associated with Irenaeus, though without mentioning him or John Hick. This is to regard suffering as a situation of trial and maturing. He considered that such a theory contains an important imperative in that it calls on people to live in such a way that suffering does not turn their attitude towards God into one of despair, but perfects them, even though the process of maturing leads them through the abysses of dying and death with Jesus. But, as other commentators have done, Rahner pointed to the lack of proportion between suffering and maturing as likely to be the result in many cases of suffering. The children burned to death by napalm bombs were not going through a process of maturing. The theory was not to be easily dismissed, however, because of the opportunities it may afford to live a life of deprivation and misery and overcome the suffering in faith, hope and love. Nevertheless, this theory remains inadequate to explain why God allows suffering.

Rahner went on to consider further answers to why God allows us to suffer; one was to regard suffering as a pointer to eternal life. He commented that no one should dismiss this answer as a 'dubious analgesic' but held also that no one can prove that suffering is the absolute necessary means for attaining eternal life. Finally, he turned to a consideration of the incomprehensibility of suffering as part of the incomprehensibility of God, a somewhat elaborate way of saying that

---

77. Ibid., 201.
78. Ibid., 202.

suffering is a mystery, thus aligning himself with many theologians who say that evil is a mystery.

He concluded by quoting an interview a certain Walter Dick had with Romano Guardini as he was dying. Guardini would ask the angel a question no book, not even the bible, no dogma ... no theodicy ... had been able to answer for him: 'Why, God, these fearful detours on the way to salvation, the suffering of the innocent, why sin?' For Rahner, an answer could only be heard, 'if we surrender ourselves in unconditionally adoring love as answer to God. ... There is no blessed light to illumine the dark abyss of suffering other than God himself.'[79]

Empirical science

It is important to remember that the issue of theodicy has been discussed over the centuries and up to modern times from a standpoint that did not include either present-day physical or biological science. Opponents of theism have of course been inspired since the nineteenth century by evolutionary theory and, on the other side, the twentieth-century theodicy of Hick has also availed of it. But neither opponents nor theists can be said to have been informed by cosmological studies. The advance in understanding of the universe, including a general awareness of the Big Bang theory of its origins, and a sense of its evolution in terms of expansion, is at a simple level for many; some see the theory of origin as an expression of the religious doctrine of creation, while many would be surprised to learn that the concept of the universe's expansion is a metaphorical one. Understanding energy and matter as having negative as well as positive value is required in order to grasp the meaning of cosmic 'black holes' and metaphor is again relevant. The gravitational field of dark matter is understood to be the force that keeps the galaxies together, and dark energy is involved in the concept of an expanding universe. It is encouraging that Barth's idea of the shadowside of creation and the more recondite idea of nothingness are stated in terms of positive and negative sides of reality; science and theology are both faced with mystery. Theologically, evil remains a mystery, while for physics 'the theory of everything' remains elusive.

It is fortunate that the findings of empirical science, both physical and biological, can have relevance to the issue of evil, its nature and to an extent its origin, if in the relationship between theology and science metaphor is employed. (Some understanding of science is naturally required.) In the area of physics, Robert J. Russell of the Centre for Theology and the Natural Sciences at Berkeley University has used the concept of entropy as a metaphor for evil.[80] In its simplest

---

79. Ibid., 208.

80. Robert John Russell, of the Centre for Theology and Natural Science in the University of California at Berkeley, pioneered this investigation with his paper 'Entropy and Evil', *Zygon*, vol. 19, no. 4 (December 1984): 449–67 and subsequently in his *Cosmology: From Alpha to Omega* (Minneapolis, MN: Fortress Press, 2008).

expression, entropy is the measure of the amount of energy no longer capable of being turned into work.[81] When heat energy is applied to water in an open container, turning it into steam, the energy applied is thereby dissipated and the process is irreversible. This can also be stated in terms of an orderly state becoming a disorderly one – what in Aquinas' terms might be described as a physical evil – and can be illustrated by the kinetic energy of a falling teacup being dissipated through shattering the cup into fragments on the ground, thereby increasing entropy.

To return to Augustine's example of sunlight injuring a person's eyes, an evil experienced by the person, which he used to illustrate his principle of changeable things giving way one to another according to laws governing the universe, his point was that natural evil had a legitimate place in creation and he declared 'cloudy and windy sky' as 'apt' for conditions on earth. He would not be concerned about the infinitesimal amount of the sun's energy being used up in the process of the injury, though its energy is in fact constantly degrading. In addition to the natural evil resulting from the sun's activity, human activity, involuntary such as drawing on the planet's resources to maintain life, and voluntary such as driving vehicles that pollute the atmosphere, living wastefully, all increase entropy in the form of additional pollution.

The traditional understanding of biological evolution has been that higher forms of life emerge from lower forms by natural selection, each succeeding species being more complex and thus better equipped as transformer of available energy – though that is a very simplistic presentation of evolution. Humankind can do so by the use of technology, technically exosomatic tools (in contrast with the endosomatic ones, eyes, ears, teeth, claws on which lesser species rely).

> The entropy law states that evolution dissipates the overall available energy for life on this planet. Our concept of evolution is the exact opposite. We believe that evolution somehow magically creates overall value and order on earth. Now that the environment we live in is so dissipated and disordered that it is apparent to the naked eye, we are for the first time beginning to have second thoughts about our views on evolution, progress and the creation of things of material value.[82]

'The Entropy Law destroys the notion of history as progress.'[83] Both quotations are from a book written in 1980, before the beginning of the series of world conferences on climate change with the Kyoto Protocol of December 1997. These have used the results of empirical science to establish ethical norms. While agnostic of morality, empirical science records the results of moral evil in its experiments.

---

81. Ludwig Boltzmann developed a mathematical formula describing the process in 1877.

82. Jeremy Rifkin, with Ted Howard, *Entropy: A New World View* (Toronto: Bantam Books, 1981), 55–6.

83. Ibid., 6.

So the metaphor of entropy can embrace all kinds of evil, both moral and natural, together described by the term 'metaphysical evil', which 'refers to the basic fact of finitude and limitation'.[84] According to the social anthropologist Ernest Becker (*Escape from Evil*, 1975) there is a 'natural and built-in evil in social life because all interaction is mutual appropriation'.[85] This led him to conclude:

> The soberest conclusion that we could make about what has actually been taking place on the planet for about three billion years is that it is being turned into a vast pit of fertiliser. But the sun distracts our attention, always baking the blood dry, making things grow over it, and with its warmth giving the hope that comes with the organism's comfort and expansiveness.[86]

The laws of thermodynamics take into account all dissipation of energy, including that emitted by the sun as part of the 'expanding' universe in which entropy is gradually increasing. What the final outcome will be can be understood differently according to what the relation actually is between the mass of the universe (taking account of black holes) and the gravitational attraction operating within it. Depending on the nature of this relationship, the universe will finally collapse, or will continue to expand forever, or will cease to expand in an infinitely far time as a closed system.

All of this would be irrelevant to Augustine, who believed that his world would come to an end with the return of Christ in an unpredictable but short time, thus finally resolving theodicy's problem of the persistence of evil in creation. He could hold this view because the Christian perception of God as creator is that all God created was good and that God's Providence works to bring creation to fulfilment. From that perspective, the Resurrection of Christ is of fundamental significance for humanity's future. The Lord's risen body was/is the transmuted form of his dead body, in what St Paul calls a 'new creation' (2 Cor. 5.17). So matter itself participates in the resurrection-transformation, and even now awaits its full redemption from decay (Rom. 8.21).[87]

---

84. Nancey Murphy, 'Natural Science', in *The Oxford Handbook of Systematic Theology*, John Webster et al., eds (Oxford: Oxford University Press, 2007), 551.

85. Ernest Becker, *Escape from Evil* (New York: Free Press, 1975), 137. He died in 1974, so a posthumous publication.

86. Ernest Becker, *The Denial of Death* (New York: Free Press, 1973), 283.

87. John Polkinghorne, *The Polkinghorne Reader. Science, Faith and the Search for Meaning*, Thomas J. Oord, ed. (West Conshohocken, PA: Templeton Press, 2010), 219-20: 'Two remarkable New Testament passages (Rom. 8.18-25; Col. 1.15-20) do indeed speak of a cosmic redemption. Just as we see Jesus' resurrection as the origin and guarantee of human hope, so we can also see it as the origin and guarantee of a universal hope. The significance of the empty tomb is that the Lord's risen and glorified body is the transmuted form of his dead body. Thus matter itself participates in the resurrection transformation, enjoying thereby its own redemption from decay.' See also John Polkinghorne, *Belief in God in an Age of Science* (New Haven, CT: Yale University Press, 1998), 21; David Wilkinson,

Among some cosmologists, there has been speculation about a future of the universe that overcomes the problem of entropy, and therefore of evil, though the speculation concerned itself not with the moral but the physical future. It focuses on the possibility of a continued existence for humanity, or what form life would ultimately take in a steady-state universe. John D. Barrow and Frank J. Tipler (*The Anthropic Cosmological Principle*, 1986) speculated about a future transition of humanity through an Omega Point, at least superficially similar to the Christian concept of the final state of creation, the *Eschaton*,[88] though the work makes no reference to God or to Christ. Their proposal envisaged the enormous computer power available at that Omega point being used to create computer simulations of the human race. In a separate book relating directly to Christian belief, *The Physics of Immortality: Modern Cosmology, God and the Resurrection of the Dead*, Frank Tipler made the assertion that 'life is a form of information processing, and human mind – and the human soul – is a very complex computer programme'.[89] He assumed that 'life goes on forever if machines of some sort can continue to exist forever'.[90]

The doyen of studies in the Science and Religion dialogue, John Polkinghorne (†2021), had serious reservations about the authors' proposal:

> I do not think that it succeeds. There are physical difficulties: the unlimited amounts of computer power are attained only in the infinitesimal dying moments, and their availability depends upon taking absolutely literally extrapolations into this unknown area of physical process. Highly conjectural properties of matter would be required. There are anthropological difficulties: … I do not think we are computers made of meat. … I regard physical eschatology as presenting us with the ultimate *reductio ad absurdum* of a merely evolutionary optimism.[91]

in *Christian Eschatology and the Physical Universe* (London: T&T Clark International, 2010), 152–6, questioned Polkinghorne's views on the transformation of matter in the new creation in relation to the issue of continuity and discontinuity.

88. John D. Barrow and Frank J. Tipler, *The Anthropic Cosmological Principle* (Oxford: Oxford University Press, 1986), 675.

89. Frank J. Tipler, *The Physics of Immortality: Modern Cosmology, God and the Resurrection of the Dead* (London: Pan Books, 1994), 124. In the joint work, *The Anthropic Cosmological Principle*, 659, the authors say:

> The essence of a human being is not the body, but the programme which controls the body; we might even identify the programme which controls the body with the religious notion of a *soul*, for both are defined to be non-material entities which are the essence of a human personality. In fact defining the soul to be a type of program has much in common with Aristotle and Aquinas' definition of the soul as 'the form of activity of the body'.

90. Tipler, *The Physics of Immortality*, 127.

91. John Polkinghorne, *Science and Christian Belief: Theological Reflections of a Bottom-Up Thinker* (London: S.P.C.K., 1994), 165.

All this illustrates the fact that empirical science can describe evil in its own terms but cannot in the end give a full account of it because of a lack of transcendent perspective. But Christianity has a definite end point for redemption from the universe's decay, which it calls the return of Christ. This will be when Christ hands over the kingdom to the Father, having destroyed all evil, including the last evil, death (1 Cor. 15-26).

PART II

A CULTURAL, HISTORICAL AND LITERARY SURVEY

Chapter 3

DOES THE DEVIL EXIST? A PERSISTENT BELIEF

The existence of evil in the world is an inescapable fact. This raises such questions as how its nature may be understood and its origin established. The issue of its nature has been discussed in Chapters 1 and 2; that of its origin will be discussed below. As previously noted, what was traditionally a theodicy discussion has become a debate between theism and atheism, with the issue of evil itself left somewhat to one side. If atheism becomes dominant in intellectual debate, there is in fact little logical basis for discussion of evil. If theism is dominant, as in the past, then it is very much a live issue, and opposition to God, especially when evidence from Scripture is taken into account, can be envisaged as some kind of being representing evil. For theists it is hard to ignore the existence of a created being – discussion of an uncreated one has always found to be fruitless – 'embodying', so to speak, evil. The presence of such a being in the world has been recognised since the era of pagan and Jewish cultures, including evidence from the *Dead Sea Scrolls*,[1] and has been attributed to the existence of gods and demons of various kinds at the centre of cultic life. As there was extensive influence of pagan practices on Israel's life and worship, there was continuous need for purification from the evil endemic to them. Old Testament writers showed familiarity with the pagan gods of the Canaanite religion and its Baal worship. In Leviticus 17, God gives detailed instructions for Israelite worship, 'so that they may no longer offer their sacrifices for goat-demons to whom they prostrate themselves' (17.7). The Book of

---

1. Among the *Dead Sea Scrolls* found in Cave 1, there is a text of the Rule of the Community, dating from 75 BC to 50 BC and probably having some older elements. As part of the Feast of the annual Renewal of the Covenant, 'the priests and their assistants, the Levites, are to recite praises of God, invoking his blessing upon the righteous, known in the Community as the Sons of Light, and his curses upon the sinful Sons of Darkness, those Jews and pagans who have sided with Belial, the evil angel or spirit who leads them'. Stephen Hodge, *The Dead Sea Scrolls: An Introductory Guide* (London: Piatkus, 2001), 112. The Damascus Document, much of which predates the Rule of the Community, has three sections entitled 'nets of Belial', namely fornication, riches and pollution of the Temple, 'which Belial is characterised as setting up as three kinds of righteousness and by which he is said to have taken hold of Israel'. Robert Eisenmann and Michael Wise, *The Dead Seas Scrolls Uncovered* (Rockford, MA: Element, 1992), 53.

Judges condemned Israel when it 'lusted after other gods and bowed down before them' (Judg. 2.17). Isaiah prophesied that God 'will punish Leviathan the fleeing serpent ... and will kill the dragon that is in the sea' (Isa. 27.1), a reference to the two monsters guarding the Ugaritic shrine of Baal, Tnn (the dragon) and Ltn (Leviathan), the serpent with seven heads.[2]

The evil forces thus described ranged from gods to beasts, with no sense of personal existence. In the Psalms, apart from frequent reference to local enemies, there is also the presence of 'the pestilence that stalks in darkness or the destruction that wastes at noonday' (Ps. 91.6), a reference, it seems, to natural evils, though underlying it there may be reference to the Mesopotamian demon-god Pazuzu, who controlled the west and south-west winds, which brought famine and malaria during the dry season and, in the rainy season, storms and locusts.[3] It is worth noting that the prayer book of the Hebrews, the Palter, contains only one specific reference to demons,[4] while there are eight or nine (depending on the translation) psalms containing references to angels.

Satan in the Old Testament

These forces lack personal characteristics, and it is difficult to give a chronology of the references in the mid-sixth-century texts to a spirit that came to be called a *satan* (a common not a proper name), with the meaning of an accuser or prosecutor. Originally, it could be used of humans as well as of spirits. Its earliest use for a spirit occurs in the Book of Numbers (22.32) where the angel or messenger said he had come out as an 'adversary' against Balaam because his way was perverse.[5] It could therefore date from the early settlement in Canaan. One author claims that 'it can be argued that the full-blown concept of Satan had already appeared in the Second Temple period prior to the rise of apocalypticism,'[6] when Satan came to be

---

2. Claude F. Schaeffer, *Ugaritica II. Nouvelles Études Relatives aux Découvertes de Ras Shamra* (Paris: Librairie Orientaliste Paul Geuthier, 1949), 46.

3. Jeremy Black and Anthony Green, *Gods, Demons and Symbols of Ancient Mesopotamia: An Illustrated Dictionary* (London: British Press, 1992), 147–8: 'Pazuzu was an Assyrian and Babylon demonic god of the first millennium BC. He is represented with a rather canine face with abnormally bulging eyes, a scaly body, a snake-headed penis, the talons of a bird and usually wings. He is often regarded as an evil underworld demon, but he seems also to have played a beneficent rôle as a protector against pestilential winds (especially the west wind).'

4. Ps. 106.37 'They offered their sons and their daughters to demons.'

5. The Hebrew *malak* being translated as ἄγγελος. Cf. Henry Ansgar Kelly, *Towards the Death of Satan: The Growth and Decline of Christian Demonology* (London: Geoffrey Chapman, 1968), 6.

6. Bernard McGinn, *Antichrist: Two Thousand Years of Human Fascination with Evil* (New York: Columbia University Press, 2000), 22.

presented in the context of a future final struggle. There is evidence in that Second Temple period of the activities of spirits predating the later identification of the Satan of the New Testament.

For example, from the time of Saul in 1 Samuel to Ahab in 1 Kings there are references to spirits with an evil purpose. In 1 Samuel (19.9) 'an evil spirit from the Lord' came upon Saul and he endeavoured to kill David. In 1 Kgs 22.19-22, the prophet Micaiah had a vision of heaven. He saw the Lord seated on his throne with the hosts of heaven standing beside him to the right and to the left of him.

> And the Lord said: 'Who will entice Ahab so that he may go up and fall at Ramothgilead?'. Then one said one thing and another said another, until a spirit came forward and stood before the Lord, saying: 'I will entice him'. 'How?' the Lord asked him. He replied, 'I will go out and be a lying sprit in the mouth of all his prophets'. And the Lord said: 'You are to entice him, and you shall succeed; go out and do it.'

In the early strata of the biblical texts and in the story of Ahab and later, God is responsible for both the good and the bad things that happen to humans. In Deut. 32.39, God says: 'See now that I, even I, am he; there is no god besides me. I kill and I make alive; I wound and I heal; and no one can deliver from my hand.' In the Psalms, Israel acknowledges God's goodness to his people, his justice, and his forgiveness of their infidelities. Overall, he is on their side, turning his face against their enemies, his eyes to the just, his ears to their appeal (cf. Ps. 34). But the total lordship of God goes beyond concepts of good and evil; in his plan that they should displace other nations, they angered him when they failed to destroy the peoples as he had given command (cf. Ps. 106.32, 34).

The situation is rather different in the Book of Job, where the Lord in the end vindicates Job, even though he yields to the promptings of Satan to allow great evils to befall Job.[7] Still, a clearer distinction between good and evil emerges, and evil now has its origin in 'one of the heavenly beings': 'One day the heavenly beings came to present themselves before the Lord, and "Satan" also came among them' (Job 1.6). Originally, these heavenly beings were 'sons of Elohim', lesser divinities, but in this anthropomorphic representation of God on his throne they are God's ministers tasked with carrying out his commands.[8] Satan is singled out, but is nonetheless one of them, with the role of a prosecutor or accuser, the translation of the Hebrew name. The story need not be read as assuming the tradition of

---

7. Henry Ansgar Kelly, *Satan in the Bible: God's Minister of Justice* (Eugene, OR: Cascade, 2017), 10.

8. Ps. 82.1: 'God has taken his place in the divine council; in the midst of the gods he gives judgment.' This scene is found in 1 Kings 22.19 as well as in Job, and has a Canaanite counterpart in Ugarit texts. See Roland E. Murphy and O. Carm, 'Psalms', in *The Jerome Biblical Commentary*, Raymond Brown, S.S. et al., eds (London: Geoffrey Chapman, 1969), 591.

the fall of some angels, as there is no account in the Old Testament of such a cataclysm.[9] The dialogue between God and Satan reflects the anthropomorphic character of much of the narrative, though Satan's wandering around the world takes away from the human imagery, while retaining the suggestion of personality. The account of creation in the Book of Genesis adds flesh, so to speak, to the character of Satan by his appearing there in the form of a serpent; Milton's *Paradise Lost* will see Satan in the form of a mist entering a reptile's body. The incident concludes with the prediction of the future conflict between the 'adversary' and the human race.

In Job and in Zech. 3.1-2, Satan is not presented as God's enemy but in Wis. 2.24 he appears as the enemy of God's plan for humankind because of envy, only to be defeated in the future by Michael and his angels in the Apocalypse (12.7). The final combat and defeat of Satan is by the angel Michael and is not presented there as a combat with God, despite the classic statement in Milton's *Paradise Lost* describing Satan as one 'who durst defy the omnipotent to arms'.

Christian culture added a profile or 'history' to this figure by regarding it as part of the creation process, the creation of non-corporeal or pure spirits, some of whom by the exercise of free will sinned against God through pride and disobedience. This belief in the origin of Satan and of evil became part of the mainstream of Christian tradition, through relying on some references in Scripture that in fact give little support in relation to the origin of Satan.

The devil in the New Testament and New Testament times

In the Old Testament, Satan had already been seen as God's enemy, and consequently appears in the New as the enemy of Christ and subsequently of the members of the Ephesian community who have to 'stand against the wiles of the devil' (6.11). The church Father, Irenaeus (+202), quoted Justin Martyr (+160) to the effect that before the advent of Christ, Satan did not dare to blaspheme God as he did not know of his own condemnation, because it was concealed in 'parables and allegories', but he learned clearly from the words of Christ and his apostles that eternal fire had been prepared for him.[10] Hence, if any other explanation were needed, the adversarial nature of all references to Satan in the Gospels is clear. Mark, in the earliest of the Gospel texts, gives an account of Jesus' baptism and goes on to speak of his temptation by the devil. This is the first naming of Satan as the devil and includes the forceful words that Jesus was 'driven' by the devil into the desert. The term 'devil' is a Latinised version of the Greek, *ho diabolos*, used in the Greek version of the Old Testament, the Septuagint, to translate Satan wherever it occurred in the Hebrew text, for example in the Book of Job. In Wis.

---

9. Two Scripture passages, Ezek. 28.14-18 and Isa. 14.12-17, satires on Israel's enemies and their fate, may be interpreted as echoes of the story of the fallen angels.

10. Irenaeus, *Against the Heresies* 5.26.2.

2.24, a book not found in the Hebrew, it says that 'through the devil's envy death entered the world', a possible reference to the serpent of Gen. 3.1-5.

Having arrived in the New Testament text, the name devil will continue to be used to describe the opposition to Jesus, and will be used by Jesus himself to name opposition to him.[11] In Mark's text, the temptation is presented simply as a fact, unlike the accounts of a triple temptation by the other two Synoptic Gospels, Matthew and Luke.[12] These latter provide a lively dialogue between the tempter and Jesus, though what source or sources there could be for such details cannot be established, except perhaps by analogy with Israel's forty years in the desert, especially as all three of Jesus' quotations are from Deuteronomy. Commentators generally hold that the text was taken from the hypothetical document Q, on which Matthew and Luke, but not Mark, are said to have relied. There were, however, literary parallels in some writings of the time. The exegete Raymond Brown suggested that, though they preceded John's text,

> the parallels between the scene of the three temptation in Mt-Lk and ... individual passages of Jn 6-7 are interesting. They raise the question of whether or not the Mt-Lk common source has not filled in Mk's vague 'he was tempted by Satan' with a dramatic synopsis of the type of temptations Jesus actually faced during his life.[13]

Matthew's account ends with the devil departing from Jesus and angels coming to minister to him (4.11) before he begins his ministry in Galilee (one of the infrequent references to angels in the Gospels), while Luke's account of the temptation concludes with 'the devil left him, to return at the appointed time' (Lk. 4.1-13), namely at the start of the Passion narrative (Lk. 22.3). At the climax of the story Luke will say that 'Satan entered Judas Iscariot' to finish his work by initiating Jesus' betrayal, arrest, torture and execution.[14] But at the beginning, Luke has him entering on his mission filled with the power of the Spirit (4.14). Mark also records the beginning of his ministry and quotes Jesus saying, 'The time is fulfilled and the kingdom of God has come near; repent and believe in the good news' (1.15).

That the kingdom of God had come near meant that this was the reality within which people would live from then on, it would govern people's lives.

---

11. Karl Kertelge, 'Teufel, Dämonen, Exorzismen in biblischer Sicht', in *Teufel, Dämonen, Bessenheit,* Walter Kasper and Karl Lehman, Hg (Mainz: Matthias Grünewald Verlag, 1978), 10–39.

12. Ibid., 18: 'As in this scene, so will Jesus be presented throughout the Gospel as the Messiah challenged by the devil, who on his path through life survives the many tests of his messianic mission' (my translation).

13. Raymond Brown, *New Testament Essays* (London: Geoffrey Chapman, 1963), 206.

14. Elaine Pagels, 'The Social History of Satan, Part II: Satan in the New Testament Gospels', *Journal of the American Academy of Religion*, vol. 62, no. 1 (Spring 1994): 17.

> The remainder of Mark's gospel will deal with Jesus' announcement of this new existence, with continuing resistance and the crisis into which it places those who hear the good news. ... Mark sees the exorcisms as a testimony to the authority of Jesus to announce God's reign; the unclean spirits recognise Jesus and his intent and cry out in an attempt at self-defence.[15]

But as John P. Meir pointed out,

> What made Jesus unusual, if not unique, was not simply his role as exorcist, but rather his integration of the roles of exorcist, moral teacher, gatherer of disciples, and eschatological prophet all into one person.[16]

This means that Jesus' role as exorcist must not dominate the perception of his ministry; other aspects of his ministry include miracles that add credibility to his identity as the Messiah, for example his miraculous feeding of large crowds. However, the exorcisms bear dramatic witness to his fundamental task of defeating the power of evil in which humanity was held and have a high profile in all three Synoptic Gospels.

In the case of a man in the Capernaum synagogue who had an 'unclean spirit' (Mk 1.24) and testified to Jesus' identity as the 'Holy One of God' (1.24), Jesus ordered the spirit to be quiet and come out of the man. After the temptations in the desert, which had no human witnesses, conflict with the devil, or demons – Mark uses the words interchangeably – will involve humans who are said to be possessed, and this type of incident will recur. The term 'holy' in the Scriptures has implications of perfection and completeness, while 'unclean' indicates defect, so that the cry of the man, 'What have you to do with us, Jesus of Nazareth?' makes the opposition more pointed.

This incident, at the beginning of a Gospel deemed the earliest of the records of Jesus' life and ministry, introduces the description of Jesus as an exorcist. It sets him apart from John the Baptist, his forerunner and from the preceding prophets, though there is evidence in the Gospels that there were other exorcists operating in the region. His exorcisms differed from those of his contemporaries by his use of single commands, rather than repeated incantations, and cannot always be distinguished from healings, but his ministry distinguished him from other healers by the obvious miraculous nature of some healings, rather than being the exercise of a natural gift, which the human Jesus may have possessed. When Jesus exorcises, it is not always clear whether a healing from physical or psychotic illness is in question rather than demonic possession; however, the fact that there is no instance in the Gospels of his words of command being unsuccessful, obviously

---

15. Virgil Howard and David B. Peabody, 'Mark', in *The International Bible Commentary*, W. Farmer, ed. (Collegeville: Liturgical Press, 1998), 339.

16. John P. Meir, *A Marginal Jew: Rethinking the Historical Jesus*, Vol II: Mentor, Message and Miracles (New York: Doubleday, 1994), 407.

because of his divinity, points to possession by a demon in some instances. The unusual case in Mk 8.24 of Jesus healing a blind man gradually by spitting on his eyes and putting his hands on them seems an example of the use of a power of healing. However, as the chapter continues with accounts of incidents that distinguish between the casting out of devils and healing of diseases, the cure of the blind man does fit into the general pattern of the bringing of good news, the advancement of the reign of God.

There is a broader context in which to consider Jesus' ministry. In a society that had no hospitals, people with psychiatric illnesses – and who manifestly had no control over themselves – wandered aimlessly about and were believed to be possessed by demons.[17] The more disruptive individuals were bound with chains, as Mk 5.4 testifies, and in that particular case the individual's extraordinary strength points to, but from a psychiatric perspective does not prove, demonic possession.

Whatever might be true in particular instances, Jesus in his ministry did not make a distinction between what would now be recognised as mental illness and the demonic influence or possession people rightly or wrongly believed to be involved.

> In one respect, Jesus seems to have transformed contemporary ideas. In Judaism, the demons were regarded predominantly – but not exclusively (Mk 3.22b) as individual beings. They were named and known one by one, as the countless names for demons show. Jesus, however, stressed the connection between the appearance of demons and Satan. He expressed this connection with a variety of pictures. Satan appears as a commander of a military force (Lk. 10.19) or even rules over a kingdom (Mt. 12.26); the demons are his soldiers.[18]

There is a dramatic example in Mk 5.1-20 of an encounter with 'a man with an unclean spirit', which Mark says occurred on 'the other side of the sea, the country of the Gerasenes'.[19] Matthew's account of the incident describes it as occurring at a different location 'on the other side of the lake … the country of the Gadarenes' (Mt. 8.28). Both locations present difficulties for the narrative.[20] The man identifies Jesus as Son of the Most High God and begs not to be tortured

---

17. Joachim Jeremias, *New Testament Theology*, Vol. 1. *The Proclamation of Jesus*, John Bowden, trans. (London: SCM Press, 1971), 93: 'We shall understand the extent the fear of demons better if we note that the absence of enclosed mental hospitals meant that illnesses of this kind came much more before the public eye than they do in our world.'

18. Ibid.

19. Andreas Hauw, *The Function of Exorcism Stories in Mark's Gospel* (Eugene, OR: Wipf and Stock, 2019), 144: 'Mark never says that the demoniac is a gentile.'

20. Gerasa is located thirty-seven miles southeast of the sea, Gadara five miles from the sea, with no sharp cliffs nearby. See Daniel J. Harrington, S. J., ed., *The Gospel of Mark. Sacra Pagina Series*, Vol. 2 (Collegeville: Liturgical Press, 2002), 163.

by him – Jesus had been telling an 'unclean spirit' to come out of him. Asked by Jesus, 'What is your name?', the reply comes in the singular and plural: 'My name is Legion, for we are many', and he begs Jesus not to drive him out of the district.[21] Jesus gives permission and the spirits migrate into a herd of pigs, which forthwith charge down a cliff and are drowned in the lake. The man is then restored to his right mind, clothed, and wishes to become a disciple. Apart from location, this incident in the Gospels of Matthew (8.28-34) and Luke (8.36-39) has other variations: it is shortened, there are two men in Matthew's account and in Matthew's and Luke's accounts the local population panics and they ask Jesus to leave the area.

It is difficult in the circumstances to reach the historical core of the event, given the diverse locations, both distant from the sea, and other elements in the accounts, but 'the sheer oddity of the geographical location … may reflect a singular historical event'.

> It could be that the unique connection of one of Jesus' miracles with a particular pagan city in the Decapolis, at a good distance from the Sea of Galilee and Jesus' customary area of activity, may have stuck in the collective memory of Jesus' disciples precisely because of the exorcism's venue.[22]

In Mark, the story follows the pattern of exorcisms performed by exorcists of that time; establishing the name of the demon was considered the critical stage as it was believed to give power to the exorcist over the demon. Here, the answer 'Legion' may indicate that the man believed himself possessed by many demons – 'for we are many'; it was well known that a Roman legion consisted of 6,000 men and it was also believed demons numbered in their thousands.[23] The suggestion by some commentators that the man may have become deranged through being ill-treated by Roman soldiers is less likely as both Gerasa and Gadara were largely Greek cities in the Decapolis and would not have considered the Roman military presence as oppressive as many Jews did.[24]

In Matthew's and Luke's accounts, the naming of the demons is lacking, but there is the same request from them to be sent into the pigs. In all three, there is the highly dramatic event of the pigs suddenly rushing down into the lake and being drowned, and while commentators link this with the Jewish revulsion

---

21. Jeremias held that as the Aramaic word, *ligyōnā'*, is ambiguous with regard to singular and plural, the reply of the man could have been: 'My name is "soldier" because there are many like me (and we resemble one another as soldiers do).' Joachim Jeremias, *New Testament Theology*, 86–7.

22. Meir, *A Marginal Jew*, 657.

23. William Barclay, *The Gospel of Mark* (Edinburgh: Saint Andrew Press, 1956²), 117: 'The queen of the female spirits had no less than 180 followers. There was a Jewish saying, "A legion of hurtful spirits is on the watch for men…".'

24. Harrington, S.J., ed., *The Gospel of Mark*, 166.

towards pigs, such an extraordinary occurrence would be difficult to explain as a consequence of psychiatric illness.

It seems easier to find an explanation for the incident recorded in Mt. 17.14-20, when Jesus cured a boy from whom the disciples had failed to 'cast out a demon'. The NRSV version says that the father described the boy as an epileptic, while the Greek text has 'a lunatic and in a wretched state', testifying to the belief that the moon could be responsible for mental illness. The symptoms of the boy's condition were in fact the same as those of an epileptic'.[25] Nevertheless, in answer to the disciples' subsequent questioning, according to Mk 9.29, Jesus says that 'this kind can only come out by prayer'.

References to the plural, demons, in the case of exorcisms – by Jesus or the disciples – seem to distinguish them from *the* devil, though these spirits are sometimes called devils also, for example in Mk 3.22, where Beelzebub is called 'the prince of devils' or in Lk. 10.17, where the disciples say the devils are subject to them. The whole issue of number in relation to demons/devils is a puzzling one in that there is no Scriptural warrant for or against them being considered numberless. In effect, demon in the singular or plural, or devil, all indicate the same dark power of opposition to Jesus and the coming reign of God. Throughout the Gospels there are incidents where what is presented as the casting out of 'a demon' or 'the devil' may, in the light of modern psychiatric medicine, seem more likely to be a case of extreme psychiatric disorder. Even though in the case of the boy, the text of Matthew (7.18) says that 'Jesus rebuked the demon and it came out', the case is more like others in which Jesus heals illnesses such as leprosy or fever by a touch, with no mention of a demon; even the bystanders did not associate leprosy with demonic possession. When demonic possession was considered by the people to be the case, Jesus did not offer any other explanation, and in answer to the challenge of the Pharisees that he cast out demons by the power of Beelzebub (Mt. 12.24), he asserted his authority to exorcise demons. When he commissioned the twelve to proclaim that the kingdom was at hand, he 'gave them authority over unclean spirits and power to cast them out and to cure all kinds of diseases and sickness' (Mt. 10.1). There were occasions when he implied that people who did not show signs of demonic possession were nevertheless in some way under the influence of Satan. These charges vary in intensity; for example, the noteworthy case in which Jesus says to Peter, 'Get behind me, Satan', concludes with him saying, 'the way you think is not God's way but man's' (Mt. 16.23).

Given the relationship of Peter to Jesus, this is very different from his saying in John's Gospel: 'Have I not chosen you, you twelve, yet one of you is a devil' (Jn 6.70). He was referring to Judas, the text says, who was going to betray him. Later in this Gospel, at the Last Supper, he says that one of the twelve will betray him. He

---

25. The Greek text in Nestle-Aland, σεληνιάζεται, means moonstruck or lunatic. This is consistent with the way people of that time would believe convulsions actually symptomatic of epilepsy were caused by some phases of the moon. Mk 9.17 and Lk. 9.38 simply refer to the presence of a spirit.

dips a piece of bread and gives it to Judas. 'At that instant, after Judas had taken the bread, Satan entered him' (Jn 13.27). In John's Gospel, Jesus performs no exorcisms of demons, instead he performs various kind of signs, including the healing of a paralytic (5.5-9) and the man born blind (9.1-7). Both events occurred on the Sabbath and led to his being challenged by the Jews, as John calls Jesus' opponents (the Pharisees in the latter case). This opposition is central to John's narrative, and causes the opponents to assert that Jesus has a demon, a charge already made when he challenged them about their descent from Abraham. They replied: 'Are we not right in saying that you are a Samaritan and have a demon?' The attitude towards him on the part of the people in general was divided:

> Many of them were saying: 'He has a demon and is out of his mind. Why listen to him?' Others were saying: 'These are not the words of one who has a demon. Can a demon open the eyes of the blind?' (Jn 10.2-21)

The entering of Satan into Judas, in John's and Luke's Gospels, accords with Jesus' earlier saying that one of the twelve was 'a devil'. It strikes a different note from the descriptions of Jesus' encountering people possessed with demons in the various accounts of exorcisms throughout the Gospel story. It could of course mean that Judas at that point cast in his lot with the devil. That possibility needs to be borne in mind in discussion today of evil in people's lives and of reports of possession.

Overall, it is clear that Jesus accepted the common belief that demons were active in the lives of the people and that he had power over them, while very often he simply healed people who were ill – sometimes at a distance – and he never attributed natural phenomena such as a storm on the lake to demons, a belief that was in the culture and remained for many centuries. Jesus' description of his opponents as evil (Mt. 7.11, Lk. 11.13) is a further indication that beneath malicious attitudes and actions, as well as what were in fact psychotic conditions, he shared the belief of the people that a deeper force for evil was at work in their world and it was variously named as demon or devil or Satan.

The devil in the life of the early Christian community

In the first account of the life of the early community, the Acts of the Apostles, the activity of the Holy Spirit is dominant at Pentecost and at later crucial moments. A good spirit, an angel, came to the rescue of the apostles (5.17) and later on Peter was woken up in prison by an angel and led out to safety (12.6-11). Similarly, Paul and Silas were miraculously released from prison in the course of an earthquake, though with no angels in attendance (16.25-34). In contrast with these wonders, evil spirits were scarcely evident in the era of the Spirit – unlike the situation in the Gospel narratives.

The persistence of evil manifested itself, however, when Ananias and Sapphira defrauded the community by pretending to give the community all of the proceeds of the sale of a property. Peter's reaction was stronger than might have been expected and the sudden deaths of the couple a harsh punishment,[26] but the environment was one where consciousness of the Spirit was still high and dishonesty seen as an offence against the Spirit.

> 'Ananias', Peter asked, 'why has Satan filled your heart to lie to the Holy Spirit and to keep back part of the proceeds of the land? While it remained unsold, did it not remain your own? And after it was sold, were not the proceeds at your disposal? How is it that you have contrived this deed in your heart? You did not lie to us but to God!' (Acts 5.3-4)

Whether Satan was actively involved, or was it simply a case of the tendency of the human heart towards evil, remains an issue, bearing in mind what the Letter of James says: 'Those conflicts and disputes among you, where do they come from? Do they not come from your cravings that are at war within you?' (4.1).

The language of the newly converted Paul was equally strong when he vigorously confronted Jews and believers alike with the Gospel message. At Paphos, in Cyprus, the efforts of a magician, Elymas Magos, to thwart him were met with: 'You son of the devil, you enemy of all righteousness, full of all deceit and villainy, will you not stop making crooked the straight paths of the Lord?' (13.10). Subsequently, an unfortunate group of itinerant Jewish exorcists thought to capitalise on Paul's wonder-working by using his name when dealing with possessed persons.

> Seven sons of a Jewish high priest named Sceva were doing this. But the evil spirit said to them in reply, 'Jesus I know, and Paul I know, but who are you?' Then the man with the evil spirit leaped on them, mastered them all, and so overpowered them that they fled out of the house naked and wounded. (19.14-16)

Paul (or his disciples) composed the earliest letters of the New Testament and in them made references to Satan or the devil, showing that this characterisation of evil was common in the early Christian community, as would be expected from the Gospels themselves.[27] In his letters, Paul also referred to powers, thrones,

---

26. 'At Qumram, a man who lied in relation to wealth was excluded from the Purity for one year and was deprived of a fourth of his food ration. But in the case of Ananias and Sapphira no casuistry applies. ... There is a note of ultimate seriousness in the New Testament which does not leave room for the gracious casuistry and second chance which the Qumran sect practices in all cases except those of downright apostasy or disloyalty.' Krister Stendhal, 'The Scrolls and the New Testament: An Introduction and a Perspective', in *The Scrolls and the New Testament*, Krister Stendhal, ed. (New York: Crossroad, 1992), 8.

27. Torsten Lofstedt, 'Paul, Sin and Satan: The Root of Evil according to Romans', *Svensk Exegetisk Årsbok*, vol. 75 (2010): 109–34: 'Paul refers to the devil on occasion, but not frequently. The word Σατανᾶς occurs in Rom. 16.20; 1 Cor. 5.5; 7.5; 2 Cor. 2.11; 11.14; 12.7; 1 Thess. 2.18; 2 Thess. 2.9. The word διάβολος, (with probable reference to the devil) is found in Eph. 4.27; 6.11; 1 Tim. 3.6, 7.

principalities, elements, spirits of wickedness 'that are not gods' (Gal. 4.8). He is referring specifically to a single power, the devil, when he speaks of 'the god of this world' (2 Cor. 4.4) and 'the ruler of the power of the air' (Eph. 2.2). He makes a direct reference to Satan when in 1 Tim. 1.20 he says he has handed over two disciples to him, 'so that they may learn not to blaspheme'. The most likely explanation for this rhetorical expression is that he has excluded them from the community until they repent. This would be similar to an incident recorded in 1 Cor. 5.5, where he instructed the community to hand a man guilty of incest over to Satan 'for the destruction of the flesh, so that his spirit may be saved in the day of the Lord'. For his part, Peter concludes his hortatory letter with a call for his readers to be alert, because 'like a roaring lion your adversary the devil prowls around looking for someone to devour' (1 Pet. 5.8). Throughout the letters, references are to the struggle of the Christian against evil in the world, and indicate a world held in thrall by evil. Traditionally this evil is described by the generic term 'principalities and powers'. Heinrich Schlier elaborated on this generic term:

> A phenomenon is being glimpsed which obtrudes on all men, and especially upon Christians. This phenomenon is described by numerous names, which the New Testament has borrowed from other sources. The use of so many names indicates that the subject is not described adequately by any one name. Fundamentally, we are dealing with a single phenomenon which is diffused and which concerns us in various manifestations.[28]

The single phenomenon takes the form of 'the lawless one' in the 2 Thess. 2.3. He represents in himself all these principalities and powers, but will in the end be destroyed by the Lord Jesus 'with the breath of his mouth' (2.8). In the meantime, he 'exalts himself above every so-called god or object of worship, so that he takes his seat in the temple of God, declaring himself to be God' (2.4). This is language used elsewhere in the New Testament for the antichrist and is effectively a description of Satan, though confusion can arise if the text, 'the coming of the lawless one is apparent in the working of Satan' (2.9), is understood to refer to two separate entities. The importance of the whole passage is to emphasise that 'the god of this world' will rule until Christ's coming. The Letter of John also manifests an apocalyptic mind when it says 'it is the last hour' and speaks of the coming of the antichrist, the 'one who denies the Father and the Son' (1 Jn 2.18-22).

There are clear indications that the abode of the god of this world and of these powers is not God's heaven but in the spheres that surround and impinge on the earth, including even the 'temple of God' (2.4), in the understanding of the cosmos in New Testament times and for many centuries to follow. The theory to be elaborated by Claudius Ptolemy (*c.* 85–165) in his *Almagest* postulated a series of concentric spheres consisting of a transparent fifth substance (differing from

---

28. Heinrich Schlier, *Principalities and Powers in the New Testament* (New York: Herder and Herder, 1961), 17.

earth, air, fire and water), of ascending degrees of purity and containing the orbits of all the bodies rotating around the earth. There were two further spheres, the last of which was the unmoved sphere causing the others to move. God's abode was beyond this. In later centuries, alternative arrangements of the spheres would be proposed, including that by the Venerable Bede.[29] The principalities and powers were invisible and embodied, but not materially, and existed in and beyond the world. This understanding forms the basis for the structure of Dante's celebrated poem, as will be seen later, and underlies the accounts of activities of demons in the lives of the desert fathers. An example of how this demonology influenced Paul's thinking is clear when in his anxiety to stress that 'God is for us' he says:

> I am convinced that neither death nor life, nor angels, nor rulers, nor things present, nor things to come, nor powers, nor height, nor depth, nor anything else in all creation, will be able to separate us from the love of God in Christ Jesus our Lord. (Rom. 8.38-9)

The mention of height and of depth reflects the cosmology of the time rather than being simply metaphorical, while the reference to 'angels' shows that the basis for belief in the principalities and powers lay in the tradition of the fall of some angels not found clearly in the Old Testament, but with their final defeat by Archangel Michael, described as an eschatological outcome in Rev. 12.7-9. This passage tells of war in heaven between Michael and his angels and the dragon, and Satan's destruction. The dragon is identified as the ancient serpent and the devil and Satan. His defeat causes him to be thrown down to the earth, where he makes war on the children of the woman clothed with the sun, who had escaped his clutches (Rev. 12.1). Chapter 20 returns to the theme, with an angel descending to bind the dragon.

> Satan's destruction is so important that it has two themes to describe it instead of one, namely his chaining and his downfall. The angel chains him for a thousand years, and locks and seals the abyss into which he places him ... Gaechter suggests that chronologically Satan's capture, 20.1-3, should precede that of the beasts, 19.19-21, but that the author chose to put the undoing of Satan last to emphasise his character as the ultimate enemy of God and man. He comes first and last in the great chiastic symmetry of chapters 12 to 20. In Chapter 12 he lost his place in heaven, and in chapter 20 he is sent below the earth.[30]

---

29. Jacques Le Goff, *Medieval Civilization, 400–1500*, Julia Barrow, trans. (Oxford: Basil Blackwell, 1988), 153: 'The Christianisation of this concept ended up in a simplified form exemplified in the twelfth-century *Elucidarium* of Honorius of Autun, who distinguished three heavens: the corporeal heaven which we see; the spiritual heaven where dwell the spiritual substances, that is to say, the angels; and the intellectual heaven where the blessed gaze on the Holy Trinity face to face.'

30. J. Massyngberde Ford, *Revelation. Introduction, Translation and Commentary* (New York: Doubleday, 1975), 330.

The Letter of Jude has its own account of the fallen angels in v. 6:

> And the angels who did not keep their own position, but left their proper dwelling, he has kept in eternal chains in deepest darkness for the judgment of the great Day.

The letter gives as its source for this event a text from 1Enoch, a non-canonical apocalyptic book, belonging to the generic category of *Pseudepigrapha*, biblically based literature with false claims to authorship.[31] The various sections belong to different dates, but overall are from the second to the first centuries BC. Chapters VI to XI are classified as Fragments from the *Book of Noah*. The story is also found in the *Book of Jubilees*, one of the Qumram texts.[32]

> And it came to pass that when the children of men had multiplied, in those days were born unto them beautiful and comely daughters. And the angels, the children of the heaven, saw and lusted after them and said to one another: Come, let us choose us wives among the children of men and beget us children. (VI.1-2)[33]

The result was the generation of giants who destroyed all before them:

> And Azâzêl (a demon associated with the desert) taught men to make swords, and knives, and shields ... and there arose much godlessness and they committed fornication. (VIII.1)[34]

According to X.4,

> The Lord said to Raphael: Bind Azâzêl hand and foot and cast him into the darkness: and make an opening in the desert, which is in Dûdâêl and cast him therein. And place upon him rough and jagged rocks, and cover him with darkness and let him abide there for ever and ever, and cover his face that he may not see the light. And on the day of the great judgement he shall be cast into the fire.[35]

---

31. Michael Patella, *Angels and Demons: A Christian Primer of the Spiritual World* (Collegeville: Liturgical Press, 2012), 108: 'The material is speculative and fictional and involves events and persons who occur in the Bible.'

32. Hodge, *The Dead Sea Scrolls*, 97: 'Like Enoch, *Jubilees* maintains that evil was introduced into the midst of humanity by the demonic offspring of the fallen angels, though it does offer some innovations of its own.'

33. R. H. Charles, trans., *The Book of Enoch* (London: S.P.C.K., 1917), 34.

34. Ibid., 35.

35. Ibid., 39.

Chapters XII–XVI recount a dream vision of Enoch and his intercession on behalf of Azâzêl, but the petition was not granted.

> In my vision it appeared thus that your petition will not be granted unto you throughout all the days of eternity, and that judgement has been finally passed on you: ... And from henceforth you shall not ascend into heaven unto all eternity, and in bonds of the earth the decree has gone forth to bind you for all the days of the world. (XIV.7)[36]

XVI.1 tells of 'the day of the consummation, the great judgment in which the age shall be consummated'.[37]

In the New Testament, Jude saw this consummation approaching in his day and urged his beloved fellow Christians to 'look forward to the mercy of our Lord Jesus Christ that leads to eternal life' (Jude 21). Though brief, this account by Jude of the origin of what came to be called the principalities and powers does testify to belief in an unseen world of evil spirits as an intrinsic part of the religious and cultural heritage of early Christianity.

There are many other apocalyptic texts from the New Testament period, inspired by the canonical Gospels[38] and Acts of the Apostles. Perhaps the most comprehensive pseudepigraphical account of the fall of Satan is in *The Gospel (Questions) of St Bartholomew* – its existence is mentioned by St Jerome in his *Commentary on Matthew*. It gives an account of the creation of the first angel, Beliar, Michael being the second. Further on in the text, Beliar becomes simply the 'devil' giving an account of his fall.

> The devil said: Suffer me, and I will tell thee how I was cast down into this place and how the Lord did make man. I was going to and fro in the world and God said unto Michael: 'Bring me a clod from the four corners of the earth, and water out of the four rivers of paradise'. And when Michael brought them God formed Adam in the regions of the east, and shaped the clod which was

---

36. Ibid., 41.
37. Ibid., 43.
38. *The Coptic Narratives of the Ministry*, apparently not earlier than the fifth century, include a dramatic encounter of Jesus and his disciples with the devil dressed as a fisherman – in the desert and with attendant demons carrying nets and hooks. 'John was sent to speak to the devil and ask him what he was catching. The devil said: "it is not a wonder to catch fish in the waters: the wonder is in this desert, to catch fish there". He cast his nets and caught all manner of fish (really men), some by their eyes, and others by their lips.' Text in *The Apocryphal New Testament, Being the Apocryphal Gospels, Acts, Epistles and Apocalypses*, Montague Rhodes James, trans. (Oxford: Clarendon Press, 1924), 149. The story is a clever adaptation of the text in Jn 21, where the miraculous catch of fish can be interpreted as symbolic of the disciples' future evangelising success, while here it symbolises the devil's conquests.

shapeless, and stretched sinews and veins upon it and established it with joints; and he worshipped him for his own sake first, because he was the image of God, therefore he worshipped him. And when I came from the ends of the earth Michael said: 'Worship thou the image of God, which he hath made according to his likeness.' But I said: 'I am fire of fire. I was the first angel formed, and shall I worship clay and matter?' And Michael saith to me: 'Worship lest God be wroth with thee.' But I said to him: 'God will not be wroth with me; but I will set my throne over against his throne, and I will be as he is.' Then God was wroth with me and cast me down, having commanded the windows of heaven to be opened.[39]

The devil in the Patristic Era

There is a long history of attempts in the Christian community since New Testament times to come to grips with how the presence of Satan in the world was to be understood. The same preoccupation has been evident in Islam[40] since the account in the *Qur'an* (Surah 7.11) of the rebellion of Iblis (the name is derived from the Greek *diabolos*), an angel who refused to obey God's command to worship Adam, giving as his reason that he had been created from fire while Adam was created from mud (Surah 7.12).[41] In Surah 7.27, the children of Adam are warned not to let Iblis seduce them. Here he is called Satan, and he and 'his tribe' see the human race, but are not seen by them. Allah says that 'he has made the devils protecting friends for those who believe not'.[42] In Christian tradition over the centuries, Satan/the devil has come to be seen from a viewpoint distinct from spirits of evil of one kind or another of the classical cultures.

Justin Martyr

The period of the Fathers showed no diminution in this climate of belief in demons, as a corollary to the more specific one of belief in the devil who opposed Jesus from the outset of his ministry. One of the earliest apologists for the Christian faith, Justin Martyr (100–165), showed familiarity with the tradition of the fall of the angels described by Jude, by referring to some angels who had transgressed against the mandate to care for humankind and all of creation given to them by God; they 'were captivated by the love of women and begat children who are those that are called demons'. He held that the demons enslaved humankind by magic writings

---

39. *The Gospel (Questions) of St Bartholomew, Apocryphal New Testament*, 178.
40. Henry Ansgar Kelly, *Satan: A Biography* (Cambridge: Cambridge University Press, 2006), 184–5.
41. This Islamic text may depend on *The Gospel of St Matthew*. See note 28 above.
42. Muhammad M. Pickthall, *The Meaning of the Glorious Qur'an: An Explanatory Translation* (Birmingham: Islamic Dawah Centre International, 2000).

and taught them to offer sacrifice and libations. But people were also possessed by the souls of the dead, who take hold of them and throw them about. But Christians were not without relief from demons as they were defeated by calling on the name of Jesus. Quoting Lk. 10.19, 'I give you authority to tread on snakes and scorpions and over all the power of the enemy', Justin added: 'And we who believe in Jesus, our Lord … exorcise all the demons and have them in subjection to ourselves'. He claimed that many Christians had healed and still healed many possessed by demons 'both all over the world and in this your city (Rome), exorcising them by the name of Jesus Christ'.[43]

Tertullian

Justin's valuable testimony to the life of the early Christian community in Rome was supplemented in the next generation by that of Tertullian (c. 155–240) in Carthage, North Africa. He devoted two chapters of his *Apologia* to demonology and consolidated an image of demons that would prevail in Christianity not as a dogmatic tenet but as the foundation of popular belief up to the beginning of modernity – including, for example, that they were equipped with wings, like the good angels.

> Every spirit is (as though it were) winged. Both angels and demons have this property. Therefore, they are everywhere in a moment. … Actually, they are always the authors of the evil but never of the good.[44]

According to the *Apologia*, they originated in the fall of Satan and his cohort:

> As for the details of how some of the angels, of their own accord, were perverted and then constituted him the source of the even more corrupt race of devils, a race damned by God together with the originators of the race and him whom we have mentioned as their leader, the account is found in Sacred Scripture. … Their business is to corrupt mankind; thus the spirit of evil was from the very beginning bent on man's destruction. The demons, therefore, inflict upon men's bodies diseases and other bitter misfortunes, and upon the soul sudden and extraordinary outbursts of violence.[45]

Their activities at both levels include the power to produce airborne diseases.

---

43. Justin Martyr, *The Works of S. Justin the Martyr*, Dialogue with Trypho, LXXVI (Oxford: J. H. and J. S. Parker, 1861), 168. A similar text occurs in the Second Apology, ibid., 62.

44. Tertullian, *Apology* 22.8 in *Apologetical Works* (Washington, DC: Catholic University of America Press, 1950), 69–70.

45. Ibid., 69.

> So it is, for example, in the case of fruit or crops, when something imperceptible in the air casts a blight upon the flower, kills the bud, and injures the development; as if in the air, tainted in some unseen manner, were spreading abroad its pestilential breath.[46]

Tertullian also attributed to demons an activity that did not persist as part of common belief in later times: he believed demons could apparently cause miraculous cures by a subterfuge.

> First, they hurt you, then they prescribe remedies that are novel or even injurious; afterwards – so that there may be a miracle – they stop hurting and are considered responsible for the cure.[47]

In the centuries immediately following Tertullian, none of the stories that emerged from chronicles of the experiences of the desert dwellers included any apparently positive, curative influence on the part of demons.

Their stories often give the impression that they were men and women of great simplicity, uninfluenced by the theological currents of the time, but modern research has shown that this was not the case, that mystical theology was the foundation on which their way of life was built. The influence of Origen's mystical theology has been found, for example, in the letters of Antony of Egypt, in many ways the prototypical desert monk.

Origen

Origen (*c.* 185–254) was an early exponent of the Christian mysticism that would have a decisive effect on monasticism.[48] Though he upheld the idea of the soul's ascent to God in mystical prayer, he also noted in his *Commentary on Lamentations* that the soul can become 'subject to the Devil or even his angels, and altogether subject to the hostile powers'.[49] He articulated his mystical teaching through reflection on Scripture, especially in his *Commentary* and *Homilies* on

---

46. Ibid.

47. Ibid., 70.

48. Because of his Platonist inheritance, Origen had an ambivalent view of the demoniacal. Plato in *Cratylus* has Socrates say in answer to Demogenes: 'Every good man is learned and skilful, that he is demoniacal, both when living and when dead, that he is properly denominated a demon.' *The Cratylus, Phaedo, Parmenides, and Timaeus* (London: B & J White, 1793), 32.

49. Joseph Trigg, *Origen* (London: Routledge, 1998), 74; Hans Urs von Balthasar, *Origen, Spirit and Fire: A Thematic Anthology of His Writings*, Robert J. Daly S.J., trans. (Washington, DC: Catholic University of America Press, 1984), 8: 'Certainly he understood that the higher one climbs, the stronger becomes the attack of the enemy and one's own inner death – but these were for him epic battles and heroic opportunities for higher trials.'

the *Song of Songs*. Though belonging to the Platonist tradition, broadly speaking, his theology was firmly rooted in the Incarnation; the mystical ascent of the soul begins in baptism.[50] In *De Oratione* XXXI, he treated of guardian angels, their presence especially when Christians assembled: 'When saints assemble together there is a twofold church, the one of men the other of angels.' His mystical theology influenced the contemplative stance of early monasticism, but, as will be seen below, other theologies, such as that of Athanasius or Evagrius or Pachomius, would in time make their contribution. Finally, Cassian's summing up of the Eastern tradition imported by him to the West had a significant effect on the understanding of monasticism articulated in his *Rule* by Benedict as the father figure of Western monasticism. While Benedict lauded the monks of the past, he made no reference to contemplation, and mentioned the devil only three times.[51] By the sixth century, the dramatic elements of the Egyptian demonology associated with the solitary combat of the contemplative monk in the desert gave way to a spirituality more in accord with that of the New Testament letters of Paul and Peter, for example.

St Antony of Egypt

In the life of Antony (250–356), the prototypical desert monk, the influence of Origen's theology was formative. Origen had expressed his views on the devil in his commentaries on Scripture and in *De Principiis*. In two places in that work, he summarised his teaching on the devil in relation to humankind.

> We have now to notice, agreeably to the statements of Scripture, how the opposing powers, or the devil himself, contends with the human race, inciting and instigating men to sin. And in the first place, in the book of Genesis, the serpent is described as having seduced Eve; regarding whom, in the work entitled *The Ascension of Moses* …, the archangel Michael, when disputing with the devil regarding the body of Moses, says that the serpent, being inspired by the devil, was the cause of Adam and Eve's transgression. (III.2.1)[52]

---

50. Andrew Louth, *The Origins of the Christian Mystical Tradition: From Plato to Denys* (Oxford: Clarendon Press, 1981), 56.

51. In the original Latin text of his *Rule*, the Prologue v. 28 includes a citation of Ps. 15 (14): 4, and uses the words *malignum diabolum*. Today's RSV simply uses the word 'wicked'. In chapter 1 of the *Rule*, Benedict spoke of the four kinds of monks, acknowledging the excellence of the Anchorites or Hermits, 'those who, no longer in the first fervour of their reformation, … go out well armed from the ranks of the community to the solitary combat of the desert'. In chapter 58, he referred to the monk who might leave the monastery because of 'having listened to the temptations of the devil'.

52. Origen, *De Principiis*, The Ante-Nicene Fathers, Vol. IV, Alexander Roberts and James Donaldson, eds (Buffalo, NY: Christian Literature Publishing, 1885), 328.

Origen did not attribute all the evil of humankind's actions to the influence of the devil, but when indulgence goes beyond a certain level of excess, the 'hostile power' presses hard to incite the person to greater sins.

> There are ... manifest reasons for holding the opinion, that as in good things the human will is of itself weak to accomplish any good (for it is by divine help that it is brought to perfection in everything); so also, in things of an opposite nature we receive certain initial elements, and, as it were, seeds of sins, from those things which we use agreeably to nature. But when we have indulged them beyond what is proper, and have not resisted the first movements to intemperance, then the hostile power, seizing the occasion of this first transgression, incites and presses us hard in every way, seeking to extend our sins over a wider field, and furnishing us human beings with occasions and beginnings of sins, which these hostile powers spread far and wide, and, if possible, beyond all limits. (III.2.2)[53]

Although Antony gave no systematic explanation of his views on the creation of the material world and on the results of the original Fall, research in recent times, based on Antony's letters, has shown that he was aware of the insights of Origen. Like Origen, he held that

> The sun, moon and stars, the holy heavens and the devil, men and women, from the beginning of creation, everything derives from one and the same.[54]

For Antony, as for Origen, the spiritual life could be described as an ascent towards the recovery of the lost unity that resulted from the Fall. Following Origen's mystical approach, he said to monks who came to consult him:

> As far as the soul is concerned, being straight consists in its intellectual part being according to nature, as it was created. ... [The] task is not difficult, for if we remain as we were made, we are in virtue, but if we turn our thoughts to contemptible things, we are condemned as evil. If the task depended on something external that must be procured, it would be truly difficult, but since the matter centres in us, let us protect ourselves from sordid ideas. (no. 20)[55]

---

53. Ibid., 330.

54. Antony, *Epistola* 5.40, cited in Samuel Rubenson, *The Letters of St Antony: Monasticism and the Making of a Saint* (Lund: Lund University Press, 1990), 65. See also ibid., 60: 'The links between the letters and Origen's theology were noted and commented on by Symphorianus Champerius as early as 1516, but have since received little attention. With the traditional image of Antony and the early monks as illiterate and unaware of Greek theological tradition the Origenism of the letters has been seen as "unexpected" and of little consequence for the interpretation of early monasticism.'

55. St Athanasius, *The Life of Antony and the Letter to Marcellinus*, introduction by Robert C. Gregg, trans. (New York: Paulist Press, 1980), par. 20.

Going out into the desert as a *monachos*, one who was single-minded in the desire for union with God, was simply a more radical way of coping with the inner struggle the Christian life involved for his Egyptian or Greek contemporaries as well as for him.

Samuel Rubenson concluded from research on the *Vita Antonii* and the *Apophtegmata Patrum* that the seven letters of Antony mentioned by Jerome and quoted by Coptic authors in the fifth century were authentic. 'It is impossible, as has often been done in the past, to accept the authenticity of the letters, while maintaining the traditional view of Antony as illiterate.'[56]

> In Antony's letters matter is at one and the same time the source of 'the power of the devil', and the precondition for progress in virtue. To Antony the chief result of the Fall is this ambivalence and insecurity. Man has not lost his likeness to God, his 'spiritual essence' or his 'mind', but the body 'weighs it down' from the spiritual to the material, and the motions of the soul and the body defy its control.[57]

In the *Life of Antony* by Athanasius of Alexandria, the inner struggle is more evident than the ascent of the 'mind' or spiritual ascent towards unity; the unity sought is that which is under threat from bodily nature and from the devil. This is compatible with the fundamentals of Antony's understanding; in Letter 1, he spoke of the three motions in the body: the first belongs to the original nature and is good; the second comes from greed and gluttony; the third comes from the devil.[58] Athanasius' concept of the Christian life was based on his theology set out in *De Incarnatione*. The Incarnation was necessary if humanity was recovered from the damaged state of the image of God in humankind resulting from the Fall. The soul was not divinised by contemplation, but by union with Christ. He said in *Contra Arianos* 2.70: 'Humanity would not have been deified if the Word who became flesh had not been by nature derived from the Father and his true and proper Word.' And more famously, in *De Incarnatione* 54 he said: 'The Word was made man in order that we might be made divine.'

The emphasis in his *Life of Antony* was not on divinising contemplation, though at the end of the work he does say that Antony was disconsolate at being annoyed

---

56. Jan Pollok, 'The Present State of Studies on the *Apophthegmata Patrum*: An Outline of Samuel Rubenson's and Graham Gould's perspectives', in *The Spirituality of Ancient Monasticism*. Acts of the International Colloquium, Cracow-Tyniec, 1994, Marek Staroewieyski, ed. (Cracow: Wydawnictwo Benedyktnów, 1995), 83.

57. Rubenson, *The Letters of Antony*, 67; Also, in the same place Rubenson: 'According to Origen, God created the world to correspond to the diversity among the spiritual beings, now no longer equal and united. In this order or hierarchy "matter" is, in the Platonic manner, regarded as the lowest level of being. But the material world is not evil. It is the result of God's providence, it is the attempt to establish an order in the diversity caused by the fall of the "minds".'

58. Antony, *Epistola* 1.35-45, cited in Rubenson, *The Letters of Antony*, 54.

by so many visitors and drawn to the outer mountain by the requests of judges, as in the inner mountain 'he rejoiced in the contemplation of divine realities'.[59] The narrative mainly concerns the solitary combat of the monk with forces within himself and with demons from without. For example, he held that evil begins with the monk's own negligence in relation to the basic drives of bodily existence, giving opportunity for devil to attack.[60]

Athanasius said in the introduction that he wrote it at the request of monks 'from abroad', to inspire them in their monastic quest, but he also said in the epilogue found in the Ancient Christian Writers No. 10 version:

> And if the occasion presents itself, read it also to the pagans, that at least in this way they may learn that our Lord Jesus Christ is not only God and the Son of God, but that the Christians by their faithful service to Him and their orthodox faith in Him prove that the demons whom the Greeks consider gods are no gods; that, moreover, they trample them under foot and drive them out for what they are – deceivers and corrupters of men.[61]

The work has an apologetic aim and from that perspective Antony is presented as a hero of anti-Arian orthodoxy.[62] Some commentators consider him a martyr. 'Athanasius combines monastic asceticism, anti-pagan apologetics and demonology by conforming Antony to the figure of the martyr, the Christian opponent of paganism par excellence.'[63]

Antony himself, addressing monks who came to him for advice, spoke of how demons tried to prevent this contemplative life, demons who had been created good, but had fallen from wisdom, and wandered the earth.

> And envious of Christians, they meddle with all things in their desire to frustrate our journey into heaven, so that we might not ascend to the place from which they themselves fell. Therefore much prayer and asceticism is needed so that one who receives through the Spirit the gift of discrimination of spirits might be able to recognise their traits – for example, which of them are less wicked, and which

---

59. St Athanasius, *The Life of Antony and the Letter to Marcellinus*, par. 84.

60. David Brakke, *Demons and the Making of the Monk: Spiritual Combat in Early Christianity* (Cambridge, MA: Harvard University Press, 2006), 16.

61. St Athanasius, *The Life of Saint Antony*, Ancient Christian Writers No. 10 (New York: Newman Press, 1978), 98.

62. Jan Pollok, 'The Present State of Studies on the *Apophthegmata Patrum*', 83: 'Rubenson emphasises the fact that the *Vita* contains arguments used in the anti-arian conflict such as the emphasis on Christ's role as divine mediator working in men. The anti-arian concepts transcend Antony's Origenist theology.'

63. Brakke, *Demons and the Making of the Monk*, 24. See also Edward E. Malone, *The Monk and the Martyr: The Monk as the Successor of the Martyr*, Johannes Quasten, ed. (Washington, DC: C.U.A. Press, 2011).

more, and in what kind of pursuits each of them exerts himself, and how each of them is overturned and expelled.[64]

The narrative includes abundant examples of the attacks of the devil and groups of demons on this desert dweller. The hostility of demons often took the form of beasts threatening the lives of the hermits, or, more often taking the form of a seductress.

> The devil, who despises and envies good, could not bear to see such purpose in a youth, but the sort of things he had busied himself doing in the past, he set to work to do against this person as well. (no. 5)[65]

The temptations centred on the details of his former life, his obligations to his sister and all the satisfactions of life he had forgone. As this attack proved fruitless, the devil

> placed his confidence in the weapons in the navel of his belly, and boasting in these (for they constitute his first ambush against the young) he advanced against the youth, noisily disturbing him in the night, and so troubling him in the daytime that even those who watched were aware of the bout that occupied them both. The one hurled foul thoughts and the other overturned them through his prayers; the former resorted to titillation, but the latter, seeming to blush, fortified the body with faith and with prayers and fasting. (no. 5)

The devil then dared to masquerade as a woman by night and 'to imitate her every gesture', again to no avail. The 'dragon', unable to defeat him, took on the form of a 'black boy' and a conversation took place between them, which concluded with Antony saying: 'From now on you cause me no anxiety, for the Lord is my helper and I shall look upon my enemies.' Hearing these words, the black one disappeared.

Athanasius' life continues: 'This was Antony's first contest against the devil, or rather, this was in Antony the success of the Saviour' (no. 7). For David Brakke, in *Demons and the Making of the Monk*, this initial contest between Antony and the devil

> is one of the most important passages in the history of monastic demonology; it provided a frame of reference as well as specific vocabulary for much subsequent literature.[66]

---

64. St Athanasius, *The Life of Antony and the Letter to Marcellinus*, no. 22.
65. Ibid., no. 5.
66. Brakke, *Demons and the Making of the Monk*, 28.

Clearly, it is fundamental for monastic demonology. However, the issue arises as to the extent to which subsequent literature and Christian spirituality have taken the view that the unique desert monastic experience should be the normative one in which to consider the existence and influence of the devil. As will be seen below in the example of Evagrius Ponticus' life and teaching, who was also a desert monk, a subtler way of treating demonic activity can be envisaged, one that has shown itself to be of perennial value even in the present-day world.

The story of Antony continues, nonetheless, to have a particular grip on the imagination of the reader. He moved from an original village setting to live among the tombs in the desert.

> He charged one of his friends to supply him periodically with bread, and he entered one of the tombs and remained alone within, his friend having closed the door on him. When the enemy could stand it no longer – for he was apprehensive that Antony might before long fill the desert with the discipline – approaching one night with a multitude of demons he whipped him with such force that he lay on the earth, speechless from the tortures. He contended that the pains were so severe as to lead one to say that the blows could not have been delivered by humans, since they caused such agony.[67]

According to Athanasius, when his acquaintance came next day and found him, he brought him back to the village where his kinsfolk sat around him and kept vigil; he regained consciousness about midnight and insisted that his friend carry him back to the tomb in which he lived. The attacks of the devil resumed.

> Now schemes for working evil come easily to the devil, so when it was night-time they made such a crashing noise that the whole place seemed to be shaken by a quake. The demons, as if breaking through the building's four walls, and seeming to enter through them, were changed into the forms of beasts and reptiles. The place was immediately filled with the appearances of lions, bears, leopards, bulls, and serpents, asps, scorpions and wolves, and each of these moved in accordance with its form. ... Struck and wounded by them, Antony's body was subject to yet more pain. But unmoved and even more watchful in his soul he lay there, and he groaned because of the pain felt in his body, but being in control in his thoughts and as if mocking them he said: 'If there were some power among you, it would have been enough for only one of you to come. ... If you are able, and you did receive authority over me, don't hold back, but attack.[68]

This time, the Lord came to help him, Athanasius related. He saw the roof opening, 'as it were', and a beam of light coming down to him, causing the demons to disappear and the pain in his body to ease.

67. St Athanasius, *The Life of Antony*, no. 8.
68. Ibid., no. 9.

Neither the author of the introduction to the *Classics of Western Spirituality* edition, Robert C. Gregg, nor Athanasius himself, draws attention to the inconsistency in the narrative arising from the accounts of Antony's injuries ('whipped with force', 'struck and wounded') and Antony's own address to the monks who came to consult him. The aim of his long address, from no. 16 to no. 43, was to encourage the monks to persevere in prayer and ascetical practices, and in that context it included a large section on demons, from no. 21 to no. 43, in which he spoke of the demons' inability to do physical harm to the monk (though in no. 40 he said that the cunning one whipped him many times). He spoke of the demons transforming themselves and imitating 'women, beasts, reptiles and huge bodies'.

> Nevertheless we need not fear their apparitions, for they are nothing and disappear quickly –especially if one fortifies himself with faith and the sign of the cross. (no. 23)

Further on, he gave greater reassurance:

> Since the Lord made his sojourn with us, the enemy is fallen and his powers have diminished. For this reason, though he is able to do nothing, nevertheless like a tyrant fallen from power he does not remain quiet, but issues threats, even if they are only words. ... [Demons] are evil and they desire nothing so much as inflicting injury on those who love virtue and honour God. But because they have no power to act, they do nothing except issue threats. ... If the capability were theirs, they would not come in great mobs, not create phantasms, nor would they work their fraud by being transfigured. It would suffice for only one to come and do what he can and wills – especially because everyone who actually possesses the power does not destroy with apparitions, nor arouse fear with large mobs, but exercises his might directly, as he wishes. (no. 28)

The reference to the Lord's sojourn could indicate some input on the part of Athanasius himself. Not only is the enemy fallen, but the conjunction of the divine and human in one person challenged the monk to reach a state of equilibrium through mastery of the basic drives. Even though demonology figures largely in Antony's address, his detailed account of the challenges facing the monk at the level of perseverance in prayer and ascetical practices shows clearly the result of long experience and mastery of the monk's craft. In fact, if less attention is devoted to the demonology, a more compelling picture emerges of the heroic nature of the desert dwellers' way of life.

According to Peter Brown in his *The Making of Late Antiquity*,

> In entering into the experiences of an Antony and a Paul, and in reconstructing what such experiences meant to contemporaries, we should not be misled by the long tradition of the iconography of the Temptation of Saint Antony. The concern of the hermit was more down to earth and less melodramatic. Antony

was grappling with his own personality. He did so in a situation of self-imposed sensory deprivation, where one may suspect that hallucination and extreme emotional states were deliberately courted so as to overcome and not entered unwittingly and then naïvely ascribed to the demonic.[69]

Brown in his *The Body and Society* also says that 'the most bitter struggle of the desert ascetic was presented not so much as struggle with his sexuality as with his belly'.[70]

Athanasius' biography is now considered soundly based on the life of a real individual, but also as belonging to the hagiographical genre. The dramatic elements need to be seen in the light of the peculiar context of the solitary life in the unrelenting heat and malnourishment of desert conditions, with the likely effects on the imagination.

---

69. Peter Brown, *The Making of Late Antiquity* (Cambridge, MA: Harvard University Press, 1978), 89.

70. Peter Brown, *The Body and Society: Men, Women and Sexual Renunciation in Early Christianity* (New York: Columbia University Press, 1988), 218:

> While the Nile valley was a zone of food, braced against the threat of famine, the desert was thought of as the zone deprived of human food: it was the zone of the non-human. For this reason, the most bitter struggle of the desert ascetic was presented not so much as struggle with his sexuality as with his belly. It was his triumph in the struggle with hunger that released, in the popular imagination, the most majestic and the most haunting images of a new humanity.

Chapter 4

STEPPING STONES TO EUROPE

Christian spirituality in Western Europe

The spirituality of the desert fathers was brought to Europe by a series of disciples who modified the awareness of the devil in the Christian life in the course of this migration. Pachomius, one of the desert dwellers, prepared the way by his form of monastic life.

Pachomius (c. 292–348)

He is credited with developing a community form of monastic life which, though still monastic, had implications for the form Christian living in society in the following centuries. He was the son of pagan parents and was reluctant, even as a child, to go with them to pagan sacrifices. According to his biography known as the *Bohairic Life*, when his parents gave him a cauldron of meat to take to some labourers,

> the devil set on him a crowd of demons under the form of dogs bent on killing him. But the boy raised his eyes to heaven and wept. At once they scattered. Right away then the devil assumed the form of an old man … (but) the boy blew his breath into his face and at once he disappeared.[1]

This incident, recounted by himself in later life, was an example of the attacks by demons recorded in his life, as in the life of Antony, who was his contemporary. As a young man he was conscripted into Constantine's army and was impressed by the charity of Christians who gave food to the conscripts as they were being ferried up the Nile. On his discharge, he went to the upper Thebaid and sought out a church in order to be baptised. He spent some years engaged in caring for the poor in that area, but then decided that his calling was to the anchoritic life.

---

1. *The Life of Saint Pachomius and His Disciples. Pachomian Koinonia*, vol. 1, translated, with an introduction by Armand Veilleux (Kalamazoo: Cistercian Publications, 1980), 25–6. This quotation is from the *Bohairic Life*.

Then, moved by the love of God he sought to become a monk. When told of an anchorite called Palamon, he went to him to share his anchoritic life.[2]

Palamon introduced him to his own ascetic practices, including overnight vigils and the practice of eating each day in summer, but only every other day in winter. He only ate bread and salt and never used oil or drank wine. In his days as a solitary Pachomius endured temptation of various kinds by demons, 'for his own training and for the benefit of others'.

> They began to attack him openly. Sometimes when he was going to bend his knees during his prayer, [the demon] would apparently make a sort of pit in front of him, to frighten him into praying no longer to the Lord. But, understanding the wiles of the tempter, he would kneel with faith and would bless God, thus giving thanks to Christ and putting the demons to shame. At other times, when he would be setting out to go about one of his tasks, they would march in front of him in double file like soldiers marching before commanders, while saying to each other, 'Make way for the Man of God' with the intention of tricking him into looking at them.' But the Man of God, through his hope in God, would not look at them, but instead would mock them as powerless creatures. And at once they would vanish from his face. Still other times they would shake his cell to make him afraid that it would collapse on him. At once he would say, Our God is our shelter.[3]

His trials, like those of Antony, included what was described as physical assault.

> He was tempted in many other cruel ways. His body was beaten and he suffered visibly from evening till morning, without any consolation except the remembrance of God who was chastening him.[4]

He spent seven years under Palamon's tutelage, before receiving a call from heaven, 'Pachomius, Pachomius, struggle, dwell in this place and build a monastery, for many will come to you to become monks with you, and they will profit their souls'.[5] Through visions he received, he founded other monasteries[6] and provided rules of life for this new cenobitic form of monastic living. Various sets of rules and precepts are extant, giving details of the requirements necessary in order that a large group of men could live together in harmony and with an ascetical lifestyle. The four sets of rules regarded as authentic – *The Precepts*, *The Precepts and Institutes*, *The*

---

2. Ibid., 301. The volume also contains the *Greek Life* (from which this quotation is taken) and fragments of three *Sahidic Lives*.
3. Ibid., 44.
4. Ibid., 310. The quotation is from the *Greek Life*.
5. Ibid., 39.
6. Ibid., 71–4 (no. 49–54) records the founding of some of them.

Precepts and Judgments, The Precepts and Laws – together provided an extremely detailed manual regulating all aspects of community life. A strict ascetical regime still contained a degree of consideration for human needs:

> The brothers shall not be forced to work excessively, but a moderate labour shall incite everyone to work. Let there be peace and contentment among them, and let them willingly submit to their superiors, either sitting, walking or standing, according to their rank, and competing with one another in humility. (*Precepts and Laws* no. 3)[7]

The Rules would provide a foundation for subsequent cenobitic monastic rules and contain no mention of demons or the devil. However, the account of life in these monasteries under Pachomius and his successor Theodore records many incidents in which demons were believed to be at work to reverse the spiritual progress made by individual monks. There were incidents also of possessed people being healed. On one occasion, brothers came to consult Pachomius, saying: 'Why is it that before the demon comes to trouble us we possess our minds in a healthy state?' They seemed to accept that they enjoyed a normal untroubled life until temptation intruded. Pachomius' response was

> Because we do not pursue the active life perfectly – this is why we do not understand all the demon's mind and versatility well enough to be able, when the troubler manifests his presence, to repel quickly the confusion of such thoughts which surrounds us by the contemplative power of the soul.[8]

On one occasion, he had trouble with ten brothers who had wicked thoughts against chastity put there by Satan, with the result that they opposed the strictness of Pachomius' teaching. He prayed for them day and night. Meeting one of them, he told him that he was aware of their struggles and that it was a case of demons fighting against them, but he knew that they had not defiled themselves.[9] This is an example of one of Pachomius' spiritual gifts, his knowledge of his monks' inner lives, as another incident also demonstrated; a brother who was being tried by a demon was brought to him from one of his monasteries.

> When our father Pachomius spoke with him, he answered well as one who is in no way tried by demons. [Pachomius] said to the brothers who had led him to him, 'I assure you, this demon is hiding in him and will not speak to me by this man's voice; but I am going to examine his whole body till I find out which of his members he is hiding in.' While he was examining his whole body he came

---

7. *Pachomian Koinonia*, vol. 2. *Pachomian Chronicles and Rules* (Kalamazoo: Cistercian Publications, 1981), 181.
8. *The Life of Saint Pachomius and His Disciples*, 33–4.
9. Ibid., 140–1.

to the fingers of his hands and said to the brothers, 'Here is the way the demon got in by, I have found it in the fingers of his hands'. Then, when he came to his neck, the place where the demon was, [the demon] made a great outcry and the man gave a violent jerk, and four men were hardly able to hold him. Our father Pachomius took hold of the place where the demon was and prayed to Christ for the brother that he might cure him. While he was praying the demon came out of the man who was immediately restored, thanks to our father Pachomius' prayers.[10]

This incident is of particular interest because similar incidents were reported in medieval times; exorcists often claimed to be able to locate in what part of the body a demon lurked in a person who was possessed. Life in Pachomius' monasteries, as recorded in volume 2 of the *Pachomian Koinonia*, did involve dealing with demonic temptation, but Pachomius' teaching encouraged the brothers to rely on the Word of God dwelling within them. 'What satanic wile is able to deceive you? For instead of having a myriad of teachers, the word of God is dwelling within you, teaching you more and making you wiser by his own knowledge.'[11]

In addition to the *Lives* there is a set of anecdotes, the *Paralipomena* (the leftovers), and among them a graphic description of an encounter Pachomius and his disciple Theodore had with a 'frightful apparition' while walking at night. It proved to be a woman, with a throng of demons running before her. Their prayer did not drive her off and instead she told them: 'I have received from Almighty God the power to tempt those whom I want. Indeed I have been asking him for this for a long time.' In response to Pachomius' question, she said: 'I am the devil's daughter and I am called "all his power" for every phalanx of demons serves me.' In the text the incident is described in three long paragraphs and reports the challenging of the spectre by Pachomius and his final dismissal, enjoining 'her never again to approach the monastery'. It all sounds like a cleverly crafted fantasy on some author's part, but, oddly, a historical note enters when the text says that Pachomius 'sent letters to the great ones who were living in the other monasteries … to inform them about the subject of the apparition.'[12]

A more obviously realistic incident is described in relation to a fig tree. Visiting the monastery at Thmoušions, he found a large fig tree in the middle of the monastery, which one of the boys was in the habit of climbing up secretly to pluck figs for the boys to eat. Pachomius 'saw an unclean spirit sitting in it,

---

10. Ibid., 162–3.

11. *Pachomian Koinonia*, vol. 2, 44.

12. Ibid., chapter 10.48–51. A similar incident is related in the life of Shenoute (348-466), the head of a federation of Coptic monasteries, two for men and one for women in his lifetime. He met the devil in the form of a local magistrate, as he was walking at night pondering whether some monks should be expelled from the monastery. He concluded that the devil was neither male or female, but a 'confusion of genders, a lack of stable identity.' David Brakke, *Demons and the Making of the Monk*, 206.

and he knew immediately that it was the spirit of gluttony. And the Holy Man knew it was he who deceived the boys'. He ordered it to be cut down, but the gardener, who had never eaten the fruit 'while all the brothers and strangers and the people living around ate their fill in the fruit season',[13] pleaded for its retention. Pachomius did not want to force compliance, but the fig tree withered away overnight.

Historical or not, the incident marks a transition that was beginning in the way of perceiving the demonic in the life of the monk and other Christians. A monk born towards the end of Pachomius' life articulated this approach to spirituality.

Evagrius Ponticus (345–399)

Evagrius, born in faraway Bithynia, Asia Minor, twelve years before Antony's death, was a friend of Basil and Gregory Nazianzen and an enthusiastic disciple of Origen's theology. Because of his acceptance of some of Origen's more dubious speculations he was condemned at the Fifth Ecumenical Council in 553, with the result that some of his own writings were transmitted to posterity under pseudonyms. He was destined to end his life as a monk in Egypt as a disciple of Macarius the Great, who had himself been a disciple of Antony. His journey there by way of Constantinople and Jerusalem was the result of his efforts to deal with his worldly ambitions and passions, and in his last years he lived an extremely ascetical life, and was an exceptional master of both moral and contemplative Christianity.

Evagrius brought to monastic life in the desert a deep understanding of the life of the soul and a new way of formulating its stages of development. He used the terms *praktike, physike* and *theologia*. The latter two concern contemplation – created reality seen in God and contemplation of God as Trinity. *Praktike* had to do with the monk's efforts to overcome temptation, to reach the stage of having overcome the passions, which he called apatheia.[14]

> Conceived by obedience, apatheia is preserved by fear of the Lord. It is nourished and grows through the practice of humility and the cultivation of sorrow for sin. Further, it never fully stabilizes; it always requires a willingness to guard and protect it, for it remains exposed to the assaults of the demons. It has limits that come from the human situation.[15]

The passions to be overcome in order to achieve apatheia were listed by Evagrius:

---

13. Ibid., chapter 12.53–55.
14. Andrew Louth, *The Origins of the Christian Mystical Tradition: From Plato to Denys* (Oxford: Clarendon Press, 1981), 103.
15. John Eudes Bamberger O.C.S.O., 'Introduction', in Evagrius Ponticus, *Praktike and Chapters on Prayer*, John Eudes Bamberger, trans. and introduction (Kalamazoo: Cistercian Publications, 1981), lxxxv.

> There are eight general and basic categories of thought in which are included every thought. First is that of gluttony and then impurity, avarice, sadness, anger, acedia, vainglory, and last of all, pride. It is not in our power to determine whether we are disturbed by these thoughts, but it is up to us to decide if they are to linger within us or not and whether or not they are to stir up our passions. (no. 6)[16]

Being 'disturbed' by these evil thoughts is to be tempted while not actually sinning, not 'allowing them to linger', and this caused Evagrius to describe attacks at the level of the various passions as *logismoi*, or 'passionate thoughts'.[17]

Demons constantly opposed progress towards apatheia, Evagrius observed throughout the *Praktike*. He spoke of demons eighty times between references in the *Praktike* and the *Chapters on Prayer*, and six times in the *Ad Monachos*. His general observations included that 'the demon of pride is the cause of the most damaging fall for the soul. For it induces the monk to deny that God is his helper and to consider that he himself is the cause of virtuous actions' (no. 14); 'The demons that rule over the passions of the soul persevere until death. Those which rule over the bodily passions depart more quickly' (no. 36).

> We must take care to recognize the different types of demons and take note of the circumstances of their coming. ... We ought to consider which of the demons are less frequent in their assaults, which are the more vexatious, which are the ones which yield the field more readily and which the more resistant. Finally, we should note the ones that make sudden raids and snatch off the spirit to blasphemy. Now it is essential to understand these matters so that when these various evil thoughts set their own proper forces to work we are in a position to address effective words against them, that is to say, those words which correctly characterize the one present. And we must do this before they drive us out of our own state of mind. In this manner we shall make ready progress, by the grace of God. We shall pack them off chafing with chagrin and marvelling at our perspicacity. (no. 43)[18]

When the depraved demon has done all he can and still finds that his efforts to prevent the prayer of the virtuous man are unavailing, he will let up for a time. But again after a while he avenges himself on this man of prayer. For he will either enkindle the man's anger and thus dissipate that excellent state established

---

16. Ibid., 16–17, no. 6.

17. Kyriakos S. Markides, *The Mountain of Silence: A Search for Orthodox Spirituality* (New York: Doubleday, 2001), 124, quoting a monk of Mount Athos: 'When human beings are attacked by such logismoi they ought to feel no guilt whatsoever. They are totally innocent and not responsible for these logismoi. The great saints faced legions of negative logismoi. No human being has ever lived without being assaulted by myriads of logismoi. Only the dead are free of logismoi.'

18. Ibid.

in him by prayer, or else he chooses to outrage the spirit by provoking it to some unreasonable pleasure. (no. 47)[19]

The attacks of the demons attract other demons to assist in the attack, but they then contended among themselves. (no. 45)[20]

Considering the logismoi in turn, a demon is specifically associated with lust, with acedia, with anger and with pride, though demonic activity is involved in all. In an interesting comment, he said: 'Anger is given to us so that we might fight against the demons and strive against every pleasure' (no. 27).[21] But the demons, for their part, draw the monk's anger to worldly desires and constrain him to fight against others. Anger is itself the 'most fierce passion' (no. 11). His account of acedia was based on the 'noon-day devil' or 'the destruction that wastes at noon' as the RSV puts it, of Ps. 91 (90):6; the Hebrew has: 'The deadly disease striking at noon.' In desert conditions the high heat of noon inevitably created lassitude, making it more likely a monk would succumb to temptation.

> When we meet with the demon of acedia then is the time with tears to divide our soul in two. One part is to encourage; the other is to be encouraged. Thus we are to sow seeds of a firm hope in ourselves while we sing with the holy David: 'Why are you filled with sadness, my soul? Why are you distraught? Trust in God, for I shall give praise to him. He it is who saves me, the light of my eyes and my God.' (no. 27)[22]

Evagrius clearly demonstrated his personal knowledge of monastic life in the desert with this observation about acedia, a uniquely monastic temptation as first articulated by him (leaving the word untranslatable), though spiritual authors have been able apply it to modern spirituality. His descriptive psychology of the monk's life provided a pattern not only for the understanding of monastic spirituality, but also a foundation for the formulation of later Christian spirituality.

As the author of the introduction to the work remarked:

> The description of the eight logismoi is surely the most original and interesting in Evagrius' present work. Not that he necessarily invented the system of eight such evil thoughts, but he has given us a classic description. His abilities as a writer and teacher are clearest in the nine chapters that comprise this section

---

19. Ibid., 62. Another way in which a demon deceives the monk is described in the *Chapters on Prayer*: 'It happens at times that the demons suggest some bad thoughts to you and again stir you up to pray against them, as is only proper, or to contradict them. Then they depart of their own choosing so as to deceive you into believing that you have conquered your thoughts of yourself and have cast fear into the demons.' Ibid., 77, no. 134.

20. Evagrius Ponticus, *Praktike and Chapters on Prayer*, 28.

21. Ibid., 23.

22. Ibid.

of the Praktikos. It would even seem that his reputation in the desert during his own lifetime was based to a large degree upon his analysis and description of these logismoi.

When the monastic movement evolved to a community rather than solitary form, the apparently physical demoniacal attacks diminished, and while temptation continued to assail individual monks the role of the father or abba became important in assisting the individual to cope or even to identify the presence of the tempter. A brother came to an abba to ask him to pray for him as he was tempted by fornication. After some time the abba became worried the brother was not finding peace.

> And God showed him what the brother was doing. He saw him sitting down, and the spirit of fornication was near him. An angel stood by, sent to help him, and was angry with the brother because he did not throw himself on God.[23]

The various collections of the sayings of the desert fathers, and the more limited collections of the saying of the desert mothers, all make many references to demons or the devil and their activities. Some refer to angels as well. In both cases, the incorporeal aspect is clear, even if it is a case of an angel 'standing by'. The role of the demon was to tempt and that of the angel to protect; to what extent a demon or an angel was an external or an internal presence in relation to the monk did not seem to need explanation, but only in some cases was there reference to a demon being in possession of a person. A fine example of 'flying' demons and angels is found in a story about Abba Moses, who was struggling with the 'demon of fornication'.

> Abba Isidore took Moses out onto the terrace and said to him. 'Look towards the west.' He looked and saw hordes of demons flying about and making a noise before launching an attack. Then Abba Isidore said to him, 'Look towards the east.' He looked and saw an innumerable multitude of holy angels shining with glory. Abba Isidore said: 'See, these are sent by the Lord to the saints to bring them help, while those in the west fight against them. Those who are with us are more in number than they are.'[24]

The 'hordes of demons flying about and making a noise' suggests strongly that the attempt to describe the inner reality of temptation was inspired by flocks of noisy birds, and the awareness of protective angels by the text in Lk. 2.9. A strong

---

23. John Wortley, ed., *The Greek Anonymous Series of Apophthegmata Patrum* (Cambridge: Cambridge University Press, 2013), 113, 169.

24. *The Sayings of the Desert Fathers: The Alphabetical Collection*, translated with a foreword by Benedicta Ward SLG (London: Mowbray, 1975), 138. There are approximately forty references to demons and nineteen to angels in that collection.

indication that demonic attacks were in fact understood as internal temptations arising from human passions is found in a discussion between Abba Poemon and a monk, Abraham, especially if it concerns the Poemon of the late fifth century.

> Abraham questioned Abba Poemon saying, 'How do demons fight against me?' Abba Poemon said to him, 'The demons fight against you? They do not fight against us at all as long as we are doing our own will. For our own will becomes the demons, and it is these which attack us in order that we may fulfil them.'[25]

The observation that 'our own will becomes the demons' presents a different picture of the demons from the usual one of external spiritual and malignant beings to which the lives of Antony and Pachomius give witness. While Evagrius spoke of demons as external forces, demons attracting other demons and then contending among themselves, his description of the logismoi points to internal struggles within the heart of the monk. In a reference to the monk's life in *Ad Monachos*, he said simply: 'An angelic dream gladdens the heart, a demonic dream agitates it.'[26] When he refers to the demon of acedia, a modern reader who does not believe in demons as traditionally articulated can understand from experience the conflict that is taking place.[27] Though belief in the existence of demons, so strongly suggested by the experience of the desert fathers, would continue in that same form for many centuries, the ascetical demand of the Christian life in the later Roman world came to be seen rather more in terms of psychological tensions of spiritual origin within the person, as it is today. Evagrius' logismoi prepared the way for a new formulation in the simpler terms of temptation to commit the Capital Sins, as Gregory the Great (r. 590–604) listed them.

Temptation as internal struggle

With time and the growth and acceptance of the Christian community under the auspices of the Emperor Constantine, Christians had become part of the establishment, while pagan rites were allowed to continue, with Emperor

---

25. Ibid., 176.
26. *Ad Monachos. Greek Text and English Translation* no. 52, translated in Jeremy Driscoll OSB, *The 'Ad Monachos' of Evagrius Ponticus: Its Structure and a Select Commentary* (Roma: Studia Anselmiana, 1991).
27. The relationship between desert monastic spirituality and that of the Christian in today's secular world is underlined in Greg Peters, *The Monkhood of All Believers: The Monastic Foundation of Christian Spirituality* (Grand Rapids, MI: Baker Academic, 2018), 142: '(1) a "monk" is someone, anyone, who has a single-minded interior focus on God rooted in her baptismal vows; and (2) asceticism, that most monastic of practices, is expected of all Christian believers by virtue of our baptism and is characterised primarily by balance and moderation.'

Constantine himself as a pagan *pontifex maximus*.[28] The freedom of the Christian community to own property, build churches, acquire assets, brought with it a change in lifestyle, and worldly temptations. Christian asceticism made demands on the Christians in society, in the form of an internal struggle with temptation, little different from those the monks endeavoured to meet, though there remained the realisation that the desert dwellers, in community or otherwise, were exceptional people and were subjected to exceptional temptations. St Jerome (c. 347–420) trained as a monk in Syria and brought with him to Rome a desert monk mentality that challenged the standards of Christian living accepted by the Christian community there. He instructed women of Christian noble families in the Scriptures and promoted an ascetical lifestyle among his followers, often criticising the attitudes and way of life of others, especially the clergy. Among his targets were ecclesiastics who made a fuss when the food and wine at their tables fell below standard.[29]

Though Antony would remain the prototypical monk and consequently a somewhat legendary figure, future generations of readers could potentially gain deep knowledge of the monastic roots of Christian spirituality through the writings of Evagrius when they were assimilated and brought to the West by Cassian.

John Cassian (c. 365–435)

Cassian was probably born in Scythia (on the border between today's Romania and Bulgaria) in the later part of Evagrius' life and as he was a contemporary of Saint Augustine as well, formed a link between two worlds. He entered a monastery in Bethlehem when he was in his early adult years. From there, Cassian and Germanus, an older companion, travelled several times to Egypt where they learned about the monastic tradition from the great desert masters or abbas. Theological controversy in Egypt led him to seek protection from the Patriarch, John Chrysostom, in Constantinople, and when Chrysostom was forced into exile, Cassian went to Rome to plead his cause. There he was invited to found a Pachomian-type monastery in Marseilles, which he did in 415, a complex of men's and women's communities.[30]

He presented his *Conferences* to the monks (and possibly the nuns) in the form of a record of twenty-four dialogues with fifteen abbas. He was highly indebted to Evagrius, but did not name him; suspicion had fallen on Evagrius because of his seeming adoption of condemned aspects of Origen's theology. Cassian had the double aim of promoting monastic life in community, while leaving room for the monk to aspire to the level of mystical union with God that characterised the

---

28. Robin Lane Fox, *Pagans and Christians* (London: Penguin Books, 1988), 666.

29. J. N. D. Kelly, *Jerome: His Life, Writings and Controversies* (London: Duckworth, 1975), 109.

30. Peter King, *Western Monasticism. A History of the Monastic Movement in the Latin Church* (Kalamazoo: Cistercian Publications, 1999), 37–40.

original hermits. These he greatly admired while accepting that the cenobitic life would not be lived on the same intense level of struggle the hermits regarded as essential to reach 'purity of heart', a term corresponding to Evagrius' apatheia – though Cassian thought it wiser not to use it. He would speak much of demons in his *Conferences*, but his more lasting influence would be through his *Institutes*.

In the *First Conference*, he spoke of the need to examine carefully a thought that arises in the heart, 'to see if it has been purified by the divine and heavenly fire of the Holy Spirit, or if it is part of the Jewish superstition or if, coming from the pridefulness of worldly philosophy, it has the mere look of piety about it'. A thought and temptation may then arise from ordinary aspects of the culture and not from demonic activity.

> But he also tries to lead us astray with counterfeits by exhorting us to pursue a certain pious work, which since it is not the legitimate coinage of the elders, leads to vice under the appearance of virtue and brings us to a bad end and by deceiving us either with immoderate and inappropriate fasting or severe vigils or inordinate praying or excessive reading. (*First Conf.* XXI.4)[31]

He stressed the difference between the new environment and that of the desert, recalling in several Conferences the experience of Jesus in the desert. But community life had the advantage that the monk could more easily unburden himself to the elders, an essential practice in order to defeat what he called the illusions (Latin *inlusio*) of the devil.[32]

Reflecting on his experience in Egypt, he saw a difference between those halcyon days and his new environment. In those early days, the attacks were so strong that the monks had to take turns in sleeping so there would always be some to keep vigil in prayer. Now things were more peaceful, but he was not sure whether demons were weaker or were allowing the monks to defeat themselves by their complacency.

> We have sufficiently learned from our own experience and from the accounts of the elders that the demons do not have the same power now that they had at an earlier time, at the beginnings of the anchorite life, when still only a few monks lived in the desert. For so great was their savagery that only a few who were very stable and advanced in age were able to endure dwelling in the desert ...
>
> Hence it cannot be doubted that one of two things has conferred this security and confidence now not only on us who seem somewhat strengthened because of the experiences of age but also on those who are younger. Either the power of the cross has also penetrated the desert and by its gleaming grace has blunted

---

31. John Cassian, *The Conferences* (New York: Paulist Press, 1997), 59.
32. Boniface Ramsey, 'Introduction' to John Cassian, *The Conferences* (New York: Paulist Press, 1997), 17: '(Deception) Cassian frequently calls by the word "illusion" (or *inlusio* in Latin, with its resonances of mockery and jeering).'

the wickedness of the demons everywhere, or our negligence has made them milder than when they first began to attack, since they disdain to fight against us with the same intensity with which they once raged against those accomplished soldiers of Christ, destroying us more ominously with deceitfulness now that visible trials have ceased. (*Seventh Conf.* XXIII. 1-2)[33]

The *Seventh Conference* he attributed to a certain Abbot Serenus (otherwise unknown). For Serenus, it was proved beyond doubt that there were as many occupations among unclean spirits as there were among humans.

For it is clear that some of them ... are such tricksters and jokers that constantly infect certain places and roads where they do not take delight in tormenting passers-by whom they can deceive but are content simply with derisions and illusions, and they strive to weary them rather than harm them. (*Seventh Conf.* XXIII. 1-2)

In contrast,

Others are given over to such fury and savagery that they are not content with troubling those whom they possess by violently lacerating their bodies but even seek to assail passers-by from a distance and to murder them brutally. (*Seventh Conf.* XXXII.1)[34]

The whole Conference was on the topic of the soul and evil spirits, evil beings from the heavenly places, and was in effect a record of Cassian's demonology. Serenus (or Cassian himself) relied on personal experience and on the Scriptures for evidence of the existence and activity of the various kinds of demons.

We find that others not only engage in lying, but even inspire people to blaspheme. We who have heard a demon openly confess that he spread abroad an impious and sacrilegious teaching through Arius and Eunomius are ourselves witnesses of this. We also read in the Fourth Book of Kings that one of this kind clearly declared: 'I will go out and I will be a lying spirit in the mouth of all his prophets.' The Apostle speaks about these in the following way when he reproaches those who are deceived by such: 'Paying attention to seducing spirits and to the teachings of demons that tell lies in hypocrisy.' ... Scriptural authority likewise teaches that there are demons of the night, of the day, and of noonday. (XXXII. 3-4)[35]

---

33. Cassian, *The Conferences*, 263.
34. Ibid., 369.
35. Ibid., 270. Henri Crouzel, in *Origen*, A. S. Worrall, trans. (Edinburgh: T&T Clark, 1989), 80, credited Cassian with formulation of the four meanings of Scripture, literal, allegorical, moral and anagogical.

He attributed corporeality of some kind to the demons, as only God was completely incorporeal.

> Nor even if a spirit is mingled with this dense and solid matter (that is, with flesh), which can very easily be done, is it therefore to be believed that it can be so united to a soul, which is also a spirit, that it can also make it the bearer of its own nature. This is possible to the Trinity alone, which so penetrates every intellectual nature that it is able not only to embrace and encompass it but even to flow into it and, being itself incorporeal, to be poured into a body. … For although we declare that some natures are spiritual, as are the angels, the archangels and the other powers, our soul itself and of course the subtle air, yet these are by no means to be regarded as incorporeal. They have a body appropriate to themselves by which they subsist, although it is far more refined than our own bodies. (XIII. 1-2)[36]

Cassian's demonology, which derived directly from the teaching of the Egyptian monks, became part of Europe's heritage up to a point in history difficult to pin down, but certainly including the period of the Reformation, to the edge at least of modernity. As will be seen in the final section of this work, there are remarkable resemblances between his demonology and beliefs current in parts of society today, especially in the United States.

His more significant contribution to Western Christianity, however, derived from his *Institutes*, a major work on the organisation and administration of cenobitic communities. It was a model on which Benedict's *Rule* drew, as the references in his text to Cassian's works make clear.[37] It is worth noting that Benedict did not follow Cassian's example of almost forty references to the devil in the *Institutes* in setting out the prescriptions for the monastic way of life in his rule – he mentioned the devil only three times (see note 37 below). It is important to note that while demonology was crucially important in Egyptian monasticism it virtually disappeared from Western monasticism, which would prove so important in the transmission of Christian culture in the West.

Another factor, however, would be influential among Christians generally, namely, the popularity of Augustine's theology. His systematic treatment of diabolical activity, arising from his exposure to apocalyptic written sources and

---

36. Ibid., 256. See Ramsey, 'Introduction', 277: 'A certain refined but nonetheless real corporeality was attributed to angels by a number of fathers. … The attribution of such corporeality to demons was almost universal. … The materiality of the soul, however, was a rare belief; its most famous exponent is Tertullian in his *De anima* 22.2. Cassian's insistence on the absolute incorporeality of God recurs in 10.3ff.' See also H. A. Denzinger and H. A Schönmetzer, *Enchiridion Symbolorum* (Herder: Barcinone, 1965), nos. 208–10.

37. Adalbert de Vogüé, 'Les Mentions des oeuvres de Cassien chez Saint Benoît et ses contemporains', in *De Saint Pachôme à Jean Cassien. Études littéraires et doctrinales sur le monachisme égyptien à ses débuts* (Roma: Studia Anselmiana, 1996), 346–57.

his personal struggle against temptation, had an effect on the large community to which he ministered, and consolidated already existing awareness of the threats from demons.

The devil in the thought of Augustine (354–430)

In the course of the vast number of his treatises, commentaries and sermons, Augustine dealt with the devil and demons from pastoral, theological and philosophical perspectives, the last of these under the heading of 'evil', where evil is the absence of good, as already noted when his theodicy was being considered in Chapter 1. The philosophical aspect of his thought was probably of less importance in the daily life of the church than his contribution to ecclesiastical *praxis*, as his sermons and commentaries on Scripture, especially the Psalms, have been in widespread circulation ever since. In his treatise on the Gospel of John he said:

> Whence is the devil himself? From the same source certainly as the other angels. But the other angels continued in their obedience. He, by disobedience and pride, fell as an angel, and became a devil.[38]

His conceptualisation of such beings as demons was derived both from Greek classical tradition and the references in Scripture. He accepted the tradition which by then established that the demons were angels who had fallen through pride and disobedience, and now inhabited the air.

> If the angels who transgressed were in the superior part of the air [because of its pure tranquillity], before they transgressed and were with their chief, now the devil, it would not be strange if after their sin they were cast down into the darkness, which is disturbed by winds and even by lightning and thunder.[39]

The reference to the 'superior part of the air' is evidence for Augustine's acceptance of the model of the universe developed by Ptolemy about AD 140. Beyond this, God, who could not be observed by astronomers, was presumed to dwell. The question of what might lie beyond the spheres had been considered by Aristotle, who concluded that since the idea of place implied the possibility of material bodies occupying it and there were no such bodies, then there could not be any place beyond the cosmos. Augustine and all others thought of the angels as belonging to a sphere of the highest purity, though not material. However, as Aquinas would hold centuries later, the angels had a relation with corporeal creatures, 'were made in a corporeal place' (*Sum Theol* 1a q61 a4 ad 1).

---

38. Augustine, *Tractates on the Gospel of John* 42.10, Fathers of the Church, Vol. 88 (Washington, DC: Catholic University of America, 1993).

39. Augustine, *Sancti Augustini Opera Omnia* Tomus 5, De Genesi ad Litteram III,10 (Paris: Paul Mellier, 1842), 231–2. My translation.

Augustine did hold that the angels, good and fallen, had a relationship with the rest of the spheres, 'had celestial bodies', in which the fallen angels were cast down. Besides, Scripture recorded the 'indubitable fact that the good angels have appeared to men in bodies that could not merely be seen but felt'.[40]

> If those transgressors before their transgression had celestial bodies, it would not be strange if as punishment they could suffer from fire and be confined to the darkness until the time of judgment.[41]

He could describe these fallen angels as embodied in an 'aerial substance' and not always so confined but free to harass humankind as Justin had testified. He was uncertain about parts of the tradition; he mentioned stories about *incubi*, whose sexual intercourse with women was attested to by 'trustworthy reporters'.

> However, I would not dare to decide, on evidence like this, whether or not certain spirits, embodied in the kind of aerial substance, whose force we can feel when it is fanned against our bodies, are subject to the passion of lust and can awake a responsive passion in women.[42]

His pastoral concerns were expressed in his *City of God*, in which he quoted the view of 'certain philosophers' that all living beings with rational souls were divided into gods, demons and men, with the demons in the middle inhabiting the air, lower than gods and higher than men. 'They have immortality of the body in common with the gods, but passions of the mind in common with men.'[43] He was discussing these matters in the context of the teachings of the Platonist philosophers, without questioning the existence of demons (or gods), but he did assume Christian teaching in making strong distinctions between the demons and the good angels, particularly in relation to knowledge; if the demons can foresee much more of the future than men, it is only because of their longer experience. They 'are often wholly mistaken, the angels never'.[44] The demons nonetheless have superior powers; because of their 'aerial bodies' they can influence bodily feelings and emotions:

> It is by no means unreasonable to suppose that beings which act with the powers of an aerial body upon our bodies, and are by the constitution of their natures able to pass unhindered through these bodies, should be capable of much greater

---

40. Augustine, *City of God* XV, Book XV, C 23 (Washington, DC: Catholic University of America, 1951), 470.
41. Augustine, *De Genesi ad Litteram* III,10, 231.
42. Augustine, *City of God* XV, C 23 471.
43. Ibid., Book VIII, C.14, 46.
44. Ibid., Book IX, C.22, 110.

quickness in moving whatever they wish, while we, though not perceiving what they do, are nevertheless affected by the results of their activity.[45]

The demons foster the idea that the human soul has so little reality that it is incapable of reaching and finding rest in unchanging and eternal truth:

> These malign spirits work secretly and with incredible hatred to fill the minds of wicked people.[46]

But they can only act with God's permission:

> [What] must be unshakeably believed is that Almighty God, whether to bless or to punish, can do whatever he wills; further that demons have no power by nature – angelic by creation and malignant only by corruption – except what he allows, whose judgments are often hidden but never unholy.[47]

Taking for granted the demonology of his day, for Augustine the pastoral issue was uppermost, 'the question of the Romans and the pagan philosophers trafficking with evil demons either for temporal or eternal goods'.[48] Asked whether parents do harm to their baptised infant children when they attempt to heal them in time of sickness by 'sacrifices to the false gods of the heathen', he replied that the children were protected by their baptism.[49] But they remain subject to temptation, because of original sin which made the human race the 'sport of demons'.[50] Overall, the Christian struggle was principally an inner one,

> its amphitheatre was the heart; … the 'Lord of this world' becomes the 'Lord of desires' – of the desires of those who love this world, and so come to resemble demons committed to the same emotions as themselves.[51]

Augustine's focus on the devil, as a distinct being from the demons, emerged from his study of the scriptures, where the devil appears at the beginning of the synoptic Gospels and is mentioned in the New Testament letters many times; Augustine

---

45. Augustine, Letter 9.3, *The Letters of Saint Augustine*, vol. I (Washington, DC: Catholic University of America, 1953), 22.
46. Augustine, *City of God*, Book VI, C. 4, 311.
47. Augustine, *City of God*, XVIII, C.18, 107.
48. Frederick Van Fleteren, 'Demons', in *Augustine through the Ages: An Encyclopedia*, Alan D. Fitzpatrick OSA, ed. (Grand Rapids, MI: William D. Eerdmans, 1991), 267.
49. Augustine, Letter 98.1, *The Letters of Saint Augustine*, Vol. II 129.
50. Augustine, *Contra Julianum*, Fathers of the Church, vol. 35 (New York: Catholic University of America, 1957), 379.
51. Peter Brown, *Augustine of Hippo: A Biography* (London: Faber and Faber, 1969), 245.

apparently used the term 'devil' over 2,300 times.[52] The word is used frequently in his sermons and his commentary on the psalms and often in the form 'the devil and his angels' of Mt. 25.41. It also comes in the form of the devil as 'prince of demons and aerial powers' and 'prince of the powers of darkness'.

> From this power of darkness, therefore, of which the devil is the prince – in other words, from the power of the devil and his angels – infants are delivered when they are baptized.[53]

He developed traditional teaching by considering the devil as head of his own body with many members in imitation of Christ with his body, the Church, of Col. 1.18, and thus present and active in the world.

> Statements are sometimes made about the devil, whose truth is not so evident in regard to himself as in regard to his body; and his body is made up not only of those who are manifestly not of this world (*foris*), but of those also who, though they really belong to him, are for a time mixed up with the Church, until they depart from this life, or until the chaff is separated from the wheat at the last great winnowing.[54]

The presence of the devil in the world he had already considered personified in the opponents with whom Christ had to contend, especially in John's Gospel:

> He himself says in the gospel, 'Lo, the prince of this world is coming', signifying, that the devil would come in the persons of his Jewish persecutors'. (Jn 14.30)[55]

But by his death Christ defeated the devil. In memorable phrases, Augustine described how the cross of the Lord became a trap for the devil.

> The devil exulted when Christ died, and by that very death of Christ the devil was overcome: he took food, as it were, from a trap. ... The cross of the Lord became a trap for the devil; the death of the Lord was the food by which he was ensnared.[56]

---

52. Van Fleteren, 'Devil', 268.
53. Augustine, *On Marriage and Concupiscence* C 22, https://www.newadvent.org/fathers/15071.htm.
54. Augustine, *Sancti Augustini Opera Omnia*, Tomus V, *De doctrina Christiana* III. 37 (Paris: Paul Mellier, 1842), 49. My translation.
55. Augustine, *Tractates on the Gospel of John* 41.7, 142.
56. Augustine, *Sermons on the Liturgical Seasons*, vol. 38, *Sermon 263* (New York: Fathers of the Church, 1959), 392.

The word he uses for a trap, *muscipula diaboli*, means a mousetrap for the devil, though in patristic writing, including Augustine's, it was commonly used to indicate temptation, a trap laid *by* the devil.[57]

The devil in the thought of Thomas Aquinas (1225–74)

Aquinas' influence on the life of the church was, like that of Augustine, both at the deep philosophical level already considered in Chapter 1 and at the level of pastoral theology. He followed Augustine's footsteps, though always prepared to introduce more nuanced thinking in such areas as sacramental theology, where he was indebted to Aristotle while Augustine had a Neo-Platonist heritage.

The heritage Augustine left to succeeding centuries gave an account of the conflict between good and evil in a way that emphasised both the devil as individual, and the demons who as the powers of darkness were part of his princedom. His thought was dominant in theology for many centuries and was greatly influential when the theologians of the 'schools' came to prominence in the early centuries of the second millennium. Peter Lombard (1096–1160), with his work, *The Sentences*, created a link between the world of thinkers like Augustine and Thomas Aquinas. Lombard dealt with demonology in his Distinctions, especially Distinction Six, chapter 6: 'On the power of Lucifer' and chapter 7: 'Whether demons, once conquered by the saints, thereafter approach other men.' Aquinas was also aware of Anselm of Canterbury's treatment of the subject, *De casu diaboli*.

Aquinas dealt with the issue of the devil and demons in the context of his treatise on angels, following the tradition about angels inherited from both the Old and the New Testaments as well as the sixth-century writings of Gregory the Great (*Hom*. 32, 8-9), and Pseudo-Dionysius (*De Coelesti Hierarchia*), both of whom speculated on the names and structure of the angelic order. Aquinas drew on Aristotelian philosophy rather than scriptural or mystical theology in his 'Treatise on the Angels' (*S. T.* Ia, qq50-64). There he treated of angels, their created nature and their characteristics (qq5-62), with a corollary on the fall of some (q63), and a final section on the demons (q64). The section on demons – as fallen angels – had to be understood in light of all he said about angels in general, with the malice of the fallen angels contrasted with the love of the faithful ones. The silence of Scripture concerning numbers of angels or devils was noted in the previous chapter; Aquinas did not consider the issue, though he might have been expected to do so. He established that angels are altogether incorporeal but can assume bodies, and in a dense argument showed that 'the movement of an angel is in time' (q53, a3) rather than instantaneous, something that would then apply to the demons as well.[58] If this angelic movement was part of commonly held beliefs,

---

57. David Scott-Macnab, 'Augustine's Trope of the Crucifixion as a Trap for the Devil and Its Survival in English Middle Ages', https://core.ac.uk/download/pdf/54198127.pdf.

58. Thomas Aquinas, *Summa Theologiae* (London: Burns, Oates & Washbourne, 1922), 39.

as seems likely, it would have lent support to the image of winged angels or demons going back to Tertullian.

He devoted five questions to the angels' knowledge and will, including love, 'the motion of the will', concluding with the contrasting situation of the fallen angels. He believed the fallen angels had reduced mental faculties, like Augustine (*City of God*, IX, 22), who held that 'they could often be mistaken'. Aquinas discussed the limitations of the demons' knowledge (q64, a1): natural knowledge was neither taken away nor lessened in the demons, because of the 'simplicity' of their nature as an intellect or mind. 'The second kind of knowledge, however, which comes of grace, and consists in speculation, has not been utterly taken away from them, but lessened; because, of these Divine secrets only so much is revealed to them as is necessary, ... but not in same degree as to the holy angels.' (It is worth noting that this limitation of demonic knowledge is not always recognised today, when accounts are given of phenomena occurring in exorcisms.)

In Question 61, he relied on Augustine (*City of God* Book XI, C. 50) to establish that the angels were not produced by God from eternity but were part of creation, even though this is not mentioned in the Genesis account of creation – Augustine had argued that they were included there under the designation of 'heavens' or 'light'. Aquinas added that Moses was addressing an uncultured people, and if it had been divulged to them that there were creatures of an incorporeal nature, it would have proved for them an occasion of idolatry. This is an example of the acceptance by both men of the Ptolemaic cosmology predicating concentric spheres of ascending purity, with the 'altogether incorporeal creatures' (*omnino*) (q50, a1), the angels, in the highest of these created spheres.

This raised the question of where the angels could be placed, given that Augustine had said they were created 'in the upper atmosphere' (*Gen. ad lit.* iii. 10). His reply was that the

> spiritual creatures were so created as to bear some relationship to the corporeal creature, and to rule over every corporeal creature. Hence it was fitting for the angels to be created in the highest corporeal place, as presiding over all corporeal nature. (q64, a4)[59]

He had already discussed (q52, a2) whether the angels can be in a 'place' in a universe so structured. His answer was that a body was in a place by being 'applied to such place according to the contact of dimensive quantity', while an 'angel is in a corporeal place by the application of angelic power in any manner whatever to any place'.[60]

In q51, a3, he dealt with angels appearing in the world in bodily form, especially whether they performed actual bodily functions. His position was that the bodies assumed by angels have no life; functions such as speech and movement that are

---

59. Ibid., 123.
60. Ibid., 27.

common to inanimate operations such as sound and movement can be performed by the assumed bodies of angels, but not those which are special to living subjects. He raised the question of demonic activity, quoting what Augustine had said about *incubi* (see above) and the belief of common folk that these demons 'have often presented themselves before women and have sought and procured intercourse with them. Hence it is folly to deny it.' Augustine had however believed that this story referred to events after the deluge. Aquinas commented:

> Still if some are occasionally begotten from demons, it is not from the seed of such demons, nor from their assumed bodies, but from the seed of men taken for the purpose.[61]

He was referring to the belief that the demon first took the form of a woman, a *succubus*, to have intercourse with a man and then the form of a man, carrying the seed with him. Aquinas explained: 'As when the demon assumed first the form of a woman, and afterwards of a man; just as they take the seed of other things for other generating purposes, as Augustine says (*De Trin.* iii.), so that the person born is not the child of a demon, but of a man'. Aquinas is here referring to the belief in demons and their activity and that 'some [children] are occasionally begotten from demons', while denying any real performance of actually bodily functions. In *De Potentia* q6 a8 ad 6, he states an objection against the ability of demons to generate human life by the process to which Augustine referred. But he answers the objection by referring to the speed by which the demon can move or by his applying potions (*fomenta*) to preserve the natural heat of the semen.[62]

In a specific discussion of 'the devil' (q63, a3) within his treatment of the fallen angels, he dealt with the devil without specifying whether the term applied to a particular and principal one of the fallen angels, so in principle his conclusions apply to all, and therefore to what he will subsequently describe as demons. The issue was whether the devil sought to be as God, and he concluded that he could not seek to be as God by equality, 'because by natural knowledge he knew that this was impossible'. But he could seek to be as God by desiring full beatitude not from grace but by the power of his own nature. The logic of this is that he sought to have dominion over others – given that 'what exists of itself is the cause of what exists of another'. Given the rigorous argumentation typical of Aquinas, which began with the discussion of incorporeal beings (following the Scriptures), his position must be taken to be that demons with significant powers exist in the universe and endeavour to exert a malign influence on humankind.

---

61. Ibid., 25.
62. S. Thomae Aquinatis, *Quaestiones Disputatae* (London: Burns & Oates, 1895), q6 a8 ad3, 212: 'Ad sextum dicendum, quod circa evaporationem seminis potest demon remedium adhibere, tum per velocitatem motus, tum adhibendo aliqua fomenta, per quae calor naturalis conservetur in semine.' See also Thomas Aquinas, *Questiones Disputatae De Potentia Dei*, English Dominican Fathers, trans. (Westminster, MD: Newman Press, 1952).

Clearly, the belief in the devil's existence stemming from the Gospels, and the Christian authors up to the time of Aquinas, is challenged in today's culture, but the logic of it at least is difficult to negate, given the starting point, the Scriptural evidence, especially the statements and practice of Jesus himself. Yet, it is also evident that Aquinas exercised the same credulity as Augustine in relation to the demon world, though he did not speak, as the latter did (*De Civ.* 15. 23) of the aerial bodies of the demons being capable of influencing bodily sensations in humans. By the time of Aquinas the popular Christian world view predicated as much reality of the world of the devil and of demons as of the good angels, with guardian angels playing an important role in the Christian's conflict with those malign forces and this would be the context for the art and literature for centuries to come.

Chapter 5

DEMONOLOGY IN MEDIEVAL LITERARY CULTURE

The plastic and other arts of the Middle Ages and beyond

The Christian imagination of the Middle Ages was employed in art and sculpture and literature to give expression to the understanding of the devil as a malignant and actively engaged agent leading people into sin, but also one mocked as in some ways a comical figure. This was in the context of a medieval popular culture arising from a world view described as 'enchantment'. The natural world was sustained by the Creator, and joined to the supernatural world by a preternatural order containing many in-between agencies, both benign and malevolent – spirits and demons, inhabitants of the environment, of the woods, the rivers, the lakes, the air itself. Ecclesiastical sculptors revelled in representing this world view not only by images of Christ in majesty, the Virgin Mary, the angels and saints but also by the creation of horrible semi-human grotesques and gargoyles, generating in the largely non-literate faithful mixed emotions of veneration, of nervousness and even amusement. The basis for mixed emotions was the overlapping of the concrete and the abstract in the framework of medieval attitudes and feelings. People swayed between

> desiring to find behind the concrete, which was perceptible, the abstract which was more real and, on the other hand, trying to make this hidden reality appear in a form which could be perceived by the senses.[1]

The concrete was exemplified by the sculptures, the abstract by beliefs both consoling and generating fear. Beliefs would also find literary expression as centuries went on and would reach a climax in the form of the popular Mystery Plays before the Reformation put an end to such outward expression in favour of a more personal inward and subjective commitment to belief.

Nervousness accompanied by amusement and mockery was the reaction of medieval people and artists who heard preachers alternate between attempts to frighten and console in their interpretation of the Gospel message, while

---

1. Jacques Le Goff, *Medieval Civilization: 400–1500*, Julia Barrow, trans. (Oxford: Basil Blackwell, 1988), 335.

ultimately adopting a reassuring tone as the liturgical seasons cycled between Christ's temptation in the desert and the glory of his Resurrection. The visual imagery kept the whole story before people's eyes, and was reinforced for those who had access to chronicles and legends recorded in monastic libraries. These were based on numerous documents from antiquity telling of monstrous people living at the edge of the known world. Belief in these marvellous races was influential throughout the Middle Ages, as ancient monster lore became part of a Christian framework.

> Men with dogs' heads, creatures with giant feet, griffins, sirens and hellish demons can all be found in the illustrated pages of medieval manuscripts. In 10th century England, descriptions of such creatures were gathered together into a text known as the *Marvels of the East*. Illustrated copies of this text enabled readers to marvel at pictures of the wondrous beings it described. ... According to medieval Christian belief, these creatures were fallen angels, whose dark, hairy, winged bodies were a perversion of the angelic form. Though not always visible, they were nevertheless believed to be ever-present. A diagram of the universe in a 14th-century *Book of Hours* shows these demons raining down from heaven towards Satan, bound in chains below the cosmos.[2]

The devil was also represented in the stained-glass windows of medieval churches. The main figures were of Christ, the Virgin Mary and the saints, and the devil a cowed and defeated figure, though this would change in later centuries with the representations in art of the Last Judgement. The eleventh-century Church of Saint Martin the Great in York has stained-glass windows depicting scenes from the saint's life, including his subduing of the devil. The Cathedral of St Stephen in Auxerre, France, begun in the thirteenth century and noted for its stained glass, has a window depicting St Eligius with a large pincers gripping the devil's nose. For a non-literate public, these images of frightful but defeated figures constantly before their eyes must have had a reassuring effect.[3]

The popular medieval and modern image of the devil as an anthropomorphic creature with hooves and horns had its origin ultimately in an ancient image of a satyr-like devil found in diverse sources, including Hellenistic mythology, rabbinic legends and early Christian texts.[4]

---

2. Alixe Bovey, 'Medieval Monsters', *The Middle Ages* (London: British Library, 2015), https://www.bl.uk/the-middle-ages/articles/medieval-monsters-from-the-mystical-to-the-demonic.

3. It is worth noting that the great rose window of the facade of Chartres Cathedral includes very small horned figures weighing souls in the representation of the Last Judgement.

4. Alexander Kulik, 'How the Devil Got His Hooves and Horns: The Origin of the Motif and the Implied Demonology of 3 Baruch', *Numen* vol. 60, no. 2/3 (2013): 195–229.

Literature and the devil

Literature in different historical periods has served well to echo the beliefs of the populace concerning Satan, whether morbid fascination, amusement, simple dread or scepticism, though one has to look below the surface of literary forms to find what attitudes are reflected. With the passing of centuries, the beliefs reflected vary and in general it can be said that, in the depictions provided by the range of literary output from medieval poetry to the modern novel, the figure of Satan becomes less obvious, less real in comparison with the art of the preceding periods. But the artistry of the cinema in the twentieth century will provide more obscure, yet powerful, evidence of the resilience of the basic concept.

The literature of the early Middle Ages up to the Renaissance contains some of the best-known evocations of the figure of Satan, with the more legendary though poetic presentations giving way over the centuries to the more subtle yet revelatory forms of the Modern era. The great number of medieval manuscripts discovered and published by the English historian George G. Coulton range from the early to late medieval period, with many undated. The devil is in evidence in many of them ranging from long anecdotes to brief references, all quite dramatic. There is a tale allegedly from the period of the Crusades, during the reign of Innocent III (+1216). A usurer 'took the Cross' but stayed at home and mocked those who went on pilgrimage. One night he found himself confronted by two black horses and 'an ill-favoured man as black as they, who cried to the boor,

> 'Quick, mount this horse, for he is brought for thee'. ... The Fiend himself mounted another; and side by side, they swept in breathless haste from one place of torture to another, wherein the wretched man saw his father and mother in miserable torments, and a multitude of others who he knew not to be dead. There he saw a certain honest knight, lately dead, Elias von Rheineck, ... mounted on a mad cow with his face towards her tail and his back towards her horns; the beast rushed to and fro, goring his back at every moment, so that the blood gushed forth.[5]

The knight had apparently confiscated a cow from a poor widow. Worse for the usurer was the sight of a flaming chair, which he was told, it would shortly be his fate to sit upon.

Many such tales are told in the collection, each with its twists and turns but leading to the recognition and disappearance of the devil. An interesting story from the Halle region of Germany concerns a priest who on his travels was hailed by a man who had been ploughing his field and ran to the priest to ask him to exorcise his wife.

---

5. George G. Coulton, *Life in the Middle Ages*. Selected, translated and annotated by G. G. Coulton (Cambridge: Cambridge University Press, 1967), 60–1.

I granted his request, coming down from my chariot and following him to his house. When therefore I looked into the woman's state, I found that she had many fantasies, for she was wont to sleep and eat too little, whence she fell into feebleness of brain and thought she was possessed by a demon; yet there was no such thing in her case. So I told her husband to see that she kept a good diet, that is good meat and drink.[6]

Dante Alighieri (1265-1321)

Dante's long poem in three parts, *Divina Commedia*, was one of the most widely read texts during the Middle Ages and survives in over 800 manuscripts. Dante gave the poem the simple title *Commedia*, but it subsequently came to be described as a 'divine comedy'. Despite that, it is more a human narrative than a divine. It is an allegorical poem in that it uses images to describe the experience of a human being's journey through life, in a story that is not solely imaginary but in many ways a true story involving historical characters. These have a symbolical function; they are introduced to illustrate the vices or virtues which are the subject of the narrative. 'He combined the conventions of allegory with the starkest realism.'[7] Dante (or someone who sought to represent him) wrote to his patron, Cangrande della Scala, describing the poem as a comedy, because 'at the beginning it is horrible and foul, as being Hell; but at the close it is happy, desirable, and pleasing, as being Paradise, and because the style is unstudied and lowly'.[8]

The way Dante presented the segments of the poem, as first the underworld, then Mount Purgatory (a projection from the underworld towards the light) and finally Heaven itself, has made it one of the most important works in literary history to give prominence to the hellish underworld as well as to Purgatory and Heaven. It has been suggested that there was an Islamic influence in his approach to the symbolical journey described, as one of the oral traditions or Haddiths of Islam gives an account of a night-time journey by Muhammad through the seven levels of Heaven. 'The structure of the Prophet's night journey – the eventual revelation of God in Heaven, the symmetric levels of Hell – does appear to be mirrored in the *Divine Comedy*.'[9] That, however, need not reveal a positive attitude towards Islam; Dante shared the Christian view of his time that Islam was the great heresy, as the description of the tortures endured (and self-inflicted) by Muhammad in the Circle reserved for 'sowers of scandal, sowers of schism' (XXVIII. 22-31)[10]

---

6. Ibid., 231–2.

7. W. T. H. Jackson, *The Literature of the Middle Ages* (New York: Columbia University Press, 1960), 356.

8. The text is reproduced in A. J. Minnis and A. B. Scott, *Medieval Literary Theory and Criticism, c. 1100–c. 1375: The Commentary Tradition* (Oxford: Clarendon Press, 1988).

9. Ian Thomson, 'Dante's Debt to Islam', *The Tablet*, 24 July 2021, 14–15.

10. Dante Alighieri, *Inferno*. Canto XXVIII. Lines 22-31 (London: J.M. Dent & Sons Limited, 1964).

makes clear. Nonetheless, that he had respect for Arabic culture is evident from his allocation of a place to three Muslims in the first Circle, the zone reserved for those neither condemned nor worthy of heaven. Saladin the Kurdish Sultan, who defeated the Crusaders and re-possessed Jerusalem in 1187, Dante sees 'aloof, alone' and probably respects him for the tolerance he showed to Christians.[11] The other two who merit a place among the philosophers, are Averroës (Ibn Rushd), through whom the West gained knowledge of Aristotle, and Avicenna, the medieval Aristotelian philosopher.

There is a broader context in that he sought to achieve a theological harmonisation of the earthly and heavenly cities by naming the great leaders of classical culture, especially in choosing tin as his guide (I 72–4) and constantly vindicating the importance of earthly life. Here he parts company with Augustine, who from an early enthusiasm for the *Aeneid* and its author, as he related in his *Confessions* (I.xiii.20),[12] later rejected the polity of the Roman Empire in expounding his idea of 'the city of God'. Dante, for his part saw the Roman Empire as 'the permanent structure of order … appointed by God to carry out his providential design of universal history'.[13] (In his *De Monarchia*, he argued for the equality of the temporal and spiritual orders.)

Dante's personal history was a troubled one; he was caught up in the intertwined political and ecclesiastical conflict of the day and spent many years in exile from his native Florence, apparently under a death sentence since 1302.[14] He probably began the poem in Verona in 1308 a few years after the French pope Clement V moved the papacy to Avignon, and this had a great effect on the poem, as emerges when the fate of various ecclesiastics is discussed by a poet who was ultimately a man of faith, the Catholic faith.

The structure of the poem reflected the context of the medieval popular culture, which derived its stability from a perception of the earth as occupying the centre of the universe, a heavy body, incapable of rectilinear or circular motion, as described in an earlier chapter. Hell, *Inferno*, is the subject of the first book of the *Divina Commedia*, and is located in the lowest part of the solid earth above a hemisphere of water, with Lucifer situated at the intersection of the two. The scene is set in an underworld that is created from the earth to which Satan had fallen. Both he and his comrades are immured in this infernal world, with Satan

---

11. If Dante's choice of Saladin was made through his knowing that Saladin believed his taking of Jerusalem occurred on the anniversary of Muhammad's night journey to Jerusalem, this could add credibility to the suggestion of Islamic influence on the structure of the poem. See Dan Jones, *Crusaders: An Epic History of the Wars for the Holy Land* (London: Head of Zeus, 2019), 294.

12. Augustine, *Confessions* (London: Sheed and Ward, 1944).

13. Giuseppe Mazzotta, *Dante, the Poet of the Desert: History and Allegory in the Divine Comedy* (Princeton, NJ: Princeton University Press, 1979), 6.

14. Thomas Cahill, *The Mysteries of the Middle Ages: The Rise of Feminism, Science and Art from the Cults of Catholic Europe* (New York: Nan A. Talase, 2006), 282.

in the lowest place. Dante envisages the earth as colder and colder the deeper the descent, but this term *inferno*, in contrast with today's usage does not imply fire. It is still terrestrial rather than a world of spirits, an 'other world'. The depiction of the underworld as a cold region by Dante was not new but was already to be found in medieval literature, and likely to be familiar to him.

There were many texts concerning the underworld in medieval Irish eschatology that could be considered precursors to Dante's poem, though by the mid-twentieth century 'critics distanced Dante from such popular texts, preferring instead to posit a Dante firmly situated in higher realms of literature and philosophy'.[15] Nevertheless, there is the 1972 study by Charles Stuart Boswell, *An Irish Precursor of Dante: A Study of the Vision of Heaven and Hell Ascribed to the Eighth Century Irish Saint Adamnán*, a text belonging to the ninth- to eleventh-century period.[16] There is also the *Visio Tnugdali*, a religious text reporting the otherworldly vision of the knight Tnugdalus, which 'stands as the most popular and elaborate text in the genre of medieval visionary infernal literature; ... by the fifteenth century it had been translated from its original Latin forty-three times into fifteen languages'.[17] *The Dialogue of the Body and the Soul* (in Middle Irish, 900–1200) brings together both cold and heat as punishment for the soul. The body says to the soul:

> Depart in the hands of the demons, and of the devil with his rebel army. A place where there will be completeness of evil with the presence of the household of the devil; that is, on bare flaming slabs, and on deep fiery valleys and on red very thick spits, on red fiery stones, on venomous streams, on hard icy rocks, on thick congealed ponds, on crooked icy trees … in a dry fiery dwelling, very putrid, very cold, very heavy, dirty, melancholy.[18]

A ninth-century Irish source, *The Martyrology of Oengus the Culdee*, a calendar of the saints, has few references to demons. It does include on 16 February Saint Juliana of Nicomedia, who was martyred during Diocletian's persecution, and was revered as patron of the sick in Europe in the Middle Ages. The thirteenth-century *Golden Legend* has an account of her martyrdom for refusing to marry a pagan

---

15. Daragh O'Connell, 'An Irish Dante, Part 1. Possible Precursors to the *Commedia*', *Studies. An Irish Quarterly Review*, no. 442 (Summer 2022): 128.

16. Charles Stuart Boswell, *An Irish Precursor of Dante: A Study of the Vision of Heaven and Hell Ascribed to the Eighth Century Irish Saint Adamnán* (London: AMS Press, 1972), 48: 'The legend which forms the ground-plan of the Vision of Adamnán and the Commedia of Dante can claim a pedigree of great antiquity that may be traced back along several widely divergent lines.'

17. O'Connell, 'An Irish Dante, Part 1', 128–9.

18. John Carey, Emma Nic Cárthhaigh and Catríona Ó Dochartaigh, eds, *The End and Beyond. Medieval Irish Eschatology*, vol. 1 (Aberystwyth: Celtic Studies Publications, 2014), 63.

suitor. Her torture included being suspended by her hair.[19] When tempted by the devil to renounce her faith she held him captive until he pleaded to be released. How medieval accounts of the devil's activities can be altered in the telling is shown by the fact that *The Martyrology of Oengus* conflates these incidents by saying she bound the devil by her hair![20]

For Dante, Satan becomes an immobile, frustrated figure. His way of portraying the prince of devils, whom he calls Lucifer, contrasts with tradition, which would make the devil for later writers an active and malignant presence in the world, intelligent and cunning, plotting the downfall of humans into hell, and with something of his previous lordly angelic status still clinging to him, though he is immersed in flames. In the poem the location of his captivity is marked by freezing winds and ice, in which Lucifer is trapped. When Dante and his guide, Virgil, reach the place where Lucifer is located, Virgil insists he must steel his soul for the encounter and with what was not life nor yet was death (XXX. 35), the 'Emperor of the sorrowful realm', a term that stresses the polarity between heaven and Lucifer. He is summarily described:

> If he was once as fair as now he's foul
> And dared outface his maker in rebellion
> Well may he be the fount of all our dole. (XXX. 37)

In Dante's model of the earth, hell's nine circles (reflecting the nine spheres of the universe) form a funnel situated in the north and terminating with the massive figure of Lucifer whose navel marks the centre of the globe. They clamber along his body, the upper part hemmed in by ice and the lower part immersed in rocks, as Dante departs from tradition in emphasising the massive body.[21] The highest and swiftest of the angels, Lucifer, the 'light bearer', is now immobile in the darkest and lowest part of hell. In contrast with previous scenes, here there is silence. Dante has no conversation with him, while in the silence three pairs of huge wings in continuous motion create the ice in which the denizens of Circle Nine are encased and the freezing wind that the two now encounter.[22] They find he has three heads

---

19. Jacopo da Varazze, *Legenda Aurea* (Tavarnazze Firenze: SISMEL Edizioni del Galluzzo, 1998), 267: 'Prefectus … jussit eam dimidia die per capillos suspendi.'

20. Oengus the Culdee, *Félire Oengusso Céili Dé*, Whitley Stokes, ed. (London: Henry Bradshaw Society, 1905), 61, 75.

21. For Dante and the culture of his time, poetry was the true artistic medium, sculpture and painting associated with the trades, but in his statuesque representation of Satan he seems to show an admiration for that art, just as he had for Giotto. See Giorgio de Santillana, 'The Role of Art', in *Critical Problems in the History of Science*, Marshall Clagett, ed. (Madison: Wisconsin University Press, 1969), 41–2.

22. Luther referred to the 'devil's icicle': 'He blows cold breath into the hearts of married people, and as a result of this the fervour of married love grows cold.' Martin Luther, *Luther's Works*, vol. 7 (Philadelphia, PA: Fortress Press, 1999), 85.

each continually munching a human body, those of Judas, Brutus and Cassius as traitors against the divine and secular. This triple imagery is intended to make Lucifer a symmetric opposite of the Trinity, a device that preceded Dante in works of art and sculpture.

> Lucifer's torments might seem relatively gentle in comparison with those of the other damned souls. This is true in terms of feeling but not to the eyes of thought. Dante purposely sacrifices the impression to the idea. ... He denies Satan a spectacular torment which might have appalled the imagination, and chooses a punishment whose unequalled horror is only apparent to the mind.[23]

As narrator of the *Divina Commedia,* Dante is a commentator on the society of his day, showing how so many of his contemporaries have fallen victim to the allures of money, power and sexual impropriety – the sections of *Inferno* are divided in accordance with the Capital sins. In *Inferno*[24] and throughout the poem, real people from history or Dante's own period are the central characters. He was critical of how in practice the hierarchical structure of the church resulted in abuse of power, as he committed even popes to the underworld. He did not go so far as to describe the papacy as 'antichrist', though this term was not uncommon in his time and was applied even to popes by their opponents. It was a term derived from the Book of Revelation, where it was used to prophesy a period when the devil would rule on earth before his final defeat.[25] But the popes he will encounter were targets of the reforming campaign of the Franciscan Spirituals who believed that the antichrist was active at that time.[26] Dante's view of the state of the church is clear from his strong allusions to the papacy in *Inferno, Purgatorio* and *Paradiso*. He mentions twenty popes by name or unmistakably alludes to them in the poem.[27]

In Circle VIII, Bowge 3, of *Inferno,* where those who committed the sin of simony are held, head down in a hole and with flames licking their feet, he encounters Pope Nicholas III, who confuses him with Pope Boniface VIII whom he expects to follow him down into the hole. In *Purgatorio,* Dante will say more about corruption of the papal regime, referring to it as a harlot. The harlot is joined by a giant and they kiss each other from time to time (*Purgatorio* xxxii, 142–60). The giant is Philip the Fair of France, who attempted to dominate Italy by his

---

23. Auguste Valensin S.J., 'The Devil in the Divine Comedy', in Anon., *Satan* (London: Sheed and Ward, 1951), 377.

24. Dante Alighieri, *The Divine Comedy 1. Hell,* Dorothy L. Sayers, trans. (Harmondsworth: Penguin Books, 1949). Citations refer to Canto and line.

25. Richard Kenneth Emmerson and Ronald B. Herzman, 'Antichrist, Simon Magus, and Dante's Inferno XIX'. *Traditio,* 29 July 2016.

26. Bernard McGinn, *Antichrist: Two Thousand Years of the Human Fascination with Evil* (New York: Columbia University Press, 2000), 171.

27. Louis C. Casartelli, *The Popes in the Divina Commedia of Dante* (London: Sands, 1921), 1.

dealings with Pope Boniface VIII and with Clement V, the pope who began the 'captivity' of the papacy at Avignon.[28] For Dante, the residency at Avignon was 'a matter of covetous Gascons striving to rob the Romans of their renown',[29] where by Romans he means the effective continuation of the Roman Empire under papal rule. In *Purgatorio* XIX, he encounters a weeping spirit, easily identified as Pope Adrian V, who died in 1276. The pope says: 'One month and little more I learned how the great mantle weighs on him who keeps it from the mire, ... My conversion ... was late; but when I was made Pastor of Rome I discovered the life which is false' (XIX.98-9).[30]

The principal denizens of *Inferno* are characters from earthly life with demons presented as playing an active but subsidiary role. There is a passing reference to 'the devil' when Virgil complains about having received false directions. A friar says he had once heard it said that among the devil's vices is that he is the father of lies (XXIII. 143). With regard to the demons, Dante appears to have in mind the fallen angels spoken of by Beatrice in *Paradiso* (XXIX. 49-55) when in *Inferno* he describes a black fiend carrying a wretched sinner and hurling him into a cauldron of pitch (XXI. 29). He had wings outspread and sharp shoulders and acted in the way devils were usually described or depicted in medieval times. In XXVII.113, Guido, an adventurer turned Franciscan (the historical Guido da Montefeltro) tells how a 'black cherub', again a fallen angel, intervened when St Francis came to rescue him, saying that he had kept Guido by the hair ever since he had given fraudulent counsel. A more extreme example of being held by a demon occurs in the case of Branca d'Oria, whose soul, Friar Alberigo told Dante, had been in 'cold storage' (XXXIII. 38) in hell for many years while his body was still on earth. Dante denied he had died – 'he wears his clothes and sleeps and drinks and eats' – only to be told that a devil now occupied his flesh (XXXIII. 45). Dante accepted a belief of the time that a person could be so given over to sin that a devil could take over the person's body and live as if the person was still alive, while the soul was in fact in hell.[31] In today's understanding, this seems a very extreme way of speaking about demonic possession.

Dante's critique of the church, to the extent even of describing the papacy as a harlot, anticipates by nearly two hundred years the criticisms which Luther will utilise in his day, though Luther will go a stage further in describing the papacy as the 'antichrist', by which he will imply that the devil occupies the chair of Peter. It is not likely that Luther ever read Dante, but he was aware that critics, including

28. Thomas Renna, 'Avignon vs. Rome: Dante, Petrarch, Catherine of Siena', *Expositions*, vol. 4, nos. 1 and 2 (2010): 49.

29. Dante's letter to the Cardinals of the Church after the death of Clement V in 1314, cited in A. C. Flick, *The Decline of the Medieval Church*, vol. 1 (London: Kegan Paul, 1930), 211.

30. J. B. McGovern, 'The Popes of Dante's Divina Commedia', *The Antiquary*, vol. 9 (December 1913): 459–63.

31. Valensin S.J., 'The Devil in the Divine Comedy', 372.

ecclesiastical writers, were using the term about opponents and even the papacy centuries before him.

Graphic illustrations of the torments of the inhabitants of Hell have been painted in the margins of a copy of the *Divina Commedia* which was made in Naples in around 1370. One of these marginal illustrations is a representation of Satan in the very centre of hell, but unlike Dante, the image shows him immersed in flames.

The final scene as Dante and Virgil escape from hell is marked by silence and icy surroundings except for a small flowing stream as they climb towards the light. Strange as compared with traditional images, Dante's representation of Lucifer is as powerful as the more famous image created by Milton of the leader of the rebel angels whom the 'Almighty Power hurled headlong flaming from the ethereal sky, with hideous ruin and combustion down to bottomless perdition' (Book 1, lines 44–6)[32] Milton introduces the reader to

> A dungeon horrible, on all sides round, As one great furnace flamed, yet from those flames No light, but rather darkness visible, Served only to discover sights of woe. (1, 61–4)

Dante's depiction of Lucifer is unique in that it emphasises not only his defeat but also his captivity, while still acknowledging demonic activity in the world. This is a more nuanced view than is found generally in Christian tradition and accords with the Scripture's account of how Christ's victorious Incarnation, death and Resurrection brought the rule of the Prince of this world to an end, though demonic activity would still persist. Dante's insight was important towards achieving a view more in accord with the reality of life in Christ, one filled with confidence in Christ's saving grace. He was also aware of the fact that the Empire of Augustus established a *pax terrena* at the time of the Incarnation and he found logical support in this temporal coincidence for his positive attitude towards the temporal order, his understanding of 'Roman history as constitutive of the redemptive process', as the Italian expert on Dante, Giuseppe Mazzotta, put it. He saw the continuation of the Roman Empire in the Italy of his day.[33] Dante's world was one where traditional religious culture held its own at a time when classical Roman and Greek cultures were also part of the fabric of society. His perception of the reality of Satan was part of a rich and complex world view and his profoundly Christian vision could take account both of the defeat of Satan and the activities of demons in the world. But culture was evolving and would bring about less nuanced approach to Satan, to demons and to evildoing, the persistence of evil.

---

32. John Milton, *Poetical Works*, Douglas Bush, ed. (London: Oxford University Press, 1966), Book 1, Lines 44–6.

33. Giuseppe Mazzotta, *Dante, The Poet of the Desert: History and Allegory in the Divine Comedy* (Princeton, NJ: Princeton University Press, 1979), 64.

The evolving culture and the devil's continuing presence evidenced in literature

The medieval popular world view, described earlier as involving enchantment, came under pressure with the decline of the rural population and the growth of towns in Europe in the centuries after the first millennium. Peasant culture had included 'cults involving trees, springs, rocks, crossroads and grave sites instead of churches and rites conducted by magicians and soothsayers, … though the church attempted either to redefine these customs in religious terms or to abolish them'.[34]

The Black Death

The plague known as the Black Death (1347–50) and the resulting deaths of one-third to half of the population, brought a new awareness of a world beyond this and fears of what awaited people. Rituals whether official or semi-pagan were ineffective against it and led to contrasting widespread convictions that it was caused by the Jews or was a punishment from God for people's sins. The Jews since the early Crusades had been held to be in league with the devil or even to be the devil incarnate[35] and were therefore likely to be the cause of the plague by poisoning wells and rivers with secret potions, but such a view could not hold in face of the evidence for it being an infectious and contagious disease spread by human contact. In his *Decameron* Boccaccio (1313–75) speculated:

> Whether it was owing to the action of the heavenly bodies or whether, because of our iniquities, it was visited upon us for our correction by the righteous anger of God, this pestilence which had started some years earlier in the Orient, … moved without pause from one region to the next until it spread tragically to the West.[36]

---

34. Hans-Werner Goetz, *Life in the Middle Ages: From the Seventh to the Thirteenth Century*, Albert Wimmer, trans. (Notre Dame: Notre Dame University Press, 1993), 133.

35. Cf. Marc Saperstein and Joshua Trachtenberg, *The Devil and the Jews: The Medieval Conception of the Jew and Its Relation to Modern Anti-Semitism* (New Haven, CT: Yale University Press, 1943), *passim*.

36. Giovanni Boccaccio, *Decameron* (Oxford: Oxford University Press, 1998), 6–7; G. G. Coulton, *Life in the Middle Ages*, 155, recounts the story of a mid-thirteenth-century Irish bishop, Thomas O'Quinn of Cloyne, who in his previous career as a Dominican preacher visited Connaught and came on a

> marvellous and miserable plague in the diocese of Clonfert, for when men went to their ploughs or walked elsewhere in the fields or the forests, then (as they told me) they were accustomed to see whole armies of demons that passed by and sometimes fought with one another. Such as saw these visions were forthwith smitten with sickness and disease, languishing and taking to their beds with all weakness of body; and many died miserably.

Boccaccio's reference to the 'heavenly bodies' seems to concern the planets and stars and their movement in the heavens, as this was a period when astrologers claimed that the movement and alignment of the stars affected people's lives, this rather than the activity of demons as was also thought in earlier centuries to afflict people physically.

The instinct to pray for relief was reinforced by preachers who insisted that

> 'man's sensuality ... now fallen on deeper malice', had provoked the divine wrath and he was now suffering just retribution for his sins.[37]

There were contrasting approaches also to the ways of bringing it to an end: quarantining was extensive in Italy and France, while penitential processions, which sometimes included flagellants, were also widely practised. As the plague kept recurring, the church in succeeding centuries, for example in Milan, provided prayers and devotions to be said at home at stated times of the day, and in the sixteenth century there Archbishop Carlo Borromeo had his clergy carry sticks to keep the people at a distance.[38] It is noticeable that, except for some references to the Jews and their unjustified diabolical associations, the issue of diabolical influence hardly arose. The reason was probably that the plague was such a physical presence and threat, and well understood to be a disease spread naturally; it was more logical for people to see it as a punishment from God rather than an attack by the devil, as there had never been a strong belief (leaving aside the special case of the early Egyptian monks) that the devil could inflict physical harm.

Though the plague returned periodically for centuries, there was a gradual recovery of the European population and this brought a more positive outlook on the future. As life assumed a more social aspect, allowing commerce to flourish once more, a celebratory dimension returned to the life of the towns, with people no longer fearful to move abroad. A feature of that town life in Germany and especially in England was the public's enthusiasm for Mystery Plays (or Miracle Plays celebrating the saints' lives).

The Mystery Plays

The origin of these plays was in the Church's liturgy. From about the eleventh century, an extension to the liturgical Latin musical text, called a *trope*, came

---

He called the people together and told them that the plague was caused by the demons but that this was because of their lack of faith that the Lord would guard and defend them against the demons.

37. Philip Ziegler, *The Black Death* (London: Guild Publishing, 1991), 211; Joseph H. Lynch, *The Medieval Church: A Brief History* (London: Longman, 1992), 306–11.

38. Samuel Kline Coen, *Hate and Compassion: From the Plague of Athens to Aids* (Oxford: Oxford University Press, 2018), 72–3.

into use to enhance its poetic quality and emphasise its meaning. Because of the large number of clerics in the sanctuary at the time, it is not surprising that *tropes* developed into dramas to explicate the text further. In general, given their liturgical origin, the texts were taken from Scripture. For several centuries, these dramas were enacted in church. One in particular, *The Harrowing of Hell*, was very popular, though not based on the canonical Scriptures but on the apocryphal Gospel of Nicodemus, which describes Christ descending into the underworld on Holy Saturday to liberate Adam and Eve and the patriarchal figures of the Old Testament. A development in the thirteenth century, a move from the sanctuary into the streets with laypeople now taking over, allowed the greater imagination and non-Biblical texts to be used; in England, especially, this liberty was availed of. The plays were performed by the guilds and gradually developed into pageants through the streets lasting several hours.

The pageants were presented in cycles corresponding to the cycle of the liturgical year and were so arranged that each guild could advertise the skills of its trade, by having a guild enact its part in the area or street where its members had their shops. The municipal authorities were in charge overall, and the guilds paid for the stages, props and costumes needed, which in some cases were very elaborate, as in the case of a Coventry Passion Play. It included hell's mouth with its fire, a barrel used somehow to produce an earthquake and three painted worlds.[39] The first pageants of the York Cycle were concerned with the different events of the Creation, culmination in the temptation and fall of Adam; they are more briefly dramatised in the other English cycles.[40]

Though Lucifer has little to say in the Scriptures, in the plays this character is often very voluble, in the York version of *The Creation and the Fall of Lucifer*, for example, which ran from the mid-fourteenth to the late sixteenth century. It was staged by the *barkers* (the tanners). Following the entry of God and the angels, Lucifer appears and proudly lists the qualities his name of light-bearer indicate:

> The beams of my brighthead (*brightness*) are burning so bright
> And I so seemly in sight myself now I see
> For like a Lord am I left to lend (*dwell*) in this light
> More fairer by far than my feres (*companions*)

Verses follow in which the angels' praises of God are alternated with Lucifer's praise of himself:

> I shall be like unto him that is highest on height
> Oh, what I am dearworth and deft!

---

39. A. C. Cawley, ed., 'Introduction', in *Everyman and Medieval Miracle Plays* (London: Dent, 1957²), xiii.

40. Ibid., xxiii.

until he says

> Oh, deuce! All goes down – *The bad angels fall from heaven*
> My might and my main are all marrand (*passing away*)
> Help, fellows, in faith I am falland! (*falling*)[41]

The next scene is set in hell and Lucifer finds himself castigated by the other fallen angels.

In the Chester Pageant of the Cooks and Innkeepers, dramatising the Harrowing of Hell, Satan speaks of the imminent arrival of Jesus and instructs the demons to 'wreak havoc on him' whose death he had caused. But Jesus comes in triumph and the stage instructions to the demons are to hurl Satan from his throne. He laments:

> Out, alas, I am shent (*ruined*);
> My might fails, verament;
> This prince that is now present
> Will spoil from me my prey.
> Adam, by my enticement,
> And all his blood, through me were blent (*deceived*);
> Now hence they shall be hent (*taken*)
> And I in hell for ay.[42]

In Dante the devil has nothing to say, but in the Miracle Plays he becomes a voluble character as in the example above.

William Langland (1332–86)

The poem by William Langland, *The Vision of Piers Plowman*, was popular over the period of the plays – at least two centuries, the fourteenth and fifteenth – and there were printings of it in the sixteenth.[43] Here also the devil speaks at length. Passus XVIII recounts the death and resurrection of Jesus and his descent into the underworld for the harrowing of hell.

> 'Stay a while', said Truth, 'for I can both hear and see
> A spirit that speaks to hell, and bids them unbar the gates'.
> From within the light, a loud voice cried out to Lucifer:
> *Attollite portas principes vestras, et elevamini portae …*

---

41. Ibid., 5–6.
42. Ibid., 165.
43. William Langland, *The Vision of Piers Plowman*, translation into Modern English Verse with introduction by Terence Tiller (London: British Broadcasting Corporation, 1981), 11. In the near-contemporary Chaucer's *Canterbury Tales*, the devil is mentioned, and in a few instances speaks, but he is mainly a figure in the background, ready to receive the souls of evildoers.

There follows an address by the devil to his companions, one interrupted by Lucifer[44] as they engage in mutual recrimination. The address ends as the Light bade them again to unlock.

> 'What Lord art thou?' asked Lucifer. '*Quis est iste?*'
> *Rex gloriae*, the Light said at once, 'The King of Glory.

A long address by the Lord follows, concluding with the sentencing of Lucifer:

> 'And Lucifer, for the lies that led Eve astray,
> You will bear a bitter sentence!' And he bound him in chains.
>
> Ashtaroth and the rest of his rout ran off to hide in corners,
> For the boldest of the lot dared not look at Our Lord.

Tiller, in his introduction to the text, says that perceptive critics have compared the poem to *Paradise Lost* and even to *Divina Commedia*, but he disagrees:

> The quest in Piers Plowman is for how to save one's soul: not so much for Heaven *per se* as for a spiritual state in which Truth and the individual are mutually indwelling, and the result of the quest is left unstated.[45]

The quest is very personal and in ways independent of the church of the late fourteenth century and of its services, which the protagonist, Will, found often below standard. In Passus 10 and Passus 11, he is critical of religious for 'gaiety and gluttony (X. 80), or priests who 'have neither learning nor lineage, but only a tonsure' (XI. 290) and of the bishop who ordains them (XI. 305; XV. 135) and this attitude was not uncommon from the beginning of the second millennium at least, from the time of Dante (as noted earlier) to the Reformation. Langland, however, should not be seen as a critic undermining authority.

In his dream, Will is critical of the radical reforming group, the Lollards (XV. 207) – an English popular movement of less-educated followers of the academic John Wycliffe (1330–85), who had been dismissed from his Oxford post for his views on the church. – He distinguished between its ideal spiritual nature and the visible, institutional reality. He also looked to the Bible as the sole doctrinal authority. The Lollards in the late fourteenth and early fifteenth centuries represented a growing anti-Roman sentiment in the English church, in part connected with the dissatisfaction at the money sent to Rome in the form

---

44. In a footnote, Tiller says: 'In common with many medieval writers, Langland treats Lucifer and Satan as different personages; nor does he make it clear which (if either!) he thinks of as the devil. Even up to the 17th century, and after, demonology remained confused, not to say illiterate, to the point of extravagance', 283.

45. Ibid., 12.

of *annates* (a tax on episcopal appointments). They were opposed to clerical authority and rejected officially sanctioned devotional practices, including belief in and devotion to the Eucharist – Wycliffe had rejected the theological doctrine of transubstantiation.[46] By the early fifteenth century they were considered heretics.

That Langland's Will, despite his anti-clerical views, would not side with them is clear from the structure of the poem based on the liturgical year and reaching a climax with his waking at Easter and urging his wife and daughter to 'creep to the Cross', to celebrate the Easter liturgy. Both the communal religious sentiment exemplified by the Miracle Plays and the privatised religion of the poem show that the figure of Satan loomed large in the consciousness of the people of those centuries.

The rise of mysticism

Jean Gerson (1363–1429)

Privatised religion adopted another form among those of a more elite culture. Jean Gerson, chancellor of Paris University, promoted Conciliarism, the theory that a general council was superior in authority to the pope at the Council of Constance (1415–18). After the Council he spent the remainder of his years away from Paris, and in exile returned to writing on the interiority of the Christian life, following the example of people like Bernard of Clairvaux. He took refuge spiritually as well as physically from the ecclesiopolitical as well as the intellectual issues of the day by promoting mysticism for the unlettered in his writing. That mystical writing was the 'most universal literature of the Middle Ages'.[47] According to William J. Courtenay,

> With Gerson not only have we reached the frontier between the fourteenth and the fifteenth century; we have reached a figure who, more than anyone else, seems to have combined the critical, analytical dimensions of late scholasticism with a thoroughgoing commitment to the mystical life.[48]

The path to mystical union he described in his *De Mystica Theologia* (1407) consisted of the traditional purgative, illuminative and unitive stages. He

---

46. See Steven Ozment, *The Ages of Reform, 1250–1550* (New Haven, CT: Yale University Press, 1980), 210: 'Lollards were for the greater part ordinary people, mainly craftsmen, opposed to the subjection of the English church to Rome, the temporal rule of the clergy, the doctrine of transubstantiation, clerical celibacy, the consecration of physical objects, masses for the dead, pilgrimages, and the veneration of the saints.'

47. Ibid., 115.

48. William J. Courtenay, 'Spirituality and Late Scholasticism', in *Christian Spirituality: High Middle Ages and Reformation*, Jill Rait, ed. (London: S.C.M. Press, 1988), 117.

emphasised the purgative step, which has been described in Evelyn Underhill's study, *Mysticism*, as

> a getting rid of all those elements of normal experience which are not in harmony with reality; of illusion, evil, imperfection of every kind.[49]

She mentions evil in the list, evidently taking it and its ultimate source, the devil, seriously. This purgative stage is necessary for all those aspiring to mystical union with God, but it is noticeable that Gerson in the programme he proposed – for 'the unlettered' – describes a simpler path, not mentioning evil but simply the dross of sin:

> Know that unless you have been purged of the love of fear by an integral and not pretended penance, unless, further, your mind has removed the dross (*scoria*) of sin and has by reform shone forth in newness of life according to the two actions of purgation and illumination, it will be vain for you to 'rise before dawn' in order to reach the height of perfection.[50]

The medieval mystic was encouraged by writers like Gerson to embrace the loved one, press close to the divine breast, enjoy the peace of God surpassing all understanding (Phil. 4.7).[51] Medieval spirituality gained considerably from the mystical current described in Gerson's Latin tradition of mysticism and the German vernacular tradition exemplified by Joannes Tauler (1300–61), both of which flourished up to the Reformation. This spirituality is evocative of that of the desert fathers, but it is noticeably free from conflicts with demons. The soul that entered by poverty and humility into the Abyss of God described by Tauler[52] was safe from the attacks of the devil.

This raises the question whether Martin Luther found attractive or availed of the consolations and the protection that mysticism offered the Christian. In fact, the young Luther praised Tauler's sermons and 'professed to know no contemporary work in either Latin or German more beneficial and in closer agreement with the Gospels',[53] but, as will be seen in the next chapter, the theological influences he encountered led him along a different path and he came to consider that the mystic's striving for union with God was an example of works righteousness, seeking salvation on the strength of one's own efforts, and therefore the Pelagian heresy. According to Heiko A. Oberman,

---

49. Evelyn Underhill, *Mysticism: The Development of Humankind's Spiritual Consciousness* (London: Bracken Books, 1995[14]), 198.

50. Jean Gerson, *De Theologia Mystica. Tractatus Secundus Practicus*, André Combes, ed. (Lugano, 1958), 112–20. My translation.

51. Ibid., 122–34.

52. See Underhill, *Mysticism*, 339.

53. Ozment, *The Age of Reform*, 239.

Luther never based his authority on special revelations or high mystical experience, nor does he write for the 'aristocrats of the Spirit', who are granted a special foretaste of the glory to come.[54]

---

54. Heiko A. Oberman, *The Dawn of the Reformation* (Edinburgh: T&T Clark, 1986), 126.

Chapter 6

THE REFORMATION: TWO MAGISTERIAL REFORMERS

Martin Luther (1483–1546)

Luther was born in Eisleben, south-west Saxony, near the end of the fifteenth century, a time when the medieval world was beginning to give way to an emerging modern one. When Luther was nine, Columbus set out for America. A major cultural change had begun with the development of movable-type printing by Johannes Gutenberg in Mainz about 1439. The ease with which knowledge could now be communicated and spread had social, political and of course religious and theological consequences. During Luther's lifetime, Nicolaus Copernicus (1473–1543) developed his heliocentric description of the universe, which was to revolutionise astronomy and in time all of science. Technological changes came slowly, but a sign of change can be seen in the move of the Luther family to Mansfeld a year after Martin's birth, as his father began a new career in copper mining and progressed to being a supervisor and joint owner with others of seven smelters. The growth of towns brought changes to a culture hitherto large rural, in which the physical environment was home to spirits and demons, the good and bad inhabitants of the woods, the rivers, the lakes, the air itself.

But this was a gradual process; religious life laden with superstitions and schooling with a pre-modern orientation remained unchanged. Luther spoke in later years of the frequency with which he was punished in school and remembered the harsh treatment he received from both father and mother. At the age of fourteen he was sent to Magdeburg where, as in Mansfeld, he was taught in a Latin School. This was a suitable preparation for his studies in Erfurt University, where he was introduced not only to the long-established scholastic philosophical theology (*via antiqua*) that provided the intellectual support for the church's doctrinal and sacramental system, but also to the new thinking (*via moderna*) of William of Ockham (1285–1347). Known as Nominalism, this new thinking had serious implications for such issues as how God's existence could be known, and was a factor in the emergence of the importance of the Bible as a way of knowing God's self-revelation.[1]

---

1. Euan Cameron, *The European Reformation* (New York: Oxford University Press, 1991), 170: 'The most persuasive evidence for a first shift away from the broadly Occamist

Though his father had expected him to study law, he joined the Erfurt community of the Observant Augustinians. His formation as a young religious included much austerity in terms of food, clothing, living conditions and discipline, as well as long hours of prayer and study. His studies built upon what he had already learned in the nearby university, and he naturally involved close attention to the works of Saint Augustine, including his doctrine of predestination and his pessimistic assessment of human nature. This Augustinian tradition affected the Erfurt community's interpretation of the fashionable *via moderna*, probably adhering to the philosophical aspects of it, but relying more on Augustine for theology.[2]

Anfechtungen

Luther was mentored in his studies and spiritual formation from 1506 by the Vicar General of the Order, Johann Von Staupitz (1460–1524), the rector of the recently founded Wittenberg University. Von Staupitz counselled him when he confided that he was very troubled by what he called his *Anfechtungen*, a word which could be translated as temptations but could also have the sense of 'attacks', indicating assaults by the devil. For a young religious in formation, a hothouse atmosphere obtained in relation to spiritualty: the struggle to maintain the right relationship between external observances and interior motivation was constant, and an almost inevitable sense of failure could be accepted with humility, complacency or mounting anxiety. The novice had to acquire the skill of survival in order to persevere. Luther survived with the help of Von Staupitz, who prudently turned him from his preoccupation with self to consideration of higher studies.[3] He saw that Luther's struggle was more than with the temptations all young religious had to endure, and had a foundation in his battle with the sin of pride, though Luther himself would only say later that his *Anfechtungen* were 'the devil's thorn in the flesh'.[4] Oddly, Staupitz seems to have been involved with Luther both in the external forum of mentor of intellectual formation and

---

consensus on salvation is found in the course of Luther's first series of lectures on the Psalms (1513–1515).'

2. This is a much disputed area of research. Heiko A. Oberman, in *The Dawn of the Reformation: Essays in Late Medieval and Early Reformation Thought* (Edinburgh: T&T Clark, 1986), 77, described the theology of the Erfurt community as the *Schola Augustiniana moderna*, with Johann Von Staupitz, the Vicar General of the Order (and soon to be Luther's mentor) making it a pastorally oriented theology. Alister E. McGrath, in *Reformation Thought: An Introduction* (Oxford: Blackwell, 1993[2]), 81, questioned Oberman's findings, mainly on the grounds of chronological inconsistencies affecting the issue of what theological trends were in place during Luther's studies.

3. Fintan Lyons O.S.B., *Martin Luther: His Challenge Then and Now* (Dublin: Columba Press, 2017), 37.

4. Lyndal Roper, *Martin Luther: Renegade and Prophet* (London: Bodley Head, 2016), 68.

in the internal forum as spiritual guide and even confessor.[5] Luther needed the challenge of objective theological study, and the implementation of that plan did in fact get him through to final religious profession. When he began his teaching career in 1513, he looked back on that period of anxiety and decided that those trials came from God, though God must have acted as a tempter 'as if he were the devil'. However, a man who impulsively sought protection in the cloister after the near miss of a lightning strike was liable to be continuously aware of demonic forces even there.[6]

After a semester teaching in Wittenberg in 1508, before completing his doctoral studies at Erfurt, he returned in 1513 to Wittenberg to lecture on the Psalms. In 1516 he discovered a manuscript of mystical theology and published it as *Theologia Germanica*, declaring in the preface that he had learned from 'this noble little book' more than from any writing except the Bible and Saint Augustine.[7] In chapter 20 of the book, the English text has: 'It is said that the devil sometimes obsesses a person and keeps him in his hold.' As the commentary notes, Luther used the word *besessen*. 'However, the text (as it progresses) suggests a distinction between a temporary "obsession" (*besessen*) and a more lasting hold on the victim, "possession" (*behafft*), which indicates a more drawn out "ownership" of the person'. As it will turn out, during his life Luther thought of the devil's activities as fundamentally external to him; he was obsessed *with* the devil but never sensed or believed that the devil 'obsessed' him or kept him 'in his hold', despite his very frequent complaints, in his letters especially, about the devil's attacks.[8] He showed himself proactive on one occasion against the devil according to a story in his *Table Talk* (*Tischreden*), his conversations at table with students, lodgers and visiting

---

5. This would be an anomalous or even non-canonical arrangement, but biographers differ as to the exact nature of the relationship. Lyndal Roper, *Martin Luther: Renegade and Prophet*, 67, held that Staupitz fulfilled both roles, as did Roland Bainton, *The Reformation of the Sixteenth-Century* (Boston, MA: Bacon Press, 1985), 33, while John M. Todd, *Martin Luther: A Biographical Study* (London: Burns & Oates, 1964), 36, gives as his 'probable' spiritual director, John Von Grafenstein.

6. But see the view of Carlos M. N. Eire, '"Bite This, Satan!". The Devil in *Luther's Tabletalk*', in *Piety and Family in Early Modern Europe: Essays in Honour of Steven Ozment*, Mark R. Forster and Benjamin J. Kaplan, eds (Aldershot: Ashgate Publishing, 2005), 80–1: 'The devil certainly played a role in all this and Luther's experience of *Anfechtung* is at the heart of his diabology. But one must make a crucial distinction: though the devil is involved in these bouts of absolute despair Luther did not ascribe them to the devil. On the contrary, for Luther, every bout of despair comes from God.'

7. Martin Luther, *The Theologia Germanica of Martin Luther*, translation, commentary and introduction by Bengt Hoffman (New York: Paulist Press, 1980), 53–4.

8. The distinction between obsession and possession is one still made in pastoral dealings with afflicted people today. The term *infestation* is also used in pastoral practice to describe environmental phenomena such as loud sounds, which may be evidence of demonic activity.

lecturers. It concerned a woman at Eisenach suffering from a list of diverse and serious maladies including paroxysms and paralysis; she took heart when Luther visited her and asked him to pray for her.

> Whereupon Luther sighed, and said: 'God rebuke thee Satan and command thee that thou suffer this, his divine creature, to be at peace'. Then turning himself towards the standers by, he said: 'She is plagued by the devil in the body, but the soul is safe and shall be preserved, therefore let us give thanks to God and pray for her' and so they all prayed aloud the Lord's Prayer. After which, Luther concluded with these words: 'Lord God, heavenly Father, ... we beseech thee, through Jesus Christ thy only beloved Son, that thou wouldst deliver this thy servant from her sickness and from the hands of the devil.' ... The night following she took rest and the following day she was graciously delivered from her disease and sickness.[9]

His intervention would be a case of what today is called a Supplication, provided for in the churches' regulations regarding exorcisms. It did involve a direct address to Satan, though not a command to depart, the core of today's Roman Catholic *Exorcism Rite*. It would appear that Luther did not feel comfortable with exorcising a demon, though in the liturgy of baptism he retained the traditional exorcism fully in the 1523 Baptismal Rite and in a slightly reduced form in the revised 1526 Rite.[10] He attached great importance to his own baptism.

> He believed deeply that baptism initiated the struggle against the devil, and it is striking how often he referred to baptism when writing about Satan.[11]

By 1518 Luther had repudiated the old scholasticism, the *via antiqua*, when he engaged in a theological disputation organised by the Augustinian Province at Heidelberg in 1518. He quoted Augustine's *Contra Julianum* 2: 'You call the will free, but it is in fact an enslaved will.' This lack of freedom of the will was a consequence Luther drew from his basic conviction about humanity's endemic state of sinfulness.[12] He was no doubt familiar with Augustine's writing about the

---

9. Martin Luther, *Table Talk* (London: Fount, 1995), 307–8.

10. Martin Luther, *Das Taufbuechlein aufs neue Zugerichtet* 1526. In the first, 1523, *Rite*, the traditional ceremonies of insufflation, salt and spittle were retained, but in 1526, these were omitted and a shortened version of the exorcism used: 'I adjure thee, thou unclean spirit, by the Name of the Father and of the Son and of the Holy Ghost that thou come out of and depart from this servant of Jesus Christ, N. — Amen.' *Luther's Works*, vol. 53, Jaroslav Pelikan et al., eds (Philadelphia, PA: Fortress Press, 1999), 108.

11. Roper, *Martin Luther: Renegade and Prophet*, 347. Roland Bainton, *Here I Stand: Martin Luther* (Oxford: Lion Book, 1994), 367: 'When the devil assailed him, he would answer, "I am baptized".'

12. Gerard O. Forde, *On Being a Theologian of the Cross: Reflections on Luther's Heidelberg Disputation, 1518* (Grand Rapids, MI: William B. Eerdman, 1997), 19, quoted Heinrich

source of the evil afflicting humankind through the role of the devil in the fall of Adam and Eve, and showed more awareness of the devil than any theologian since Augustine.

> Luther presents a doctrine about the devil on the authority of the Holy Scriptures and in continuity with ecclesiastical tradition. What he says about the devil, however, and the way in which he says it, goes far beyond biblicism and traditionalism. He does not merely develop further a piece of theological and popular tradition; rather on the basis of his own experience, he bears witness to the reality and the terribleness of the power of the devil.[13]

He referred frequently in a sober way to the devil in his writings, for example, in his *Commentary on Galatians*,[14] where the devil is mentioned eight times, but more vividly in his letters to his friends, especially his close assistant and colleague, Philip Melanchthon. If very much aware of both the devil's temptations and God's protective hand in his own life, he was also very conscious of the devil in everyday affairs, and where his influence might be found, especially in the administration of the church. Unlike Augustine's diabology, Luther's account was a record of his personal experience and of the devil's activity that he perceived in the abuses perpetrated or permitted by the authorities in the church. The abuse that seems first to have concerned him as a theologian was the widespread granting of Indulgences.

The Ninety-Five Theses

In the *Ninety-Five Theses* he posted for debate on Indulgences on 31 October 1517, he targeted the papacy for its part in what he judged the financial scandal and theological deviancy of the Indulgence system but made no mention of the devil. He asked in no. 86: 'Why does not the pope, whose wealth is today greater the riches of the richest, build just this one church of St Peter with his own money, rather than with the money of poor believers?'[15] The controversy raised by his document led in 1518 to an interview lasting several days with Cardinal Cajetan, and as a result the hardening of his position against the papacy.

Bornkamm's argument that 'as far as the theology of the Reformation is concerned, the Heidelberg Disputation is the most important of all Luther's disputations'.
    13. Paul Althaus, *The Theology of Martin Luther*, Robert C. Schultz, trans. (Philadelphia, PA: Fortress Press, 1966), 161.
    14. See John Dillenger, *Martin Luther: Selections from His Writings* (New York: Anchor Books, 1961), 99–165, for Luther's *Commentary on Galatians*.
    15. Lyons, *Martin Luther: His Challenge Then and Now*, 225.

The antichrist and the papacy

By 1520, he was hinting – at the least – that the papacy was the antichrist, where antichrist meant, as 2 Thess. 2.3-10 put it, the 'man of sin' or 'lawless one', the agent of Satan, who would rule until destroyed by Jesus 'with the breath of his mouth'. In June of that year, he had written to George Spalatin, the Elector Friedrich's secretary, saying that the antichrist would soon be revealed.[16] He concluded his attack on the Papal Curia in *On the Papacy at Rome* of the same month, by saying that if the Curia's claims regarding the pope's authority were to be accepted by Pope Leo X, then he would say 'right out' that the pope was the antichrist. His response to the Papal Bull of June of that year, *Exsurge Domine*, was entitled *Against the Execrable Bull of Antichrist* (November). In it, he speculated whether Leo was responsible for the Bull (knowing that he was). When called to defend his theological position at the imminent Synod of Worms in 1521, he said:

> This shall be my recantation at Worms: 'Previously I said the pope is the Vicar of Christ. I recant. Now I say the pope is the adversary of Christ and the apostle of the devil.'[17]

He retained this polemical attitude towards the papacy throughout his career, notably in his final publication, *Against the Papacy at Rome Founded by the Devil* (1545). In his *Preface to His Works* (1545), he concluded by asking the reader to pray 'that the Word may be further spread abroad, and may be strong against the miserable devil'.

> For he is mighty and wicked, and just now is raving everywhere and raging cruelly, like one who well knows and feels that his time is short, and that the kingdom of his Vicar, the Antichrist in Rome, is sore beset.[18]

The scatological images of the papacy which he commissioned for the work on the papacy, showed the pope excreting devils, making the papacy part of the connection between excrement and the devil.

His association of the papacy and its curia with the devil on the external level could well have been a projection of the conflict he felt in his own inner

---

16. Theodore Smauk, Introduction to Project Gutenberg's *The Works of Luther* Vol. 1 2010, n28, quoting the letter to Spalatin: 'Endlicheinmal mussen die Geheimnisse des Antichrist offenbart werden. Denn so drangen sie sich selbst hervor, und wollen nicht welter verborgen sein.' About Luther's *Address to the German Nobility* (1520), Peter Matheson, *The Rhetoric of the Reformation* (Edinburgh: T&T Clark, 1998), 121, said: 'The devil and the forces of hell are already on stage, and antichrist is in the wings. Scarcely embarked on reading the pamphlet, the reader is swept headlong into a cosmic struggle.'

17. *D. Martin Luthers Werke, Briefwechsel* I, 391, Weimar, 1930 (WAB).

18. Final sentence in *R. Martin Luther to the Christian Reader* 1545. Project Gutenberg's *Luther's Works*, Vol. 1, 2010.

life, which from the beginning of his career was one of constant struggle with his *Anfechtungen*. Werner Elert in *The Structure of Lutheranism* suggested that there was a close bond between Luther and nature, and that between him and the activities of nature there was no boundary line. Luther's belief in demons, he believed, was part of this awareness of nature.

> These poltergeists, satyrs, and all the rest of the devil's vermin affect our senses with all kinds of strange phenomena. The devil himself makes use of all the means provided by the world of nature.[19]

Luther claimed he was particularly subject to these attacks when, after his condemnation at Worms, he was lodged for his own safety from 1521 to 1522 in the Wartburg Fortress, above the town of Eisenach (where he had been in school). He mentioned almost casually the many attacks he experienced and even how he ignored or reacted to the devil's poltergeist activities.[20]

A natural explanation was suggested by Heinrich Bornkamm:

> The lofty Wartburg was exposed to the full force of the winds, and poltergeist noises might well sound like the devil throwing nuts at the ceiling from the chest on the table, or like kegs being rolled down the stairs. ... As in everything else Luther told about the devil's deeds and wiles, there is here hidden a fantastic reality. Luther's was a fantasy rich in imagery and knowledgeable concerning the reality of the great Enemy confronting him in a thousand disguises at every turn. To be sure, the tale of Luther hurling the inkpot at the devil is a later invention.[21]

Bornkamm's interpretation that it was not a case of *infestation* is likely to be correct, as Luther did not seem to realise that the conflict at an apparently poltergeist level with Satan reflected an inner spiritual struggle, a fight against temptation independent of his fantasies. His letters from the Wartburg have frequent references to diabolic attacks. In November 1521 he wrote to his friend Nicholas Gerbel about his temptations:

> Believe me in this idle solitude I am subjected to Satanic attacks. It is much easier to fight against the incarnate Devil – that is, against men – than against spiritual wickedness in the heavenly places. Often I fall and am lifted again by God's right hand.[22]

---

19. Werner Elert, *The Structure of Lutheranism*, Vol. 1, Walter A. Hansen, trans. (Saint Louis: Concordia, 1962), 452.
20. Jeffrey Burton Russell, *Mephistopheles: The Devil in the Modern World* (Ithaca, NY: Cornell University Press, 1986), 39.
21. Heinrich Bornkamm, *Luther in Mid-Career, 1521–1530*, E. Theodore Bachmann, trans. (Philadelphia, PA: Fortress Press, 1983), 13.
22. WAB 2 435.

His mood was affected by the hardships of life in the fortress; he suffered from the cold, possibly from the diet provided by the keeper of the fortress, and from the isolation, all of which could bring heightened awareness of the devil's activities. In a letter to Melanchthon in May 1521, he complained that the Lord had stricken him with severe pains in his abdomen and described in some detail the emptying of his bowels.[23] In a letter to Spalatin, from the Wartburg on 9 September 1521, he said it was time to pray hard against Satan as he was planning a deadly tragedy in Germany, while Luther himself was lazy and snoring instead of praying against him.[24] He could on occasion repel the devil with some humorous rebukes, seeing him, in C. S. Lewis's words, 'as the salacious, grotesque, half bogey, half buffoon, of popular tradition'.[25]

Tischreden

That he was obsessed with the devil is clear from the number of times he refers to him, in his writings and, especially in his *Tischreden*. Much of what he said about diabolical activity was recorded there by the students. Accordingly, it consists not so much of systematic theological comment as personal reminiscence, pithy statements or even invention. But it is a very rich source of reference to and stories about the devil. As Carlos Eire established, in it there are 447 references to the devil, under 138 subject headings.[26] He comments:

> Nowhere else does Luther deal as often with the devil, or on more personal terms; nowhere else is his diabology as raw or sharp-edged.[27]

It contains some concise statements about the devil's activities, for example:

> The devil seduces us at first by all allurements of sin in order thereafter to plunge us into despair; he pampers up the flesh, that he may, by and by, prostrate

---

23. WAB 2 407.
24. WAB 2 429.
25. C. S. Lewis, *A Preface to Paradise Lost* (London: Oxford Paperbacks, 1960), 99.
26. Carlos M. N. Eire, '"Bite This, Satan!" The Devil in Luther's *Table Talk*', in *Piety and Family in Early Modern Europe: Essays in Honour of Steven Ozment*, Marc R. Forster and Benjamin J. Kaplan, eds (Aldershot: Ashgate Publishing, 2005), 70. Another major source of references to the devil is in his 'Against the Heavenly Prophets', where in many passages he accuses Karlstadt of being under the influence of the devil: 'Since he had invited the devil to be his sponsor up to this point so that the masses without due process were to destroy images, as enjoined by God's commandment, then he had to continue and press the auxiliary commandment, which follows from it, and commands the people to murder.' Martin Luther, *Luther's Works, Vol. 40*: Church and Ministry II, Jaroslav Pelikan et al., eds (Philadelphia, PA: Fortress Press, 1999), 104–5.
27. Ibid.

the spirit. We feel no pain in the act of sin, but the soul after it is sad, and the conscience is disturbed.[28]

Unsurprisingly, it also contains dramatic anecdotes to impress his audience, for example, the case of the musician at Mohlberg in Thuringia, who made his living by playing at merrymakings, but was under constant attack by the devil's threat to 'carry him off'. The pastor prayed for him and with some pious people watched over him day and night, fastening the doors and windows.

> At length the musician said: 'I feel that Satan cannot harm my soul, but he will assuredly remove my body', and that very night at eight o'clock, though the watch was doubled, the devil came in the shape of a furious wind, broke the windows and carried off the musician, whose body was found next morning, stiff and black, stuck on a nut-tree. 'It is a most sure and certain story', added Luther.[29]

The *Tischreden* contains many crude comments, something which can be explained in part by the context of a gathering involving university students, food, copious consumption of beer, the absence of female company – his wife, Catherine von Bora, served them but did not participate – and the earthiness of a man who gave detailed accounts of his bowel problems in his letters to Melanchthon.

Luther's preoccupation with his buttocks and bowels may well have had its root in his relationship with his parents as a child, their repression and punishment of him by beatings on the buttocks. The suffering inflicted on him by the devil then seems to have become associated with his abdominal pains and their origins in his treatment by his parents. In later life, when he suffered badly from constipation and kidney stones, he associated the pains he had in the abdominal and anal region (from constipation generally) with the oppression he felt from the devil and the papacy. Some of his cruder remarks express this obsession, for example, his saying to the devil: 'I have defecated in my pants and you can hang them around your neck and wipe your face with it'.[30] On another occasion he told the company:

> The devil seeks me out when I am at home in bed, and I always have one or two devils waiting to pounce on me. They are smart devils. If they can't overwhelm my heart, they grab my head and plague me there, and when that proves useless, I show them my ass, for that's where they belong.[31]

---

28. Martin Luther, *Table Talk*, William Hazlett, trans. (London: Fount Paperbacks, 1995), 282.

29. Ibid., 296.

30. *D. Martin Luthers Werke: Tischreden* II n. 1557.

31. *D. Martin Luthers Werke: Tischreden* 1. n.491, cited in Carlos M. N. Eire, '"Bite this, Satan!" The Devil in Luther's *Table Talk*', 70. Eire spoke of an alternative version: 'An alternate reading of this line has Luther using an even more aggressive verb, substituting shove or throw for show: "so will ich sie in Ars werfen" (WAT I.217)'.

An incident which occurred on the day of his first celebration of Mass, the *Primitz*, may throw some light on how parental oppression came to be linked with harassment by the devil. It was a day overloaded with emotion for the intensely devout Luther, and it reached a climax as he began to recite the central prayer of the Mass, the Canon. He became, in his own words, 'utterly stupefied and terror-stricken'.[32] With the help of the assistant priest, he recovered and after Mass, still in a heightened state of emotion, he went to take his place at the celebratory breakfast.

This was the first time he was with his father since he departed for the cloister. His father must be regarded as having shown goodwill in attending – there is no mention of his mother – and bringing a gift of twenty gulden to the community, but in his presence Luther was inevitably uneasy. After his ordeal of addressing God the Father, he may now have looked for some words of reassurance from his earthly father. The events that followed are described in a different sequence in the accounts Luther gave of the occasion many years later, but it is clear that there was an altercation between father and son, the sort of thing that can arise unexpectedly and against the participants' own wishes in a situation highly charged with emotion. It is likely that Luther took the initiative of suggesting to his father how everything had turned out well, despite past disappointment on his part. He was justifying his decision to enter the cloister, and referred to the vow he had taken on the day of the storm. This brought an unfortunate reaction from his father, who retorted that he hoped his decision had not been an illusion of the devil.[33]

From a larger perspective, the struggle with the devil was in Luther's world view part of the conflict between God and the devil.[34] In *Luther: Man between God and the Devil*, Heiko Oberman presented him as a man driven by a sense of a cosmological struggle between God and the devil, where the devil and the papacy become conflated and this certainly was the case for Luther by the end of his life. As Oberman puts it, for Luther,

> the condition of man does not depend on the breadth of his education but on his existential condition as a 'mule' ridden either by God or the devil, but

---

32. Bainton, *Here I Stand: Martin Luther*, 41.

33. As Todd remarks, 'it was typically ham-handed, this poking rough and ready German fun at his son'. It was the wrong thing to say to a man who so often felt besieged by the devil and had just gone through moments of self-doubt and even of panic. The situation worsened when Luther presented the life of the cloister as one of quiet – a safe haven from such temptations – causing Hans to take the high moral ground and remind him of the commandment to honour one's parents'. Todd, *Martin Luther: A Biographical Study*, 41. See also Gordon Rupp, *The Righteousness of God* (London: Hodder and Stoughton, 1953), 85.

34. In his sermon no. 6 for the year 1530, he spoke of the activities of the devil: 'The devil brews one misfortune after another, for he is a mighty, evil and restless spirit. Therefore, it is time that God be concerned about his honour', WA 32, 37.

with no choice in the matter, no freedom of decision, no opportunity for self-determination.[35]

Apocalypticism

As he grew older, Luther's outlook became apocalyptic and he speculated about when the world would end, as indicated by the title of his Supputatio Annorum Mundi of 1541, a book that exists only in manuscript.

> Heightening Luther's sense of cosmic struggle was his conviction that the End Time was nearly at hand; that with the exposure of the papal antichrist seated within the church, Satan had unleashed all his minions for one final climactic battle. Luther's own ill-health and expectation of death, combined with his disappointment about the reception of the gospel within Germany, fed his sense of the imminence of the Apocalypse and his desire to do final battle with the devil.[36]

Luther's unique preoccupation with the devil was a consequence of his family background, his world view, his relation with nature and the intense spiritual struggle with temptation that resulted in part from his religious formation. In his pastoral practice, he acted against what he regarded as superstitious rituals, pilgrimages, for example,[37] and old customs such as the fears going with the spilling of salt,[38] but did little to promote de-sacralisation of the world view of enchantment he had inherited. As noted above, he retained the exorcism used in the baptismal ceremony, albeit abbreviated, and his strong defence of the Real Presence in the Eucharist brought heaven and earth close together, though he repudiated ways of contacting the next world through such rituals as Masses for the Dead. He retained shrines in the churches, though the saints in heaven were stripped of their intercessory role. He believed in guardian angels as firmly as he believed in demons. Because of his lasting influence, the beliefs that marked the religious culture of the following centuries retained a deep sense of the reality of the devil, as is clear from such practices as the witch-hunt and, at the literary level, the prestige in which Milton's *Paradise Lost* would be held.

---

35. Heiko A. Oberman, *Luther: Man between God and the Devil* (New Haven, CT: Yale University Press, 1989), 219.

36. Mark Edwards Jr, *Luther's Last Battles: Politics and Polemics 1531–1546* (Minneapolis, MN: Fortress Press, 1989), 9.

37. In his last sermon, preached in Eisleben three days before his death, 18 February 1546, he expressed his indifference at the fact that people continued to go on pilgrimage to the shrine of the *heileger Rock* of Christ at Trier. See F. Lyons O.S.B., 'Luther's Last Sermon. In Commemoration of the 450th Anniversary of Martin Luther's Death', *Pro Ecclesia*, vol. 5, no. 3 (1996): 203–14.

38. WA TR 5. 6373.

Though Luther lived on the boundary between the medieval and modern eras, he remained in many ways a medieval man. He was aware of astronomers' speculations about the spheres surrounding the earth, whether there might up to twelve,[39] but his attitude to more revolutionary ideas being proposed by a 'new astronomer who wished to prove that the earth moved' was one of incredulity: 'the fool wants to change the whole of astronomy. … But the Holy Scripture clearly shows us that Joshua commanded the sun, not the earth, to stand still." (Josh. 10.12, 13).[40] Nonetheless, forces were at work to further the de-sacralisation process that would lead on the part of prominent thinkers to Satan's relegation to the status of a discarded myth.

John Calvin (1509–64)

Born in Noyon, Picardy, France, in 1509, John Calvin was the son of Gérard Cauvin – a lawyer who was procurator of the diocesan Cathedral Chapter, and was thereby in a position to provide his son with an income by having him tonsured as a cleric at the age of twelve. (He subsequently received two curacies, but eventually resigned from all those positions.) His father's intention that he should have a lucrative clerical career led to him, aged fourteen, being sent to study in Paris, first at the Collège de la Marche and then at the more prestigious and very strict Collège de Montaigu. There he encountered the latest thinking in Nominalist theology, the orthodox critique of Luther's theology, and the new humanist learning. Because of difficulties in relations with the diocese on Gérard's part, excommunication in fact, he abruptly redirected his son to legal studies at Orleans, though Calvin later explained in the preface to his *Commentary on the Psalms* that it was his father's decision because the legal profession raised those who followed it to wealth. He also spent a year in Bourges, where his interest in humanism developed.[41]

---

39. Martin Luther, *Commentary on Genesis*, vol. 1, John L. Lenker, trans. (Project Gutenberg: E Book #$8193, 2015) Part II, vol. 6.

40. Martin Luther, *Conversations with Luther: Selections from Recently Published Sources of the Table Talk*, Preserved Smith and Herbert Gallinger, trans., ed. (New York: Pilgrim Press, 1815), 104:

> Mention was made of a new astronomer who wished to prove that the earth moved and went around, not the sky or the firmament or the sun or the moon. It was just as when one was sitting on a wagon or boat which was moving, it seemed to him that he was standing still and resting, and that the earth and trees moved by. 'So it goes,' [said Luther], 'whoever wants to be clever must not be content with what anyone else has done, but must do something of his own and then pretend it was the best ever accomplished'.

41. John Calvin, *Commentary on the Psalms*. https://ccel.org/ccel/calvin/calcom08/calcom08.vi.html.

His conversion

In the same preface, he spoke of his conversion to the reform that had originated with Luther, but had taken hold among many students of humanism in France. Though too 'obstinately devoted to the superstitions of Popery to be easily extracted from so profound abyss of mire ... God by a sudden conversion subdued and brought my mind to a teachable frame'.[42] His move was influenced by friendship with others, including Nicholas Cop, who became rector of the University of Paris, and was joined there by Calvin in 1533. Both Cop and Calvin fled from Paris after Cop had delivered an address in the Church of the Mathurins on 1 November 1533, in which he extolled some idea of the reform.[43] Calvin was suspected of having made an input to the text – his rooms were searched two days after the event. Thus began a period of flight for him and some friends during which he spent the spring of 1535 in Basel, before risking a return visit to France in the summer. On his return journey to Basel he diverted through Geneva to avoid the French and Imperial armies and on being recognised there was constrained by the Swiss reformer Guillaume Farel to remain and assist in the reform of the city.[44] Because of the rigour of the reform programme he introduced he was ousted by local opposition and went into exile in Basel from 1538 to 1541, when because of chaotic conditions in the city, the authorities recalled him, and there he continued to promote his programme of reform until his death in 1564.

This conversion from immersion in humanist studies to evangelical fervour did not mean a total change of course, as the reform movement among his fellow students based on Luther's campaign in Germany was in the cultural milieu of the *Rhétoriquers*, people like Clément Marot (1496–1544), who produced a French translation of the Psalms in 1541. This followed on the first French translation of the Bible by Jacques Léfevre d'Etaples in 1530, whom Calvin met at the court of the reform-minded Marguerite of Navarre in 1534. At that time he intended to write a catechetical treatise in French to aid the reform movement, and after the publication of his *Institutes of the Christian Religion* in Latin in 1536, he did produce a French edition in 1541,[45] and ultimately a French edition of the 1559 *Institutes*. Though he spoke disparagingly about humanists[46] like d'Etaples (and

---

42. Ibid.

43. Timothy George, *Theology of the Reformers* (Nashville, TN: Broadman and Holman, 1988), 176: 'On All Saints' Day, Cop did not praise the saints but rather proclaimed Christ as the only mediator with God. Cop was forced to flee for his life.'

44. A. G. Dickens, *Reformation and Society in Sixteenth-Century Europe* (London: Thames and Hudson, 1966), 152.

45. It is worth noting that in sixteenth-century French, *Institutions* meant instruction. Cf. Ruth Whelan, 'Biodegradable Calvin', *Doctrine and Life*, vol. 60, no. 1 (January 2010): 36–42.

46. John Calvin, *Institutes of the Christian Religion*, John T. Neill, ed., F. L. Battles, trans. (Philadelphia, PA: Westminster Press, 1960), II.ii.18: 'I do not deny that one can read competent and apt statements about God here and there in the philosophers, but these always show a certain giddy imagination. ... They are like a traveller passing through a field

of course Erasmus) who remained loyal to Rome, 'Calvin did not cease to be a humanist after he became a reformer'.[47]

The contrast with Erasmus

The particular interest here is the extent to which humanist influence may have altered Calvin's diabology, to what extent it resulted in a difference between his and Luther's diabology. Obsession with the devil, so characteristic of Luther, and fear of the devil, a major factor in the lives of medieval people are not evident in Erasmus' *Enchiridion*, though he did warn against the attacks of the devil when speaking of the *enchiridion* or dagger carried by the Christian. 'Since our enemy is incessant in his attacks, we must be constantly on the battle line, constantly in a state of preparedness.'[48]

> Don't look on Christ as a mere word, an empty expression, but rather as charity, simplicity, patience and purity – in short, in terms of everything he has taught us. Consider as the devil, on the other hand, anything that deters us from Christ and his teaching.[49]

Erasmus and Calvin did not necessarily differ in regard to the importance of the devil's attacks on the Christian, but, as will be seen, the humanist Erasmus was not as much concerned as Calvin with the evil propensities of the human heart. In any case, in contrast with the war of words between Luther and Erasmus in the enslaved or free will controversy, Erasmus and Calvin did not engage directly with each other. Erasmus was indeed 'caught in the crossfire'[50] between the conservatives and radical reformers like Carlstadt, Müntzer and then Farel, who all spent time in Basel in 1535, the year he arrived there. The complications of the situation have been described as follows:

> John Calvin arrived in Basel in early 1535 during his flight from Paris – the same journey that would eventually find him in Geneva. Desiderius Erasmus also arrived in Basel during 1535. Calvin had published his treatise on Seneca by then and was working on the *Institutes of the Christian Religion*, but his was a career yet unforeseen. Erasmus was sick and frail. He was the greatest living humanist, but his friends and colleagues were now mostly gone. Erasmus was

---

at night who in a momentary lightning flash, sees far and wide, but the sight vanishes so swiftly that he is plunged again into the darkness of the night before he can take even a step.' *Institutes* quoted hereafter by Book, Chapter and paragraph number.

47. George, *Theology of the Reformers*, 176.
48. Desiderius Erasmus, *The Handbook of the Militant Christian* I.2 in John P. Dolan, *The Essential Erasmus* (New York: Mentor-Omega Books, 1964), 35.
49. Ibid., 58.
50. Roland Bainton, *Erasmus of Christendom* (Tring, Herts: Lion Publishing, 1988), 264.

often bedridden and rarely left his room in the house of Hieronymus Froben. Calvin was immersed in the humanist culture of Basel and interacted with some of Erasmus's associates and protégés in the city, but the young Frenchman never met the aged titan. Calvin left Basel in the early spring; Erasmus too made plans to move on from Basel – but he developed dysentery and died in July 1536, just as Calvin was taking on more and more pastoral duties in Geneva.[51]

It was after Erasmus' death in 1536 that differences would emerge in relation to their approach to the Christian life. While both looked back to the early Fathers, Erasmus' advice in the *Enchiridion* was,

> I would suggest that you read those commentators that do not stick so closely to the literal sense, ... Origen, Ambrose, Jerome and Augustine.[52]

Calvin, on the other hand, was dedicated to establishing the original text, yet made more use of Erasmus' translation than any other, 'although he criticised him and contested his position more than regularly'.[53] An interesting example of disapproval and difference arose in the exegesis of the Letter of James. The context is the passage in James 1, that 'one is tempted by one's own desire, being lured and enticed by it.' (1.14). Calvin said,

> We conclude that it is a vain manoeuvre for man to attempt to throw the blame for his errors on God, for whatever the evil, it comes from no other source than the perverse affections of man himself. ... The reason why the devil chases us into sin is precisely that he is himself all aflame with a mad passion for it.[54]

He disagreed with Erasmus' humanist translation of the chapter; the humanist did not recognise the responsibility of the human being, while he reinforced it.[55] This assertion that 'evil comes from no source than the perverse affections of man himself' was a statement that Calvin later qualified in his explicit treatment of the devil in his major work, *The Institutes of the Christian Religion*, published in

---

51. Greta Grace Kroeker, 'Calvin, Erasmus, and Humanist Theology', in *Calvin and the Early Reformation*, Brian C. Brewer and David M. Whitford, eds (Leiden: Brill, 2019), 11.
52. Erasmus, *The Handbook of the Militant Christian*, I.2.37.
53. Max Engammare, 'John Calvin's Use of Erasmus', *Erasmus Studies*, vol. 37 (2017): 176.
54. John Calvin, *A Harmony of the Gospels: Matthew, Mark, Luke, and the Epistles of James and Jude*, vol. III, A. W. Morrison, trans. (Edinburgh: Saint Andrew Press, 1972), 268.
55. Towards the end of the chapter, verse 26 (RSV) says: 'If any think they are religious and do not bridle their tongues, but deceive their hearts, their religion is worthless'. Calvin did not favour Erasmus' translation of the Greek ἀλλὰ ἀπατῶν καρδίαν (but deceiving the heart) which was 'He allows it to go astray (*sinit aberrare*)'. 'This is the source of the invective [*sic*] to which the hypocrites are addicted, and we are to see how, blinded with excessive self-love, they persuade themselves to be far better than they are.' Ibid., 274–5.

successive editions from 1536 to 1559. Quotations here will be from the 1559 edition.

Calvin's references to the devil

Calvin based his treatment of the devil on his theology rather than on personal experience – as far as can be known, as his reticence in personal matters rarely deserted him. Unlike Luther, 'Calvin was by nature uncommunicative about his personal history'.[56] In his references to the devil something of the old culture of vulnerability in relation to mysterious forces remained. For example, in a letter to the Lausanne Reformer, Pierre Viret, in November 1546, he spoke of a man in Geneva, noted for his dissipated way of life, who fell ill and 'seemed to fly away despite attempts to hold him', no trace remaining of him except his cap on the side of the river, which had led to a fruitless search for his body. Calvin recounted all this as the work of the devil and mentioned it in a sermon the following Sunday.[57] Like Luther, he subscribed to the cosmology of his time, which envisaged the spheres inhabited by angels and demons.[58] But he showed more openness to the beginnings of the self-confident, scientific mentality that marked modernity.[59]

56. François Wendel, *Calvin: The Origin and Development of His Religious Thought*, Philip Mairet, trans. (London: Collins, 1969), 15: '(A) certain timidity, an aristocratic inclination to screen himself from the public, and finally his conviction that the individual is nothing in himself but only in so far as he is an instrument of the Divine will, caused him to remain silent about many events that would have interested biographers.'

57. John Calvin, *Joannis Calvini opera quae supersunt omnia*, Tome 12 (Brunswige: C.A. Schwetschke et Filium, 1864), 413–14: 'Ambae quum retinere eum vellent, evolavit procul tanto impetu, ut ferri, non currere, ipsum appareret' (413–14).

58. In his *Commentary on Genesis*, Calvin declared his respect for the 'astronomers' of his day while, like Luther, defending Moses' simple, even literal, interpretation of the biblical text: John Calvin, *Commentary on the First Book of Moses*, vol. 1, J. King, trans. (Edinburgh: Calvin Translation Society, 1847), 86: 'Moses wrote in a popular style things which, without instruction, all ordinary persons, endued with common sense, are able to understand; but astronomers investigate with great labour whatever the sagacity of the human mind can comprehend.' What his view of Copernicus was is more difficult to determine, though it has been established that a statement previously attributed to him was without foundation, and the facts are now well documented. The statement, 'Who will venture to put the authority of Copernicus above that of the Holy Spirit?', became well-known because of its appearance in a book by Andrew D. White, *History of the Warfare of Science with Theology*, in 1896. As recently as 1965, it was included in a new edition of White's work. Owen Gingerich, 'Did the Reformers Reject Copernicus?', *Christianity Today*, Issue 76 (2002), explained how this persistent attribution to Calvin came about.

59. Donald K. McKim, ed., *The Westminster Handbook to Reformed Theology* (Louisville, KY: Westminster John Knox Press, 2001), 206: 'John Calvin's interest in Aristotelian physics is reflected in his sermons and commentaries. Like Martin Luther and Huldrych Zwingli, Calvin accepted the basic Aristotelian picture as a description of universal Providence.'

He articulated his fundamental teaching on 'devils' early in *The Institutes of the Christian Religion*:

> All that Scripture teaches concerning devils aims at arousing us to take precautions against their stratagems and contrivances, and also to make us equip ourselves with those weapons which are strong and powerful enough to vanquish these most powerful foes. (I.xiv.13)

Recalling many passages in Scripture concerning Satan's activities, he said:

> We have been forewarned that an enemy relentlessly threatens us, an enemy who is the very embodiment of rash boldness, of military prowess, of crafty wiles, of untiring zeal and haste, of every conceivable weapon and of skill in the science of warfare. (Ibid.)

In the context of this language of incessant warfare, he urged a similar response on the part of the Christian with perseverance until death. In subsequent paragraphs, he spoke of continuous struggle, but also of the assurance of victory, because the devil 'can do nothing unless God wills and assents to it'. He returned to this issue in Book II, the logic of his approach being that God was actively involved in everything that happened. He referred to a saying of Augustine:

> Somewhere Augustine compares man's will to a horse awaiting its rider's command, and God and the devil to its riders. 'If God sits astride it', he says, then as a moderate and skilled rider, he guides it properly. ... But if the devil saddles it, he violently drives it far from the trail, like a foolish and wanton rider, forces it into ditches, tumbles it over cliffs, and goads it into obstinacy and fierceness'. (II.iv.1)

Because he believed, as Augustine did, that God predestines humankind either to salvation or damnation, he assigned a role to Satan in the carrying out of God's purposes.

> For those whom the Lord does not make worthy to be guided by his Spirit he abandons, with just judgment to Satan's action. (II.iv.1)

Even in the case of the Christian not thus predestined, he believed that the devil exercised a major role. This followed his very developed doctrine of Divine Providence in three chapters of the *Institutes* (I.xv–xvii). Meditating on Providence was a necessary means to avoid yielding to the temptations of the devil or 'wicked men'.

> But let them recall that the devil and the whole cohort of the wicked are completely restrained by God's hand as by a bridle, so that they are unable to hatch and plot against us or, having hatched it, to make preparations or, if they

have fully planned it, to stir a finger toward carrying it out, except as far as he has permitted, indeed commanded it. (I.xvii.11)

The final phrase, 'commanded it', results from Calvin's conviction that God by his Providence can direct anyone, good, wicked or even the devil, so to act as to carry out his plans. His doctrine of predestination is then the means by which he reconciles the two positions that 'evil comes from no other source than the perverse affections of man himself' and the suggestion that the devil is a malignant enemy capable of whipping away the dissolute invalid or riding a person to destruction.

Unlike Luther, he was distrustful of the 'liberty of the Christian', which Luther extolled in a famous publication in 1520 – though he could not deny it. But the religious regime imposed by him in Geneva was marked by regulation and restriction, and he lamented the extent to which people sought licence to decide for themselves. 'They attend not to what pleases God, but give licence to their own imaginations.'[60] With his mind focused on an idealised early Christian community, in exercising his ministry in Geneva he had great concern for order, so much so that in an interesting speculation on what would happen if the papacy were to end, allowing everyone to follow his own will as his law and creating dreadful confusion, he concluded:

> It is better that the devil should rule men under any sort of government, than that they should be set free without any law, without any restraint.[61]

The papacy, controlled by the devil, was preferable to disorder!

He wrote a tract against a group he called Libertines, who, he said, 'babble of devils as nothing else than evil emotions or perturbations which come upon us from our flesh'.[62] For him there were 'not a few' clear testimonies of Scripture on the matter.

The testimony of Scripture was enough to establish the existence of the devil. His commentaries on the Gospels, which took the existence of the devil for granted, were pastorally motivated and therefore his exegesis of passages frequently referred to the implications for the life of the Christian; he also tended to use his exegesis to introduce a polemic against Roman usages. For example, his account of Jesus' fast in the wilderness – the purpose of which he said, oddly, 'was to gain him more authority in being set apart from the common lot of men'– led to a diatribe against those 'who pretend to be imitators of Christ'.[63] The pastoral note was evident when

---

60. John Calvin, *Commentaries on the Book of the Prophet Jeremiah and the Lamentations*, vol. 4 (44:8), John Owen, trans. (Edinburgh: Calvin Translation Society, 1854), 532.

61. John Calvin, 'Commentary on Jeremiah 30:9', https://biblehub.com/commentaries/calvin/jeremiah/30.htm.

62. Calvin, *Institutes of the Christian Religion*, I.xiv.19.

63. Calvin, *A Harmony of the Gospels*, vol. I, 134.

the discussion was of a passage where Jesus encountered the devil – or Satan, the term he used more frequently.[64] In the temptations in the desert, he noted that the Son of God willingly underwent temptation 'and met the devil in a set trial of strength, that by his victory he might win us the triumph'.

> So as often as Satan attacks us, let us remember that we can in no other way sustain and repulse his assaults than by the protection of that shield.[65]

In discussing those temptations, he lacked today's exegetical tools and made no reference to the issue of how they came to be recorded in the absence of eye witnesses. He did not take any special notice of the fact that the three temptations had parallels in Deuteronomy.

In his *Harmony of the Gospels* he followed the sequence of Matthew's text, harmonising the texts of Luke and Mark with it. Accordingly, he took the story of the Gadarene demons from Matthew and dealt at the outset with the issue of the number, saying that Augustine's conjecture was probably right, that there were two, but excused the mention of only one (in Luke and Mark), 'on the ground that this was the more notorious, and indeed because of the savagery of his affliction, was the subject of a more striking miracle'.[66] In commenting on this one man, he held that 'the unclean spirit (of Mark's text) kept the poor man at the tombs to rend him with unending terror at the gloomy spectacle of death. … It makes a gloomy and awful scene, yet one which warns of the misery and horror of being subject to Satan's tyranny'.[67] The demons' interaction with Jesus and their plea to escape, Calvin saw as a futile exercise. His description of the outcome used language that showed the depth of his conviction about the reality of such an encounter and, incidentally, could well provide some insights for those engaged in the ministry of the church's exorcising rituals today:

> So we see how the devils breathe nothing but fury against God, and yet with all their swelling pride they fall like broken creatures in a twinkling: for their malice and perversity is never tamed, never ceases to resist God's rule, and yet it meets its match and surrenders.[68]

His view, however, of the exorcisms carried out by the church of his day was less than positive. He was commenting on the charge against Jesus that he cast out demons by the power of Beelzebub and his concern was to vindicate Jesus' mastery over the devil during his ministry.

---

64. The Index to the three volumes of *A Harmony of the Gospels* lists fifty-two entries for Satan.
65. Calvin, *A Harmony of the Gospels*, vol. I, 135.
66. Ibid., 284.
67. Ibid.
68. Ibid., 285.

> We know what tricks Satan sometimes uses to deceive men, presenting an appearance of dissension to ensnare their minds in superstitions. Thus the exorcisms in the papacy are nothing but counterfeit fights of Satan against himself. But no such suspicion rests on Christ. He casts out demons from men to restore them sane and whole to God. When the devil enters into this conspiracy with himself, he pretends to be overcome, but in such a way that he emerges victorious. But Christ attacked the devil in open battle, and cast him completely down and left him with nothing. He did not strike him down in one respect and set him up on his feet in another, but destroyed his weapons of war everywhere.[69]

Calvin's many references to the devil were characterised by both belief in the reality of the devil and a confidence that the believer's union with Christ provided armour against the devil's attacks. This was because of particular characteristics of his theology. In addition to the doctrine of justification by faith rather than works, within the overall envelope of predestination, he introduced a new note with his emphasis on the utter sovereignty and transcendence of God.[70] In his *Commentary on Psalm 145*, he said that David, extolling the immensity of God's greatness, admonishes us to praise God, 'since by the immensity of God's greatness we are almost struck dumb, or caught up in ecstasy'.[71] For Calvin, transcendence, or sovereignty, implied the total incapacity of man 'of his own nature either to aspire to good through resolve or struggle after it through effort',[72] but it also underpinned his doctrine of the union of the Christian with Christ through the gift of the Spirit. His theology of the Word had a richness of content that came from his theology of the Spirit; the internal witness of the Spirit to the Word effected the union of the believer with Christ.

> There is good reason for the repeated mention of the 'testimony of the Spirit', a testimony we feel engraved like a seal on our hearts, with the result that it seals the cleansing and sacrifice of Christ. ... To sum up, the Holy Spirit is the bond by which Christ unites us to himself. (*Inst.* III.i.1)

---

69. Calvin, *A Harmony of the Gospels*, vol. II, 41.

70. This had implications for his doctrine of the Eucharist; he complained that his opponents (in the context, Lutherans) did not understand 'the manner of descent by which he lifts us up to himself' (IV.17.16). Cf. *Joannis Calvini Opera quae supersunt omnia, Epistola: Calvinus Polonis* (1557), G. Baum et al., eds (Brunsvigae: Schwetschke, 1863-1900), 16, 677: 'Christus secundum carnem suum in caelo manens, admirabili Spiritus sui virtute ad nos descendit, et simul nos ad se sursum attollit.'

71. John Calvin, *Commentary on Psalm 145*, v. 1, *Joannis Calvini opera quae supersunt omnia*, G. Baum et al., eds, Tome 32, CR 60 413: '(David) admonet tunc rite demum a nobis Deum laudari quum ad immensitatem potentiae eius quasi obstupescimus, vel rapimur in ecstasin.' My translation in text.

72. Calvin, *Institutes of the Christian Religion*, II.iv.1. Hereafter referred to by Book, Chapter and paragraph number.

The Christian should not think of Christ as afar off but of dwelling within.[73]

> For we await salvation from him not because he appears to us as afar off, but because he makes us, engrafted into his body, participants not only in all his benefits, but also in himself. ... We ought not to separate Christ from ourselves or ourselves from him (III.ii.24).

In consequence, true believers have armour protecting them against evil, and when it comes to the issue of temptation a principal cause of concern for Calvin was not the workings of the 'spirit who holds power over the air' (Eph. 2.2) to which he referred in *Inst.* I.xiv.13, but the temptation of unbelief because of the depravity of human nature. Union with Christ and depravity of human nature were held together in his perspective. In a disquisition on faith and its properties in *Inst.* III.ii, he acknowledged the difficulties experienced by believers:

> In recognising the grace of God toward themselves, they are not only tried by disquiet, which often comes upon them, but they are repeatedly shaken by gravest terrors. For so violent are the temptations that trouble their minds as not to seem compatible with (the) certainty of faith. (III.ii.17)

These temptations come from within, from human weakness. But he also maintained a balance by frequently drawing attention to the wiles of the devil and his never-ceasing activity. He used a series of sermons on the Acts of the Apostles from 1549 to 1551 to compare and contrast the two communities – the original community described in Acts and the congregation in the Genevan Cathedral, in terms of hearing and heeding the Word of God. His comments were often quite pointed and drew attention quite often to the incursions of the devil into the life of people.

> Calvin is only too aware of this field of tension between God and the devil for the hearers. Only Sermon 14 lacks the words *diable* and *Sathan* entirely. In other sermons, the number of times *diable* is mentioned varies from 1 to 19 times per sermon, and as far as *Sathan* is concerned, 1 and 12 times per sermon.[74]

---

73. Wilhelm Niesel, *Reformed Symbolics: A Comparison of Catholicism, Orthodoxy, and Protestantism* (Edinburgh: Oliver and Boyd, 1962), 182:

> For both Calvin and the Heidelberg Catechism, 'that joining of head and members, that indwelling of Christ in our hearts, in short that mystical union', is fundamental. 'We do not therefore, contemplate him outside ourselves from afar in order that his righteousness may be imputed to us, but because we put on Christ and are engrafted into his body – in short, because he deigns to make us one with him.'

74. Wilhelmus H. Th. Moehn, *The Relation between God and His Audience in Calvin's Sermons on Acts*, Lydia Verburg, trans. (Genève: Librairie Droz, 2001), 80.

His doctrine of the church and attitude to 'superstitions'

Book IV of the *Institutes* contained an extensive treatment of the Church and the sacraments leading to the conclusion that the Roman rituals are 'diabolical'. His fundamental concept of the church can be gathered from the title of the book: 'The External Means or Aims by which God Invites Us Into the Society of Christ and Holds us Therein'. Here, more than in other parts of the *Institutes*, the background of opposition to the papal church becomes evident and it is hardly possible to understand fully the positive idea of the church as such he put forward without taking account of the negative image which for him the papal church provided. If in earlier editions of the *Institutes* he tended towards the idea, found in the *Augsburg Confession* (1530), of the invisible church as the *ecclesia proprie (dicta)*,[75] his contacts with Martin Bucer in Basel, and the development of his own theology of ministry, as he took charge in Geneva, quickly led him to create his own balance between the visible and invisible aspects of the church.

In the succeeding chapters of Book IV, Calvin set out his teaching on Word and sacrament, with a sacrament being what might be called a visible aspect of the Word:

> [A sacrament] is an outward sign by which the Lord seals on our consciences the promise of his goodwill toward us in order to sustain the weakness of our faith; and we in turn attest our piety toward him in the presence of the Lord and of his angels and before men. (IV.xiv.1)

He argued that the sacraments were necessary for anthropological reasons: 'now because we have souls engrafted in bodies, he imparts spiritual things under visible ones'. But he added a note of warning: 'Not that the gifts set before us in the sacraments are bestowed with the nature of the things, but that they have been marked with this signification' (IV.xiv.3).

'Gifts not bestowed with the nature of things', depending on what *with* means, may indicate an understanding at odds with the Roman liturgical tradition about the rites involving bread and wine and water and oil, especially as further on he spoke of 'those who attach to the sacraments some sort of secret powers with which one nowhere reads that God has bestowed them' (IV.xiv.14). It has to be said that Calvin did point to a weak spot in medieval Catholic sacramental theology, according to which the sacraments conferred grace on those who did not (in Calvin's words) set up a barrier of mortal sin. This he understood to mean someone without faith, though that was not in fact the official position with regard to the conferring of grace.

> How deadly and pestilential this notion is cannot be expressed. ... Of a certainty it is diabolical. For in promising a righteousness apart from faith, it hurls souls

---

75. *Articuli Fidei Praecipui*, VIII, in H. J. Kidd, *Documents of the Continental Reformation* (Oxford: Oxford University Press, 1911), 264.

headlong to destruction. Secondly, because it draws the cause of righteousness from the sacraments, it binds men's pitiable minds ... in this pitiable superstition, so that they repose in the appearance of a physical thing rather than in God himself. (IV.xiv.14)[76]

In considering the traditional sacramental teaching, he saw superstition and idolatry in the Roman doctrine and worship of the Eucharist (IV.xvii.35–7). These negative judgements brought about an increasing dichotomy between the Protestant and Catholic mentality, with Catholic rites regarded as part of medieval magical practice. While many in the church were aware, independently of the Reformation, of the need for reform, the approach adopted by Calvin and others disparaged the notion of rituals that appeared to be magical.

> [The people] were now taught that their practical difficulties could only be solved by a combination of self-help and prayers to God. The substitute action involved in the practice of magic was condemned as both impious and useless. The strong emphasis upon the virtues of hard work and application, which was to become a pronounced feature of religious teaching of the sixteenth and seventeenth centuries, Catholic as well as Protestant, both reflected and helped to create a frame of mind which spurned the cheap solutions offered by magic, not just because they were wicked, but because they were too easy.[77]

De-sacralisation

The repudiation by the Protestant tradition of the rites and devotions characteristic of medieval Catholicism resulted in an austere form of churchmanship and worship that relied on the subjective nature of the converted person's faith rather than the objective saving act of God in Christ celebrated in the liturgy.[78] Theology lent itself to a process of de-sacralisation nourished by the growth of empirical science. Charles Taylor's view of the disenchantment process, as he calls it, that 'cast aside all the myriad rituals and acts of propitiation of the old religion', had two aspects:

---

76. Carlos M. N. Eire, *War against the Idols: The Reformation of Worship from Erasmus to Calvin* (Cambridge: Cambridge University Press, 1986), 227: 'A final consideration Calvin takes into account is that all impure worship not only displeases God, but goes to Satan as well. Those who become embroiled in idolatry, he points out, are handing themselves over to the devil, because the ultimate result of false worship is abandonment by God.'

77. Keith Thomas, *Religion and the Decline of Magic* (New York: Scribner, 1971), 278.

78. Howard G. Hageman, 'Reformed Spirituality', in *Protestant Spiritual Traditions*, Frank. C. Senn, ed. (New York: Paulist Press, 1986), 62.

First negative, we must reject everything that smacks of idolatry. We combat the enchanted world, without quarter. At first, the fight is not carried on because enchantment is totally untrue, but rather because it is necessarily ungodly. If we are not allowed to look for help to the sacred, to a 'white magic' of the church, then all magic must be black. All spirits now are ranged under the devil, the one great enemy.[79]

The second he described as a positive energy:

We feel a new freedom in a world shorn of the sacred, and the limits it set for us, to re-order things as seems best. We take the crucial stance, for faith and the glory of God. … We are not deterred by the older taboos, or supposedly sacred orderings. So we can rationalise the world, expel the mystery from it (because it is all now concentrated in the will of God).[80]

The consequences of the drive to reorder society and rationalise the world came to fruition in the centuries after Calvin in societies with a Calvinist heritage, such as Geneva and Scotland,[81] Puritan and Presbyterian New England. In the newly fledged United States, a civil religion acknowledging a Supreme Being or Providence served to underpin the political establishment and owed its origin partly to Calvin's transcendence doctrine but partly also to Deism. How true to Calvin later Calvinism was has always been disputed. Calvin himself, with his

---

79. Charles Taylor, *A Secular Age* 80, in *The Myth of Disenchantment Magic, Modernity, and the Birth of the Human Sciences* (Chicago: University of Chicago Press, 2017), Jason Ā. Josephson-Storm maintained that disenchantment could have several meanings, but took issue with the thesis that disenchantment characterised the rise of modernity. In a contribution to the Correspondence section of *New Atlantis* (Summer/Fall 2018), be wrote:

> Many theorists have argued that what makes the modern world 'modern' is that people no longer believe in spirits, myth, or magic – in this sense we are 'disenchanted.' However, every day new proof arises that 'modern' thinkers do in fact believe in magic and in spirits, and they have done so throughout history. … As I show in my book, over the course of 'modernity,' many people continued to believe in the reality of spirits, moral forces, and demons (and even came up with new ones) and the majority continue to hold such beliefs today.

80. Taylor, *A Secular Age*, 80.

81. The association of the Catholic cause with the devil in the minds of reformers like John Knox in Scotland is evident in a covenant made by Protestant nobles in 1557, in which they declared: 'We, perceiving how Satan in his members, the Antichrists of our time, cruelly doth rage, seeking to overthrow and destroy the Evangel of Christ and his Congregation, ought, according to our bounden duty, strive in our Master's cause, even unto death.' See Hans J. Hillerbrand, *The Division of Christendom: Christianity in the Sixteenth Century* (Louisville, KY: Westminster John Knox Press, 2007), 352.

concept of God's transcendence or sovereignty, was not one to expel mystery from the world. He believed too in the existence and activity of the devil and this belief was carried through into European Reformed society for at least a century.

> On the one hand, the reformers' emphasis on complete divine sovereignty should have seriously challenged Christianity's more dualistic tendencies. But, on the other, Protestantism was too driven by a profound sense of human sin to be able to jettison the devil.[82]

---

82. Nathan Johnstone, 'The Protestant Devil: The Experience of Temptation in Early Modern England', *Journal of British Studies*, vol. 43, no. 2 (April 2004): 174; E. V. Walker, 'Demons and Disenchantment', in *Disguises of the Demonic: Contemporary Perspectives on the Power of Evil*, Alan M. Olson, ed. (New York: Association Press, 1975), 17: 'Since the time when Max Weber identified "intellectualisation", "rationalisation" and "disenchantment of the world" as an overwhelming trend of Western civilisation, counter-movements resisting that trend have gathered strength and shown unexpected endurance. To some extent the revival of demonology and what is called "the occult" ... may be understood as part of the resistance.'

Chapter 7

THE CATHOLIC REFORM: THREE OUTSTANDING REFORMERS AND CONFLICT WITH THE DEVIL

With regard to the belief in the existence and activity of the devil, the early division between the Protestant Reformation and the Catholic Reform did not bring with it any significant difference, though that shared belief would later divide along diverging lines. Calvin and Saint Ignatius Loyola saw the devil's temptations in a similar light. However, the term *reformatio* quickly assumed the meaning attributed to it by Protestant theologians, namely, the movement and doctrines originating from Martin Luther.

> [Protestant writers] ignored the original broader meaning of the word *reformatio* as it was used in ecclesiastical circles from the late Middle Ages until well into the sixteenth-century: 'renewal of the church in head and members', but without alteration of its essence in dogma, liturgy or discipline.[1]

The diverse Protestant churches embarked on their own lines of development. Belief would in time diverge from the original understanding and place of the devil in the life of the Christian, while the Catholic traditional belief remained unaltered, and doctrinally defined, in this as in other respects.

Ignatius Loyola is generally regarded the representative or even the leading figure in the Catholic Reform, which consisted of an articulation of the original *reformatio* and a reaction to the Reformation tenets. The movement was referred to in less ecumenical times as the Counter-Reformation, as it does suggest an aggressive counter-attack on the other side – and certainly a spate of polemical documents, including the attribution of diabolical characteristics, was part of the weaponry of each. Counter-Reformation could suggest that little reform took place, or little perception of the need for reform, without the challenge of the Reformation.[2]

---

1. Hubert Jedin, 'Catholic Reformation or Counter-Reformation', in *The Counter-Reformation*, David M. Luebke, ed. (Oxford: Blackwell Publishers, 1999), 26.
2. Michael Mullett, *The Counter-Reformation and the Catholic Reformation in Early Modern Europe* (London: Methuen, 1984), 5. Mullett, as the title indicates, believed

Why there should have been a Reformation and a counter movement in the first place is generally seen as having the character of inevitability about it, because of widely recognised ecclesiastical abuses: 'At the beginning of the sixteenth-century everyone that mattered in the Western church', Owen Chadwick said, 'was crying out for reformation'.[3] One of the most prominent of these was Erasmus, whose biting satires did not, however, prevent him from remaining loyal to the church of the time until his death in 1536. A reforming church council, the Fifth Lateran Council, did take place from 1512 to 1518, and though it decreed various reforms, they were overtaken by events with the beginning of Luther's campaign against abuses.

Saint Ignatius Loyola (1491–1556)

Ignatius Loyola was a leading Catholic reformer, but in fact, he first set out to reform himself. Before his death in 1556, the community he founded, the Society of Jesus, had become the very active instruments of the papacy's plan to regain last ground from the communities established by Protestant leaders in sixteenth-century Europe and on into the following centuries. In his native Spain, a reform movement was in train before the beginning of the century. Cardinal Francisco Ximénes de Cisneros (1436–1517) reached prominence when he became Archbishop of Toledo, the Primatial See, in 1495. He undertook a moral and intellectual reform, concentrating especially on clerical formation. His initiative in relation to scriptural studies led to the compilation of the *Complutensian Polyglot Bible* (from *Complutum*, the Latin name for Alcalá, where he founded a university) in Latin, Greek and Hebrew, a process that went on for decades and added a humanist emphasis to the reform process in the church.

His reform would find its counterpart in Italy especially after the ending of the last phase of the Council of Trent in 1563, as the old church marshalled its forces

---

there was a case for the term Catholic Reformation or even simply for 'Reformation' as a comprehensive term for the Christian revival of the late middle ages. See Carlos M. N. Eire, *Reformations: The Early Modern World 1450–1650* (New Haven, CT: Yale University Press, 2016), 393:

> While it is neither necessary nor useful to think of the 'Counter-Reformation' as the only label for early modern Catholicism (a term originally conceived by the German Protestant historian, Leopold Von Ranke, in the nineteenth-century), it is extremely important indeed to acknowledge that the Catholic Reformation did include a certain amount of deliberate reacting to Protestantism, a process of self-fashioning in which the traits of the 'other' were wilfully shunned and countervailing traits were enlivened and given greater definition and prominence.

3. Owen Chadwick, *The Reformation* (Harmondsworth: Penguin Books, 1972), 10.

against the advance of Protestantism. Some special impetus was needed, however, at a pastoral level, and Providence – a designation of God's involvement in the world much used at the time – provided it. Saint Ignatius of Loyola appeared on the scene along with what Henri Daniel-Rops described as the awakening of the Catholic soul.[4]

Early life

He was born to Basque parents in 1491 in the Castle of Loyola, while his father, Don Beltrán, was away fighting in Granada as part of the military campaign recommended by Cisneros to King Ferdinand and Queen Isabella to recover the ancient Christian territory from the Moors. After his mother's early death, his father accepted the invitation of a friend, Don Juan Velásquez, to send his young son to Arévalo to be educated as a Castilian gentleman, in preparation for life at Court. The boy, Iñigo (the name he used as his signature all his life), and his companions in the Velásquez household engaged in sports, music and dance – the Basques were very musical. They were introduced to chivalric literature, especially the novel *Amadís de Gaula*, the love story of the knight Amadís and Oriana (which would become a favourite of the young Teresa of Ávila). Accounts of those formative years, but dating from the last years of his life and written by his closest associates, his successor Lainez, his secretary Polanco and others, all 'give in broad outline the picture of a person who up to the age of thirty led an almost completely worldly life, intent only on his pleasures and ambitions'.[5] This seems a sanitised version of his lifestyle, as Polanco, on the basis of his conversations with the ailing Ignatius, declared more openly:

> Though he was attached to the faith, he lived nowhere in conformity with it and did not avoid sin. Rather he was much addicted to gambling, and dissolute in his dealings with women, contentious and keen about using his sword.[6]

At the age of seventeen, he opted for a military career, in this case against the French, and entered the service of the Duke of Nájera. The war between the France

---

4. Henri Daniel-Rops, *The Catholic Reformation*, Vol. 1, John Warrington, trans. (New York: Image Books, 1962), 91:

> History has vindicated the assessment of Ignatius as a major contributor to the Catholic Reform, despite the opposition of Pope Paul IV to the Jesuit movement. He was known for his anti-Spanish sentiments. He wished to impose on the Jesuits the obligation of the choral office that obtained in the other religious orders and suppressed the clause in the *Constitutions* that the General would be elected for life.

5. James Broderick S.J., *Saint Ignatius Loyola: The Pilgrim Years* (London: Burns & Oates, 1956), 30–1.
6. Cited by Broderick S.J. 45.

of Francis I and the Spain of the young Emperor Charles V entered a new phase in 1521 with a crossing of the Pyrenees by the French in order to recover the former territory of Navarre. At Pamplona they besieged a fortress held by a small garrison under the command of the thirty-year-old Iñigo Lopez of Loyola, whose leg was shattered by a ricocheting bullet. The French officers gallantly arranged for him to be carried in a litter about one hundred kilometres along the rugged roads of Navarre[7] to his birthplace, where after some excruciatingly painful attempts to reset his broken leg, he settled down to recuperate.

But the outlook for a return to a soldiering career was bleak and, as is well known, in his isolation he turned to the sparse collection of literature in the castle, pious treatises, which, rather than nourishing his chivalric dream, introduced him to the saints. They included a Spanish translation of Jacob de Voragine's hagiographical account of the saints in his *Golden Legend* and the four volumes of the *Life of Christ* by the Carthusian, Ludolph, which Cisneros had had translated into Castilian.[8] His dreams of heroism began to divert to imitation of great saints such as Dominic and Francis. He said later in life that 'God was beginning to overcome the devil in my soul'.[9]

He engaged in the discernment of spirits, a spiritual practice going back to the early Christian centuries. In the fourteenth century, its format changed from being a gift of the Spirit to a theological science with rules established by ecclesiastical authority, especially by Jean Gerson.[10] In the case of Iñigo, it is more likely to have been of a charismatic nature, though by his time there would be general awareness of the *alumbrado*[11] issue, making him cautious in his discernment.[12] Discernment of spirits would in fact become the fundamental theme of his *Spiritual Exercises*. He spent his time alone for long periods in his room at the top of the castle,

---

7. Daniel-Rops, *The Catholic Reformation*, 47.

8. Ibid., 48. As part of his rudimentary education, Iñigo apparently learned, but never mastered Castilian, though in later life he wrote various documents in that language, including his *Diary*, which was important for its insights into his spiritual life. See Broderick S.J., *Saint Ignatius Loyola*, 30–1.

9. Daniel-Rops, *The Catholic Reformation*, 48.

10. His doctrine on discernment of spirits was formulated in, among other treatises, *De distinctione verarum visionum a falsis* (1401), *De probatione spirituum* (1415) and *De examinatione doctrinarum* (1423).

11. An *alumbrado* (*alumbrada*) in Spain was a person who gave priority to mystical states of prayer to the extent of neglecting vocal and liturgical prayer. In extreme, heterodox cases, union with God in prayer was believed to be permanent and the person incapable of sin. Only loosely organised as a movement in Spain in the sixteenth and seventeenth centuries, where its members were targeted by the Inquisition, it had an equivalent in Italy, *Illuminismo*.

12. That there was something of both dimensions to his discernment then and later was argued by Fabián Alejandro Campagne, 'Ignacio de Loyola y Teresa de Ávila. Inspectores de Espíritus: Institución y Carisma en los albores da la Era confesional', in *Via Spiritus: Revista de História da Espiritualidade e do Sentimento Religioso* 01/2014, Vol. 21, 111: 'San Ignacio

looking out on the mountains, with competing visions in his mind for days on end. His thoughts went back to the chivalric literature of his early days, how he might devote himself to the service of a lady, the journey he would undertake with all its hazards in order to reach her, the speeches he would make, the feats of arms he would perform, in order to win her approval. Tiring of this he would turn to what he had read of the lives of Francis and Dominic; his aspiration now would be to imitate their heroism and this vision too would fill his mind as he looked towards the mountains, to a world waiting to be evangelised. He came to notice that when he finished engaging in his worldly vision his mood was desolate and restless, while the vision of a life spent in service of the Lord ended with his mind at rest and spiritually uplifted. A new vocation became increasingly attractive, as he took to re-reading and copying the spiritual treatises; a conversion from old ways was occurring, a decision was gradually forming in his mind.

His conversion

His conversion can be seen as a gift from God, a purely spiritual grace, but can also be analysed from a psychological perspective, as has been done by a present-day psychoanalyst, who is himself a member of the Jesuit Order, W. W. Meissner S.J., MD.[13] The traumatic events of Iñigo's childhood – the early death of his mother, the prolonged absence of his father fighting wars, his being sent very young to the Vélasquez household, his military defeat –provide material for psychoanalysis at a distance, and the author admits that lack of detailed knowledge poses a problem for the enterprise. He does not endeavour to explain away the spiritual reality of the conversion, but applies analytical tools to identify the psychological factors of which Iñigo would not be aware. His technical conclusion is summarised in the note below.[14]

Iñigo followed up his discernment and conversion in a radical way by vowing to go as a pilgrim to Jerusalem. He was still dressed in his military attire, riding

---

de Loyola fue un ejemplo acabado de este nuevo intento de reconciliación entre poder institucional y poder carismático: un genuino visionario que, tras haber sido instruido de manera directa por el Sumo Hacedor, aceptó someterse al severo examen de la justicia religiosa ordinaria y extraordinaria.'

13. W. W. Meissner S.J., M.D., *Ignatius of Loyola: The Psychology of a Saint* (New Haven, CT: Yale University Press, 1992).

14. Ibid., 367–8:

> I would offer the ... general hypothesis that in his conversion experience Iñigo abandoned the identification with his phallic, powerful, narcissistic, authoritarian, and domineering father and turned to an equally powerful identification with his passive, vulnerable, pious, religious and idealised mother. ... The pattern of phallic narcissistic masculine identification was in some degree motivated by the need to counter and deny the unconscious but decidedly threatening feminine identification. The tension between these internalised

a mule and accompanied by his brother and two servants, when he set out in late February or early March 1522 for the Benedictine Abbey of Monserrat at the other side of the country. They spent the night at a little shrine, Our Lady of Aránzazu, before he dismissed his companions and went on alone. At Monserrat, he laid his uniform, sword and dagger at the feet of the statue of Our Lady and then gave away the rest of his clothes to a beggar, leaving himself with only a long sackcloth garment he had bought during his journey. From there he went to Manresa and stayed in what was officially a hospital, but was more likely a hostel.

A diabolical vision

He later wrote an account (in the third person) of an incident that occurred during his stay:

> While he was staying in the hospital, it chanced that he often saw in broad daylight something in the air close to him, which gave him much satisfaction, because it was exceedingly beautiful. He could not clearly determine what exactly it was, but it seemed somehow to have the form of a serpent, with many things that shone like eyes, though they were not eyes. He found great delight and consolation in seeing that thing, and the more often he saw it the greater grew his pleasure. Its disappearance from his sight left him discontented.[15]

He reflected after a few days that while his feelings up to then had been consistently joyful, during the period of the visions, 'he was vehemently assailed and troubled in his mind by the thought of the difficulty of his life, as though voices spoke within his soul, saying "How can you possibly endure such a life for the seventy years you have still to live?"'[16] He decided that the question came from the 'enemy'; he conquered the temptation and remained at peace. (The serpent vision continued to trouble him for fifteen years afterwards.) Meissner noted:

> It is tempting to put this apparition in an archetypal context, where the serpent would represent the unconscious libido, the symbolism expressing phallic erotic conflicts.[17]

>> configurations in his internal psychic world would have been maintained in large part by a powerful narcissistic cathexis. When this structure was shaken by the severe narcissistic trauma of his defeat and injury, the masculine pattern of identification could no longer be maintained adequately, some effective substitute had to be found. No surprise that the narcissistic resolution was purchased at the cost of a feminine identification and the substitution of a masochistically tinged submission to the power and will of God.

15. Cited in Broderick, *Saint Ignatius Loyola*, 92.
16. Ibid.
17. Meissner S.J., *Ignatius of Loyola*, 71.

That does make sense at the psychological level, at a depth of which Iñigo would be unaware, but his own interpretation of the vision as a spiritual experience also makes sense, if one accepts that the 'enemy' is real and can manifest itself in the form of psychological processes related to deep-seated needs of the person. This suggestion is all the more persuasive if the devil is not thought of as a person, but a malign force, an issue to be discussed towards the end of this work. Again, the spiritual experience must not be easily explained away.

There were years ahead of him, in which he would prepare to be a soldier of Christ. They began with a pilgrimage to Jerusalem and then involved periods of rudimentary education, gradually progressing to higher levels until he received his master's degree in theology at the University of Paris in 1535 at the age of forty-three, and having changed his name to Ignatius, a more acceptable one in the academic environment than the Basque original. Jesuit authors are not agreed on the stages in which he wrote the *Spiritual Exercises*, but he did have some parts already in a notebook when he stayed in Manresa. That is not surprising because he was very familiar with the contents of Ludolph's *Life of Christ*. 'The sequence of topics contained in Ludolph's *Vita* became the nucleus of Ignatius' thought, which at Manresa he would soon express in his *Exercises*.'[18] However, *The Spiritual Exercises* derived from his personal experience of discernment and conversion rather than from Ludolph's model, useful though that was.[19]

The spiritual exercises

It is a hugely detailed book of instructions for someone who aspires to living the Christian life 'in the service of Christ, the Eternal King', as the First of the Four Weeks puts it. He added 'Rules for the Discernment of Spirits' (an abbreviation of his long title) to the *Exercises*, considering them useful for the First Week. The full title is 'Rules to Aid Us towards Perceiving and Then Understanding, at least to Some Extent, the Various Motions Which Are Caused in the Soul; the Good Motions That They May Be Received, and the Bad That They May Be Rejected'. The Rules were based on his own discernment and have achieved over the centuries a considerable degree of importance as a way to access Ignatian spirituality, though discernment of spirits has always been important in Christianity, inspired, for example, by St Paul's teaching in 1 Cor. 12.10. The word 'motions', according to one commentator, had a particular meaning for Ignatius; when he spoke of motions caused in the soul, he was concerned with 'motions' caused by good or evil spirits for their respective ends.

---

18. George E. Ganss S.J., ed., *Ignatius of Loyola: The Spiritual Exercises and Selected Works* (Mahwah, NY: Paulist Press, 1991), 20.

19. Ibid., 5: 'This small book, begun in 1522, ... reveals much of his personality as well. From 1522 to about 1541, his own spirituality developed side by side with his revisions of and additions to the pages, which were to become the book published in 1548, twenty-six years after its inception.'

Ignatius clearly believed in the existence of angels and devils, and for him the spirits, whether good or evil, are always persons, intelligent beings.[20]

In the Rules, he dealt with consolation and desolation as two opposite motions; consolation included 'every increase in hope, faith and charity, and every interior joy which calls and attracts one to heavenly things' (316).[21] By desolation he meant everything contrary to consolation, 'for example darkness of soul, turmoil within it, an impulsive motion toward low and earthly things, or disquiet from various agitations or temptations' (317). In desolation one should never make a change.

> For just as the good spirit is chiefly the one who guides and counsels us in time of consolation, so it is the evil spirit who does this in time of desolation. By following his counsels we can never find the way to a right decision. (318)

The fall of the angels and the vision of hell

The first exercise of the week includes contemplation of the fall of the angels: 'How they were created in grace and then, not wanting to better themselves by using their freedom to reverence and obey their Creator and Lord, they fell into pride, were changed from grace to malice, and were hurled from heaven to hell' (50). The Week ends with a meditation on hell, without mention of its chief inhabitant. The meditation begins with the composition of place, the length, breadth and depth of hell. The five senses are employed to enable sensory experience: the huge fires and souls within bodies full of fire, the wailing and shrieking and blasphemies against the Lord, the smell of smoke, sulphur, filth and the rotting things – the bitter flavours of hell. 'By my sense of touch, I will feel the flames touch the souls and burn them' (70). This technique, known as composition of place, is used throughout the *Exercises* and is simply the use of the imagination to create an image that is meant to cause a motion (as mentioned above) of the soul.

The fourth day of the Second Week introduces the well-known idea of the Two Standards. The Standard of Satan is presented first, and the composition of place centres on the great plain of Babylon. 'He is seated on a throne of fire and smoke, in aspect horrible and terrifying' (140). The retreatant is asked to consider
how he summons uncountable devils, disperses some to one city and others to another, and thus reaches into the whole world, without missing any provinces, places, states, or individual persons. ... Consider the address he makes to them: How he admonishes them to set up snares and chains; how first they should tempt people to covet riches ... so that they may more easily come to vain honour from the world, and finally to surging pride (141–2).

---

20. Ibid., 424.
21. The Rules are identically numbered in all editions of the text.

The meditation on the Two Standards particularly indicates the essentials of the Ignatian approach. Ignatius' thinking, from the beginning to the end of the *Exercises* and his own life, is dominated by commitment to service, here the service of God under the banner of Christ. The lines of battle are clearly drawn; the enemy is known and identified. He is the devil, the tempter of men, who uses every device, exploits every weakness, and loses no opportunity to attack and destroy the souls of men. No man is secure from his ambushes. His subtlety and trickery are such that he often deceives men into doing evil in the name of good.[22]

That comment by a present-day Jesuit psychoanalyst poses the question whether the 'essentials of the Ignatian approach' apply only to Ignatius himself or are to be considered perennially applicable. This is an important question because unlike statements about the devil attributed to Luther or Calvin, lying unread in history books, the *Exercises* are a text in full use today. Presumably, some clash of cultures occurs on occasion, as retreatants interpret their own life experience and spiritual needs according to their beliefs. Meissner notes that 'the influence of Iñigo's experience is unmistakable here,'[23] indicating a degree of subjectivity, calling for reinterpretation today. He takes up the issue a little later:

We ... note projective elements written into the *Exercises*. ... The exact psychological mechanisms are difficult to pinpoint in this context because Iñigo's allusions were common among the spiritual writers of his day and reflect a long-standing Christian usage. That tradition tends to personify the devil as an actual spiritual force, going about like a roaring lion seeking to devour men's souls. ... Despite this traditional rhetoric, I would argue that projective mechanisms are also at work in this depiction of the spiritual struggle.[24]

Ignatius' mystical visions

Throughout the weeks, there are many references to combating the 'enemy' and this could give the impression that, unlike Teresa of Ávila, he did not enjoy mystical visions.[25] But it must be remembered that the *Exercises* were for beginners, those on a journey of conversion, and not yet capable of mystical union.

---

22. Meissner S.J., *Ignatius of Loyola*, 100.
23. Ibid.
24. Ibid., 106-7.
25. It is worth remembering what a twentieth-century Jesuit, the theologian, Karl Rahner S.J. wrote in his *Theological Investigations*, Vol. 20, Edward Quinn, trans. (London: Darton. Longman & Todd, 1981), 145: 'The Christian of the future will be a mystic or will not exist at all.'

His *Autobiography* corrects any false impressions. There he recorded a number of incidents in which he believed he was favoured with mystical encounters with God or the Virgin Mary. They have the same quality of interior communication and enlightenment typical of Teresa's visions. He was accustomed to pray to the three persons of the Holy Trinity separately and wondered one day why he also thought it right to add a fourth prayer, simply to the Holy Trinity. 'One day ... his understanding began to be elevated so that he saw the Holy Trinity in the form of three musical keys',[26] indicating harmony. On another occasion, God gave him insight into creation. 'He seemed to see something white from which some rays were coming, and God made light from this. He did not know how to explain these things.'[27]

He described these events as visions, and seemed to see something in an internal sense, but he also stressed the element of 'enlightenment' or understanding the visions gave him. This was true especially of a vision he had about five years after the Manresa events, when he was now leader of a small band of companions and they were on their way to Rome to offer their services to the pope. In a small wayside chapel at La Storta, near Rome – it is still there – he was praying to Our Lady, asking her to give him a place with her Son. As he explained to his companions afterwards, he 'experienced such a change in his soul and saw so clearly that God had placed him with Christ, his Son, that he would not dare to doubt it.'[28] Diego Lainez, his close companion since 1534, wrote in 1559 that Ignatius had told him that at La Storta God had impressed upon his heart the words, 'I shall be propitious to you in Rome.'[29]

God was propitious; the religious community Ignatius dreamed of founding received the approval of Pope Paul III in 1539, and the spread of Society of Jesus was rapid in Europe and beyond.

Ignatius suffered greatly from abdominal pains from the beginning of his pilgrim phase and during all his time in Rome (caused by gallstones, an autopsy discovered) and this limited his travels to short trips in Italy. He maintained an extensive correspondence, both administrative and for pastoral counselling. Some of the correspondents were ladies of the same noble families with whom Teresa of Ávila, his younger contemporary, also corresponded.[30] He died in 1556 without ever having returned to Loyola or the Arévalo of his formative years. Eight years after he left to join the army, Teresa was born in Ávila just over fifty kilometres from Arévalo.

26. Ganss S.J., ed., *Ignatius of Loyola (The Autobiography)*, 79.
27. Ibid., 80.
28. Ibid., 96.
29. Ibid., 42.
30. Philip Caraman S.J., *Ignatius Loyola: A Biography of the Founder of the Jesuits* (San Francisco, CA: Harper and Row, 1991), 152.

Saint Teresa of Ávila (1515–82)

Ávila, a walled town about one hundred kilometres north-west of Madrid in the Province of Castile-Leon, was the birthplace in 1515 of Teresa Sánchez de Cepeda y Ahumada, her parents being Don Alonso Sanchez de Cepeda and Doña Beatriz de Ahumada y Cuevas. Her father was a *hidalgo*, a member of the lower nobility, a certain distinction in a highly stratified society. Her grandfather was the son of a Jewish *converso*, a Jew who had converted to Catholicism. As Teresa in her reforming career would be in danger of delation to the Inquisition with its suspicions regarding anyone with Jewishness even remotely in their ancestry, it was fortunate that this fact did not become public in her lifetime, though whether she knew about it is disputed.[31] Teresa was one of twelve children: three sisters and nine brothers, the two eldest being the children of Don Alonso's first marriage.[32]

Early life

In the *Prologue* to her autobiography,[33] an extraordinarily lucid account of her mystical life written at the behest of her confessors, she insisted that her life was 'much more wicked than I am allowed to say'. She made an unfavourable comparison between her life and that of the saints, who once called by God never turned away from him again. This disclaimer, though it has something of a rhetorical flourish, shows that Teresa was very much aware of her human frailty; it made her account of the graces she received a continuous exclamation of wonder at the goodness of God and made the book the very attractive narrative so many generations have enjoyed. The preamble, if not ignored, enables the reader to appreciate the depth and the seriousness of the narrative. It is not simply about distractions at prayer for a woman deeply committed to it; it is about mystical union with God, threatened by the 'world, the flesh and the devil'.[34] Today, the

---

31. Carlos Eire, *The Life of Saint Teresa of Ávila: A Biography* (Princeton, NJ: Princeton University Press, 2019), 2; Rowan Williams, *Teresa of Ávila* (London: Chapman, 1991), 1; See also Francisco de Ribera S.J., *Vida de Santa Teresa de Jesús* (Barcelona: Gustavo Gili, 1908); Alison Weber, 'Saint Teresa, Demonologist', in *Culture and Control in Counter-Reformation Spain*, Anne J. Cruz and Mary Elizabeth Perry, eds (Minneapolis: University of Minnesota Press, 1992), 171–95.

32. Teresa of Ávila, *The Life of Saint Teresa of Jesus*, David Lewis, trans. (London: St Anselm's Society, 1888), I, 6. Mirabai Starr's modern translation, *Teresa of Avila: The Book of My Life* (Boston, MA: New Seeds, 2008), has much to recommend it, but it does not number the paragraphs as David Lewis's and Alison Peers's translations did. The traditional chapter numbers, followed by paragraph number will indicate the references in the text. Cf. Rowan Williams, *Teresa of Ávila*, 1.

33. It remained in manuscript form until after her death.

34. The phrase originated with Peter Abelard, *Petri Abelardi Omnia Opera, Expositio de Symbolo Apost.* PL 178, 617: 'Tria autem sunt quae nos tentant, caro, mundus et diabolus'.

threat to the Christian life envisaged in modern spiritual writing is from the world and the flesh in a secularised and sexualised culture, with the idea of evil somehow subsumed under these two. In contrast, Teresa's writings have many references to the devil.

> The Devil and his minions are named over two hundred times in Teresa's *Complete Works*, not including the references to Lucifer, Satan or his peculiarly Spanish sobriquet, Patillas. The imposing presence of the Devil in the writings of a sixteenth-century nun is not surprising, considering that this was an era of heightened preoccupation with the demonic powers.[35]

A selection of her perceptions of the devil's interference in her life will be given below, including the dramatic 'almost public' events recorded by her in chapter XXXI, and often not mentioned in accounts of her life and mystical visions, probably because they jar with the otherwise elevated spiritual level of the narrative.

As the contemporary phenomenon of the witch-hunt made clear, the common profile of women included a tendency to carnal pleasure combined with less intelligence, so that women were considered likely prey for the devil. The terms *incubus* and *succubus* were common. For women like Teresa, given to the cultivation of mysticism and literary accounts of experience, there was the added hazard of encounters with the Inquisition, whose officials had that perception of women and suspected a priori diabolic influence was involved. Teresa was well aware of this and worried not only about the Inquisition, but also that her visions might come from the devil.

She wrote her autobiography in 1561–2 at the request of her spiritual advisers and as an *apologia* at a time when she feared she would be accused of unorthodoxy. She wrote it in simplicity of heart as an honest record of her spiritual experiences, and would not have realised how profound a discourse it was, though she used no esoteric words, or that it would eventually become one of the great classics of spiritual writing. It was for limited circulation among her advisers and was addressed to one person, a typical phrase being: 'if you, my father approve' (XXII.1).

> The most elemental fact to bear in mind as one reads the *Vida* is that it was written for an authority figure who is never mentioned by name but is constantly addressed throughout the text as 'Vuestra Merced' ('Your Grace' or 'Your Reverence').[36]

The adviser addressed was Fra García de Toledo O.P., of the Dominican community in Ávila, who required her to do so when he became her confessor after she founded, against much opposition, the monastery of Saint Joseph in Ávila. Her

---

35. Weber, 'Saint Teresa, Demonologist', 171.
36. Ibid., 44.

project aroused hostile gossip, raising the possibility that she would be delated to the Inquisition. In fact, however, the Inquisitor, Francisco de Soto, had also been involved in advising her and found no grounds for action against her on reading the text.[37] Though Teresa did not worry about these disturbing comments, and even laughed internally at them (XXXIII.5–7), the tone of her writing was nevertheless supplicatory in places.

> In the case of the expression 'Vuestra Merced', translated variously in English, but never accurately, Teresa's choice of words is revealing, for an exact translation is 'Your Mercy', not 'Your Reverence 'or 'Your Grace'.[38]

She began her autobiography with a tribute to her parents, 'who were devout and feared God'. She had great praise for her father, 'who was much given to the reading of good books' – books in Spanish so that the children might read them. That, combined with her mother's 'carefulness' that the children would say their prayers, led to Teresa being serious about her Christian devotion when she was 'six or seven years old'. Inspired by the accounts of the heroic lives of the saints, she and her older brother, Rodrigo, ran away from home to find martyrdom among the Moors; an uncle happened to meet them and persuaded them that it was not a good idea.[39] Her mother, she said, was a 'woman of great goodness' and 'purity in all her ways', but a woman who suffered much from ill-health all her life, and in fact died very young, when, according to Teresa herself, she was only twelve or less, leaving her grief-stricken. Her father's books were of a serious kind, but her mother had delighted in the novels of the time, tales of romance and chivalry, among them the novel *Amadís de Gaula*, which had also been on the reading list for the young Iñigo de Loyola at Arévalo.[40] As a teenager, Teresa immersed herself in such books. Her father became concerned, not only by this habit, but also because, in her own words, she 'learned every evil from a relative who was often in the house' (II.4).

A twentieth-century female biographer commented on this confession:

> It must be remembered, first, that the woman writing this autobiography, already in her late forties, was writing it uneasily and only as an imposed penance; but, much more importantly, we must remind ourselves that this woman, when she wrote of her past life, was only then emerging, very anxiously, very wearily, and very humbly, at the victorious end of a twenty-five years' struggle of the soul. … An effort of imagination is required of us here. We have to try to conceive

---

37. Williams, *Teresa of Ávila*, 42.
38. Eire, *Saint Teresa of Ávila*, 45.
39. An account of the adventure was given by Francisco de Ribera S.J., *La Vida de la Madre Teresa de Jesús, Fundadora de las Descalças y Descalços*, I. c4., Jaime Pons, ed. and intro. (Barcelona: Gustavo Gili,1908).
40. Kate O'Brien, *Teresa of Ávila* (Cork: Mercier Press, 1951), 21.

how the curiosities, fantasies and sensual experiments of an averagely worldly adolescent might appear to a woman who had fought a severe, long road to the highest and most exacting form of sanctity, and who now, habituated to the beatific vision, believed herself to be the intimate friend of God. It is possible that to one grown so far out of contact with our average human appetites, which once were also hers, those appetites even at their most immature and trivial might seem to her, transfigured before eternity, more shocking, more grotesque and alarming than they could possibly appear to us.[41]

These escapades, involving her cousin, did not last more than three months before her father sent her to a boarding school at an Augustinian convent, not because he thought her wicked, but after her older sister's marriage he did not think she should be in charge of younger siblings. Her time there created mixed emotions; though she 'hated to be a nun' she enjoyed the life of the school, was 'made much of' and greatly admired the nuns for their prudence, observance and recollection. However, at seventeen she became suddenly and seriously ill and had to return to her family home. From there, when sufficiently recovered, her father brought her to stay with her married sister and on the way they stayed a few days with his brother.

> Though I remained here but a few days, yet, through the impression made on my heart by the words of God both heard and read, and by the good conversation of my uncle, I came to understand the truth I had heard in my childhood that all things are as nothing, the world vanity, and passing rapidly away. I also began to be afraid that if I were then to die, I should go down to hell. Though I could not bend my will to be a nun, I saw that the religious state was the best and the safest. And thus, by little and little, I resolved to force myself into it. (III. 6)

Her entry to Carmel convent

But she was subject to fainting-fits and fever, her health 'was always weak'. Encouraged by reading good books, she decided to tell her father of her decision and met strong opposition on his part. She and her brother set out early one morning in 1535, he to become a Dominican friar in Ávila and she to present herself as a postulant at the local Carmelite Convent of the Incarnation. Reluctantly, her father accepted the fait accompli. She was full of joy as she began her religious life, but the demands of the life there, including the change of food, caused a relapse into ill health, and a recurrence of fainting-fits. Her father took her, first to her sister's house and then to a place in the mountains, 'there to undergo treatment by a famous *curandera*, or woman-quack'.[42] She suffered greatly from the treatment, which lasted three months. Her father then took her home in such a condition

---

41. Ibid., 23–5.
42. Ibid., 36.

that her death seemed imminent. It seemed to take place on 15 August 1539, but in the most dramatic of circumstances she came back to life a couple of days later.[43] She was in a terrible state, totally paralysed and in need of constant care, but a few months later she asked to be brought back to the convent, where she made a slow recovery to health. She was cured of her paralysis, she later claimed, by St Joseph (VI. 13), but it took four years for her to return to full observance of convent life. For the rest of her life, however, she suffered from various ailments, such as headaches, fevers and the original fainting-fits.

She came to realise that life in a convent that was not enclosed was doing her harm and would have led her 'straight to hell'. Trying not to be judgemental, she decided that such things as visits from outside might not pose the perils for others that they would for her. Then she had a vision in which Christ sternly warned her about the dangers of friendships with outsiders.

> Christ stood before me, stern and grave, giving me to understand what in my conduct was offensive to him. I saw him with the eyes of my soul more distinctly than I could have seen him with the eyes of the body. The vision made such a deep impression on me that, though it is more than twenty-six years ago, I seem to see him present even now. (VII. 11)

This is the first recorded example of the series of visions central to the story of Teresa and included in her autobiography. Her mystical visions and trances made her the great saint she became, but are not the focus of interest here, except in so far as, at times, her spiritual advisors misinterpreted them as diabolical delusions, leaving her distressed. Interleaved with her account of mystical experiences are incidents when she was examined or even disbelieved by authority, and occasions when she showed great independence of judgement, though, as a woman, she was in a subordinate position to the clerics who were her confessors and guides.

In those first few years after her return to the convent, her observance of the religious life left something to be desired; she abandoned prayer apart from the daily round of community prayer. She wrote in her autobiography about the subtle temptation that afflicted her:

---

43. Eire, in *The Life of Saint Teresa of Ávila*, 15–16, gives and account of the incident:

   > No one could detect any signs of life, and when a mirror was pressed to her nostrils to determine whether or not she was still breathing, the absence of any moisture on the mirror made it seem clear that she was dead indeed. ... Teresa's grieving father could not reconcile himself to the circumstances and insisted, against custom, that her burial be delayed for a day or two. Family members kept vigil next to her corpse constantly, taking turns around the clock. Late on the third night of this vigil, shortly before she was about to be buried, her brother Alonso accidentally knocked over a candle, setting a curtain on fire. During the ensuing commotion, much to everyone's surprise and delight, Teresa gasped for air and sprang back to life.

It was the most fearful delusion into which Satan could plunge me – to give up prayer under the pretence of humility. I began to be afraid of giving myself to prayer, because I saw myself lost. I thought it would be better for me, seeing that in my wickedness I was one of the most wicked, to live like the multitude – to say the prayers I was bound to say, and that vocally: not to practise mental prayer nor commune with God so much; for I deserved to be with the devils and was deceiving those who were about me, because I made an outward show of goodness. (VII. 2)

Tempted by Satan

This was the first of her many references to temptation by Satan, 'a fearful delusion into which Satan could plunge' her, and it was a temptation which anyone in her position might endure, not the typical temptations of later years which were accompanied by psychosomatic symptoms. It was not hypocrisy on her part; as soon as she felt any such temptation, she would feel such pain (spiritual, most likely) that the devil would depart from her 'with loss', leaving her with gain.

Like Ignatius, she gave priority to the virtues of humility and a consequent ready obedience, as the famous incident shows, when her confessor, not believing in the authenticity of her vision of Christ, required her to make an obscene gesture.

> As my visions grew in frequency, one of those who used to help me before –it was to him I confessed when the father-minister could not hear me – began to say I was certainly under the influence of Satan. He bade me, now that I had no power of resisting, always to make the sign of the cross when I had a vision, to point my finger at it by way of scorn, and be firmly persuaded of its diabolic nature. If I did this, the vision would not recur. … This was a great hardship for me; for, as I could not believe that the vision did not come from God, it was a fearful thing for me to do; and I could not wish … that the visions should be withheld. (XXIX. 6)[44]

Chapter XIII was devoted to temptations and the humility needed to deal with them:

> Satan, I believe does great harm; for he hinders those who begin to pray from going onwards, by suggesting to them false notions of humility. He makes them think it is pride to have large desires, to wish to imitate the saints, and to long for martyrdom. (XIII. 5)

---

44. Ibid., 40: 'Dealing with the devil on his own level with obscenities and insults was fairly common in monastic culture, as common as common as the belief that the devil could deceive anyone.'

She obviously had her own history and aspirations in mind, as became clear further on when Satan's temptation that she was ruining her health, in her determination to pursue religious ideals, led her to say to him that her death was of no consequence. She wanted the Cross, not rest. She realised that Satan took advantage of the virtues people had in order to lead them to evil (XIII. 10–12). Going on to treat of instructions for those who had attained the prayer of quiet, she said that they would know whether their state came not from the Spirit but from Satan, because if from him it 'leaves trouble behind, and scant humility, and poor dispositions'. But 'Satan can do little or no harm, if the soul directs to God the joy and sweetness it then feels' (XV. 16).

> The great source of our deliverance from the cunning devices and the sweetness that Satan sends is to begin with a resolution to walk in the way of the Cross, from the very first. (XV. 21)

Several of the following chapters were devoted to states of prayer and the visions that accompanied these states. Her visions can be thought of as the culmination of a life of prayer in which she experienced – if that is the appropriate term – union with God, the highest stage of a person's interior life, which she described in the autobiography:

> In this fourth state, there is no sense of anything, only fruition, without understanding what that is, the fruition of which is granted. It is understood that the fruition is of a certain good containing in itself all good together at once, but this good is not comprehended. (XVIII. 2)[45]

In the course of those chapters, she returned to a former theme, her failure to pray:

> What a proud humility was that which Satan devised for me, when I ceased to lean upon the pillar, and threw away the staff that supported me, that my fall might not be great. I make the sign of the cross this moment. I do not think I ever escaped so great a danger as this device of Satan, which he would have imposed on me in the disguise of humility. (XIX. 15–16)

45. Williams, *Teresa of Ávila*, offered his explanation, 67:

> Up to the fourth and final level, Teresa says, the created subject is still *doing* something, even if it is only registering with wonder the gifts that are being given. In the final stage, we enter upon a prayer in which self-awareness itself is suspended, at least to the extent that, in prayer, it becomes quite impossible to verbalise what is going on, to be in any way distanced from what is happening. This is what she will here call 'union': a fairly natural projection from the way she has been using the term throughout as a gauge of the increasing degree and scope of absorption felt by the mind (or 'soul' or 'spirit' – Teresa declares in XVIII. 2 that she cannot see what the difference really is).

When a soul develops a certain trust and confidence that there is no falling away, Satan, through this confidence, robs it of the distrust that it ought to have in itself (XIX. 22).

Resuming the history of her life, Teresa spoke of the graces the Lord began to bestow on her 'as one, so it seemed, willing to receive them'. Referring, without naming her, to Magdalena of the Cross, who in the course of a serious illness had confessed that her publicised mystical trances had been feigned, Teresa said that she began to be afraid, because 'in these days, women have fallen into great delusions and deceits of the devil'. She, however, had a very deep conviction that God was with her, especially when she was in prayer.

> But if I was a little distracted, I began to be afraid, and to imagine that perhaps it was Satan that suspended my understanding, making me think it to be good, in order to withdraw me from mental prayer, hinder my meditations on the Passion and debar me the use of my understanding. (XXIII. 3)[46]

She knew it was important to conquer fear and came to realise that if her progress in prayer was the work of the Spirit, Satan could do her little harm, and on the contrary must lose in the struggle. A problem arose when she consulted a 'learned ecclesiastic' and his friend, a 'nobleman', to whom she gave what she had written up to then. The two of them came to her and said that the opinion of both was that she was deluded by an evil spirit; the best thing for her to do was to apply to a certain Jesuit. This man, after hearing her confession told her that what was happening in her life was the work of the Holy Spirit. The Jesuits remained her guides and friends thereafter (XXIII. 16–19).

Locutions

From chapter XXIV onwards, she said much about her 'inability to resist the graces of God' and the locutions she received, – words 'very distinctly formed' addressed to her by Christ or the 'Good Spirit' – but she felt it necessary to distinguish these from those that come from an evil spirit. She was confident that she could do so: 'I know by experience in many ways when these locutions come from God' (XXIV. 3). She gave an extensive account of divine locutions before devoting six paragraphs to the issue of Satan's locutions.

---

46. Dyan Elliott 'Raptus/Rapture', in *The Cambridge Companion to Christian Mysticism*, Amy Hollywood and Patricia Beckman, eds (New York: Cambridge University Press, 2012), 197: 'During the thirteenth century there were already incidents in which Satan appeared as an angel of light, or even as Christ, during a female mystic's revelations. William of Auvergne (d. 1249), archbishop of Paris, also raised the possibility of an individual being raptured into evil.'

> Locutions that come from Satan do not leave any good effects behind, but do leave evil effects. This has happened to me; but not more than two or three times. Our Lord warned me at once that they came from Satan. (XXV. 13)

She spoke of the 'sweetness and joy, which Satan gives', after which, 'the soul is never gentle, but is, as it were, terrified, and greatly disgusted'. But it was for her a certain truth that 'the devil will never deceive, and that God will not suffer him to deceive, the soul which has no confidence whatsoever in itself'. If a locution varied 'ever so little' from the Sacred Scriptures, she was convinced that it came from Satan (XXV. 14–17).

After reflecting on her own anxieties, she declared confidently:

> Seeing ... that Our Lord is so powerful, – as I see and know he is, – and that evil spirits are his slaves, of which there can be no doubt, because it is of faith, – and I a servant of this Our Lord and King, – what harm can Satan do unto me? Why have I not strength enough to fight against all hell? I took up the cross in my hand, I was changed in a moment into another person and it seemed as if God had really given me courage enough not to be afraid of encountering all the evil spirits. It seemed to me that I could, with the cross, easily defeat them altogether. So I cried out, Come on, all of you; I am the servant of the Lord: I should like to see what you can do against me. (XXV. 24)

She made a significant comment on her relations with her confessors:

> Do we not know that (Satan) cannot stir without the permission of God? ... I am really much more afraid of those people who have so great a fear of the devil, than I am of the devil himself. Satan can do me no harm whatever, but they can trouble me very much, particularly if they be confessors. (XXV. 17)

The chapters from XXVI to mid-way in Chapter XXX were devoted to the assurances she received that her prayer was the work of the Holy Spirit, assurance too about the visions she had of Christ's sacred humanity, including the transverberation of her body by a sword held by an angel (XXIX. 17). By XXX. 10, however, doubts and suspicions had returned, but she recognised them as the invention of Satan. 'This invention of Satan', she warned her confessor, was 'one of the most painful, subtle, and crafty that I have ever known him to possess'.[47] She interpreted this situation as one in which Our Lord had given him 'leave and licence' to tempt her as he gave him of old to tempt Job. In Holy Week, he tempted her over matters so trivial that in other circumstances it would be laughable (XXX. 12–13).

Throughout the autobiography, she felt that despite her union with God in prayer, the devil was never far off, ready to tempt or delude her. As noted earlier,

---

47. Ch. XXX. 12: 'Es esta una invención del demonio de las más penosas y sutiles y disimuladas, que yo he entendido de él.'

the devil and his minions are mentioned over two hundred times in her works, apart from references to him under other sobriquets. It is difficult to classify the references apart from the obvious category of internal and external appearances. The chapter on the latter, XXXI, offers a striking contrast to everything else in the book by its dramatic visual content. In comparison with the realistic narration of the events in her life, her illnesses, discussions with her confessors, the many temptations in which she sensed the devil internally, and especially her profound description of her visions as real but not perceived with the bodily eye, this chapter exudes an atmosphere of fantasy, uncharacteristic of Teresa. It tends to be ignored in writings about her and her spirituality.

Her own foundation

However, it is true also that the humble, obedient Teresa was a woman with an active imagination – as well as the obvious qualities of energy and determination needed when she set out, in a reforming spirit, to found her own community, the Convent of St Joseph in Ávila in 1562. Her imagination showed also in her depiction of the *Interior Castle*, with its seven rooms or mansions. She even peopled the first two rooms, with demons. The visual presentations or apparitions of the devil in chapter XXXI are very different in nature from her visions, they seem to be external, visible to the bodily eye, even three-dimensional and moving – and they must have some connection with the state of her health.

Just over a century before Teresa wrote her book, there was a report of an apparition of Our Lady to a little girl, in a village called Cubas, about 120 kilometres from Ávila. In 1449, it was claimed that Inés Martínez, a twelve-year-old girl, saw the Virgin six times, from 3 to 19 March. Dressed in gold, the beautiful Lady appeared to the girl while she was herding pigs. On 9 March, Mary took a cross from Inés and planted it to mark the location of her desired shrine, which later became a Franciscan convent. (It survived up to its destruction in the Civil War, but the nuns managed to preserve a full transcription of the documents of the canonical enquiry into the event.) For many years, on the anniversary of the apparition, a procession took place from the town to the rural sanctuary, where the nuns would expose the cross.[48]

It is not possible to establish whether Teresa knew about the Cubas apparition,[49] but the fact that such a tradition existed is a reminder that reports of apparitions were commonplace in sixteenth-century Spain, as William A. Christian has shown in relation to Castile,[50] and came out of, as well as contributing to, the religious culture. The apparitions were almost always of Our Lady. Those not proven to be fake (though possibly the fruit of an over-imaginative temperament) were the

---

48. William A. Christian, *Apparitions in Late Medieval and Renaissance Spain* (Princeton, NJ: Princeton University Press, 1981), 57.
49. Francisco de Ribera S.J., *Vida de Santa Teresa de Jesús*, makes no mention of it.
50. Christian, *Apparitions in Late Medieval and Renaissance Spain*, 100–10.

consequence of a deep faith and devotion, which was in some sense rewarded by God.

An important distinction is needed: Teresa's visions of Christ and Mary were graces received because of her mystical union with God, and apparitions are a different matter; the whole tenor of her life's narrative indicates that her visions were of a different order from apparitions. They were internal events, not involving the eyes of the body, not the kind of eyewitness to details of clothing that was typical of apparitions. She mostly saw light and detected the divine presence.[51] But Teresa must have felt the influence of the religious culture that was her heritage. This was not the same as the chivalric culture that fascinated her as a girl, but rather more a cultural background to the life of the rural population, and had, no doubt, superstitious elements within it. Because of the seriousness of her spiritual quest, she differed from her contemporaries, who were prone to seeing apparitions, and sometimes, at least, had their claims ratified through investigation.[52]

The devil's appearances

In her case, she had no need of apparitions, and the temptations by the devil, which plagued her all her life, were real and internal. It seems odd that they might on occasion have taken the form of an apparition, but did so according to chapter XXXI.[53] She distinguished between interior, secret temptation and almost public temptations and troubles. More accurate, perhaps, would be a distinction between interior temptation and external troubles, as the appearances of the devil she described were in fact more troubles than temptations, annoying interruptions of her schedule of prayer, and sometimes frightening. The fears of the devil she shared with the population generally, her ailments and her lively imagination, may have been significant factors in these events.

---

51. The vision she had while at Mass in the church of St Thomas (XXXIII. 16), might seem more like an apparition: She saw herself clothed with a garment of excessive whiteness and splendour; she did not see at first who was putting it on her, but then realised it was Our Lady and St Joseph. ('La vestían una ropa de mucha claridad y blancura. No veía al principio quién se la vestía; pero después vió que Nuestra Señora de la parte derecha, y de la izquierda el glorioso San José, eran los que se la ponían.') But the mystical dimension became clear: she understood that she was cleansed from her sins.

52. Christian, *Apparitions in Late Medieval and Renaissance Spain*, 204: 'Validation was itself in the hands of the town government and clergy. ... New grace threatens no one. ... Hence the inquiries that have come down to us of early Spanish visions [sic] were not primarily investigations, but rather ratifications.'

53. Eire, *The Life of Teresa of Ávila*, 82: 'The devil plays a key role in Teresa's *Vida*, but only as a foil to the power of God and to Teresa's confidence in her closeness to God. Her visions of demons are numerous and often detailed, but each and every one of them is an occasion for victorious struggle.'

> I was once in an oratory, when Satan in an abominable shape, appeared on my left hand. I looked at his mouth in particular, because he spoke, and it was horrible. A huge flame seemed to issue out of his body, perfectly bright, without any shadow. He spoke in a fearful way, and said to me that, though I had escaped out of his hands, he would yet lay hold of me again. I was in great terror, made the sign of the cross as well as I could, and then the form vanished – but it reappeared instantly. This occurred twice. I did not know what to do; there was some holy water at hand; I took some and threw it in the direction of the figure, and then Satan never returned. (XXXI. 1)

(Later in this work, the issue of whether a devil can speak will be considered in the context of exorcism rites, and a negative conclusion drawn.)

Her way of depicting the devil was in accord with ancient tradition, but her visual image also has affinity with the artistic style of artists like her near contemporary, El Greco (1541–1614), who in his famous painting of Philip II, *Alegoria de la Liga Santa*, included a gaping hell mouth behind him, unseen by Philip.[54] The baroque period which followed shortly after El Greco was one of 'pictorial hallucination, bleeding crosses, fantastic battles filling the air, magic, possessed women'.[55]

On another occasion, the situation in which she experienced the devil's presence was a period of five hours in which she suffered 'terrible pains, inward and outward sufferings'. Obviously, it could have been a case of the pains being at the origin of the perceived diabolical visitation rather than the other way round – the psychosomatic element in her internal suffering cannot be ignored, though it is only from a materialistic perspective that her mystical experiences can be discounted, as they have so often been.

> [When] I found myself suffering so cruelly, I relieved myself by making these [interior] acts and resolutions, in order that I might be able to endure the pain. It pleased Our Lord to let me understand that it was the work of Satan; for I saw beside me a most frightful little [dark creature] gnashing his teeth in despair at losing what he attempted to seize. When I saw him, I laughed and had no fear. (XXXI. 3)

(One could speculate as to whether she knew of Antony of Egypt in his day seeing a similar black figure.)

There were others present, helplessly watching her body, head and arms violently shaking and could do nothing about it. She did not ask for holy water, as this would reveal the nature of her trouble.

---

54. See E. C. Graf, 'The Devil's Perspective in El Greco's "Alegoria de la Liga Santa", San Juan de la Cruz's "Cántico Espiritual" and Cervantes's "La Numancia"', *Romance Notes*, vol. 53, no. 1 (2013): 54.

55. Robert Muchembled, *History of the Devil: From the Middle Ages to the Present*, Jean Birrell, trans. (Cambridge: Polity Press, 2003), 130.

> I know by frequent experience that there is nothing which puts the devils to flight like holy water. They run away before the sign of the cross also, but they return immediately: great then must be the power of holy water. As for me, I am conscious of a special and most distinct consolation whenever I take it. (XXXI. 4)[56]

At length, she asked the others to bring holy water and sprinkle her with it, which they did, but her pains continued. She took some and threw it herself in the direction of the creature, who then disappeared. On another occasion, she asked for holy water when the devil had gone, and the two nuns who brought it 'perceived a most offensive smell, like that of brimstone. I smelt nothing myself, but the odour lasted long enough to become sensible to them'. (XXXI. 5)

> At that time, too, I thought the evil spirits would have suffocated me one night, and when the sisters threw much holy water about, I saw a great troop of them rush away as if tumbling over a precipice. These cursed spirits have tormented me so often, and I am now so little afraid of them – because I see they cannot harm me without Our Lord's permission. (XXXI. 9)

The nuns perceiving a most offensive odour, and Teresa not, indicates a quite extraordinary phenomenon, beyond any empirical explanation. Otherwise, the apparitions of the devil in physical form would seem an example of hallucinations on Teresa's part.

As her story unfolded in chapter XXXI and subsequent chapters, it became an account of struggles within herself, rather than from outside, regarding her place in the community – how she was regarded, and her assessment of herself – until in chapter XXXII she recorded a vision she had of hell. She understood that it was the Lord's will to show her the place the devils kept in readiness for her, and which she had deserved for her sins. The physical pains she had endured through life were as nothing compared with what this vision brought her.

> I was placed as it were in a hole in the wall; and those walls, terrible to look on of themselves hemmed me in on every side. I could not breathe. There was no light, but all was thick darkness. (XXXII. 5)

Her final success

This clearly psychosomatic experience seems to have been the climax of a long struggle going on within her in relation to life in the community, a fundamental discontent with life hemmed in by the mitigated Rule observed there. It occurred

---

56. 'De muchas veces tengo experiencia que no hay cosa de que los demonios huyan más para no tornar. De la cruz también huyen, mas vuelven luego. Debe ser grande la virtud del agua bendita.'

to her, and to others, 'that it was possible to find means for the foundation of a monastery, if we were prepared to become nuns like those of the Discalced Orders' (XXXII.13). She had a vision of Our Lord, who commanded her to labour with all her might for this end. Her struggles now became the external ones caused by those opposed to the idea, and there was only occasional reference to the devil – she did see his hand in the situation when there was talk that she might be brought before the Inquisition.

As this struggle went on, with approval by the authorities being given and then withdrawn, appeals to Rome and support from powerful people, she remained content and did not even speak of the project for 'five or six months'. In chapter XXXVI. 4, she was able to record how with 'full sanction and authority ... our monastery of our most glorious father St Joseph was founded in the year 1562'. Litigation had been involved and continued after their occupancy, causing, in Teresa's view, confrontation with Satan. She promised before the Blessed Sacrament to do all in her power to ensure permanence and make a vow of enclosure.

> When I had done this, the devil fled in a moment, and left me calm and peaceful, and I have continued so ever since. (XXXVI. 9)

This was twenty years before her death; she embarked on a successful programme of foundations in the intervening years, convinced that this was for the good of the Church, and did so with extraordinary physical energy despite her poor health. It is evident throughout Teresa's account of her life that she, like Ignatius, had serious medical problems, and it is tempting to consider what would happen if she lived now rather than then. Modern medical practice could both diagnose and treat her ailments without great difficulty. Today's psychotherapy would probably also have a role, without either discipline being in a position to adjudicate on her spiritual progress. Such speculation is less inappropriate than that which has also taken place in modern times. For some, reading texts has concentrated on diagnosing possible temporal lobe epilepsy or other neuropathological conditions, missing the point by trying to explain away the spiritual realm.[57]

Teresa wholeheartedly accepted the Church's teaching and authority with regard to every detail of her life. She thought of herself as a great sinner, and therefore constantly under the threat of being led astray by Satan, whom she perceived, as did everyone else, as the enemy prowling around like a lion seeking whom he might devour (1 Pet. 5.8). It may be that only one with such severe assessment of self as she had could find the determination to set out on a path towards the discovery of God's mercy and love, leading to mystical union with God in prayer. Mediocrity has been the more common lot of the Christian, though some consolation is available to anyone who reads the text – and finds Teresa too great a challenge. The medieval concept of *medietas virtutum* describes the state of virtue the ordinary

---

57. See Eire, *The Life of Saint Teresa of Avila*, 182–6, for an account of this type of speculation.

person reached through relying on the support of the communal adherence to the basic tenets of the faith and their liturgical enactment. There has always been a leaven of chosen souls in the community to encourage the faint-hearted and provide the challenge of higher aspirations for the strong. Teresa of Avila and Ignatius Loyola may be seen as chosen souls raised up by God's Providence at a critical time of challenge to the community's adherence to the faith.

Saint John of the Cross (1542–91)

Early life

This Carmelite Friar, whose name would always in later years be associated with that of St Teresa, was born at Fonteviros near Ávila, when Teresa was in her teens. His father, Gonzalo de Yepes, himself parentless, was the nephew of rich silk merchants, whose business he managed, but he was disowned by them when in 1529 he met and married a girl, Catalina Álvarez, also parentless, but without means, who worked as a weaver in Fonteviros. Gonzalo had to have recourse to weaving also, and their living was a poor one. 'The house was humble, its furniture, such as there was, plain, the food none too plentiful.'[58] They had three children, Francisco, Luis and John. Tragedy struck when Gonzalo died shortly after the birth of John. Now destitute, Caterina decided to travel with her children – John still an infant to be carried – the hundred miles to the Province of Toledo, where Gonzalo's reasonably prosperous relatives lived. The visit did not go well; at Gálvez, she left Francisco with his uncle, a doctor who promised to care for him, and trudged back to Fonteviros with the other two to resume her penurious way of life as a weaver. (A year later, she went back to Gálvez to bring the ill-treated Francisco home and train him to work with her.)

Luis died, probably from malnourishment, and she moved with Francisco, now a young adult, and John, in search of work to Arévalo, the town where Ignatius had spent his formative years. There John received basic education at a school for poor children. When he was nine, the family moved again, this time to Medina del Campo, twenty-four miles away, a busy commercial centre of about 30,000 inhabitants, where his mother and Francisco and a girl who had joined them in Arévalo, worked at their trade. In all these towns of his early years, the family lived in Islamic neighbourhoods.[59] John attended a Catechism School, served Mass at an Augustinian Convent and was taken on as a messenger at a local hospital. When he was seventeen he began to study the humanities at the Jesuit College in the town.

---

58. Crisógono de Jesús O.C.D., *The Life of St John of the Cross*, Kathleen Pond, trans. (New York: Harper Brothers, 1958), 3.

59. Antonio T. de Nicolás, *St John of the Cross: Alchemist of the Soul* (New York: Paragon House, 1989), 19.

His entry to a Carmelite monastery and encounter with Teresa

Four years later, he entered the newly endowed Carmelite monastery at Medina and after profession was sent to the Carmelite monastery in Salamanca for biblical studies at the University. After ordination in 1567, he became attracted to the more solitary life of the Carthusian Order,[60] but while visiting Medina he met Teresa, who was there to establish a community of her newly established Order of Discalced Carmelites, the first since her foundation of the monastery of St Joseph in Ávila. John and Teresa were clearly like-minded, and under her influence in 1568 he also founded a new branch of the Carmelite friars at Duruelo in Segovia – in a derelict house and farm which had been donated to Teresa. There he took the name John of the Cross.[61]

He maintained close contact with Teresa until her death, and spent five years, 1572–7, at her convent in Ávila, though in that period, he visited various communities he had founded. He sometimes travelled with her to her convents, and also began his writings. His best-known literary output include the poems *Spiritual Canticle, Dark Night of the Soul* and *The Living Flame of Love*. The *Ascent of Mount Carmel* was a study in ascetical theology. Among his Minor works, there were communications of spiritual guidance and ten Romances on theological topics.

The interest here is to establish how much impact the existence of the devil had on his life. Unlike the considerable amount known in Teresa's case, what there is in the life of her friend, John, has to be inferred mostly from his writings; he left reminiscences, mostly verbal, but no autobiography. There have, however, been numerous biographies beginning with one in 1595 by a friar who had been appointed an annalist. But it was not regarded with favour by the authorities. Others followed up to 1873, and in 1888 one composed by David Lewis from the various previous ones. Modern authoritative biographies include *Vida de San Juan de la Cruz* (Madrid, 1955, to be quoted below) by Crisógonó de Jesús O.C.D., for which the author claimed to have had access to all primary MS sources, and *San Juan de la Cruz* (Barcelona, 1980) by Gerald Brenan.

His first exorcism

In Ávila, he was confessor for the nuns, who were quite numerous. At some time in 1573, he became involved in a remarkable incident that occurred in an Augustinian

---

60. Ibid., 44: 'If Fray John was thinking of exchanging the Carmelite Order for the Carthusian straightaway, considering his studies in Salamanca finished, he must have kept his intention secret from his superiors. Otherwise, after the conversation with St Teresa, it would not have been easy for him to return to the university.'

61. Daniel A. Dombrowski, *St John of the Cross: An Appreciation* (Albany: State University of New York Press, 1992), 38: 'John of the Cross was persuaded from joining the Carthusians by Teresa of Avila herself, who had, as a spiritual mother, adopted the much younger John of the Cross, if only to work him to the bone for the rest of his life in the work of the reform.'

Convent outside the walls. There was a young nun there, about twenty, who had come to the convent at the age of five. Without any further education, she proved to be a wonderful expositor of the Scriptures, with many from outside coming to hear her. The Superiors began to be uneasy and called in theologians from Salamanca University to assess her. They returned a verdict that her spirit was good and her wonderful knowledge infused. Nevertheless, suspicion remained and it was decided to ask Fray John to intervene. He at first refused, then thought better of it and consulted the Inquisition in Áquila. The officials gave him permission and he then crossed the city to the Convent for the first of many visits. He began by meeting her in the Confessional and after an hour announced to the community and officials that she was possessed. He was asked to exorcise her and did so in visits once or twice a week for several months.

> At the first exorcism, Fray John made the possessed nun confess that she had handed herself over to the devil when she was six years old, the year, that is, she entered the convent. The contract was made solemnly. The child drew blood from one of her arms and with it wrote a script in which she testified that she was giving herself to the devil for ever.[62]

The dramatic events that followed formed a pattern well known in such situations, one exchange being of particular significance. Asked by Fray John to translate the words, *Verbum caro factum est et habitavit in nobis'*, she responded at once: 'The Son of God became man and lived with you.' He objected that the words do not say 'with you' but 'with us', and the nun replied: 'It is as I say, for he did not become man to live with us, but with you', leaving those present in no doubt that Lucifer was speaking through her mouth.[63] The devil sought revenge for the ongoing exorcism by a ruse:

> One day, two discalced friars came to the turn (the revolving hatch) saying they were Fray John and his companion. They wore the same habit, had their physical features and spoke in the same tone of voice. They came, as was usual, to talk with the possessed nun. The turn-sister informed the nun and the latter went to the confessional. When she came out, she was in despair.[64]

This was, of course, noticed and Fray John was sent for. He came at once and exorcised her once more. This occurred during the months in which the extended exorcism was taking place.[65]

---

62. Ibid., 81.
63. Ibid., 83.
64. Ibid., 82.
65. Gerald Brenan, *San Juan de la Cruz* (Barcelona: Editorial de Laia, 1980), 36: 'Presumiblemente perdió también su anterior familiaridad con las Sagradas Escrituras. Su éxito en éste y en otros casos de posesión diabólica le dieron una gran reputación en

Another case of a possessed nun occurred on the vigil of the Feast of the Holy Trinity while Fray John was in Ávila. He began an exorcism in the afternoon and interrupted it to go the Vespers of the Vigil, and the nun went also. When at the beginning, the choir began to sing the doxology to the Trinity, the possessed nun was lifted into the air, and left hanging upside down. Fray John commanded the devil, in the name of the Trinity, to return her to her place and she was immediately restored a normal position. When Vespers were finished, the exorcism continued 'until the nun was freed'.[66] During those years Fray John was continually in combat with the devil and suffered accordingly.

Assaults by the devil

On another occasion, he told Fray Francisco that the devils treated him so badly that he did not know how he remained alive; his confrère knew that on some nights when he was in bed ' the devil would rip off the bedclothes, leaving him in his under-tunic in the terrible cold of a winter's night in Ávila.'[67]

As the tradition from the time of Augustine held that the devil could not physically assault a person, it seems preferable to look for some other explanation of these occurrences: nightmares, perhaps! Accounts of St Teresa's diabolical encounters did not include physical assaults.

Imprisonments and escapes

Harassment by the devil was not the only opposition he endured. There was much opposition from the members of his former community, especially as the new way of life led to several foundations, still under the authority of the Father General, but different in their observance of the Carmelite tradition. As the founder of the new, Discalced male Carmelites, John was targeted by the Calced branch and was twice imprisoned by them. In the first incident he was kidnapped by the Calced in early 1576 and taken to their community in his home town of Medina. He was freed after a brief period by the intervention of the Papal Nuncio, Ormaneteo. During his second detention, in a Carmelite monastery in Toledo for almost a year,[68] he was kept under very harsh conditions and yet, with paper smuggled to him by a sympathetic friar composed part of his most famous poem *Spiritual Canticle*. He was then thirty-six and very malnourished.

---

la ciudad; las monjas de la Encarnación, que eran testigos de su austeridad, lo tenían por santo.'
    66. Crisógóno de Jesús, *The Life of St John of the Cross*, 83.
    67. Ibid., 84.
    68. Brenan, *San Juan de la Cruz*, 204.

He escaped in August 1578 and was nursed back to health by Teresa's community in Toledo and by a stay in hospital.[69] From then on, he continued to promote Carmelite reform and with others petitioned Rome for a separation from the existing Order and to be constituted as the Discalced Carmelite Order. While conflicts continued, he was able to establish new communities until his early death at forty-nine.

References to the devil throughout his writings

In *Ascent of Mount Carmel*, Book II, chapter 11 (II. xi.) he dealt with supernatural knowledge reaching the intellect by way of the exterior bodily senses. It was not to be relied upon.

> He who esteems these apprehensions is in serious error and in danger of being deceived or at least he will hinder his spiritual growth. ... These manifestations ought always to be considered diabolical more certainly than divine. For the devil possesses greater leeway in influencing the exterior and corporal part of man. He can deceive the soul more readily through this action than through a more interior and spiritual kind. (II. xi. 3)

In II. xxi, he dealt with people's desires for revelations and locutions, and the dangers involved.

> [The devil] imparts facsimiles of God's communications so that, disguised among the flock like the wolf in sheep's clothing, his meddling may be hardly discernible. Since the devil through conjecture makes many reasonable manifestations that turn out to be true, people may be easily misled, thinking that the revelations must then be from God. These people do not realise the ease with which the devil, with his clear natural light knows, through their causes, many past or future events. (II. xxi. 7)

In succeeding paragraphs he gave examples of the devil's knowledge of the future, not only in a natural way but also because 'supernatural events can be known in their causes' – the devil can observe God's Providence. He concluded:

> The devil can learn and foretell that Peter's life will naturally last only a certain number of years. And he can determine many other events through such various ways that we would never finish recounting them all, nor could we even begin to explain many because of their intricacy and the devil's craftiness in inserting lies. One cannot be liberated from him without fleeing from all revelations, visions, and supernatural communications. (II. xi. 11)

---

69. Carlos M. N. Eire, *Reformations: The Early Modern World 1450–1650*, 370: 'Had he not escaped in August 1578, in the dark of night, he might not have survived.'

Chapter XXVI was devoted to the knowledge of pure or 'naked' truths, the intellectual understanding or vision of truths about God. It is a knowledge that can be received only by a person who has arrived at union with God, 'for it is itself that very union'. 'It is so sublime and lofty that the devil 'is unable to meddle or produce anything similar'.

> He could, nevertheless, in his apery and in an effort to persuade the soul that its experience is from God, proffer to it a certain sensory feeling of grandeur and fulfilment. But this diabolical communication does not enter the substance of the soul and renew and enamour it as does a divine touch. (II. xxvi. 6)

He could expand, he said, a great deal on the deceptions the devil can and does with regard to this kind of knowledge. The devil could implant clearly, but falsely, knowledge of the sins of others, in order to have it made known publicly to bring about defamation and distress, something he said of which he had much experience (II. xxvi. 17).

In *The Dark Night of the Soul*, after each stanza of the poem there is a Book consisting of several chapters of commentary. Book I, deals with the imperfections of beginners.[70] The stanza speaks of the soul's departure from love of self and of all things. This departure is described as a 'dark night'.

Book I, chapter IV, treated of lust as a spiritual imperfection proceeding from spiritual things – in spiritual exercises, impure movements or rebellions experienced in the sensory part of the soul. This can happen especially at the time of Communion, when the soul receives joy and gladness, and the sensory part takes its share.

> The second origin of these rebellions is the devil. To bring disquietude and disturbance on a soul when it is praying, or trying to pray, he endeavours to excite impure feelings in the sensory part. And if a person pays any attention to them, the devil does him great harm. Some souls, through fear, grow slack in their prayer – which is what the devil wants – in order to struggle against these movements, and others give it up entirely, for they think that these movements come when they are engaged in prayer rather than at any other times. (I. iv. 3)

Book II dealt with the night of the spirit, commenting towards the end on stanzas 2 and 3 of the poem. Chapter II dealt with habitual and actual imperfections, the first being the natural dullness everyone contracts through sin, and a distracted and inattentive spirit, 'the stains of the old man lingering in the spirit'. 'The spirit must be illumined, clarified and recollected by means of the hardships and conflicts of this night.' The actual imperfections affect those who receive abundance of spiritual communications and apprehensions in the sensory and spiritual parts of their souls.

---

70. Colin Thompson, *St John of the Cross: Songs in the Night* (London: S.P.C.K., 2002), 202.

This is the stage in which the devil induces many into believing vain visions and false prophesies. He strives to make them presume that God and the saints speak with them, and frequently they believe their fantasy. It is here that the devil fills them with presumption and pride. Drawn by vanity and arrogance, they will allow themselves to be seen in exterior acts of apparent holiness, such as raptures and other exhibitions. They become audacious with God and lose holy fear which is the key to and guardian of all virtues. (II. ii. 3)

Book II. xxiii. 2 commented on the fourth line of the stanza, 'In darkness and concealment', the soul's hiding place, which the devil cannot reach.

> The reason the darkness of this contemplation frees and hides the soul from the wiles of the devil is that the contemplation experienced here is infused passively and secretly without the use of the exterior and interior faculties of the sensory part of the soul. (II. xxiii. 2)

But the devil can become aware that the soul is receiving very interior and secret communications, because of the quiet state they produce in the sensory part. So he does everything possible to disturb the sensory part, 'which he can affect with sufferings, horrors and fears'. But the devil's assiduity in disturbing the soul is often to no avail.

> [When] the spiritual communication is not bestowed exclusively on the spirit, but on the senses too, the devil more easily disturbs and agitates the spirit with these horrors by means of the senses. The torment and pain he then causes is immense, and sometimes it is ineffable. (II. xxiii. 5)

In a rather strange explanatory process, the combat between the good angel and the devil in relation to communications to the soul was the subject of II. xxiii. 6. God permits the devil to recognise favours granted through the good angel so that the outcome of a struggle between the two will mean a more abundant reward for the victorious and faithful soul. A certain parity between the two spirits is assumed.

This estimation of the devil's status was given in more detail in the *Spiritual Canticle*. The 'wild beasts' of stanza 3 are first of all the 'world'. (Here John used the same triad as Teresa in *Autobiography*, ch. 23, the world, the flesh and the devil).

> She [the soul] calls the devils, the second enemy, 'strong men', because they strive mightily to entrap her on this road and because, too, their temptations are stronger, and their wiles more baffling, than those of the world and the flesh, and, finally, because the devils reinforce themselves with these other two enemies, the world and the flesh, in order to wage a rugged war. ... The prophet Job ... remarked concerning this strength that there is no power on earth comparable to that of the devil. Only the divine power is sufficient to conquer him and only the divine light can understand his wiles. (*Stanza* 3. 9)

Stanza 24 says

> Our bed is in flower
> Bound round with linking dens of lions.

> In this state the soul is so protected and strong in each of the virtues – and in all of them together while at rest upon this bed in flower of union – that the devils not only fear to attack her, but they do not even venture to appear before her. For they become greatly frightened on seeing her so exalted, courageous, and bold, with the perfect virtues in the bed of her beloved. When she is united with him in transformation, they fear her as much as they do him, and they have not even the courage to look at her. The devil has an extraordinary fear of the perfect soul. (*Stanza* 24. 4)

The final Stanza says:

> No one looked at her
> Nor did Aminadab appear;
> The siege was still
> And the cavalry
> At the sight of the waters, descended.

The name Aminadab here, as in several places in St John's Works, is to be understood as referring to the devil, as the modern commentary, based on early manuscripts indicates:

> In Sacred Scripture, Aminadab, speaking spiritually, symbolises the devil, the soul's adversary. He endlessly combated and disturbed her with the countless ammunition of his artillery to prevent her entry into this fort and hiding place of interior recollection with the Bridegroom.[71]

In his life, St John felt the impact of the devil in different ways. There seem to have been assaults on his person and he felt the pressure of the diabolic presence when he exorcised the afflicted. These encounters were, however, external signs of the internal combat with the devil in the soul, about which he wrote in such detail as to indicate that he was testifying to evidence gained from his personal experience or from his spiritual direction of nuns. How much came from his personal struggle to

---

71. St John of the Cross, *The Collected Works of St John of the Cross*, Kieran Kavanagh O.C.D and Otilio Rodriguez O.C.D, trans. (Washington, DC: ICS Publications, Institute of Carmelite Studies, 1979), 564; See also Gerald Brenan, who quotes John's own commentary, *San Juan de la Cruz*, 199: 'El nombre Aminadab aparece tres veces en la Biblia: primero en Éxodo, 6.23, en una lista de genealogías; luego en el Cantar de los Cantares, 6.12, y por último en Mateo, 1.4, en la genealogía de Jesucristo, donde figura equidistante entre

reach mystical union despite all the obstacles the devil put in his way is obviously not known, but there is the question of how else he could have had such detailed knowledge. The fact that he lived a life of extreme austerity is a clue that he felt the need to be always on his guard against yielding even to the most trivial of moral laxity. Yet he does not seem to have been obsessed with the challenge evil posed. While there is much about the devil in the Works already quoted, there are two treatises written at the request of others that do not mention the devil at all – though they do treat of human weaknesses. *The Spiritual Canticle. Beyond the Dark Night* he wrote at the request of Sister Ana de Jesús in 1584 and *Love's Living Flame* was for Dona Aña de Peñalosa.

Abraham y David. La cita en el Cantar de los Cantares, según la Vulgata, es: Nescivi: anima mea conturbavit me propter quadrigas Aminadab.' See also Terence O'Reilly, 'The Figure of Aminadab in the Writings of St John of the Cross', in *Humanism and Religion in Early Modern Spain. John of the Cross, Francisco de Aldana, Luis de Leon* (London: Routledge, 2022), 116–22.

Chapter 8

THE DEVIL IN THE ERA OF MODERNITY: POETRY AND LITERATURE IN A NEW AGE

Christopher Marlowe (1564-93)

Persistent belief that the devil was active was true of Elizabethan England when Christopher Marlowe was born in Canterbury in February 1564, two months before the death of Calvin in April, and the birth of William Shakespeare that month. The Catholic restoration under Queen Mary had been reversed, but much of the old culture remained. During the rise of the reform movement in the 1530s, a promoter of the Protestant faith, Hugh Latimer, sometime Bishop of Worcester, was a noted preacher. He preached a sermon before the Convocation of Clergy about 1537 (reprinted soon after execution in 1555) in which he said that the 'children of this world' had an evil father and an evil grandfather, the devil, whom he could not adequately describe.

> I wot not what to call him, but a certain thing altogether made (of) hatred of God, of mistrust in God, of lyings, deceits, perjuries, discords, manslaughter heaped up and made of all kind of mischief. This alonely I can say grossly and as in a sum ... the devil to be a stinking sentine of all the vices; a foul, filthy channel of all the mischief.[1]

The Elizabethan Age

By 1558, the religious upheavals of the previous decades had consolidated the English version of the Reformation, with Elizabeth I (r. 1558-1603) firmly in charge - though of a people with divided religious loyalties, as Eamon Duffy has clearly established.[2] Her conservative mind favoured a religion of rituals with little outward change from the Catholic past, including a hierarchical structure not only supportive of monarchy, but including it, as the monarch was the supreme

---

1. Hugh Latimer, *Sermons by Hugh Latimer, Martyr 1555*. Parker Society, G. Corrie, ed. (Cambridge: Cambridge University Press, 1844), 42.
2. Eamon Duffy, *The Stripping of the Altars: Traditional Religion in England 1400-1580* (New Haven, CT: Yale University Press, 1992).

governor of the church,[3] while a radical reforming group looked to Geneva and a more congregational polity. The England into which Marlowe was born was one in which continental influence on religious thinking went hand in hand with the politics of defensiveness against the great powers of Europe, an unstable situation that would break down into religious and political strife in the following century. As John Bossy remarked about the continent's Reformed doctrines: 'Perhaps we should think of them as spores secreted in a Christian culture, guaranteed to produce mushrooms at a certain temperature.'[4] Marlowe received the new humanist education in which the classics dominated, but the emphasis was on reconciling Christianity in its Anglican formulation with classical learning, and thus one in which Scripture, following the lead of Desiderius Erasmus, was given great prominence.

Understanding Marlowe

From the fact that Marlowe was being sought by the authorities at the time of his death on charges of atheism, which at that time meant dissent from church teaching, it appears that he had become a critic of Scriptural doctrines and Anglican orthodoxy, and this may explain the circumstances of his violent death during a row in a tavern. Speculation about him was prompted by his interest in the magic arts, his spying for the Elizabethan authorities, allegedly heretical views, proclivity for brawling and even possibly same-sex interests, the last of these because of his references to homosexual relationships in his plays, *Edward II*, *Dido* and *The Massacre*. A specialist in Marlowe studies, Emily C. Bartels, contributed to the speculation with the assertion:

> As a spy, possibly an associate of the freethinking School of the Night (if it existed), probably a homosexual, and certainly a playwright, Marlowe was alienated within his society and demonized by accusations that are now well known.[5]

But her biography was in the historical context of England's nascent imperialism as the title incorporating 'Imperialism' showed, creating an image of him from a perspective more political than biographical or literary. The reality seems more elusive.

---

3. Eamon Duffy, *A People's Tragedy* (London: Bloomsbury Continuum, 2020), 89: 'In her early years, Elizabeth was very conscious of being a Protestant queen of a still pervasively Catholic people. "Softly, softly" was her motto in religious matters and she distrusted anyone or anything that might rock the ship of state.'

4. John Bossy, *Christianity in the West: 1400–1700* (Oxford: Oxford University Press, 1985), 110.

5. Emily C. Bartels, *Spectacles of Strangeness: Imperialism, Alienation, and Marlowe* (Philadelphia: University of Pennsylvania Press, 1993), 11.

> In truth, we know little about Christopher Marlowe's life. ... Given the paucity of information about (him), his biographers inevitably draw heavily on contextualising his life within the late Elizabethan world or drawing inferences about Marlowe from his plays and poems. ... In particular, what the majority of his biographers understandably succumb to is a tendency to allow Marlowe's life to attain a significance that few of his contemporaries likely held it possessed.[6]

During his brief life, he was both revered and reviled.

> 'Wit sent from heaven, but vices sent from hell' was how one contemporary summed him up, simplistic reaction, but perhaps a typical one.[7]

His significance as a playwright, despite the future dominance of his contemporary, Shakespeare, was vindicated in subsequent centuries, and his influence can probably be seen in the late nineteenth-century play, *The Picture of Dorian Gray*, by Oscar Wilde, where Faustian themes are clearly present. On seeing his finished portrait, Dorian Gray lamented that he would grow old and horrible, while the picture would always remain young and he wished it were only the other way.

> For that – for that – I would give everything! Yes, there is nothing in the whole world I would not give! I would give my soul for that.[8]

Gray had come under the influence of a hedonistic older friend, Lord Henry Wotton, whose conversation evoked the cleverly cynical remarks of Marlowe's Mephistopheles. After some time, he fell in love with a young actress, but cruelly rejected her. That evening he went home and his eye fell on the portrait. There was no doubt that the whole expression had altered. Suddenly he remembered what he had said the day the portrait was finished.

> He had uttered a mad wish that he himself might remain young, and the portrait grow old, that his own beauty might be untarnished, and the face of the canvas bear the burden of his passions and his sins.[9]

Word reached him the next day that she had committed suicide. By using the story of the portrait, Wilde devised a very imaginative way to describe the gradual

---

6. Thomas Healy, 'Marlowe's Biography', in *Marlowe's Biography in Context*, Emily Bartels and Emma Smith, eds (Cambridge: Cambridge University Press, 2013), 334.

7. Charles Nicholl, ' "Faithful Dealing": Marlowe and the Elizabethan Intelligence Service', in *Marlowe, History, and Sexuality: New Essays on the Life and Writings of Christopher Marlowe*, Paul Whitfield White, ed., Studies in the Renaissance (New York: AMS Press, 1998), 1.

8. Oscar Wilde, *The Picture of Dorian Gray* (Harmondsworth: Penguin Books, 1962), 33.
9. Ibid., 103.

descent into evil of the Faustian legend. In the text, a denizen of an opium den that Gray frequented described him as the 'worst one' that came there: 'They say he has sold himself to the devil for a pretty face.'[10] Wilde may have had Marlowe's version in mind; the text refers to a visit by Gray with the painter to Marlo, probably the present-day Marlow.

Marlowe's 'Doctor Faustus'

Marlowe's play was very familiar to Victorian critics of the 1880s. They judged that

> in recounting the story of an educated unbeliever, who sold his soul to the devil, the author achieved a mature perspective on his own excursion into free thought. As an intellectual, he identified with the protagonist, as a Christian he repudiated him. The precise balance of his sympathies remained an open question and this supplied an infinite quantity of grist for the mills of interpretation.[11]

The tendency for literary criticism to draw inferences about him from his work can be fruitful, particularly in the case of his *Doctor Faustus*, where the diabolic holds centre stage and may throw light on the author's view of the devil as much as on the reasons why he himself was demonised by society. In Marlowe's time, the Calvinist doctrine of predestination was a disputed issue in England, and especially in Cambridge where he studied, as Puritanism's adherence to the doctrine met with opposition from mainstream Anglicanism. The Puritan interpretation of the play was that Faust's fate was inevitable, while others considered that interpretation repulsive. An analysis by James Ross Macdonald of the play in terms of the diabolic theme raised the issue of what he described as the contrast between 'the Calvinist conception of the devil as a mental tempter in Faustus's interactions with Mephistopheles and the "popular" notion of him as a physical tempter that characterises the low-comedy subplots.'[12] This contrast, insofar as it reflected Marlowe's actual intention, does throw light on the diabology of the day; educated people like Marlowe probably did have a less primitive image of the devil than others, but it would also be true that, as in the case of Calvin himself, both the mental and physical understandings must have been part of society's outlook. Marlowe in fact played on the susceptibilities of his audience by introducing the prince of devils at one point, but only briefly. The prince of devils appears in a form

---

10. Ibid., 213.
11. David Riggs, 'Marlowe's Quarrel with God', in *Marlowe, History, and Sexuality: New Essays on the Life and Writings of Christopher Marlowe*, Paul Whitfield, ed., Studies in the Renaissance, vol. 35, 17. (New York: A.M.S. Press, 1997).
12. James Ross Macdonald, 'Calvinist Theology and "Country Divinity" in Marlowe's "Doctor Faustus"', *Studies in Philology*, vol. 111, no. 4 (Fall 2014): 824.

described by Faustus as 'looking so terrible' (719).[13] He remains the mysterious power of evil controlling all its terrestrial manifestations, while allowing many scenes in the play to adopt a comic, even slapstick, character as Faustus and Mephistopheles, both invisible travellers through the world, indulge in pranks on the Pope at his banquet (887–909).

That he chose to write a play about Faust could be explained by a variety of reasons: his esoteric interests, or the fact that Calvinist predestinarian theology was a topic of the day, or even more obviously because a book of interest to a playwright had become available in English, *The English Faust Book* (an abbreviation of the original title), a translation of the original German story. His *Dr Faustus* depends on this book, though with many omissions yet often literally, and draws on the fantasies surrounding the life and doings of the legendary character. Marlowe's interest in magic provided material for the career of Dr Faustus.

Mephistopheles

Of principal interest here is Marlowe's treatment of Mephistopheles, the devil who appears in answer to Faustus's appeal (lines 254–60) and is to be distinguished from Satan or Lucifer, the prince of devils.[14] Mephistopheles is the first in a new line of devils that will appear in literature, including the homonymous character in Goethe's *Faust,* Satan in Milton's *Paradise Lost* and Philip Traum in Mark Twain's *The Mysterious Stranger*. Apart from *Paradise Lost*, the devil will appear in human form, as in the case of Marlowe's devil, who is told by Faustus that he is too ugly to attend on him and is required to return as an 'old Franciscan friar. That holy shape becomes a devil best' (260–1).

It emerges straight away that Mephistopheles is not his own master but a servant of Lucifer, as other devils will be in the course of the play. Mephistopheles is an ambivalent character. When he explains that he is one of the unhappy spirits who fell with Lucifer and are 'forever damned' with him in hell, Faustus asks how it is that he is out of hell. Mephistopheles replies:

> Why, this is hell, nor am I out of it.
> Thinkest thou that I, who saw the face of God
> And tasted the eternal joys of heaven,
> Am not tormented with ten thousand hells
> In being deprived of everlasting bliss? (317–21)

His ambivalence shows itself when despite his role of luring Faustus towards damnation, he does not hesitate to describe the terrors of hell that would await

---

13. Christopher Marlowe, *Dr Faustus* (The A Text), David Ormerod and Christopher Wortham, eds (Nedlands: University of Western Australia Press, 1985), Line 719. Further number references refer to lines of the text.

14. Marlowe, *Dr Faustus*.

him there, if he made a pact with Lucifer. When about to make his pact, Faustus asks what good will it do to do so and why Lucifer tempts him. Mephistopheles quotes in Latin the adage: 'It is a consolation to the wretched to have companions in misery' (483).

Faustus is the protagonist of Marlowe's play, but the dialogue shows Mephistopheles as no less central and it reveals much about him. His exchanges with Faustus show him to be capable of anticipating his victim's train of thought as well as recognising his ambitions. Whether the play's audience would be led by this to greater conviction about the existence of both Lucifer and his disciples cannot be known, but the play would hardly have been the success it was without a popular conviction that it reflected life. Marlowe's own ambition may have been to comment on the people of his day, the credulity that existed in relation to magic, the self-aggrandising tendency of the people who had shrugged off the norms and outlook of medieval Catholicism. When Mephistopheles refuses to answer Faustus's direct question, 'Who made the world?' (698), there could be a hint that for Marlowe and for at least some of his contemporaries this was now a question to be asked in light of the new understanding of the universe that was emerging with the questioning of the old Ptolemaic theory – the nature of the universe is in fact one of Faustus's questions.

Society's acceptance of the devil's existence

Marlowe's life and play, and the culture of his day, can assist in assessing the extent to which Satan was a reality for that society. At first glance, given that the culture was officially Anglican, with its inheritance of Luther's theology, belief in the devil could be taken for granted, though Marlowe's own views cannot be established with certainty. In the play, good angels and bad angels appear, giving Faustus contrasting exhortations, with the result that he oscillates between fear of eternal punishment and rejection of a life after death. When Mephistopheles asserts that hell has no limits, he retorts 'Come, I think hell's a fable' (574). It has been claimed that the bad angel is speaking for Marlowe himself, as a way of expressing his dismissal of an afterlife. According to his contemporary, the playwright Thomas Kyd, who once shared a room with him, he used to 'gybe at praiers' and 'jest at the devine scriptures'.[15] Belief in the devil was not necessarily linked with the widespread practice of magic, which had its own tradition going back to writing attributed to a Hermes Trismegistus – hence hermetic magic. An interest in magic, the investigation of secret powers in nature, was common among those dedicated to emerging empirical science, perhaps including Marlowe, and could even be a

---

15. Paul H. Kocher, 'Viewpoints', in *Twentieth Century Interpretations of Doctor Faustus*, William Farnham, ed. (Englewood Cliffs, NJ: Prentice Hall, 1969), 103.

threat to religious belief, especially belief in the devil, as magical explanations were sought for mysterious phenomena in nature.[16]

But magic could also be seen in a different light, as linked with the activities of the devil, and in fact in the sixteenth century the magic arts were more often seen as under the control of the devil, which led to belief in what was known as witchcraft and consequently to the witch-hunt. Official documents, the institution of the Inquisition, books such as the *Malleus Maleficarum* (1486) by Sprenger and Kramer, all testify to how much of a threat to society the belief in witchcraft was seen to be, belief that continued through the sixteenth century and beyond. People charged with witchcraft were believed to have made a pact with the devil in order to be given extraordinary powers, malevolent or benevolent, but mostly the former. The sad story of the witch-hunt reached its height in the sixteenth century in Europe and the late seventeenth in America in the infamous Salem trials, and caused the death of many innocent people. The extremes to which witch-hunts led finally brought about the end of those trials as common sense prevailed. Much of the evidence was now seen to the products of diseased or even malevolent minds.[17]

The preternatural

In the age of modernity, empirical science was affected by the decline of Aristotelianism with its world view based on causality and certainty, and a clear distinction between the spiritual and the corporeal as articulated by Aquinas. While science sought certainty, it was faced with experimental findings, or at least claimed results, that remained puzzling and a challenge to Aristotelian physics. An interest in Platonism and Neoplatonism's concept of 'world-soul' (going back to Plato's *Timaeus*) grew, as it allowed greater room for the existence of occult forces, including demons.

A zone called the preternatural, between the natural and the supernatural, became recognised even by empirical science, as explanations were sought for the age-old phenomenon of magnetism. Awareness of this zone was sufficiently powerful to give rise to an art or science around 'demons', no longer clearly Mephistophelian disciples of Satan, but some kind of preternatural forces with malevolent powers. The result was a belief in 'demonology' in the sixteenth and on

---

16. Jeffrey Burton Russell, *Lucifer: The Devil in the Middle Ages* (Ithaca, NY: Cornell University Press, 1984), 293: '[The] new magical world of the fifteenth and sixteenth centuries revived a natural view of the occult, and offered occult explanations within a highly sophisticated and coherent intellectual system. Many early modern "scientists" such as Ficino and Giordano Bruno (*c*. 1548–1600) were really magicians in this sense.'

17. Diarmaid MacCulloch, *A History of Christianity: The First Three Thousand Years* (London: Allen Lane, 2009), 686: 'Maybe forty or fifty thousand people died in Europe and colonial North America on witchcraft charges between 1400 and 1800, most noticeably from around 1560.'

into the seventeenth century, at least. It had little foundation in scriptural doctrine relating to Satan, rather more in ancient pagan beliefs and practices.

Seventeenth-century demonology

The concern was with the hidden forces of nature, which produced storms that destroyed crops or property or sudden outbreaks of disease in people or livestock, phenomena that could have a natural explanation but for simple people could be the work of demons, if they were not a punishment from God. Science continued to investigate nature, gradually moving the boundary between nature and the preternatural in favour of establishing natural laws, but even when the proximate causes of climatic events, for example, were established, for a demonologist a doubt could remain as to whether there was beyond them a more remote cause, the action of a demon. In seventeenth-century France, the physician Albert Kyper (1614-1655) assured the readers of his *Institutiones physicae* 'that many things are done in this world by the force of demons which we in our ignorance attribute to natural causes'.[18]

However, in England a contemporary physician, John Webster (1610-1682) paid tribute to the work of members of the Royal Society for advancing the boundaries of science into the territory of the hidden laws of nature and to gradual curtailment of the preternatural:

> [They] plainly evince that hitherto we have been ignorant of almost all the true causes of things, and therefore through blindness have usually attributed those things to the operation of Cacodemon that were truly wrought by nature and thereby not smally [sic] augmented and advanced this gross and absurd opinion of the power of Witches.[19]

Webster was a contemporary of the poet John Milton.

Puritanism and de-sacralisation of the culture

If Calvin had a high theology of the Holy Spirit and the church, as is evident in the *Institutes*, the subsequent development of Reformed Christianity, precisely because of the centrality of the subjective act of faith, led to a de-emphasising of the rites of the church apart from baptism (without exorcisms) in which the saving act of

---

18. Albert Kyper, *Institutiones physicae* (Lugduni Batavorum: apud Adrianum Wyngaerden et Franciscum Moiardum, 1745), Preface, cited in Mark A. Waddell, *Jesuit Science and the End of Nature's Secrets* (Farnham: Ashgate, 2015), 31.

19. John Webster (1610-82), *The Displaying of Supposed Witchcraft Wherein It Is Affirmed That There Are Many Deceivers and Impostors* (London: Printed by J.M., 1677), 268.

Christ was sealed. Faith as a response to the Word, and the internal witness of the Spirit, formed the basis for a theology of covenant with God. This in turn created a world view in which the Christian had an autonomous status and took on a responsible role in the world's affairs, answerable in the end to God's judgement. This theology and world view helped to establish a new religious culture, freed from the medieval dependence on rites, a state which can be described as secularisation or de-sacralisation of the culture – the term used by Carlos Eire 'to isolate those conceptual factors in Protestantism that created a culture decidedly uneasy with the mixing of heaven and earth or the sacred and the mundane'.[20] This would be typical of the Puritan understanding of religion, which emerged in seventeenth-century England and was in conflict with the established Anglican Church, leading to the Civil War and the temporary triumph of Oliver Cromwell's Commonwealth.

John Milton (1608–74)

As a Puritan, Milton flourished during the period of Cromwell's Commonwealth, but with the return of the monarchy at the Restoration (1660) he belonged to a dissident and often persecuted minority. Puritans had a 'this world' approach to spirituality, as seen, for example, in Bunyan's *Pilgrim's Progress*, yet Milton chose to emphasise the unseen world of Satan's campaign against humankind, in what appears to be a subtle anti-monarchist motive.

Satan the hero of Paradise Lost?

n *Paradise Lost* (1647),[21] Milton's approach supported the reversal of the trend towards hominisation of the devil that was evident in Marlowe's play. Satan is then the construct of a poet's imagination as well as a reflection by a Puritan Christian on the biblical witness and on seudepigraphic sources, such as *1 Enoch*.[22] In the

---

20. Carlos Eire, *Reformations: The Early Modern World 1450–1650* (New Haven, CT: Yale University Press, 2016), 748: 'As used here, the term desacralization refers strictly to paradigm shifts within the Christian religion itself. More specifically, it refers to the way Protestantism redefined the realm of the sacred and numinous and realigned the relation between creation and the Creator.'

21. *Poetical Works*, Douglas Bush, ed. (London: Oxford University Press, 1966). The numbers here, VII.24-5, refer to lines of the poem in Book VII of the twelve books. Further quotes from the poem will be be indicate by Book and line.

22. Grant McColley, 'The Book of Enoch and Paradise Lost', *Harvard Theological Review*, vol. 31, no. 1 (January 1938): 24: 'The first fact which develops from comparative analysis of I Enoch and Paradise Lost is that, with the possible exception of Genesis, there is no single book in the Old or New Testaments or in apocryphal or pseudepigraphic literature, in which are concentrated more conceptions fundamental to Milton's epic.' Of the branch of the Pseudepigrapha known as the Hexamera, Michael Patella, *Angels and Demons: A*

course of his developing narrative, especially in *Paradise Regained*, he may depart significantly from the scriptural text. His authorship of *Paradise Lost* (1667) is usually deemed to belong to his anti-monarchist writing and reflect his own experience of being a fugitive, though he was finally included in the Act of Pardon. This flight may have influenced his invocation of the muse Urania in Book Seven:

> More safe I sing with mortal voice, unchanged, To hoarse or mute, though fall'n on evil days. (VII, 24-5)[23]

It has been suggested that his personal history influenced his portrayal of Satan. This is an important issue, the question of whether his description of God is poetically less impressive and whether God or Satan is the protagonist in the poem. It may be that Milton was opposed to Charles II and was influenced by anti-monarchist sentiments when speaking of God.[24] There are flaws in how he depicts God: for example, when God introduces his Son to the heavenly court and the rejoicing leads 'from dance to sweet repast':

> Tables are set, and on a sudden piled/ With angels' food and rubied nectar flows/ In pearl and diamond, in massy gold/ Fruit of delicious vines, the growth of heav'n. (V, 632-5)

God is 'the empyreal host' (5, 584) and the comparison with Olympus is obvious. Divine laughter in the poem has a somewhat ambiguous nature. Laughter at humanity's quaint opinions 'when they come to model heav'n and calculate the stars' (8, 79-80) makes God rather condescending towards human scientific endeavour, though the laughter in heaven at the efforts of the builders of the tower of Babel is a clear reference to Ps. 2.4.

> Among the Builders; each to other calls
> Not understood, till hoarse, and all in rage,
> As mockt they storm; great laughter was in Heav'n. (XII, 57-9)

Christian Primer of the Spiritual World (Collegeville: Liturgical Press, 2012), 109, says: 'Of these two versions on the origin of evil beings, the Hexamera becomes the more popular and is, in fact, the basis of the great English epic poem, *Paradise Lost*.'

23. John Milton, *Poetical Works*, Douglas Bush, ed. (London: Oxford University Press, 1966).

24. Nathan Johnstone, *The Devil and Demonism in Early Modern England* (Cambridge: Cambridge University Press, 2006), 235: 'In a pamphlet justifying the execution, John Milton overturned Charles' claim to theocracy. Theocratic power was, by definition, exercised for God or for the devil. Royal power that was not exercised to the "terror" of evil was not of God, but "of the Devill, and by consequence to be resisted".' Citing John Milton, *The Tenure of Kings and Magistrates* (London, 1649), 15-16.

Milton does seem, as one commentator remarks, to allow in the course of the conflict that Satan has the best laugh, but God has the last laugh.[25] One has to wait for the beginning of *Paradise Regained* (*PR*)[26] for a denouement: there Milton acknowledges the victory of God (the Son):

> by one man's firm obedience fully tried,
> Through all temptation and the Tempter foiled
> In all his wiles defeated and repulsed. (*PR* I. 3–6)

William Blake and Percy Bysshe Shelley

William Blake (1757–1827), like Milton, was a critic of the Anglicanism of his day and was to an extent influenced in his rationalist approach to religion by the Enlightenment. In his lapidary comments on religion, he neatly described the tensions he believed Milton must have felt in composing *Paradise Lost*: 'The reason Milton wrote in fetters when he wrote of Angels & God, and at liberty when of Devils & Hell, is because he was a true Poet and of the Devil's party without knowing it.'[27] Blake anticipated the emergence of the Romantic Movement, which was beginning with poets like Percy Bysshe Shelley (1792–1829) and will be discussed below. Shelley, in the introduction to his *Defence of Poetry* began the re-evaluation of Milton's Satan, which was to become a major theme for discussion by the critics.

> Nothing can exceed the energy and magnificence of the character of Satan as expressed in *Paradise Lost*. It is a mistake to suppose that he could ever have been intended for the popular personification of evil. ... Milton's Devil as a moral being is far superior to his God, as one who perseveres in some purpose, which he conceives to be excellent, in spite of adversity and torture. ... Milton has so far violated the popular creed (if this shall be judged to be a violation) as to have alleged no superiority of moral virtue to his God over his Devil.[28]

The issue becomes one of whether Satan is really the hero of *Paradise Lost* and therefore embedded in English culture at a time when science continued to make inroads on a belief system that still officially recognised the old order embracing both heaven and hell in their traditional roles.

---

25. T. A. Birrell, 'The Figure of Satan in Milton and Blake', in Anon., *Satan* (London: Sheed and Ward, 1950), 385.

26. John Milton, *Poetical Works*, Douglas Bush, ed. (London: Oxford University Press, 1966). *Paradise Regained* is also in this work, in four Books. Quotations by book and line.

27. William Blake, *The Marriage of Heaven and Hell: In Full Color* (New York: Dover Publications, 1994), 30.

28. Percy Bysshe Shelley, *A Defence of Poetry* (Indianapolis, IN: Bobbs Merrill, 1904), 64.

Maximilian Rudwin, a twentieth-century specialist in the European traditions of the fantastic in literature, as related in particular to various manifestations of the devil, concluded that 'it is generally agreed that the hero of *Paradise Lost* is none other than Satan'.[29] However, neither his nor Blake's comment was fair to Milton, who never fully departed from his Puritan orthodoxy, but it does reflect how he depicts Satan as a warrior from the beginning.

John D. Shawcross summed up the history of this depiction of Satan as hero:

> The reading of Satan as the hero of John Milton's *Paradise Lost* has had a long history. The view of the Romantics like William Blake and Percy Bysshe Shelley and later commentators has often been cited, and we are aware of the statements of John Dryden, Charles Batteux, and William Godwin preceding them.[30]

Samuel Johnson (1709-84)

The critical attitude of Samuel Johnson towards the poem was presumably influenced by the fact that he was himself a conservative Anglican and opponent of Puritanism. Johnson acknowledged Milton's genius:

> Nature had bestowed upon him more bountifully than upon others the power of displaying the vast, illuminating the splendid, enforcing the awful, darkening the gloomy, and aggravating the dreadful.[31]

But his overall assessment was that:

> The reader finds no transaction in which he can be engaged, beholds no condition in which he can by any effort of imagination place himself; he has, therefore, little natural curiosity or sympathy. ... The want of human interest is always felt. *Paradise Lost* is one of the books the reader admires and lays down, and forgets to take up again.[32]

Johnson's judgement that the 'want of human interest is always felt' could well have sprung from an aversion to the dramatic *persona* of Satan and from the rationalist spirit that was already prevalent in England. He did not share the view

---

29. Maximilian Rudwin, *The Devil in Legend and Literature* (Chicago: Open Court Publishing, 1931), 14.

30. John T. Shawcross, 'An Early View of Satan as Hero of Paradise Lost', *Milton Quarterly*, vol. 32, no. 3 (1998), 104–5.

31. Samuel Johnson, *Lives of the English Poets* (Oxford: Oxford University Press, 1961), 123.

32. Samuel Johnson, *Life of Milton* (1779), 73 in http://www.umsl.edu/~gradyf/2310/miltonrep1.htm#:~:text=The%20plan%20of%20Paradise%20Lost.

that Milton had in mind the world of his own day, the clash between Puritans and Royalists represented in allegory by the struggle between Satan and God, 'Heavn's awful Monarch' (IV. 960). In history, the 'monarch' had the victory in the end.

Milton does treat Satan as a warrior bloodied but unbowed, who is introduced at the beginning of the poem as defeated but resolute in his determination to resume the battle. He discerns, 'weltring by his side one next himself in power and crime, Beelzebub.' Breaking the 'horrid silence', he addresses him:

> What though the field be lost?
> All is not lost; the unconquerable will
> And study of revenge, immortal hate,
> And courage never to submit or yield. (I. 114–15)

Beelzebub in turn responds to his prince, his chief 'of many throned powers' (I, 78–128), lamenting that their strength undiminished and their eternal being serves only to undergo eternal punishment. To which Satan replies:

> To do aught good will never be our task.
> But ever to do ill our sole delight. (I. 159–60)

This dialogue gives the impression that Satan is to be seen as the protagonist in the narrative, but C. S. Lewis, in his *A Preface to Paradise Lost*, held that Milton would not have agreed with those who regarded him as the hero, but that

> Milton has chosen to treat the Satanic predicament in the epic form and has therefore subordinated the absurdity of Satan to the misery which he suffers and inflicts.[33]

According to Lewis, it would be a mistake to hold that, for Milton, Satan 'should be able to rant and posture through the whole universe without, sooner or later, awaking the comic spirit'.[34]

The succeeding books of the poem show Satan as a powerful leader who says, 'I give not heav'n for lost' (2, 14) and begins his campaign against God's other creation. In Book IX, through entering in the form of a mist into a serpent, he has achieved his object of seducing mankind and in Book X returns to receive the acclaim of the 'Stygian throng' but instead is greeted on all sides with 'a dismal universal hiss, the sound of public scorn'. An anthropomorphic note enters as he feels his visage and arms alter, 'his legs entwining each other, till supplanted down he fell, a monstrous serpent on his belly prone' (X, 824). This together with references to divine laughter creates an overall impression of a figure belonging to

---

33. C. S. Lewis, *A Preface to Paradise Lost* (London: Oxford Paperbacks, 1960), 95.
34. Ibid.

this world as well as to the 'dungeon horrible' and 'darkness visible' and 'furnace flamed' to which he and his companions had been cast down (1, 62–3) and not really a hero, even if unbowed and determined to continue the conflict. If like Dante's Lucifer, he has in some sense lost the battle, Milton's Satan is a force to be reckoned with in the world of human affairs.

Satan's dismissal

However, literary evidence as well as the chronicle of the eighteenth century show that awareness of the devil was transformed, as the thinkers of what became known as the Enlightenment brought all religion before the bar of reason. The Enlightenment came as a challenge to the religious orthodoxy of the Protestant culture that dominated Europe for centuries. Its rationalistic critique of religion meant that all of the Christian tradition including the text of the Bible had to be submitted to the judgement of reason in accordance with the scientific progress of the day. Such empiricism quickly ruled out the existence of Satan. But the repression of a fundamental instinct for belief resulted in a resurgence of belief expressed in a more disguised way in literature, simply as a mysterious human – always male – in the plots of plays and novels.

Johann Wolfgang Goethe (1749–1832)

Goethe was born into a Lutheran family, but was decidedly a freethinker, who felt himself under the influence of fate and the gods, and once described himself as 'not anti-Christian, nor un-Christian, but most decidedly non-Christian'; orthodox Christian beliefs were 'blasphemies against the great God and his revelation in Nature'.[35] He was in effect a Deist, yet his version of the Faust legend, *Faust*, opens with a dialogue between God and Satan, based on the Book of Job, This sets the tone for Faust's dealing with a spirit Goethe calls Mephistopheles, who presents himself as a travelling scholar,[36] though really the devil called up by Faust's incantation and 'part of the darkness which brought forth light', an enemy of creation. He admits to his limitations, unable, for example, to cross the Pentagram at the threshold of the room – though by Goethe's time this once Christian design had become an ambiguous symbol. Faust recognises from the beginning that Mephistopheles is the devil and makes a pact with him.

---

35. Nicholas Boyle, *Goethe: The Poet and the Age*, vol. 1, *The Poetry of Desire (1749–1790)* (Oxford: Oxford University Press, 1991), 353.
36. Goethe, *Faust. A Dramatic Poem*, A. Hayward, trans. (London: Edward Moxon, 1834), 53

Mephistopheles a composite figure

Goethe presents Mephistopheles as a composite figure derived from the age-old devil myth of pagan and Christian culture, and this allows him to range widely in behaviour and identity from posing as Faust in an interview with a student to taking part in a witches' coven in the Harz Mountains. He sometimes presents himself as Satan and sometimes as Satan's disciple.

> Mephistopheles is much too complex, diverse, and ambiguous to be identified with the Christian Devil. Goethe gladly used and developed the myth, but he always vehemently denied the literal existence of the Christian devil.[37]

Throughout the play Mephistopheles is Faust's constant companion, leading him to the love affair that will finally undo him, while in Marlowe's play the frequent appearance of a good and a bad angel signals opportunities for Faust to repent and adds complexity to the narrative when he muses on this possibility.

Goethe and the Enlightenment

Goethe's play, which is as much concerned with evil as Marlowe's, reflects the interests of Enlightenment thinkers such as Voltaire, who called for compassionate treatment of poor girls guilty of infanticide.[38] A girl, Margaret, had been seduced by Faustus and had drowned the child of their union. She was arrested and condemned to death, and in the final part of the play, Faust sets out to free her with the help of Mephistopheles. But she refuses to flee with him and the play ends with her death and salvation as a voice calls from heaven, while Mephistopheles says she is 'judged' and to Faust 'Hither to me'. Faust is led away to his fate.

Goethe had centred his version of the Faust legend on one man's tragic search for total satisfaction in a way of life characterised by sensuality, but in a previous publication, *Die Leiden des jungen Werthers* (1774), Goethe had published a supposed collection of letters by a young man who had committed suicide out of despair over his hopeless love for a married woman, a work that to an extent must have influenced his *Faust*.

The concentration on unrequited love (and perhaps Goethe's own unhappy experiences) could be regarded as the beginning of a cultural movement with its own literature that was developing in reaction to the Enlightenment culture in Germany and in France in the late eighteenth century. What might be called the mechanisation of the world through industrialisation and urbanisation, planned economies and emerging consumerism, was the fruit of the Enlightenment's culture

---

37. Jeffrey Burton Russell, *Mephistopheles: The Devil in the Modern World* (Ithaca, NY: Cornell University Press, 1986), 158.

38. Voltaire had written a Commentary on the work of the philosopher Beccaria against the laws that condemned to death poor young women guilty of infanticide.

of progress, based on submitting everything to the judgement of reason. Material progress was the key concept; the sense of personal identity and individuality, the whole realm of experience with its emotions, artistic sensibility, awareness of the beauty of the world, had to be subordinated to the march of progress. The Romantic Movement was a reaction to this; it included an idealisation of women and an embrace of isolation and melancholy.

The Romantic Movement

The beginning of Romanticism, as the new culture came to be called, was encapsulated in the work of Jean-Jacques Rousseau (1712–78), who wrote a book on the education of children, *Emile*. In it he railed against the rigidities of adult life and proposed the freedom of the child as a new norm for living. In England, Romantic love, as distinct from the typical calculating approach centred on dowries and family fortunes, found its expression in the poetry of Wordsworth and Coleridge published in the collection, *Lyrical Ballads* in 1798, and may have marked the start of the movement there.

Victor Hugo's 'La fin de Satan'

How all this affected belief in God and the devil was real yet subtle. The new idea of progress, especially for Victor Hugo (1802–85) was to release the spirituality latent in the universe. He conceived a plan for an immense epic poem to assert 'the immanence of spirit and of good and the objective non-existence of matter, which is the cause of evil'[39] – thereby showing a tendency towards Manicheism. By the time he worked on the poem, he had come to believe that evil itself did not exist, evil was a 'transitory hypothesis'; when people came to understand the nature of things, evil would disappear. From analysis of social evils, he moved to the metaphysical. In its cause and in its essence, which was nothingness, it was a mere absence of divine light. This void he called Satan. The objective non-existence of Satan would become clear when revolution would abolish social evils, but in the meantime, there was need for a myth that led people to a new understanding of reality. The title of the poem, which remained unfinished at his death, was 'La fin de Satan'.[40]

The poem echoes Milton's portrait of Satan but with the fundamental difference that it involves soul-searching, so to speak, on Satan's part and his sense of being rejected by the cosmos, though he loves the God who rejected him. A feather falls from the wing of this ruined angel and becomes a beautiful angel called Liberty, showing that even within Satan's rebellion there is a sign of a return to future

---

39. Paul Zumther, 'The turning-point of Romanticism', in Anon., *Satan* (London: Sheed and Ward, 1951), 406.
40. Ibid., 406–7.

liberty and love. When he protests that God rejects his love, God replies that if he releases the angel Liberty, his daughter and God's, she will encourage humanity to rebel against evil, destroy the prison, symbolised by the Bastille, that keeps people in darkness and from a life of love.

Like Goethe and Voltaire, Hugo's world view was greatly influenced by the injustices and the evils they perceived in the world and they looked for a transformation of society in their day. Hugo thought that by giving the traditional symbol of evil, Satan, a fiendishly fascinating and inherently sympathetic character, a new light could be made to transform people's perception of the world, generating love among them. It meant that the shadow of Satan was cast over all the works of the Romantic period. According to one of the more severe critics of the Romantic culture,

> It may well be said without any levity that Satan was the patron saint of the Romantic School. He impressed it with his personality to such an extent that it was soon named after him. The expression 'Satanic School' applied by Robert Southey to the Byronic group in England was accepted by Victor Hugo as an epithet of honour for the corresponding movement in France.[41]

Baudelaire's 'Le Joueur Généreux'

A short piece published by Charles Baudelaire, 'Le Joueur Généreux' in *Le Figaro* in 1864 was later published in English in a collection of his works, *Baudelaire, His Prose and Poetry*.[42] The narrator told of encountering a mysterious stranger, who he recognised as the devil.

> Yesterday, in the crowd of the boulevard, I felt myself grazed by a mysterious Being whom I have always wished to know, and whom I recognised at once, though I had never seen him.[43]

They spent the evening together in a resplendent subterranean abode, eating and drinking, until dawn broke. The devil explained to him the absurdity of the different philosophies that had taken possession of the human brain, and 'deigned even to confide to me certain fundamental principles, the property and the benefits of which it does not suit me to share with the casual comer'. He did not bemoan his bad reputation around the world and

> had never feared for his own power save once, on the day when he had heard a preacher, more subtle than his colleagues, cry from the pulpit: 'My dear brethren,

---

41. Rudwin, *The Devil in Legend and Literature*, 61.
42. Charles Baudelaire, *Baudelaire: His Prose and Poetry*, T. R. Smith, trans. (New York: Boni and Liveright, 1919), 80–4.
43. Ibid., 80.

never forget, when you hear the progress of wisdom vaunted, that the cleverest ruse of the Devil is to persuade you he does not exist!'[44]

Asked for news of God and whether he had recently seen him, he replied,

> We greet one another when we meet, but as two old gentlemen, in whom an innate politeness cannot extinguish the memory of ancient bitterness.[45]

Before parting, the devil said he wanted to show that despite all the ill that was said of him, he could be a good devil and offered his new friend prodigious powers for his future happiness, but the narrator, on reflection, dared not believe in such munificence, but in his habitual, silly prayers asked God to bring it about.

By the mid-nineteenth century, rather earlier than in the United States, there was a revival of interest in the figure of Satan, and Baudelaire represents both the fascination and the ambiguity of attitude, the attraction and rejection at the same time of this figure. The story of 'Le Joueur Généreux' represents a stage in Baudelaire's development, a more complex attitude than he revealed in a poem, 'Les litanies de Satan', published as part of *Les Fleurs du Mal*:

> O you, the most learned and the most beautiful of the Angels,
> God betrayed by fate and deprived of praise.[46]

Such ambiguity is an indication of the confused attitudes towards the existence of Satan, which were destined to give way to a lack of interest as the new century approached and a renewed struggle between traditional Christian teaching and Enlightenment attitudes was experienced in Europe and in the United States.

The Romantic Movement in the United States

The European Romantic movement reached America in the early nineteenth century. Apart from the English heritage of much of the population, a French cultural influence made a contribution because of the links established with France by the diplomat and polymath, Benjamin Franklin (1706–90), in the eighteenth century. In America the movement had a significant anti-Calvinist or anti-Puritan element, a positive attitude to the natural world, yet still a strongly moralistic

---

44. Ibid., 82. In the French version the quote and its context were: 'Mes chers frères, n'oubliez jamais, quand vous entendrez vanter le progrès des lumières, que la plus belle des ruses du Diable est de vous persuader qu'il n'existe pas!'

45. Ibid., 83.

46. Charles Baudelaire, *Oeuvres Complètes de Charles Baudelaire* (Paris: Éditions de la Revue Française, 1918), includes 'Les Litanies de Satan' at page 175: 'O toi, le plus savant et le plus beau des Anges, Dieu trahi par le sort et privé de louanges'.

approach to the ills of society. The infamous witch-hunt had ceased in the previous century but a preoccupation with evil was evident in the works of such writers as Nathaniel Hawthorne (1804–64) and Mark Twain (1835–1910).

Nathanael Hawthorne (1804–64)

Hawthorne's *Scarlet Letter* (1850), set in the Massachusetts colony in the mid-seventeenth century, found evil at the heart of the clerical establishment as a young woman is subjected to a church trial on giving birth to a child while her husband has not yet arrived to the colony. The story begins with Hester Prynne, carrying the infant in her arms, being made to stand on the pillory, a platform shoulder-high, outside the church, with the letter A embroidered in scarlets on her dress, while her judges led by the governor are on a balcony above her. In a scene full of tension and – as will emerge later – dramatic irony, the minister calls on his junior colleague, Arthur Dimmesdale, 'to exhort her to repentance and confession', in effect to reveal the name of the child's father.[47] Despite the demand, she refuses to name the father of the child and is condemned to a life of social stigma, eking out a meagre living by her sewing skills. Hawthorne presents her husband as a nefarious character, older than Hester; he had come to the village seeking revenge and was recognised only by her. She perceived 'what a change had come over his features – how much uglier they were, how his dark complexion seemed to have grown duskier and his figure more misshapen – since the days she had familiarly known him'.[48] Assuming the name Roger Chillingworth and posing as a physician, he treats Dimmesdale, now suffering from a heart condition, forcing him to reveal the nature of his illness to be the spiritual one of guilt. The climax of the novel comes when the young minister, Dimmesdale, on emerging in procession from the church one day, climbs on to the pillory and confesses his guilt as the father. He dies in Hester's arms and the letter A is found seared on his chest. Roger Chillingworth also dies and Hester lives out her life in respectability in the village.[49]

The novel became a classic of American literature in the nineteenth century and has inspired imitators in recent times, for example, in the trilogy by John Updike, the last one being the novel, *Roger's Version*, based on Hawthorne's Roger Chillingworth, exploiting what seems to have been behind Hawthorne's use of the name Chillingworth – a chilling reality of evil lurks behind the appearance of worth.

---

47. Nathaniel Hawthorne, *The Scarlet Letter* (Ware: Wordsworth Editions, 1992), 86–8.
48. Ibid., 137.
49. See also, John R. May, 'American Literary Variations on the Demonic', in *Disguises of the Demonic: Contemporary Perspectives on the Power of Evil*, Alan M. Olson, ed. (New York: Association Press, 1975), 36: 'Nathaniel Hawthorne is the American master of the romance concerned with exposing the devil's lasting influence on the race sprung from Eden's shadows, and the *locus classicus* in his *oeuvre* is doubtless the conclusion to (the short story) *Earth's Holocaust*.'

Like Hawthorne's Roger Chillingworth, Updike's Roger Lambert is a fictional version of the satanic principle, a portrait of evil.[50]

The Romantic Movement's highlighting of emotion and the hypocrisy of the social and religious establishments continued, though without identifying the source of evil as the influence of Satan. In England and America it ignored the criticism of Robert Southey (1774–1843) who, though originally a Romantic poet, had become conservative in his views and, as already noted, coined the term 'Satanic School' to describe his erstwhile friends Byron and others. Nonetheless, there was need to find some way of symbolising the evil that was targeted. Though Hawthorne had set his novel in seventeenth-century Massachusetts, in the Romantic culture he could not appeal to beliefs in the devil and witchcraft to add depth to his depiction of the story, though one of the villagers is identified as a 'lady-witch'. A suggestion of occult forces was needed; his solution was the introduction of the mysterious scarlet letter as a kind of physical stigma appearing on Dimmesdale's breast.

Mark Twain (1835–1910)

A writer somewhat younger than Hawhorne and destined to outlive him, Mark Twain had a reputation as a humourist, but introduced a sinister theme into one of his novels and, in a sense, revived the fortunes of the devil in literature. A satanic theme appeared in slightly different forms in collections of his writings such as *The Mysterious Stranger and Other Stories* from 1908 to 1916. Set in the winter of 1590 in a remote Austrian village, it chronicled the activities of three boys who, as they wandered in their rural district and relaxed near a wood, were visited by a youth of their own age, very well dressed and handsome, who took it upon himself to join them. The three wanted to be friendly but didn't know how to begin until one of them, the narrator, Theodor, thought of offering him his pipe, though he himself had no means of lighting it. That this was no ordinary youth became clear when he blew on the pipe and the tobacco glowed red. There followed a whole series of wonders and Theodor eventually asked him who he was.

> 'An angel', he said, quite simply, and set another bird free and clapped his hands and made it fly away.[51]

He knew the boys' names without being told, causing one of them to ask him what his was. Quite tranquilly, he said it was Satan. When one said it seemed a strange name for an angel, he said the Satan they knew about was his uncle and the only one of the family who had sinned. The rest of the family were 'ignorant of sin;

---

50. Frank G. Novak Jr., 'The Satanic Personality in Updike's *Roger's Version*', *Christianity and Literature*, vol. 55, no. 1 (Autumn 2005): 4.
51. Mark Twain, *The Mysterious Stranger Manuscripts*, vol. 7, Edited with introduction by William Gibson (Berkeley: University of California Press, 1969), 11.

we are not able to commit it; we are without blemish'.[52] During this conversation, he casually squashed the life out of various little human figures he had brought into existence before their eyes, 'just as if they had been flies'.[53] They judged in their minds that this was a cruel act, but realised he was without feeling and wished to make them as he was, and was always reading their thoughts. One of his revelations was that as an angel he was without Moral Sense, a characteristic of humans, of which he spoke disparagingly, pointing to injustices perpetrated by those who claimed to be guided by it.

Satan assumed the name Philip Traum as he began to involve himself in the village's affairs and alter events in such a way as to cause disaster for those who at first appeared to benefit from his activities. A poor young woman who suddenly began to have full and plenty was suspected to be benefiting from witchcraft. She put her prosperity down to Providence, having dismissed thoughts of witchcraft, as she and her serving woman were both devout. She invited villagers to a party, to which Philip Traum came uninvited, and bizarre events occurred including the expanding and then shrinking of the contents of a wine bottle, leading the priest to declare the house bewitched. Further wonders followed, causing the villagers to flee and believe the whole village to be bewitched; it could lead to the community being put under Interdict by the church. As a result, the villagers engaged in a witch-hunt which ended in the hanging of a woman who used natural remedies to cure illnesses.

Satan offered to show the boys the history of the human race and its future progress and it proved to be a succession of wars and bloodshed, leaving them upset and causing what Theodor, the narrator, described as an 'evil chuckle'[54] on Satan's part, as he insisted on the futility of human civilisation. This is the first and only time in the narrative that evil is attributed to Satan, though the three boys had often been shocked by his indifference to human suffering and his seeming cruelty. Theodor remained nonetheless fascinated and attracted by him.

Satan disappeared for a long time but came eventually to say good-bye to Theodor for good, saying he had investigations and undertakings in other corners of the universe.[55] To Theodor's expressed hope of seeing him again, he replied:

> Nothing exists; all is a dream. God – man – the world – the sun, the moon, the wilderness of stars – a dream, all a dream; they have no existence. Nothing exists save empty space – and you! 'I?' [Theodor said]. And you are not you – you have no body, no blood, no bones, you are but a thought. I myself have no existence; I am but a dream – your dream. [56]

---

52. Ibid., 13.
53. Ibid., 14.
54. Ibid., 78.
55. Ibid., 96.
56. Another version of the ending has: 'There is no God, no universe, no human race, no earthly life, no heaven, no hell. It is all a dream – a grotesque and foolish dream. Nothing

Twain left various unfinished versions of the story after his death, so it is difficult to establish what his own belief was in relation to Satan, though it does seem clear that despite the ending in which Satan says he has no existence, the author was not trying to construct a narrative around what he considered a nonentity. The story is a commentary on the waywardness of humanity as seen in the history of wars and injustices towards the poor, which Satan chronicles. It may be that Twain is paradoxically using Satan to point to the evils he sees in society, and though Satan initially presents as a non-fallen angel, in the course of the story, his real character become evident as a result of a nagging feeling in Theodor and his companions.

In any case, he continued in his writing to give prominence to Satan:

> By the summer of 1897, Twain was writing *Letters to Satan*, inviting His Grace to make a pleasure tour through the world, assuring him 'You have many friends in the world, more than you think'.[57]

His opening allegations in *Concerning the Jews*, published in 1899, is that he has no prejudices of race, colour, caste or creed – not even a prejudice against Satan on account of his not having a fair show.[58]

The decline of Romanticism

By the 1880s, however, psychological and social realism were competing with Romanticism in the novel and the image of the patron saint of the Satanic School was fading before the scientific pragmatism of psychologists like William James, a believer 'who did not feel obliged to protect Christianity by excising its integral parts'.[59] In his *Varieties of Religious Experiences* (1902) he chose to limit his study to direct and immediate religious experiences and conceded that in the healthiest-minded type of religious consciousness there is a shadow side – 'a higher happiness holds a lower unhappiness in check'.[60] Referring to a picture by Guido Reni of St Michael with his foot on the devil's neck, he says,

> The world is all the richer for having the devil in it, so long as we have our foot on his neck. In the religious consciousness, that is just the position in which the fiend, the negative or tragic principle, is found.[61]

---

exists but you. And you are but a thought – a vagrant thought, a useless thought, a homeless thought, wandering forlorn among the empty eternities!'
57. Twain, *The Mysterious Stranger Manuscripts*, vol. 7, 17.
58. Ibid., 18.
59. Russell, *Mephistopheles*, 218.
60. William James, *The Varieties of Religious Experience* (Harmondsworth: Penguin Books, 1982), 49.
61. Ibid., 50.

George Bernard Shaw (1856–1950)

James's well-known positive assessment of religious experience manifested the balance that G. B. Shaw called for in his play, *The Devil's Disciple*, one of three 'Plays for Puritans'. In a long introduction, Shaw inveighed against the sensuousness of the dramas of the time, which allowed every penman to play on people's romantic illusions. It is set in late-eighteenth-century New England as the defeat of the English army is imminent. Shaw called on the Puritans to rescue '[the theatre] again as they rescued it before, when its foolish pursuit of pleasure sunk it in "profaneness and immorality" ... I have always, I think, been a Puritan in my attitude towards Art'.[62]

In the Devil's Disciple, Shaw makes it clear that he is a critic of Puritan religion as it has been practised, at least in the eighteenth-century new world, by saying that his principal character, Dick Dudgeon, the devil's disciple, is a

> Puritan of the Puritans ... brought up in a household where the Puritan religion has died, and become, in its corruption an excuse for his mother's master passion in all its phases of cruelty and envy. ... In such a home, the young Puritan finds himself starved of religion, which is the most clamorous need of his nature. With all his mother's indomitable self-fulness, but with Pity instead of Hatred as his master passion, he pities the devil; takes his side; and champions him like a true Covenanter, against the world.[63]

In the play, Dick is one of the 'American' rebels. In the First Act at the reading of his father's Will, he introduces himself as the black sheep of the family:

> I knew from the first that the Devil was my natural master and captain and friend. I saw that he was in the right, and that the world cringed to his conqueror only through fear. I prayed secretly to him; and he comforted me, and saved me from having my spirit broken in this house of children's tears. I promised him my soul, and swore an oath that I would stand up for him in this world and stand by him in the next.[64]

Additional opprobrium falls on this young man who has been living with smugglers and criminals when the Will reveals that he is the principal beneficiary. The story unrolls of his problematic relationship with the family, especially his mother, and his involvement in the rebellion, a struggle that the Presbyterian minister, Anthony Anderson, and the rest of the family wish to avoid. But the English forces converge on the village and in an attempt to assert control over the area are intent

---

62. G. B. Shaw, 'Why for Puritans?', *Three Plays for Puritans* (Harmondsworth: Penguin Books, 1946), 21.
63. Ibid., 25–6.
64. Ibid., 66.

on executing the minister as a representative of the whole community. By chance, Dick is in the Anderson's house and the minister out when they come to arrest him, and Dick dons the minister's coat, pretending to be him. He is taken away and a court martial scheduled. In the paradoxical way favoured by Shaw, he is saved by the arrival of Anderson, now representing the rebel militia, who are in a position to rout the English.

Shaw gives no obvious reason for Dick's heroic act, nor does he think there is any need for one; he points to Dick's disavowal of the motive of love for the minister's wife, as she had mistakenly believed.

> I had no motive and no interest: all I can tell you is that when it came to the point whether I would take my neck out of the noose and put another man's neck into it, I could not do it. I don't know why not: I see myself as a fool for my pains; but I could not and I cannot. I have been brought up standing by the law of my own nature; and I may not go against it, gallows or no gallows.[65]

Anderson pays tribute to Dick in a way that implies his turning away from being the devil's disciple:

> This foolish young man boasted himself the Devil's Disciple; but when the hour of trial came to him, he found that it was his destiny to suffer and be faithful to the death.[66]

He goes further by asserting that Dick will take his place as the Reverend Richard Dudgeon, while he will become a captain of the militia. The reaction of Dick is to say he has 'behaved like a fool':

> [If] I had been any good, I should have done for you what you did for me, instead of making a vain sacrifice.[67]

Dick asserts he is being true to his own nature, but what that nature is, is an issue. Is he in some sense the devil's disciple, or has he been and is no longer? Shaw believes he does not have to engage with that question; instead, he reminds his readers of recent literary history.

By setting *The Devil's Disciple* in New England a century after the Salem witch trials, he is reacting to the most recent of a series of cultural upheavals, one following another, that had begun with the Protestant Reformation's repudiation of the medieval world view. The Enlightenment generated a reaction in the form of Romanticism in literature, and to this Shaw looks back.

---

65. Ibid., 94.
66. Ibid., 117.
67. Ibid., 118.

A century ago William Blake was, like Dick Dudgeon, an avowed Diabolonian: he called his angels devils and his devils angels. His devil is a Redeemer.[68]

Nietzsche, Shaw says, turned good and evil inside out. So he seems committed to this reversal of other-worldly roles, but the issue still arises as to where the devil is in all this drama – functioning as a device to add dramatic tension to the interaction between the characters, or presented as a real force in Dick's life as his master. Shaw does not give an answer, but provides the details needed to confer a sense of realism by the cynical remarks constantly on Dick's lips, his sardonic tone, his banning his mother from her home, but there is also his righteous indignation at the way his niece has been treated and his own kindness to her, his self-assessment at the end as one who had not been 'any good', but above all his heroic act of self-sacrifice. Shaw says that this is something inexplicable that happens in real life 'once a week or oftener' and playgoers were left, as are readers today, with a literary contribution to the enigma of Satan's place in the contemporary world.[69]

C. S. Lewis (1898–1963)

C. S. Lewis famously responded to the tensions inherent in this approach to Satan's place in the world by producing a book of letters from a devil to his nephew, *The Screwtape Letters*.[70] It avoids presenting the devil in human form – as a 'devil's disciple'. But the effort to enter into a devilish spiritual world Lewis found costly, as he admitted some years later:

> Though I had never written anything more easily, I never wrote with less enjoyment. … It would run away with you for a thousand pages if you gave it its head. But though it was easy to twist one's mind into a diabolical attitude, it was not fun, or not for long. The strain produced a sort of spiritual cramp.[71]

This was because Lewis brought back the old view of Satan and his existence in the nether world of Dante's and Milton's poetry that had been rejected by the Romantics, and by Lewis's time consigned to history, while evil was now portrayed effectively yet ambiguously in the characters and lives in modern fiction and in an emerging film genre. But, for Lewis, Satan had to be taken very seriously as the prototypical example of evil and had to be completely shorn of the heroic status the Romantics had accorded the subject of Milton's poem and the often confusing image of a modern enigmatic male figure. Lewis had written *A Preface to Paradise Lost* in 1942, the fruit of several years of lectures at Oxford, and at a time when

---

68. Ibid., 26.
69. Ibid., 28.
70. C. S. Lewis, *The Screwtape Letters* (New York: Macmillan, 1948).
71. C. S. Lewis, *Essay Collection and Other Short Pieces* (London: HarperCollins, 2010), 752.

Milton's epic had been the subject of much adverse comment by 'anti-Miltonist' scholars. It 'remains arguably the most influential work of Milton criticism ever written'.[72] It is a work of literary criticism and of theological analysis, answering the charges of critics like a certain Professor Saurat on both levels. In *A Preface to Paradise Lost*, Lewis had written:

> In so far as *Paradise Lost* is Augustinian and hierarchical it is also Catholic in the sense of basing its poetry on conceptions that have been held 'always and everywhere by all'. This Catholic quality is so prominent that that it is the first impression any unbiased reader would receive … this poem was accepted as orthodox by many generations of acute readers well-grounded in theology.[73]

Lewis had no difficulty with the mise en scène depicted by Milton nor with Satan's movement within it. 'Satan has been in the Heaven of Heavens and in the abyss of Hell and surveyed all that lies between them.'[74] He makes clear his rejection of the Romantic view both for its transfer of the story to an earthly landscape and its sympathetic treatment of Satan: 'To admire Satan is to give one's vote not only for a world of misery, but also for a world of lies and propaganda, of wishful thinking, of incessant autobiography.'[75]

Beneath the surface then, *The Screwtape Letters* is a very serious book dealing with the challenges posed to the Christian in the modern world, the world in which Satan still operates. The world it describes includes the 'patient', one of the 'two-legged animals' assigned to Wormwood, Screwtape's nephew. The patient recently converted to Christianity – presumably from agnostic Anglicanism – lives in the very material world of newspapers and buses and daily meals and has an idea of the church mostly centred on a sham Gothic building.

There is also a world below, which seems rather more like Milton's than Dante's nether world. There the Father dwells, directing all remotely, and Lewis adds a touch of humour to this infernal scene by peopling it with bureaucratic officials.

As Lewis admitted, he found it hard to give a role to operatives of a world above, who might on behalf of God, the unnamed Enemy, counteract the efforts of Wormwood. Their operations in the patient's world take place in a church the reality of which the patient hardly knows. This setting proved a remarkably convincing one for Lewis's readers in wartime Britain with its necessary concentration on material survival, and has lost none of its relevance today, even though many people now spend much time in the virtual world of the digital era – because the material world still has a decisive grip on people's lives. Lewis wrote about people's enfleshed existence as the theatre of their encounter with Wormwood and his

---

72. David V. Urban, 'C. S. Lewis and Satan: *A Preface to Paradise Lost* and Its Respondents, 1942–1952', *Connotations*, vol. 28 (2019): 192–234, at 192.

73. C. S. Lewis, *A Preface to Paradise Lost* (London: Oxford Paperbacks, 1960), 82.

74. Ibid., 102.

75. Ibid.

seemingly many colleagues, all engaged in a struggle to counteract the care for his 'sons' by the Enemy, who has an 'inveterate love of degrading the whole spiritual world by unnatural liaisons with the two-legged animals'.[76]

In 1940, Lewis had written a short book on the 'the problem of pain' at the request of a publisher, a treatment of the issue which he had considered quite tentative and lacking in authority yet had profound insights on evil and, in particular, on the topic of hell. This was as war began again in Europe and years before the post-war reflections of theologians on evil. In the intervening work, the *The Screwtape Letters*, Lewis takes account of the wartime effects on the Christian life in what might be called a more homely way, but actually provides the basis for the more theological reflections of the post-war era. Screwtape wants a full account of the reactions of the patient to the war, whether, for example, Wormwood can do more good for the infernal cause by making him an extreme patriot or an ardent pacifist. Of the war itself, he says:

> We may hope for a good deal of cruelty and unchastity. But, if we are not careful, we shall see thousands turning in this tribulation to the Enemy. ... And how disastrous for us is the continual remembrance of death which war enforces. One of our best weapons, contented worldliness, is rendered useless.[77]

(Lewis lived long enough to see how quickly contented worldliness would return when war ended.)

In letter No. 7, Screwtape discusses the issue of the patient's ignorance of Wormwood's existence, the policy of concealment which has not always been followed.

> The fact that 'devils' are predominantly comic figures in the modern imagination will help you. If any faint suspicion of your existence begins to arise in his mind, suggest to him a figure in red tights, and persuade him that since he cannot believe in that ... he cannot therefore believe in you.[78]

A large section of the book is devoted to the patient's spiritual progress or otherwise in the context of his family and social contacts, while Wormwood's efforts to direct him often come in for adverse comments from the uncle. It is this issue of the constant involvement of the devil in the patient's life that gives the work its spiritual depth; many books today on spirituality include a psychological perspective but lack the depths which the presence of the tempter gives this chronicle. As temptation can be very subtle, a note of drama can reinforce its reality. The patient is killed in a bombing raid, which is described in very realistic terms, and his sentiments at this moment of salvation are particularly powerful: he

---

76. Lewis, *The Screwtape Letters*, 17.
77. Ibid., 31–2.
78. Ibid., 40

sees both Wormwood and 'Them', God and the angelic host. 'You die and die and then you are beyond death. How could I ever have doubted it?' are his final thoughts, leaving Wormwood reeling back dizzy and blinded.[79]

The letters are signed 'your affectionate uncle', seeming to introduce a touch of human warmth, but from the start this is a shallow sentiment, given that the whole leitmotiv of the chronicle is the exaltation of hatred. So it is not surprising that the book ends with Wormwood's failure and Screwtape looking forward to devouring him.

It would be easy to regard Lewis's theme as fantasy, and in fact, the literature and movies of the following generation reverted to presenting evil as embodied in characters, though an exception to this approach was certainly presented by William Blatty's novel, *The Exorcist*. Its subsequent movie version was directed by William Friedkin, an unbeliever who some twenty years later visited the famous Vatican exorcist, Fr Gabriele Amorth, and found himself beset with questions as to the reality of the scenario he had thought to be fantasy. The issue of exorcism will be treated in another chapter.

79. Ibid., 158.

Chapter 9

TWENTIETH-CENTURY CHRONICLES OF EVIL

The First World War

Evil has been the subject of speculation not only by philosophers and theologians but also by writers who have experienced profound evil in their own lives. Chronicles of sufferings endured, sometimes to a degree that leaves the reader dumbfounded that the narrator survived, exist over the course of centuries, but the literature that emerged in the twentieth century from what seemed a great civilisation has a particular depth as a record of good turned to evil, of depravity the enormity of which it is difficult to grasp. In that new century, technological progress in Britain was built on the heritage of the Crystal Palace Great Exhibition of 1851 (which did not include armaments). It could now also assist in the development of weaponry. Even such devices as the telephone could now have military application in the form of the field telephone. This meant that helpful technical progress could become a retrogressive programme of aggression.

The literature of the Holocaust is an obvious record of such evil, while other examples recording deep evil are also well known. But they are often on a scale difficult to compare with the evil done to millions of the Jewish population and other ethnic groups of several European countries in the 1940s.

On the last page of his authoritative *The First World War*, the historian John Keegan described that war as a mystery.

> Its origins are mysterious. So is its course. Why did a prosperous continent at the height of its success as a source and agent of global wealth and power ... choose to risk all it had won for itself and all it offered to the world in the lottery of a vicious and local internecine conflict? Why, when the hope of bringing the conflict to a quick and decisive conclusion was everywhere dashed to the ground within months of its outbreak, did the combatants decide nevertheless to persist in their military effort, to mobilise for total war and eventually to commit the totality of their young manhood to mutual and existentially pointless slaughter?[1]

---

1. John Keegan, *The First World War* (London: Pimlico, 1999), 456.

It seems all the more strange when the cultural connections between the two sides are borne in mind, when men who had been educated together in England's public schools became officers in the opposing armies, wearing ornate and similar uniforms, but different decorations derived from their nations' battle history. The two sides were rooted in proud and chivalric, but romanticised traditions, and when war was in the air in 1914 an atmosphere of excitement grew. A generation of young English men thought of war as an adventure akin to school cricket, strenuous but entertaining, with a team spirit and confidence of emerging victorious in a combat that would be over quickly. It is no surprise that a literary genre evocative of past triumphs should have marked the response to this situation. But when the quick and decisive victory proved a chimera, the literature too took a new turn. As it emerged, 'the problem for the writer trying to describe elements of the Great War was its utter incredulity, and thus its incommunicability in its own terms'.[2]

The War Poets

Initially, some of the poetry continued in the Romantic vein of the previous century. Rupert Brooke (1887–1915) was one of the first of the War Poets to be published, as the *Times Literary Supplement* included two sonnets 'The Dead' and 'The Soldier', on 11 March 1915, a month before his death. He was commissioned in the Royal Navy Volunteer Reserve at the outbreak of war in August 1914 and was engaged in one expedition to Antwerp in October that year. Brooke had a romanticised idea of war; writing to a friend in December 1914, after his sojourn in Belgium, he declared that it was 'all great fun'.[3] Without seeing action in trench warfare, which would come to be the main inspiration for other poets, he died from sepsis on board ship on 23 April 1915. Two of his five war sonnets repeat the theme of sunset and dawn that marked pastoral poetry and which he had used several times in 'The Old Vicarage, Grantchester', written in Germany in 1912. The theme is evident in 'The Dead', one of two sonnets with the same title, written in 1914 before departure for Belgium:

> The years had given them kindness. Dawn was theirs,
> And sunset, and the colours of the earth.[4]

---

2. Paul Fussell, *The Great War and Modern Memory* (Oxford: Oxford University Press, 1975), 139.

3. Geoffrey Keynes, ed., *The Letters of Rupert Brooke* (New York: Harcourt, Brace and York, 1968), 645: 'It's all a terrible thing. And yet, in its details, it's great fun. And – apart from the tragedy – I've never felt happier or better in my life than in those days in Belgium.'

4. Mike Read, *Forever England: The Life of Rupert Brooke* (Edinburgh: Mainstream Publishing, 1997), 230.

Of those who came to be called the War Poets, Siegfried Sassoon (1886–1967), Wilfred Owen (1893–1918) and Isaac Rosenberg (1890–1918) – all three subjected to the horrors of trench warfare – were among the best: Sassoon for his poems of protest and for his anti-war writings, Owen for poems that have led to his being considered the best of the War Poets, and Rosenberg for what one critic considered the greatest poem of the war, 'Break of Day in the Trenches'.[5]

One of the most popular and frequently quoted poems of the war, and the origin of the custom of wearing a red poppy, was 'In Flanders Fields', by the Canadian John McCrae published in *Punch* magazine on 8 December 1915. It uses the theme of dawn, sunset and sky of pastoral poetry, but introduces recruiting poster rhetoric:

> In Flanders fields the poppies blow
> Between the crosses, row on row,
> That mark our place; and in the sky
> The larks, still bravely singing, fly
> Scarce heard amid the guns below.
> We are the Dead. Short days ago
> We lived, felt dawn, saw sunset glow,
> Loved and were loved, and now we lie,
> In Flanders fields.
> Take up our quarrel with the foe:
> To you from failing hands we throw
> The torch; be yours to hold it high …

It was used for recruitment, in propaganda efforts, and to sell war bonds. The red poppy symbolised heroism; today it more soberly commemorates all who have died in combat.

Isaac Rosenberg (1890–1918)

Isaac Rosenberg was born of Jewish immigrant parents and grew up in poverty. He studied art at the Slade School, and while there his interest turned to poetry. His health was poor and job prospects during the war very few. He joined the army in 1916 and was killed in action in April 1918. His own ill health and poverty led him to fear what evils for all of society the war would bring in its train. He had a shrewd idea of the dangers the war posed not only to recruits like him but also to England, and felt the need to record the death of a civilisation. His biographer wrote:

---

5. Fussell, *The Great War*, 250.

Death, he realised, had long stalked the cities and through the war spread to the countryside, devastating the normal intercourse of life, rooting out and eradicating the sustaining force of human love.[6]

One of his poems, 'A Worm Fed on the Heart of Corinth', records his fear that England was betrothed to the 'incestuous worm', the 'shadowless' Satan, and that, if consummated, England and civilisation would come to an end, like Babylon and Rome.

> A worm fed on the heart of Corinth,
> Babylon and Rome.
> Not Paris raped tall Helen,
> But this incestuous worm,
> Who lured her vivid beauty
> To his amorphous sleep.
> England! famous as Helen
> Is thy betrothal sung.
> To him the shadowless,
> More amorous than Solomon.[7]

'Break of Day in the Trenches' talks of darkness rather than sunset, of the bowels of the earth rather than sky, while the athletic young men, in contrast with the sardonic rat, are doomed to die. The poppy is there, but marked with the dust of death.

> The darkness crumbles away.
> It is the same old druid Time as ever,
> Only a live thing leaps my hand,
> A queer sardonic rat,
> As I pull the parapet's poppy
> To stick behind my ear.
> Droll rat, they would shoot you if they knew
> Your cosmopolitan sympathies.
> Now you have touched this English hand
> You will do the same to a German
> Soon, no doubt, if it be your pleasure
> To cross the sleeping green between.
> It seems you inwardly grin as you pass
> Strong eyes, fine limbs, haughty athletes,

---

6. Joseph Cohen, *Journey to the Trenches: The Life of Isaac Rosenberg 1890–1918* (London: Robson Books, 1975), 165.

7. Max Egremont, *Some Desperate Glory: The First World War the Poets Knew* (New York: Farrar, Strauss and Giroux, 2014), 131.

Less chanced than you for life,
Bonds to the whims of murder,
Sprawled in the bowels of the earth,
The torn fields of France.
What do you see in our eyes
At the shrieking iron and flame
Hurled through still heavens?
What quaver – what heart aghast?
Poppies whose roots are in man's veins
Drop, and are ever dropping;
But mine in my ear is safe –
Just a little white with the dust.[8]

Siegfried Sassoon (1886–1967)

On his father's side, Sassoon was of Jewish ancestry, though throughout his life he made few references to it. It was only in his last years that he recognised how his paternal side had given him religious, poetic and prophetic insights – 'the daemon in me is Jewish'.[9] His mother very early encouraged him to read poetry and become a poet; his talent for prose he discovered after the war. In the last days of July 1914, rumours of war with Germany were in the air and young men of his social class were enthusiastic about the adventure which seemed in prospect, and believed, like his neighbours of similar social class, in the rightness of the cause. One of the attractions ahead was the continuing involvement with horses.[10] Years later, in his fictionalised autobiography, *Sherston Trilogy*, 'carefully structured to enact the ironic redemption of a shallow fox-hunting man by terrible events',[11] Sassoon described his situation at the time of his enlisting:

> The years of my youth were going down for ever in the weltering western gold, and the future would take me far from the sunset-embered horizon.[12]

Sassoon's pre-war poetry had been like that of Rupert Brooke, reflecting his pastoral environment. He was like many others of the time, who 'with varying degrees of talent sought through poetry to portray the war not as tragedy so much as heroic opportunity'.[13] His first posting, to a position some distance from the

---

8. Ibid., 141.
9. John Stuart Roberts, *Siegfried Sassoon* (London: Richard Cohen, 1999), 3.
10. Britain 'called up 165,000, mounts for the cavalry and draught animals for the artillery and regimental transport wagons'. Keegan, *The First World War*, 83.
11. Fussell, *The Great War*, 102.
12. Roberts, *Siegfried Sassoon*, 56.
13. Ibid., 61.

front lines, inspired a poem titled 'To Victory', still in pastoral mood, but hinting at a revised view of the war 'adventure'.

> Return to greet me, colours that were my joy,
> Not in the woeful crimson of men slain,
> But shining as a garden; come with the streaming
> Banners of dawn and sundown after rain.[14]

The death at the front of one of his friends was the beginning of a change in his view of the war; first a desire for revenge gripped him and then dismay at the great number of casualties.[15] Invalided back to England, he was dismayed at how his contemporaries there retained a romantic view of the war. Some of the poems written in France during this period show his new realistic view:

Prelude: The troops
And through some mooned Valhalla there will pass
Battalions and battalions, scarred from hell;
The unreturning army that was youth;
The legions who have suffered and are dust.[16]

Banishment
Love drove me to rebel.
Love drives me back to grope with them through hell.[17]

Does It Matter?
Does it matter? – losing your legs?
For people will always be kind,
And you need not show that you mind
When others come in after hunting[18]

Hero
'Jack fell as he'd have wished,' the Mother said,
And folded up the letter that she'd read.
'The Colonel writes so nicely.' Something broke
In the tired voice that quavered to a choke.[19]

---

14. Siegfried Sassoon, *Collected Poems* (London: Faber and Faber, 1949), 13.
15. Siegfried Sassoon, *Memories of a Fox-Hunting Man* (London: Faber and Faber, 1967), 305: 'I went up to the trenches with the idea of trying to kill someone. It was my idea of getting my own back.'
16. Siegfried Sassoon, *Collected Poems* (London: Faber and Faber, 1949), 67.
17. Ibid., 89.
18. Ibid., 76.
19. Ibid., 29.

Sassoon's war came to an end when after a period of convalescence in England he took a stand against the official policy of continuing the war despite the loss of so many young lives. He wrote to his commanding officer a letter subsequently read out in the House of Commons by a sympathetic MP and published next day in *The Times*.

'Finished with War. A Soldier's Declaration', written on 15 June 1917:

> I am making this statement as an act of wilful defiance of military authority, because I believe that the War is being deliberately prolonged by those who have the power to end it. I am a soldier, convinced that I am acting on behalf of soldiers. I believe this War, upon which I entered as a war of defence and liberation, has now become a war of aggression and conquest. ... I have seen and endured the sufferings of the troops, and I can no longer be a party to prolonging those sufferings for ends which I believe to be evil and unjust.

While he could have been court-martialled, his connections were such that he was sent instead to Craiglockhart Military Hospital in Scotland to be treated for a nervous disorder and never returned to service in France. It seems that his was not the only protest; more than 300,000 offences were dealt with by the military courts, some for desertion, but there must have been some that involved principled protest.[20] After the war, Sassoon continued military service until he relinquished his commission in 1919. In civilian life he became a novelist and editor and was instrumental in introducing the war poems of Wilfred Owen, whom he had met in Craiglockhart and encouraged to record the horrors of the war for a wider audience. The pacifist movement, the Peace Pledge Union, founded in the 1930s by Reverend H. R. L. Sheppard, attracted Sassoon's support and that of various celebrities, but with the rise of the Nazi regime in Germany, Sassoon's relationship with it became strained.[21]

Wilfred Owen (1893-1918)

Son of a station master, Tom Owen, and of Susan (Shaw), a very devout mother, Wilfred was himself a devout Anglican in his early and young adult years, though he became disillusioned about religion when working as an assistant to a parish clergyman, feeling that the Anglican Church was insensitive to the needs of the poor.[22] He is thought to have begun composing poetry at about seventeen, though all his early manuscripts were burned by his mother on his death, as he had instructed.[23] After a period teaching English in France and having considered

---

20. Peter Frankopan, *The Silk Roads: A New History of the World* (London: Bloomsbury, 2015), 319.
21. Roberts, *Siegfried Sassoon*, 276.
22. Dominic Hibberd, *Wilfred Owen: A New Biography* (Chicago: Ivan R. Dee, 2003), 69.
23. Jon Stallworthy, *Wilfred Owen: A Biography* (London: Chatto and Windus, 1974), 53.

joining the French army – and briefly even the Italian – he returned to England and joined the army in 1915. His early war experience in France at the beginning of 1916 involved much physical hardship as well as danger; he kept his mother informed in considerable detail. In 1917, he wrote to his mother that the aim of war was the extinction of militarism, beginning with Prussianism – he was not a pacifist. In September, he wrote: 'I hate washy pacifists, as temperamentally as I hate whiskied Prussianists.'[24]

In a letter Owen spoke also of the devastated landscape, 'not a blade of grass, not an insect':

> Hideous landscapes, vile noises, foul language and nothing but foul, even from one's own mouth (for all are devil ridden), everything unnatural, broken, blasted; the distortion of the dead, whose unburiable bodies sit outside the dugouts all day, all night, the most execrable sights on earth. In poetry we call them the most glorious.[25]

The last sentence hints that he will abandon the style of writing, imitative of Keats, which had been his since his teenage years. From his experiences at the front, his poetry would acquire a new tone. The transition was aided by the fact that after two traumatic incidents – in one he was left unconscious for several days – he was invalided out and sent to the Craiglockhart Military Hospital where Siegfried Sassoon was already a patient. He shyly introduced himself to the older man and formed a friendship in which Sassoon mentored him, counselling him to combine realism reflecting his war experience with his own romantic approach, which he did very effectively. His focus was on individuals, young men whose wounded bodies were described graphically, in effect a homoerotic style that Sassoon concealed in his own poetry.

> Owen's poetic response to the war is unique. Unlike Sassoon, Blunden and Graves, with their 'university' bent toward structured general ideas, Owen, as Bergonzi has noted, 'rarely attempts a contrast, nostalgic or ironic, between the trenches and remembered English scenes.' Rather he harnesses his innate fondness for dwelling on the visible sensuous particulars of boys to promote an intimate identification with them.[26]

Owen's poems were published after his death in action exactly a week before Armistice Day, 11 November 1918. His best known poems include: 'Anthem for Doomed Youth', 'Futility', 'Dulce Et Decorum Est', 'The Parable of the Old Men and the Young' and 'Strange Meeting'.

---

24. David Roberts, ed., *Minds at War: The Poetry and Experience of the First World War* (West Sussex: Saxon Books, 1996³), 147.
25. Stillworthy, *Wilfred Owen*, 159.
26. Fussell, *The Great War*, 291.

'Anthem for Doomed Youth' is a poem that contrasts the funeral rites he knew from his Anglican parish past and the manner in which soldiers on the front met their end. As well as expressing his rejection of religion, his aim was to make his readers face the obscenity of men dying like cattle. It is an example also of his use of 'sensuous particulars', the eyes of the soldiers.

> What passing-bells for these who die as cattle?
> – Only the monstrous anger of the guns.
> Only the stuttering rifles' rapid rattle
> Can patter out their hasty orisons.
> No mockeries now for them; no prayers nor bells;
> Nor any voice of mourning save the choirs –
> The shrill, demented choirs of wailing shells;
> And bugles calling for them from sad shires.
> What candles may be held to speed them all?
> Not in the hands of boys, but in their eyes
> Shall shine the holy glimmers of goodbyes.
> The pallor of girls' brows shall be their pall;
> Their flowers the tenderness of patient minds,
> And each slow dusk a drawing-down of blinds.[27]

The poem 'Dulce et Decorum Est' was based on an incident in which Owen was involved, a sudden gas attack, which caused the soldiers to try desperately to get their masks on. One soldier was too late and suffered an agonising death. Again attention is directed to his eyes. This poem emphasises suffering and shocks the reader with an invitation to become part of the scene:

> Bent double, like old beggars under sacks,
> Knock-kneed, coughing like hags, we cursed through sludge,
> Till on the haunting flares we turned our backs,
> And towards our distant rest began to trudge.
> Men marched asleep. Many had lost their boots,
> But limped on, blood-shod. All went lame; all blind;
> Drunk with fatigue; deaf even to the hoots
> Of gas-shells dropping softly behind.
>
> Gas! GAS! Quick, boys! – An ecstasy of fumbling
> Fitting the clumsy helmets just in time,
> But someone still was yelling out and stumbling
> And flound'ring like a man in fire or lime. –
> Dim through the misty panes and thick green light,

---

27. Max Egremont, *Some Desperate Glory. The First World War the Poets Knew* (New York: Farrar, Strauss and Giroux, 2014), 193.

> As under a green sea, I saw him drowning
> In all my dreams before my helpless sight,
> He plunges at me, guttering, choking, drowning.
>
> If in some smothering dreams, you too could pace
> Behind the wagon that we flung him in,
>
> And watch the white eyes writhing in his face,
> His hanging face, like a devil's sick of sin;
> If you could hear, at every jolt, the blood
> Come gargling from the froth-corrupted lungs,
> Obscene as cancer, bitter as the cud
> Of vile, incurable sores on innocent tongues.
> My friend, you would not tell with such high zest
> To children ardent for some desperate glory,
> The old Lie: *Dulce et decorum est
> Pro patria mori*.[28]

'The Parable of the Old Man and the Young' is based on the story of Abraham's willingness to sacrifice his son, Isaac, but has his hand stayed by an angel at the last moment. The poem's last two lines are a condemnation of the leaders whom he considered responsible for the death of the Europe's youth. 'One by one' indicates their callous indifference.

> But the old man would not so, but slew his son
> And half the seed of Europe, one by one.

The War Poets used their talent and their sensuous approach to human life to impress on the minds of the population at home, and especially the generals such as Douglas Haig, the horror that was life in the trenches.[29] As the generals understood it, their role was to follow the tradition inherited from previous, even recent, wars, and direct the operation from the safety of positions far behind the lines. The difference by the time of the Great War was that now the number of soldiers was enormous and spread out over long front lines, while the armaments were vastly more powerful and capable of fairly accurate aim. Highly efficient communications would be necessary to coordinate action, but the technology for this, though theoretically advanced, was in practice easily damaged; long telephone

---

28. Ibid., 215.
29. Artists also took part in the protest; men such as Paul Nash, C. N. W. Nevinson, and Sir William Orpen painted protest canvases, despite being commissioned as war artists. See David Stevenson, *The History of the First World War. 1914–1918* (London: Penguin Books, 2004), 576.

wires submerged in mud rarely functioned well. The result of pursuing warfare in those conditions is seen in startling numbers:

> Year groups 1892–95 [in Britain], men who were between nineteen and twenty-two when the war broke out, were reduced by 35–37%. Overall, of the sixteen million born between 1870 and 1899, thirteen per cent were killed, at the rate of 456,600 for each year the war lasted [1,826, 400]. ... In all 2,057,000 Germans died in the war, or of wounds in its aftermath.[30]

The evils which the troops of both sides suffered, the death, mutilation, permanent injury and psychological trauma, these cannot be considered natural evils, but were the result of decisions taken by others – military and political authorities. The evils suffered by the civilian population, bereavement above all, the demolition of homes, and the destruction of crops in France especially – these were brought down on them by others, in the first place by the military authorities.

> In their time, almost all the leading commanders of the war were seen as great men, the imperturbable Joffre, the fiery Foch, the titanic Hindenburg, the Olympian Haig. Between the wars their reputations crumbled, largely at the hands of memoirists and novelists ... whose depiction of the realities of 'war from below' relentlessly undermined the standing of those who had dominated from above. ... The impassive expressions that stare back at us from contemporary photographs do not speak of conscience or feelings troubled by the slaughter over which these men presided.[31]

Kaiser Wilhelm II could reasonably be included with those men (as he was in German photographs) and in the end the responsibility for all that happened from 1914 to 1918 must be sought in the stance of the empires of the time.

> Europe was a continent of empires: Italy, France, Austria-Hungary, Germany, Russia, Ottoman Turkey, Britain, Portugal, the Netherlands, even tiny Belgium, only formed in 1831.[32]

They had defensive attitudes towards each other since the beginning of the century at least, because of their competition to retain far-flung colonies with their natural resources and their attempts to suppress internal dissent – a problem especially for the Hapsburgs because of integrated but unassimilated Bosnia, where the assassination of Archduke Franz Ferdinand sparked off the conflagration. Despite the fact that the various dynasties were related to each other and publicly maintained cordial relations – for example, the Kaiser was the colonel of the British

---

30. Keegan, *The First World War*, 7.
31. Ibid., 337–8.
32. Frankopan, *The Silk Roads*, 321.

First Dragoons and his cousin, George V, was the colonel of the Prussian Ist Guard Dragoons – there was mutual suspicion and rivalry, and in most of the countries (Britain excepted) there was conscription of young men in order to build up reserve armies. Obviously, the manufacturers of armaments could only approve.

The War Poets, looking at things from below, very effectively brought the end result of this situation to public notice, but it would be difficult to establish how deeply they understood the final nature of the evils they chronicled. Rosenberg did mention the 'shadowless' Satan, 'the incestuous worm', and Sassoon in his 'A Soldier's Statement' made the damning accusation that a war of defence and liberation had become a war of aggression and conquest. But men like the young Sassoon and Owen, lacking religious conviction, lacked also the language which could have identified a conflict that went deeper than the political or economic.[33] An explanation could have been found in the primeval struggle between good and evil, which the Anglican Church of their earlier days in its creed and its liturgy recognised, It was a 'struggle not against enemies of flesh and blood but against the rulers, against the authorities, the cosmic powers of this present darkness, against the spiritual forces of evil in the heavenly places' (Eph. 6.12). But by then, the young were not listening.

After the war, Sassoon had a successful career as a poet, an editor and a writer of fictionalised autobiography, but he had a troubled personal life involving affairs with men, marriage at forty-seven and the birth of a boy, but separation from Hester after ten years. He struggled with conflicting desires for solitude and friendship, but throughout the years was, according to his friends and biographers, on a spiritual journey. In one volume of his 'autobiography', *Siegfried's Journey*, he described how, faced with a manuscript of Pope's *Essay on Man*, he had reflected on his disordered existence, 'in which God within the mind was being obliterated. It was a relief to be reminded of one's own unimportance'.[34]

> These two sentences are vital clues to the nature of his religious poetry. In the first place, even then, an inward sense that the spiritual was real, and secondly an ingrained humility about the significance of the worldly self. … Yet so scrupulous is the search that it issues in no firm belief until more than thirty years have passed.[35]

In the last decade of his life, a significant but seemingly chance encounter brought his search to a new level of insight. He received a letter from a nun who had read

---

33. Sassoon, *Memories of a Fox-Hunting Man*, 304: '[The] innocuous blasphemings of the holy name were a peculiar feature of the war, in which the principles of Christianity were obliterated or falsified for the convenience of all who were engaged in it.'

34. Siegfried Sassoon, *Siegfried's Journey (1916–1920)* (London: Faber and Faber, 1946), 184.

35. Michael Thorpe, *Siegfried Sassoon: A Critical Study* (London: Oxford University Press, 1966), 208.

his *Sequences*, a short book of poems published in 1956. She had noted a change in his writing, suggesting a new spiritual awareness. He replied by return, expressing how much comforted he had been by it. In the course of a long letter, he said:

> When I wrote 'spiritual' poems in the past they were only emotional attitudes. Of late years I have had to think it all out for myself unemotionally. And the state of the world hasn't aided optimism, has it? It seemed as though the world were pervaded by evil, and the powers of darkness really showing their hand.[36]

The evils he and the others had identified as resulting from decisions by people safely distanced from the horrors of the war, he now ascribed to more sinister forces and was on his way, with the help of that same sister, to a deeply Christian understanding of the world. He had a moment of enlightenment when he read a letter from Hilaire Belloc to a mutual friend, in praise of the Catholic faith and Church; he entered the Church ten years before his death in 1967.

Realignment of forces and regional conflicts

The realignment of political forces and boundaries after the First World War sowed the seeds for future conflicts, making the twentieth century one in which regional conflicts succeeded each other from Korea to Vietnam and on into the twenty-first, with various repressive regimes throughout the world trampling on the human rights of millions, as still happens. The Khmer Rouge regime in Cambodia, for example, led by Pol Pot in the 1970s, involved ruthless enforcement of Communist social policy, causing the resettlement of the Cambodian population and the death of between a million and a half and two million people from starvation and brutal treatment.

Two notorious regimes in Europe, those of Nazi Germany and Stalin's Russia, were chronicled by writers who suffered under them. The Gulag writings of Aleksandr Solzhenitsyn (1918-2008) and the memoirs of Primo Levi (1919-87) are a record of the evils perpetrated by those regimes. In the United States, the writings and speeches, as well as the life, of the assassinated Martin Luther King laid bare an evil at the heart of that society in the policies of segregation and injustice of which remnants still remain.

Martin Luther King (1929-68)

Son of a Black Baptist minister in Atlanta, Georgia, he was at first named Michael, but subsequently given the name Martin Luther by his father, who inspired him to resist racial segregation and social injustice in general. After training for the ministry, he was appointed pastor of a Baptist church in Montgomery, Alabama,

---

36. Roberts, *Siegfried Sassoon*, 314.

and there began his campaign against segregation with the Montgomery Bus Boycott, which lasted over a year.[37] In the course of his short life of thirty-nine years, he preached and wrote against segregation and participated in many marches and sit-ins as part of the non-violent Civil Rights Movement. He won the Nobel Peace Prize in 1964, but was arrested many times and finally assassinated in 1968.

A gifted preacher and writer, many of his sermons appeared in print, and his writings included his autobiography. Among his more noteworthy writings was his *Letter from Birmingham City Jail* in which he addressed the issue of violence in the Civil Rights Movement, in a response to the concerns of white religious leaders. He spoke of the two opposing forces among the Black population, those who for various reasons accepted their segregated status and those who formed a force of

> bitterness and hatred (that) comes perilously close to advocating violence. It is expressed in the various black nationalist groups that are springing up over the nation, ... This movement is nourished by the contemporary frustration over the continued existence of racial discrimination. It is made up of people who have lost faith in America, who have absolutely repudiated Christianity, and who have concluded that the white man is an incurable devil.[38]

This analysis shows what a difficult path he followed in combating evil by what he called the more excellent way of love and non-violence that was evident in all his speeches and writings. In his *Strength to Love*, he devoted a chapter to 'The Death of Evil upon the Seashore', based on the text of Exod. 13.30: 'And Israel saw the Egyptians dead upon the sea shore.' His fluent style is evident here as is in all his writings and includes a literary device that made a great impression on his readers and hearers; the last sentence alludes to Isa. 61.10, but the reader of the text is meant to be shocked when 'clothed in the garments' refers not to 'salvation' as in the biblical text, but to calamitous wars, a device King used also elsewhere.

> Is anything more obvious than the presence of evil in the universe? Its nagging, prehensile tentacles project into every level of human existence. ... Evil is stark, grim and colossally real. ... Within the wide arena of everyday life, we see evil in all of its ugly dimensions. We see it expressed in tragic lust and inordinate selfishness. We see it in high places where men are willing to sacrifice truth on the altars of their self-interest. We see it in imperialistic nations crushing other people with the battering ram of social injustice. We see it clothed in

---

37. His account was published as *Stride toward Freedom* (Eastford, CT: Martino Fine Books, 2015).
38. https://www.csuchico.edu/iege/_assets/documents/susi-letter-from-birmingham-jail.pdf, 4.

the garments of calamitous wars which leave men and nations morally and physically bankrupt.[39]

The chapter's origin in the biblical text allowed King to refer to the fact that just as the Hebrews' liberation from slavery in Egypt led them to the Red Sea, they still had to cross and continue their search for the Promised Land. So also King's own people had achieved a certain freedom because of a Supreme Court decision that separate educational facilities were inherently unequal – the forces of segregation were 'dying on the seashore'. He reflected:

> The problem is far from solved and gigantic mountains of opposition lie ahead, but at least we have left Egypt and with patient and firm determination we shall reach the promised land. Evil in the form of injustice and exploitation shall not survive forever.[40]

His allusions to biblical texts enhanced the appeal of his writing to the largely Baptist Black population. His most famous speech, with succeeding sentences beginning 'I have a dream', was made before an enormous throng that included whites as well as Blacks and reached its climax with a sentence alluding to and quoting the well-known text, Isa. 40.4-5:

> I have a dream that one day every valley shall be exalted, and every hill and mountain shall be made low, the rough places will be made plain, and the crooked places will be made straight; 'and the glory of the Lord shall be revealed and all flesh shall see it together'.

As a college student, he had written a long essay with the title 'Religion's Answer to the Problem of Evil', summarising and critiquing the classical treatment of the problem, such as the free will argument, though his analysis relied more on contemporary philosophers of religion, such as the Methodist Edgar Brightman of Boston University. He made some telling comments on the failure of many to give full recognition to the goodness and power of God. His conclusion began:

> The existence of evil in the world still stands as the great enigma wrapped in mystery, yet has not caused Christians to live in total despair. ... [W]ith all of the new light that has been shed on the old problem, we still come to a point beyond which we cannot go. Any intellectual solution to the problem of evil will come to an inevitable impasse. The ultimate solution is not intellectual but spiritual. After we have climbed to the top of the speculative ladder, we must leap out into the darkness of faith. But this leap is not a leap of despair, for it eventually cries

---

39. Martin Luther King, *Strength to Love* (New York: Harper & Row, 1963), 58–9.
40. Ibid., 63.

with St Paul, 'For now we see through a glass darkly ... but then I shall know even as I am known'.[41]

His approach to the problem of evil was spiritual rather than intellectual and gave him the strength to confront evil in the course of his life; it must also have enabled him to face the ultimate evil of his own martyrdom. Some decades later, Aleksandr Solzhenitsyn would bring his prophetic message to the United States and reflect also on the problem of evil.

Aleksandr Solzhenitsyn (1918–2008)

Solzhenitsyn, a graduate in mathematics and literature as well as a Second World War veteran, fell foul of the Russian authorities because of a letter he wrote criticising Joseph Stalin. He spent eight years in prisons and in the Gulag, the enforced labour camps, followed by three years in exile in Kazakhstan. On release he worked as a mathematics teacher and began to write. His first novel, *One Day in the Life of Ivan Denisovich*, appeared in 1962 at a time of loosening government restraints on cultural life that proved to be short-lived. It was based on his own experience. In it he concentrated on

> the killing monotony of prison life, the convict's constant confrontation and coping with the brutal yet ordinary, often uninteresting but always essential necessities of existence.[42]

Solzhenitsyn gave a Baptist fellow prisoner Denisovich advice on what to pray for, anticipating an idea that will become central to Solzhenitsyn's thinking in later years, the issue of evil:

> Ivan Denisovich, you shouldn't pray to get parcels or for extra skilly, not for that. ... We must pray about things of the spirit – that the Lord Jesus should remove the scum of evil from our hearts.[43]

When denied the right to publish, he resorted to illegal private circulation of his works and to publishing abroad; this resulted in the first parts of *The Gulag Archipelago* being published in Paris in 1973. It was an attempt to compile a literary-historical record of the system of prison and labour camps since the Bolshevik Revolution, and was inspired not only by his own experience but also by

---

41. Martin Luther King, *The Papers of Martin Luther King, Jr*, vol. 1, *Called to Serve*, Clayborne Carson et al., eds (Berkeley: University of California Press, 1991), 415–32.
42. Robert Louis Jackson, 'Criticism', in *One Day in the Life of Ivan Denisovich: A Critical Companion*, Alexis Klimoff, ed. (Evanston, IL: Northwestern University Press, 1997), 44.
43. Aleksandr Solzhenitsyn, *A Day in the Life of Ivan Denisovich* (London: Victor Gollancz, 1970), 185.

the fact that the famous Russian writer Maxim Gorky had been a supporter of the labour camps – though near the end of his life he became an opponent of Stalin's regime. Publication of the first volume of the *Gulag* led to Solzhenitsyn's arrest on a charge of treason in 1974 and to his exile to the United States until 1994, when he returned to Russia. The second and third parts of the work appeared in 1974–5, with the second of particular importance in relation to his reflections on evil; these sprang from his conviction 'about the need for human beings to exercise their moral freedom by fighting for justice and by actively struggling against evil'.[44]

In 2006, he was asked in an interview for a German literary and political review, *Cicero*, whether simple human decency could be an adequate response to absolute evil. He replied that radical evil, in his view, is not reducible to madness or stupidity, but has a dense nucleus or core, with the capacity to strike out in every direction. Given its power, nothing less than an 'active struggle' is necessary to combat it.[45] This view arose from his experience of the labour camps and his observations about the effect on prisoners, including himself. Reflection on the low incidence of suicide among prisoners, the determination to survive at all cost, led him to recognise that in the camp there were two ways to go, to the right or to the left. 'One of them will rise and the other will descend. If you go to the right – you lose your life, and if you go to the left – you lose your conscience.'[46] So in the camps there were many examples of prisoners who survived at any cost, 'at any cost' meaning at a cost to someone else, the cost of goods and even the cost of lives. Prisoners committed murder because of a grudge or of resentment against those suspected of being informers or 'stool pigeons'.

But there was also the possibility of 'ascent'.

> And as soon as you have renounced that aim of 'surviving at any price' and gone where the calm and simple people go – then imprisonment begins to transform your former character in an astonishing way. To transform it in a direction most unexpected to you.[47]

In his own experience, a transformative incident occurred when, as a patient recovering from surgery in the prison hospital, he was visited late in the evening by one of the doctors, Boris Kornfeld, who wanted to share with him the story of his conversion from Judaism to Christianity in the prison. Kornfeld's personal testimony ended with the assertion that he had become convinced 'there is no punishment that comes to us in this life on earth which is undeserved'.

---

44. Daniel J. Mahoney, *The Other Solzhenitsyn* (South Bend: St Augustine's Press, 2014), 26.

45. Ibid., 27.

46. Aleksandr Solzhenitsyn, *The Gulag Archipelago*, vol. 2, Part IV, 'The Soul and the Barbed Wire' (London: Collins/Fontana, 1976), 585.

47. Ibid., 592.

> Superficially it can have nothing to do with what we are guilty of in actual fact, but if you go over your life with a fine-tooth comb and ponder it deeply, you will always be able to hunt down that transgression of yours for which you have now received this blow.[48]

The shock the prisoner felt on discovering the next morning that Kornfeld had been brutally murdered during the night, and the last words that now 'lay upon' him as an inheritance, led him to reflect that 'for my whole conscious life I had not understood either myself or my strivings'.

> What had seemed for so long to be beneficial now turned out in actuality to be fatal, and I had been striving to go in the opposite direction to that which was truly necessary to me. ... It was granted to me to carry away from my prison years on my bent back, which nearly broke beneath its load, this essential experience: *how* a human being becomes evil and *how* good. In the intoxication of youthful successes, I had felt myself to be infallible, and I was therefore cruel. ... In my most evil moments, I was convinced that I was doing good, and I was well supplied with systematic arguments. And it was only when I lay there on rotting prison straw that I sensed within myself the first stirrings of good. Gradually it was disclosed to me that the line separating good and evil passes not through states, nor between classes, nor between political parties either – but right through every human heart – and through all human hearts. (emphasis in the original)[49]

This profound insight did not cause Solzhenitsyn to confine himself within an introspective mood; rather his attitude to the Russian state remained as condemnatory as its Bolshevik ideology, its injustices and its cruelties warranted. In a subsequent chapter of *Gulag* 2, 'Our Muzzled Freedom', he used an analogy to describe the condition of the state. He had suffered from an abdominal cancer that terrified him by exuding poisons infecting his whole body. This tumour occupied only less than half of 1 percent of his whole body, whereas the Archipelago consisted of 8 percent of the state. 'And in this same way our whole country was infected by the poisons of the Archipelago.'[50]

On the day he was arrested and sent into exile, 12 February 1974, Solzhenitsyn released the text of 'Live Not by Lies'. He equated 'lies' with ideology, the illusion that human nature and society can be reshaped to form a new humanity.

> Solzhenitsyn knew that the Bolshevik regime was unimaginable without the gulag archipelago and the terror that accompanied it. But he always emphasised that 'the universal, obligatory force-feeding with lies' was 'the most agonising aspect' of life in the USSR, worse than 'material miseries', worse than any lack

---

48. Ibid., 594.
49. Ibid., 597.
50. Ibid., 614.

of civil liberties. It might be said that the Lie, the illusion of creating a radically New Man and Society, which in decisive respects were beyond good and evil, takes 'ontological' precedence over violence and brutality.[51]

Given such a radical critique of his own country, one could expect that he would find the liberal society of the Western world a breath of fresh air, when he began his twenty years of exile in 1974, during which he addressed numerous European and American audiences and later visited Japan and Taiwan. But he cautioned against the misuse of freedom, apparently favouring a benevolent authoritarianism and was distrustful of democracy – 'a society with no other scale than the legal one is not quite worthy of man'. He sensed spiritual poverty in the West as in the East, a materialistic departure from 'the moral heritage of the Christian centuries with their rich reserves of mercy and sacrifice', as he put it in his Commencement Address at Harvard on 8 June 1978. It was a forceful expression of this critique and proved the most controversial of his speeches. In it, he used the terminology of good and evil, a way of speaking that went far beyond the platitudes – or even inspiring phrases – that can mark such an occasion.

In a criticism of Western democracy, he said:

> Life organized legalistically has shown its inability to defend itself against the corrosion of evil. ... When a government starts an earnest fight against terrorism, public opinion immediately accuses it of violating the terrorist's civil rights. ... Such a tilt of freedom in the direction of evil has come about gradually, but it was evidently born primarily out of a humanistic and benevolent concept according to which there is no evil inherent to human nature.[52]

In a comment that showed awareness of a future ecological as well as a political crisis – a situation so obvious today – he made explicit reference to evil:

> [The] fight for our planet, physical and spiritual, a fight of cosmic proportions, is not a vague matter of the future; it has already started. The forces of Evil have begun their offensive; you can feel their pressure, and yet your screens and publications are full of prescribed smiles and raised glasses.[53]

He elaborated on the issue of moral principles:

> Very well-known representatives of your society ... say: We cannot apply moral criteria to politics. Thus, we mix good and evil, right and wrong, and make space for the absolute triumph of absolute Evil in the world.[54]

---

51. Mahoney, *The Other Solzhenitsyn*, 79.
52. Aleksandr Solzhenitsyn, *A World Split Apart* (New York: Harper & Row, 1978) 21
53. Ibid., 37.
54. Ibid., 39.

His most profound analysis of Western society showed – despite his use of *we* – that he was himself a man from the East with its own spiritual heritage, one now repudiated by Russian Communism, but still a force to be reckoned with in the lives of the many simple people whom he had praised in his writing. He went back to the European Renaissance to show what had gone wrong, he claimed, in the West.

> The Middle Ages had come to a natural end by exhaustion, becoming an intolerable despotic repression of man's physical nature in favour of the spiritual one. Then, however, *we* turned our backs upon the Spirit and embraced all that is material with excessive and unwarranted zeal. This new way of thinking, which had imposed on us its guidance, did not admit the existence of intrinsic evil in man nor did it see any higher task than the attainment of happiness on earth. It based modern Western civilization on the dangerous trend to worship man and his material needs. (Italics in the original)[55]

Probably without knowing it, the literary Solzhenitsyn was endorsing the views of theologians who for more than a generation had inveighed against theological liberalism in both Europe and the United States. The most powerful critique was probably that of the Reformed theologian Helmut Richard Niebuhr (1894–1962), who in his *The Kingdom of God in America* (1937) made the famous summing up of liberal Protestantism's creed: 'A God without wrath brought men without sin into a kingdom without judgment through the ministrations of a Christ without a cross.'[56] It is interesting that while Solzhenitsyn mentioned evil ten times, he made no reference to sin in his address and referred to God only twice. While he held that radical or absolute evil had a dense nucleus or core, he did not speculate about it from a religious perspective.

Mikhail Bulgakov (1891–1940)

Bulgakov was born in the then Russian city of Kiev and died at a comparatively young age in Moscow, after a career as a doctor, a dramatist and a novelist, during Stalin's regime, when censorship was as big a problem for him as it would be for Solzhenitsyn. In his initial career as a dramatist, he enjoyed critical acclaim (and even Stalin's approval), but as the regime became more oppressive, he was required by the secret service to burn the manuscript that was the basis of *The Master and Margarita*. He burned half of it and subsequently wrote that part from memory, continuing his work privately until his death. The manuscript had a chequered history; a censored version with some text removed appeared in *Moskva* magazine in 1966, and – as would happen with Solzhenitsyn's *Gulag Archipelago* six years

---

55. Ibid., 43.
56. H. Richard Niebuhr, *The Kingdom of God in America* (Middletown, CT: Wesleyan University Press, 1988), 193.

later – a smuggled version was published in Paris in 1967. The full text was printed and distributed by hand in the Soviet Union in a practice known as *samizdat* at that time and finally was openly published in Russia in 1973.

Bulgakov followed the tradition of the great Russian novel by introducing twenty characters in what was by Russian standards a book of moderate length. Many literary influences on him have been identified, with Goethe's *Faust* the most obvious in a book about the devil's activity, the demonic aspect of the Soviet regime, and, it emerged, of the elite citizenry. One of the first characters to appear is a newspaper editor, Mikhail Berlioz, clearly named after Hector Berlioz, composer of *The Damnation of Faust*. There may well have been an evocation of Mark Twain's *Mysterious Stranger*, in that the first chapter describes Berlioz and a poet, Ivan Poniryov, engaged in conversation, and a stranger who invites himself to join them. As with Twain, this stranger becomes the principal protagonist of the novel and, as with Twain, displays superhuman powers in the initial encounter, even to the extent of producing the brand of cigarette desired by the poet. Bulgakov evidently intended that the reader would recognise the clues to the identity of the stranger, while Twain was less subtle, as in his book the young stranger soon identified himself as Satan.

The two friends' conversation was about the non-existence of Jesus Christ, the subject of a poem the editor had published and now wanted the poet to improve, as 'his Jesus had come out, well, completely alive, a Jesus who had really existed, although admittedly a Jesus who had every possible fault'.[57] Having joined in the conversation, the stranger (a Frenchman? a German? they pondered silently) expresses his delight at their professed atheism, but then says: 'But this is the question that disturbs me – then who, one wonders, rules the life of man and keeps the world in order?'.[58] The poet replies angrily at once that 'man rules himself'.

The poet Ivan's angry though possibly conflicted reply reveals the Soviet ideology, which 'combined a discourse of modern self-fashioning with a narrow, prescriptive definition of what it meant to be a good Communist'.[59] Being a good Communist involved two contradictory positions: 'The first stressed personal responsibility, while the other asked for the renunciation of the self in the interest of a common cause.'[60] As the story of Jesus' trial and execution becomes the second narrative interspersed in the book, beginning with chapter 2, it is clear that the ruling regime's world-view parodies the Christian understanding of life, which also demands renunciation of self. It is difficult to keep up with the double narrative of the book, even if this was Bulgakov's intention; evidence that it was emerges in the book when the author of Jesus' trial is identified simply as the master, a man whose

---

57. Mikhail Bulgakov, *The Master and Margarita*, Michael Glenny, trans. (London: Fontana, 1984), 13.

58. Ibid., 18.

59. Jessica E. Merrill, 'The Stalinist Subject and Mikhail Bulgakov's "The Master and Margarita"', *Russian Review*, vol. 74, no. 2 (April 2015): 293.

60. Ibid., 294.

manuscript of the story was burned by the authorities. The stranger's probing and the poet's response seem to be Bulgakov's way of expressing the tension, which in fact was felt by independent-minded people like himself during the Stalinist period, as well as hinting – in the course of the narrative – that the stranger 'keeps the world in order'.

> A man decides to go to Kidlovodsk ... a trivial matter you may think, because for no good reason he suddenly jumps up and falls under a tram! You're not going to tell me that he arranged to do that himself. Wouldn't it be nearer the truth that someone quite different was directing his fate? The stranger gave an eerie peal of laughter.[61]

Bulgakov was here following the traditional presentation of the devil as ruler of the world, an idea suggested by various Scripture passages and used explicitly by John's Gospel: 'The ruler of this world' (Jn 12.31; 14.30; 16.11). This concept of the devil is essential to the development of the narrative, because the stranger, soon to be identified as Professor Woland, goes on to work wonders and cause disaster in subsequent chapters, though without doing any direct harm himself to anyone. (A further Faustian connection can be seen in his name; in *Faust,* Mephistopheles spoke of the arrival of Squire Voland.) His numerous entourage includes a very large cat, appropriately named Behemoth, that walks on its hind legs and speaks, and in the final part of the story will be revealed as a demonic pageboy.[62] It can also appear as 'a large fat man in a tattered cap, with vaguely feline looks and carrying a primus stove', as he and Koroviev, Woland's principal assistant, proceed to cause havoc in an upmarket department store, where payment has to be made in foreign currency.[63]

The same two perform extraordinary marvels at a variety show, billed as a performance by Professor Woland, who had introduced himself at the beginning of the book as a professor of black magic. A farcical event occurs when Fagotto and the cat perform magic tricks that shower down money from the ceiling, and the latest fashions from Paris are given to the ladies, though all the magic gifts disappear afterwards. Both the chaos in the department store and the variety show reflect Bulgakov's attitude to the grasping, materialistic nature of Moscow's elite.

In *Faust* and in Marlowe's version, extraordinary powers were attributed to the devil. Bulgakov continued that tradition; his presentation of Woland and of his team of assistants introduces an element of fantasy, not excluding horror and humour, which made the book a literary masterpiece. But it was not a treatise on demonology. The Christian tradition has generally not seen the devil as responsible for physical evils. However, Bulgakov's intention was perfectly clear: the Soviet

---

61. Mikhail Bulgakov, *The Master and Margarita*, Michael Glenny, trans. (London: Fontana, 1984), 18.
62. Ibid., 399.
63. Ibid., 365–70.

regime and the successful citizens were in the power of whatever the reality for Bulgakov was behind the concept of the 'devil'. The way the plot develops makes Woland more a comic character than an evil one.

Bulgakov drew on the real life situations and events in the Moscow of his time: the scarcity of accommodation, for example, that allowed Woland and his strange entourage to magically take over the deceased Berlioz's apartment, and especially the spectacular real event marking the Spring Festival of 1935. The US ambassador to the Soviet Union, despite the Great Depression, hosted an extravagant reception for the elite of Moscow, featuring amazing displays of flowers and trees and collections of wild animals and birds.[64]

Margarita of the book's title comes on the scene when a parody of the real event takes place in a midnight ball. She is married to a devoted husband, but is lovelorn because her lover, the master of the title, has disappeared. She is persuaded to become the hostess at the ball, held in a vast pavilion decorated in a similar fashion to the US ambassador's actual event. The conductor of the orchestra is a Johann Strauss, the cat informs her.[65] Now Queen Margarita, she is required by Koroviev, who stands beside her, to receive the guests beginning with a man and woman who just before had been two skeletons that emerged from their coffins. Margarita shows little interest in Emperor Caligula and Messalina, 'as in the rest of the procession of kings, dukes, knights, suicides, hangmen, informers, traitors, madmen, detectives and seducers'.[66]

The second narrative, woven into the book beginning with chapter 2, serves Woland's purpose of demonstrating his existence through the ages as well as the issue of Jesus' historical existence he had raised in the first chapter. It deals with the trial of a certain Jeshua before an official described as Pontius Pilate the Procurator. In this way, the main narrative serves as a frame story, allowing the intercalation of the core of the Christian story in several chapters throughout the text and keeping Woland's claim to be a witness to the trial to the forefront. It emerges that a man referred to as the master is the narrator of the story of Pilate in this and subsequent chapters. His history is somewhat similar to the real-life author, Bulgakov, in having difficulties with the secret service and being required to burn his manuscript. This device allowed Bulgakov to comment on the official view of the historical Jesus as a lunatic or deceiver in the society of his day, influenced by the writings of Renan and Nietsche.

64. The Reception was organised by a staffer, Irena Wiley, who gave an account of it in her memoirs. The Ambassador commissioned her to do so – 'the sky is the limit'. Irena Wiley, *Around the Globe in Twenty Years* (New York: David McKay Company, 1962), 32: 'As the party was to be at the end of April, we decided to make it a green, white and gold Spring Festival: green trees, green grass, white tulips, white lambs with gilded horns and hooves, and white roosters in gold and glass cages.'
65. Bulgakov, *The Master and Margarita*, 278.
66. Ibid., 285.

The final chapter presents a party of riders on flying horses, as Woland and his entourage return to from whence they came.

> Night thickened, flew alongside, seized the riders' cloaks and pulling them from their shoulders, unmasked their disguises … and when a full purple moon rose towards them over the edge of a forest, all deception vanished and fell away into the marsh beneath as their magical, trumpery clothing faded into the mist.[67]

The night strips away Behemoth's fluffy tail and fur. 'The creature who had been the pet of the prince of darkness [is] revealed as a slim youth, a page–demon, the greatest jester that has ever been.' Koroviev becomes 'a knight clad in dark violet, with a grim and unsmiling face'.[68] Woland explains that once when they were talking of darkness and light, the knight had made an unfortunate pun and as a penance he had spent more time as a practical joker than he had bargained for. 'Both Azazello's eyes were alike, empty and black, his face white and cold. Azazello was now in his real guise, the demon of the waterless desert, the murderer-demon'.[69] In the moonlight a vague figure of a man could be seen seated on a massive stone chair. Woland says to the master, 'Now is your chance to complete your novel with a single sentence.' The master calls out to the seated Procurator, 'You are free. He is waiting for you' – Jeshua had pleaded for him in the completed narrative.

Margarita and the master ride with Woland. They had been poisoned by Azazello but brought back to life so that they could live a new life together, which Woland likens to that of Faust: 'Don't you want, like Faust, to sit over a retort in the hope of fashioning a new homunculus? That's where you must go where a house and an old servant are already waiting for you and the candles are lit.… In the first rays of the morning, the master and his beloved crossed a little moss-grown stone bridge. They left the stream behind them and followed a sandy path'.[70]

> Then the black Woland, taking none of the paths, dived into the abyss, followed with a roar by his retinue. The mountains, the platform, the moonbeam pathway, Jerusalem – all were gone.[71]

Bulgakov's novel ranks with the best of twentieth-century fiction, but because of the mixed genre to which it belongs, incorporating the supernatural, political satire, humour and fantasy, it has not received the acclaim of single theme works such as Pasternak's *Dr Zhivago* or Solzhenitsyn's *Gulag Archipelago*. As a modern novel, however, it stands out for its treatment of evil through the device of personifying it as a Satanic figure who does battle with an evil regime. Woland and his retinue are themselves the devil and his angels, but their involvement in the world amounts

---

67. Ibid., 398.
68. Ibid., 399.
69. Ibid.
70. Ibid., 402–3.
71. Ibid., 404.

to identifying the evil of the Soviet elite. What Bulgakov himself believed about Christianity may be hidden in his and in the master's story of Jeshua, but is no more accessible than what he, as so many authors of recent centuries, believed about the devil. The same could be said about the Italian Jewish writer Primo Levi.

Primo Levi (1919–87)

Levi's powerful work, *If This Is a Man* (1958), is an account of his experiences during a year spent in Auschwitz and its outlying Buna camp from February 1944 to its dissolution in March 1945. It is probably the most powerful example of Holocaust literature, even though Elie Wiesel's *Night* is also a well-known account of life in Auschwitz-Birkenau, but one described by critics as fictionalised-autobiography. It is certainly an eye-witness account of the fifteen-year-old Wiesel and his father, and Wiesel described it as his 'deposition, of which he would change nothing even if he waited another ten years to publish'.[72] But because of the history of the original very large manuscript, its editing by various publishers in various language editions, and Wiesel's own admissions about stories he invented, it is less impressive than the autobiography of the twenty-five-year-old Levi, all of whose characters are real and described by him in more detail in his later works.

Despite the setting, of cold and hunger, of cruelty and death, Levi's measured yet passionate style presented an account of human dignity constantly under attack from the Nazi regime, the victory of good over evil, and a harrowing tale of loss and of survival in extremely harsh conditions of forced labour, starvation and climate. But he acknowledged that moral integrity could hardly, if at all, survive in those conditions. In a later book, *Moments of Reprieve* (1981), he explained to a new, innocent and upright prisoner that it

> was necessary to get busy, organise illegal food, dodge work, find influential friends, hide one's thoughts, steal and lie; that whoever did not do so was soon dead.[73]

In the same book, he described Auschwitz as '*anus mundi*, ultimate drainage point of the German universe'.

If This Is a Man was followed by *The Truce*, a celebration of life over death and a recovery of the joy of living as he made his way homeward to Italy by a very circuitous route through Poland, Russia, Romania, Hungary and Austria.

The incident that gave the book its title reveals the evil that was at the heart of the Nazi regime and its policy of extermination in the concentration camps: the Jews and various other groups were considered less than human. In 1938, Heinrich Himmler in addressing a conference of SS Generals said that the

---

72. Elie Wiesel, *All Rivers Run to the Sea* (New York: Knopf Doubleday, 2010), 79.
73. Primo Levi, *If This Is a Man: The Truce* (London: Abacus, 1987), 109.

Jews were the 'primary matter of everything negative' (*Urstoff alles Negativen*).[74] Levi's memory and description of the incident were detailed, yet as he wrote his memoir a few years later, the whole event with its life-saving sequel now seemed a fantasy: 'Today, at this very moment, as I sit writing at a table, I myself am not convinced that these things really happened.'[75] But they had of course happened, and were so embedded in his consciousness as to have a reality all their own and therefore possibly a chimera. There had been a call from the authorities for prisoners who were industrial chemists to be put to work in a chemical plant, and this had involved a preliminary oral examination. When it came to Levi's turn, he was escorted into the office of Doktor Pannwitz. The interview, which did lead to his new employment, provided him with an insight into how he and his fellow prisoners were perceived simply by the way Pannwitz looked at him; it also served to give him a perception of evil.

> Pannwitz is tall, thin, blond; he has eyes, hair and nose as all Germans ought to have them, and sits formidably behind a complicated writing-table. I, Häftling 174517, stand in his office, which is a real office, shining, clean and ordered, and I feel that I would leave a dirty stain on whatever I touched. When he finished writing, he raised his eyes and looked at me. From that day I have thought about Doktor Pannwitz many times and in many ways. I have asked myself how he really functioned as a man; how he filled his time outside of Polymerisation and the Indo-Germanic conscience; above all when I was once more a free man, I wanted to meet him again, not from a spirit of revenge but merely from a personal curiosity about the human soul.
>
> Because that look was not one between two men; and if I had known how completely to explain the nature of that look, which came as if across the glass window of an aquarium between two beings who live in different worlds, I would also have explained the essence of the great insanity of the third Germany ... The brain which governed those blue eyes and those manicured hands said: 'This something in front of me belongs to a species which it is obviously opportune to suppress'.[76]

---

74. Josef Ackermann, *Heinrich Himmler Als Ideologe* (Göttingen: Musterschmidt, 1970), 160, cited in Daniel J. Goldhagen, *Hitler's Willing Executioners: Ordinary Germans and the Holocaust* (London: Little, Brown and Company, 1996), 412.

75. Levi, *If This Is a Man: The Truce*, 109; Hannah Arendt, *The Origins of Totalitarianism* (Cleveland, OH: Meridian Books, 1958), 444:

> There are no parallels to the life in the concentration camps. Its horror can never be fully embraced by the imagination for the very reason that it stands outside life and death. It can never be fully reported for the very reason that the survivor returns to the world of the living, which makes it impossible for him to believe fully in his own past experiences.

76. Levi, *If This Is a Man*, 111–12.

Levi thought of it in terms of insanity, and in *The Truce*, as he began his homeward journey via Russia, he reflected on the difference between the Russians and the Germans:

> [Under] their slovenly and anarchical appearance, it was easy to see in them, in each of those rough and open faces, the good soldiers of the Red Army, ... gentle in peace and fierce in war, strong from an inner discipline born from concord, from reciprocal love and from love of their country; a stronger discipline, because it came from the spirit, than the mechanical and servile discipline of the Germans.[77]

But he was soon disillusioned. At a railway station in Poland, he saw a painter covering the slogan 'Workers of the world unite!' with a coating of whitewash; 'in its place we saw, with a subtle sense of chill, another quite different slogan appear, letter by letter: "On towards the West".[78] War, as his Greek friend had told him, does not cease.

The insanity of the German regime was an example of a deeper malaise; the soul of a country, not just of a regime, was infected with evil. It cannot be said, however, that a new evil simply originated in Germany. It is true that Luther's diatribe of 1543 against the Jews, *On the Jews and Their Lies*, belonged to the history of German Lutheranism, but antisemitism was widespread in the Christian Middle Ages and persisted. His polemical treatise fell into the hands of the National Socialists and the propagandist, Julius Streicher, at his trial in Nuremberg in 1946, attempted to show there was nothing novel in current German antisemitism by appealing to Luther's call in the treatise for the burning of Jewish synagogues.[79] Luther's modern biographers point out that his opposition to the Jews was based on religion, on their anti-Christian stance and supposed practices, while the National Socialist attitude was racist. The religious element was nonetheless prominent in the overall approach to the Jews and contributed to the acceptance of the idea that they were enemies of the people, *das Volk*.

> One of the moral pastors of the nation, for example, the General Superintendent of the Kurmark Diocese of the Evangelical (Lutheran) Church in Prussia, Bishop Otto Dibelius, in a letter shortly after the April 1933 Boycott (of Jewish businesses) said that he had 'always been an antisemite'. 'One cannot fail to appreciate' he continued, 'that in all the corrosive manifestations of modern civilisations Jewry plays a leading role'.[80]

77. Ibid., 232.
78. Ibid., 292.
79. Fintan Lyons O.S.B., *Martin Luther: His Challenge Then and Now* (Dublin: Columba Press, 2017), 178.
80. Goldhagen, *Hitler's Willing Executioners*, 108.

In Germany's recent history, Jews had been accused of not serving in the military during the First World War, of not defending the Fatherland.

> Instead Jews were alleged to have been staying safe at home and using the wartime conditions to exploit and immiserate the Germans for their own profit in the black market.[81]

The economic hardship experienced by the population during the Weimar Republic, which came after the First World War, did nothing to alleviate this resentment and the antisemitic climate that prevailed in educational institutions. It created a generation of young people who became a large segment of the National Socialist movement. It is understandable that Jewish writers put great emphasis on the antisemitism that was endemic to German society leading up to the second war and during it, so it is interesting to read a 'confessional memoir' about how the Jewish population was perceived, written to her lost former childhood Jewish friend by an educated, devoted member of the Hitler Youth.

> *Those* Jews were and remained something mysteriously menacing and anonymous. They were not the sum of all Jewish individuals. … They were an evil power, something with the attributes of a spook. One could not see it but it was there, an active force for evil. … One was friendly with individual Jews, just as one was friendly as a Protestant with individual Catholics. But while it occurred to nobody to be ideologically hostile to *the* Catholics, one was, utterly, to *the* Jews. (Emphasis in the original)[82]

Clearly, the writer felt she was reflecting the attitude of the German population as a whole, and this is borne out by photographs from the 1930s as persecution of the Jews became widespread. A photo shows crowds lining the street in Regensburg the night after the attack on Jewish premises *Krystallnacht* to watch the deportation of Jewish men to Dachau.[83]

Cultural and religious antisemitism are in themselves insufficient to explain the progression from boycotting trade, to sequestration or destruction of Jewish property, to forced emigration, to deportation to concentration camps, to the so-called Final Solution. The evolution of evil was fed by an additional factor not confined to Germany, the growth over decades of the Western world's acceptance of eugenics. The world's first professorial chair in eugenics was established in 1909 at University College, London.[84] Eugenics meant the practice or advocacy of improving the human species by selectively mating people with specific desirable hereditary traits, with the added aim of reducing human suffering by breeding

---

81. Ibid., 81.
82. Ibid., 89.
83. Ibid., 100.
84. Michael Burleigh, *The Third Reich: A New History* (London: Macmillan, 2000), 346.

out diseases, disabilities and so-called undesirable characteristics from the human population. 'Breeding out' could mean controlling who might be allowed to create progeny, but it could also mean eliminating the unsuitable from the bloodline by compulsory sterilisation or, more radically, by forced euthanasia (from the Greek 'good death'). The eugenic policy was being promoted actively in the United States in the form of forced sterilisation of mentally handicapped men in various states from the beginning of the twentieth century. Modern eugenics is more often called human genetic engineering. Today the concept of self-chosen, assisted euthanasia is enshrined in the legislation of a growing number of countries and is considered an aspect of human rights legislation, though it remains controversial.

Eugenic research was being pursued in Germany before the National Socialist regime came to power in 1933 with the election of Adolf Hitler as chancellor on 30 January. Research by specialists in eugenics concluded that people inherited mental illness, criminal tendencies and even poverty, and that these conditions could be bred out of the gene pool. The high numbers of institutionalised mental illness patients led to growing acceptance that medical science's inability to treat these cases suggested that enforced euthanasia, or 'mercy killing', might be the only solution. This perception was already present among professionals in the mid-1930s. The National Socialist regime saw it somewhat differently as an opportunity to introduce 'Aryan cleansing' and thereby produce the purified Aryan race that was their goal. This programme under the direction of Hitler's physician, Karl Brandt, began in the early summer months of 1939 and initially targeted institutionalised disabled children, who were killed by injection or starvation, their parents being subsequently informed and a death certificate falsely indicating death from natural causes. It was gradually extended to include youths up to seventeen and by October a full-scale campaign, known as Aktion T4 (after the programme's coordinating office address, Tiergartenstrasse 4) included the killing of people with severe psychiatric, neurological or physical disabilities. Gassing chambers were placed in various secret locations. All of this preceded Hitler's decision in 1941 to implement the Final Solution, the extermination of the Jewish population in Germany and the occupied territories, but it provided the necessary experience and techniques that came to be used in Auschwitz and elsewhere.

There were protests as the secret campaign became known, including a sermon by the Archbishop of Münster, Clemens Count Von Galen, on 3 August 1941, a man whom the Nazi authorities feared to apprehend because of his great prestige. But there was a temporary halt in Germany itself on Hitler's orders, though it resumed in 1942 and continued until the end of the war.

This phased campaign included the introduction in March 1941 of *Einsatzgruppen*, the mobile killing units, in the occupied territories such as Poland. The policy of elimination, which soon included the gassing technique, was exposed for what it was in the trial of Adolf Eichmann in Jerusalem in 1961 for crimes against the Jewish people, for crimes against humanity and for war crimes. The role of Eichmann in the campaign described in the book by the Jewish writer Hannah Arendt, *Eichmann in Jerusalem: A Report on the Banality of Evil*,[85] served to reveal the activities of the whole hierarchy and levels of responsibility from Hitler downwards. It emerged very clearly in the course of the trial that Hitler – the 'madman', the 'demon' and 'incarnation of evil', as Count Claus Von Stauffenberg's little conspiracy group had seen him – was not the only architect of the extermination campaign. While there was a larger opposition to him motivated by the realisation that Germany faced defeat under his leadership, the high-ranking Nazis were indifferent to the horrors in which they were implicated. They were confident that with Hitler out of the way they could negotiate with the Allies as with equals, insensitive to the perception of the Allies and the population of the West generally that they were monsters.

An extremely efficient bureaucracy had been created to administer the extermination campaign in which Eichmann seems to have been a naïve man whose main characteristic was loyalty to the Führer. He was pushed around from one department to another, so that his responsibility for the campaign was not easily established. What was clear was that his and others' concentration on efficiency meant that inadvertence to its ultimate aim could be widespread among officials who were in competition for higher positions; Arendt's book clearly demonstrates the banality of evil.

As Daniel Goldhagen put it:

> From the accumulated evidence one can only conclude that conscience as such had apparently got lost in Germany, and this to a point that people hardly remembered it and ceased to realise that the surprising 'new set of German values' was not shared by the outside world.[86]

By 1943 many of the military leaders saw that the war could not be won but most could not bring themselves to overthrow Hitler:

> With no tradition of opposition to tyranny to guide them, the generals found it difficult to overcome inherent moral scruples. They reasoned that Germany was engaged in total war and that the majority of Germans still supported their führer. All soldiers had sworn a personal oath to Hitler.[87]

---

85. Hannah Arendt, *Eichmann in Jerusalem: A Report on the Banality of Evil* (London: Penguin Books, 1965).

86. Goldhagen, *Hitler's Willing Executioners*, 103. 'The member of the Nazi hierarchy most gifted at solving problems of conscience was Himmler' 105.

87. Klaus P. Fischer, *Nazi Germany: A New History* (London: Constable, 1995), 537. The final blow for Hitler, causing him to commit suicide, was the Reuter report that Himmler was endeavouring to negotiate a surrender through Swedish diplomatic officials. Fischer, *Nazi Germany*, 565.

The civilian population can hardly be condemned along with the regime as monsters. Awareness of the killing campaign at home, and of that less known abroad in the occupied territories, must inevitably have lessened as people looked to the war-front where their own relatives were at risk or were injured or killed in action. The atrocities in Auschwitz and the other camps seem to have been largely unknown to the general population.

As Arendt pointed out, evidence is hard to come by,

> but a few priceless stories (are) to be found in the war diaries of trustworthy men who were fully aware of the fact that their own shocked reaction was no longer shared by their neighbours.[88]

She relayed an account given by a physician in Königsberg, East Prussia, in January 1945, of his attempt to persuade a woman to leave the area as the Russian army approached.

> Where do you want to go? I ask her. She does not know, but she knows that they will all be brought into the Reich. And then she adds, surprisingly: 'The Russians will never get us. The Führer will never permit it. Much sooner he will gas us.' I look around furtively, but no one seems to find this statement out of the ordinary.[89]

Though quite far from Berlin, this woman was apparently aware that the extent of the destruction of human life included Germany itself, and out of loyalty to the Führer she was willing to be included in it. There was also the almost carpet-bombing campaign of the Allies, laying the country waste and killing thousands of people, especially in Dresden. This showed how evil infected the whole period. The Nazi regime was obsessed with creating a new Germany, cleansed of Jews (*Judenrein*) and all others that prevented the implementation of their policy. But their evil plan devoured them as well when the Nuremberg trials proceeded in 1946.

Siegfried Sassoon had been able to recognise and protest against those he held responsible for the suffering and deaths occurring during the first war. Most others, except for the most jingoistic, regarded it as a tragedy or perhaps an unfortunate necessity. This was before the Just War Theory, with its principles to establish whether a war is morally justified, had been accepted by most countries. According to it, a just war is permissible because it is a lesser evil, but it is still an evil. The theory relies on a distinction already made by Sassoon in his 1917 protest between defence and aggression.

The memoir of Primo Levi obviously made it clear that Hitler's policy of making Germany *Judenrein* was aggression of an ethnic cleansing kind, while his

---

88. Arendt, *Eichmann in Jerusalem*, 110.
89. Ibid., 111.

Lebensraum policy, space needed for the purified Aryan race, led to aggression and occupation of territories. He has rightly been held responsible for the evils of the Second World War, though others obviously shared that responsibility. Martin Luther King faced institutional evil as the ultimate source of his persecution by police and the judiciary, and paid the price of his life for his non-violent response. Stalin has been held responsible for the evils of the *Great Purge* (1936–8) in Russia, which led to Solzhenitsyn's imprisonment and exile, but Solzhenitsyn's own analysis went deeper and led to his famous conclusion that the line separating good and evil passes not through states, nor between classes, nor between political parties either but right through every human heart and through all human hearts.

Looking back on those chronicles of evil, many of those observers could take their reflections only so far, if they lacked the transcendent perspective and the language that Christian faith could provide. Christian faith has a historical dimension that deepens the understanding of evil by linking it with demonic activity. Historically, it was understood that dependence on God's grace, an ascetical way of life, and also on occasion, exorcism, were needed to defeat it.

PART III

EXORCISM: A HISTORICAL AND THEOLOGICAL ANALYSIS

Chapter 10

EXORCISM: THE HISTORICAL CONTEXT

A discussion of the history of exorcism in the course of a single chapter is necessarily selective. Below, examples will be presented from various centuries, countries and religious traditions, and the chapter will conclude with an account of contemporary attitudes towards its practice and of the extent of its use.

Exorcism in the early centuries

Exorcism rituals always existed in the ancient religions, and they persist today through the use of holy books in Buddhism, Hinduism and Taoism.[1] Exorcism is also found in Islam. Exorcism was part of the Jewish religion at the time of Christ, but today it is associated with the followers of the mystic movement, Kabbalah, rather than mainstream Judaism. It has been part of the Christian church's rituals throughout its history, though its use has had varying degrees of prominence according as crises arose from divisions in the church or from fear of an external spiritual enemy – at the time of the witchcraft trials, for example.[2]

Belief in the existence of the devil was part of the Christian tradition from the beginning, though not included in the various creeds. These profess what

---

1. John Nicola, *Diabolical Possession and Exorcism* (Rockford, IL: Tan Books, 1974), 110–14, reproduces an eyewitness account of a Taoist exorcism ceremony held sometime before 1961. It was of a man of about twenty-five and the Taoist priest was dressed in ritual robes. He read at length from Taoist scriptures and repeatedly called on demons to leave the man. The man suffered very violent convulsions, while expressions of refusal poured out of his distorted mouth in a shrill voice. Gradually, the priest became very weak and had to be supported by other monks, but eventually declared that he had won, while the man twisted and rolled on the bed and suddenly became still. According to local people, this ritual had a devastating effect on the health of the priests involved.

2. Francis Young, *A History of Exorcism in Catholic Christianity* (Switzerland: Palgrave Macmillan, 2016), 2; Diarmaid MacCulloch, *A History of Christianity: The First Three Thousand Years* (London: Allen Lane, 2009), 686: 'Maybe forty or fifty thousand people died in Europe and colonial North America on witchcraft charges between 1400 and 1800, most noticeably from around 1560.'

Christians believe *in*, which is different from believing *that* the devil exists. The belief was first formulated in chapter 1, no. 800 of the Fourth Lateran Council (1215–18). According to it, the devil and other demons were created good, but made themselves (per se) evil.[3] The doctrine was reiterated at the Council of Trent (1545–63). Irrespective of official decisions, it has always been a Christian instinct to respond to the existence of evil by endeavouring to name it.[4]

Little is known about the baptism rituals in the earliest Christian centuries – in some cases, as in Acts 10.44, it may even have been a baptism of the Spirit rather than a Johannine water baptism.[5] From the time of Tertullian, however, exorcisms were part of the baptismal rite in a threefold form of renunciation of the devil, his works and pomp, and indicated a belief that the unbaptised person was in some way under the sway of the devil. This was true even for one born of Christian parents, who were part of a believing community, as by then baptism of infants was common, despite Tertullian's disapproval. According to the third-century *Apostolic Tradition* (probably by Hippolytus), the bishop blessed the oil of exorcism, which the presbyter then applied to the one to be baptised, saying: 'Let all evil spirits depart from you.'[6]

In the second century, Justin Martyr (+160) did not distinguish between ordinary illness and demonic influence and so associated demonic possession with all illnesses, considering the essence of Christian exorcism to be healing: 'Many of our people, the Christians, by exorcising them in the name of Jesus Christ, … have healed and do even now heal, when they were not cured by all the other exorcists, and practisers of incantations and charmers.'[7]

Throughout the early Middle Ages, all extraordinary symptoms of diseases were viewed as the result of demonic possession. In short, the whole of creation was seen as assailed by demonic powers, which Christianity alone could overcome. There were periods when exorcism was in decline, according to André Goddu, mainly because they were not always successful in relieving symptoms.[8] Bert Roest offered

---

3. H. Denzinger and A. Schönmetzer, *Enchiridion Symbolorum* (Barcinone: Herder, 1965), 259.

4. Frédéric Le Gal, 'L'exorcisme: La Dépossession du Corps Surmontée', *Stress et Trauma* 8 (2) (2008): 107–13, at 108: 'Doesn't the figure of the devil, at least that of the Christian tradition, represent an attempt to shed light on this elusive reality of evil which, by means of a personal figure [the devil, Satan, the Evil one], becomes graspable because it is named?' (my translation).

5. K. W. Noakes, 'From New Testament Times until St Cyprian', in *The Study of the Liturgy*, Cheslyn Jones et al., eds (London: S.P.C.K., 1992), 114.

6. Bernard Botte O.S.B., *La Tradition Apostolique* (Paris: Les Éditions du Cerf, 1946), 50.

7. Justin Martyr, *Second Apology*, 6, in *The Works of S. Justin the Martyr* (Oxford: J.H. and J.S. Parker, 1861), 62.

8. André Goddu, 'The failure of exorcisms in the Middle Ages', in *Witchcraft, Magic and Demonology: A Twelve Volume Anthology of Scholarly Articles*, Brian Levack, ed., vol. 9, *Possession and Exorcism* (New York: Garland, 1992), 4.

an explanation for Goddu's view, by distinguishing between charismatic exorcisms and professional exorcism based on procedures with a semi-sacramental status, which were on the rise:

> Goddu developed his thesis on the decline of charismatic exorcism on the basis of frequency of references to exorcisms in later medieval saints' lives within the October volumes of the *Acta Sanctorum*. ... [There was] an increase in the thirteenth-century, a relative decline in the fourteenth, and a massive decline in the fifteenth.[9]

Francis of Assisi (1181?-1226)

Saint Francis was probably the best known of the charismatic healers and exorcists in the Middle Ages. As a deacon, he was not authorised to use official rituals. Thomas de Celano wrote the first hagiographical account of his life, the *Vita Prima*, shortly after his death, and despite early controversies in the Franciscan movement leading to the destruction of de Celano's works, it was in later generations regarded as objective.[10] A number of chapters recorded Francis's healing and exorcism ministry. There are homely touches to these accounts, even suggesting authenticity; in one case Francis showed reluctance when implored by the parents to heal a child a few years old who was weak and lame and still confined in a cradle:

> The saint refused for a long time, judging himself useless and unworthy of such power and such grace. But at last, overcome by the persistence of the father's entreaties, Saint Francis prayed, laid his hands on the head of the boy, and blessing him, lifted him up. Immediately, the boy stood up healed, and with the onlookers rejoicing, began to walk all around the house.[11]

This was an example of his healings; exorcisms were also chronicled and again an attractive human touch was evident – some thought he was dealing with possession in a case where he himself did not seem to know. One of his brethren suffered from what would seem to have been epileptic symptoms – though the man, stretched out rigid on the ground, was also suddenly lifted up into the air and bounced back on to the ground:

> The holy father Francis took pity on his condition, went to see him, and, after praying, signed him and blessed him. The man was suddenly healed.[12]

9. Bert Roest, 'Demonic possession and the practice of exorcism: An explanation of the Franciscan heritage', *Franciscan Studies*, vol. 76 (2018): 301–40, at 316.
10. Jacques Le Goff, *San Francesco d'Assisi* (Roma-Bari: Editori Laterza, 2000), 21.
11. Thomas de Celano, *Vita Prima Sancti Francisci* 23.65 in *Francis of Assisi: Early Documents*, vol. 1, The Saint, Regis J. Armstrong O.F.M. Cap. et al., eds (New York: New City Press, 1999), 240.
12. Ibid., 25.68, 241.

One day Francis and three of his brothers came to a village called San Gemini (today the multi-towered San Gimignano). They stayed in the house of a man whose wife was said to be troubled by a demon, 'as all the people living in the area were aware'. The husband, trusting in his holiness, implored him to heal her:

> But since the blessed Francis preferred in his simplicity to be held in contempt rather than to be lifted up by worldly honour for some display of holiness, he refused to do it. ... Since so many people kept asking, he gave in to their pleas. He called over the three brothers who were with him, and set one in each corner of the house, 'Brothers,' he said, 'let us pray to the Lord for this woman, that God may shake off the devil's yoke from her, to his praise and glory.' He added: 'Let us stand apart in the corners of the house to prevent the evil spirit from fleeing or deceive us by trying to hide in the corners.'

When they finished praying, Francis approached the woman and said:

> In the name of Our Lord Jesus Christ, I command you, demon, under obedience, to come out from her and not trouble her any more. He had scarcely uttered the words, when the demon came out.

It did so with such swiftness and the woman's cure was so sudden that Francis 'thought he was deceived and he left the place right away, ashamed'.[13]

Thomas de Celano wrote a second life of Francis at the request of the General Chapter of the Order held in 1244. It contained information he had acquired after the first publication. It chronicled the development of the life in more detail, omitted the healings and exorcisms of the first life, but added a *Treatise on the Miracles of Blessed Francis*. The *Vita Secunda* dealt with the inner life of Francis and his brothers and the temptations by the devil they endured. It included an incident in which devils assaulted Francis during the night, leaving him very weak.[14]

From charismatic to official exorcism

The move away from accounts of charismatic exorcisms evident in the course of one generation continued with the life of Francis written by Saint Bonaventure in 1269, as the development of sacramental theology by the scholastic theologians gave more precision to the concept of a sacrament as an instrumental cause of grace, and placed more emphasis on its importance. This had implications for the status of exorcisms, as their role in the conferring of the sacrament of baptism

---

13. Ibid., 25.69, 242.
14. *St Francis of Assisi: Writings and Early Biographies*, Marion Habig, ed. (Chicago: Franciscan Herald Press, 1972³). Chapters LXXXI to LXXXV deal with his temptations, LXXXVI with the assault, 462–3.

was prominent. In effect, were exorcisms an unnecessary extra? Peter the Chanter (+1197), who devoted his *Summa de Sacramentis* to baptism, pondered why some exorcised children died before baptism, while un-exorcised children survived.[15] Precision was needed with regard to demonic possession, if the place of exorcism was to be vindicated.

The solution that emerged among scholastic theologians such as Aquinas in the thirteenth century was to interpret demonic possession as demonic influence on a person internally and externally:

> Aquinas claimed that angels, being purely intellectual creatures, were not in any way corporeal. Their immaterial constitution explains how they could exist in great numbers. Since demons were believed to be fallen angels, they too were spiritual beings. Unless angels and demons were pure spirit, it would have been hard to imagine how hundreds or even thousands of demons could have occupied the body of a demoniac at the same time. Designating demons as immaterial spirits obviated the problem of explaining how even one of them could penetrate a human body, a feat that would be difficult if they were in any sense corporeal.[16]

Exorcists believed, therefore,

> the power of the devil can be strengthened through sin, but exorcism protects one from this internal influence. The physical effects of demonic influence, however, may remain after a successful exorcism.[17]

---

15. Goddu, 'The failure of exorcisms in the Middle Ages', 11. Cantor was concerned also about how the unbaptised (un-exorcised) could be saved and held that deceased baptised children should be honoured with the feast of a Confessor. Petrus Cantor, *Summa de Sacramentis et Consiliis*, vol. 3 (Beauvechain: Nauwelaerts, 1952), 347.

16. Brian Levack, *The Devil Within: Possession and Exorcism in the Christian West* (New Haven, CT: Yale University Press, 2013), 58: 'Demons and angels were not central concerns for Thomas, but in his massive *Summa Theologica* he conducted a systematic investigation of the nature of spirits and of demonic power.' Aquinas had said in *S.T.* Ia q110 a2 that 'corporeal matter does not obey either good or bad angels at their will', but in q114 a4 he said that demons can employ certain seeds that exist in the elements of the world in order to transmute matter by natural powers (such as putrefaction) from one form to another. So demons can produce transformations of matter 'into serpents and frogs'. But if the transformation cannot be produced by natural powers, the transformation by the operation of the demon is not real but 'a mere semblance of reality'. However, 'just as [the demon] from the air can form a body of any form and shape and assume it so as to appear in it visibly: so in the same way he can clothe any corporeal thing with any corporeal form, so as to appear therein'. See also Chapter 3.

17. Goddu, 'The failure of exorcisms in the Middle Ages', 13.

This insight, that the effects of exorcism were restricted to the spiritual, was common to the thirteenth-century scholastics, including Thomas Aquinas in *Sententiae* IV, d6, q2, art 3. As will be seen in the next chapter, the practice of repeated exorcisms, which sometimes occurs today, does not seem to take account of this distinction.

In the later Middle Ages, the use of exorcisms was restricted to official formulas because of the abuses stemming from popular usage and the practices of heretics, especially the threat posed by the dualism of the Catharist[18] heresy that had emerged in the twelfth century:

> The Catharist heresy challenged orthodox Christian teaching on the origin of evil, forcing theologians to return to the question of Satan, his agents and how to deal with him.[19]

Orthodoxy and exorcism

The Byzantine Church derived its exorcism customs from the early centuries and as a result did not restrict the practice of exorcism to official formulas or ministers in the way the Western Church did, though it did develop an official rite, *Un Office byzantin d'Esorcisme*.[20]

> Exorcising is practised in the Greek Orthodox Church today in the Sacraments of Baptism, in exorcising satanic powers in the case of the evil eye (*Vaskania*) and in exorcising the devil in the case of a possessed person.[21]

18. Steven Runciman, *The Medieval Manichee: A Study of the Christian Dualist Heresy* (Cambridge: Cambridge University Press, 1988); Adriaan H. Bredero, *Christendum and Christianity in the Middle Ages*, Reinder Bruinsma, trans. (Grand Rapids, MI: William B. Eerdmans, 1994), 29:

> The Cathari (or Albigensians) ... first appeared in Western Europe in the twelfth-century in a number of urban centres, being noted first in the Rhineland around 1143. It is probable that their movement originated in the Balkans. ... Both Catharism and Manichaeism presupposed an evil power operating independently from the power of good. Matter, both groups said, belongs to the realm of evil, while the spiritual was of the realm of the good. ... The Cathari rejected both baptism, except by the Spirit, and the Eucharist.

19. Young, *A History of Exorcism in Catholic Christianity*, 62; Bredero, *Christendum and Christianity*, 363: 'Catharism ... may well have begun precisely as resistance against changes in the church, resulting from the church's increasing interaction with society, changes that the Cathars refused to come to terms with.'

20. Louis Delatte O.S.B., ed., *Un Office byzantin de l'Esorcisme* (Bruxelles: Académie royale Belgique, 1957).

21. George C. Papademetriou, 'Exorcism and the Greek Orthodox Church', in *Exorcism through the Ages* (New York: Philosophical Library, 1974), 52.

Today the *Orthodox Book of Prayers* (Ευχολόγιο στο μέγα) is used extensively.[22] This book has prayers of exorcism from the early centuries, attributed to Saint Basil and Saint Chrysostom.

But a study by Charles Stewart of current exorcism customs on the island of Naxos, *Demons and the Devil: Moral Imagination in Modern Greek Culture*[23] established that popular belief and exorcistic practices persist regarding demons long associated with streams and places and that the faithful themselves actively engage in exorcism rites. For example, some old women told him of the *Hyalou* prayer used to prevent a demon strangling a child at night, the prayer being 'partly a saints' legend and partly an exorcism'.[24] He gave an example of such a popular exorcism:

> An exorcism text dating from the sixteenth century records how the devil was sworn out of the body and ordered to descend into the big toe of the left foot, where presumably it would be alright to remain.[25]

In 1486, Heinrich Institor and Jacob Springer published *Malleus maleficarum*, a treatise principally directed against witches. In it they maintained the efficacy of official exorcisms, though not against injuries caused by witches or demons, and explained that any failures were due to lack of faith. The popular belief that demons could cause physical injury as well as symptoms of mental derangement persisted.

Apparitions

In addition to alleged cases of witchcraft and possession, claims to have seen an apparition also needed investigation. In early modern Spain, where there was a multitude of such incidents, the Inquisition investigated cases to establish whether reported visions were of diabolical origin and sometimes inflicted punishment. More often, it was dealing with accounts from simple rural dwellers rather than intense religious people and allowed the establishment of shrines, which the seers claimed the Virgin Mary or others saints instructed them to establish:

> Mary was the most important saint in terms of the number of images and district or regional shrines. As the use of images spread through the West in the twelfth and thirteenth centuries, Mary's popularity as a helping saint gradually eclipsed

---

22. Nicholas Papadopolous, ed., *Euchologion to Mega* (Athens: Michael Salivou Press, 1927).
23. Charles Stewart, *Demons and the Devil: Moral Imagination in Modern Greek Culture* (Princeton, NJ: Princeton University Press, 2016).
24. Ibid., 100.
25. Ibid., 178.

Jeanne d'Arc (1412-31)

The case in France of Jeanne d'Arc (1412-31) was very different: her visions of St Michael the Archangel led to her involvement in the struggle against the English occupation of the greater part of France, and her trial was not one where the Inquisition might have vindicated, punished or exorcised her, but instead a politically motivated one.

An official of the French Inquisition was present, though not in charge, when she was tried for heresy by a pro-English bishop, Pierre Cauchon, in a case arising from the military struggle between King Charles VII and the English forces occupying France. Heresy was the charge against anyone accused of religious deviancy, though in her case the trial clearly did not have to do with religious deviancy. Her short career began after an interview with King Charles, in which she convinced him that she had a vision of the Archangel Michael and St Catherine of Siena instructing her to come to his aid militarily. After a short and very successful campaign, she was captured and put on trial in Rouen, in January 1431, in order to eliminate the threat her military leadership posed to the English. She was executed on 30 May of that year.

The interrogators at her trial set out to demonstrate the falsity of her visions by showing that she had no miraculous signs to prove their authenticity; she claimed that the help she received from the saints in her military success was such a sign:

> Asked how, if the enemy, the devil, transformed himself in the form or visage of an angel, would she know if it was a good or bad angel, she said she would know well enough if it was Saint Michael or something disguised as him. She also said that the first time she was very unsure if it was Saint Michael. And the first time she was very afraid; and she saw him many times before she knew it was Saint Michael.[27]

The interrogators could not impugn Jeanne's visions any more than she could prove them. From the start, they 'were convinced that her voices were evil spirits. ... [They believed] that in fact they were evil spirits in disguise with whom she had an idolatrous pact'.[28]

Historians have generally sought to explain her visions in terms of mental or even physical illness, but such studies tended to rule out genuine religious experience too easily. King Charles VII, while initially sceptical, trusted her,

---

26. William A. Christian, Jr, *Apparitions in Late Medieval and Renaissance Spain* (Princeton, NJ: Princeton University Press, 1981), 13–14.
27. Ibid., 189.
28. Ibid., 190–1.

though he had witnessed the symptoms of mental illness in his own father. Two inquests ordered by Charles VII led to a re-trial established by the Inquisition and a declaration in 1455 nullifying the original. She was canonised by the Catholic Church in 1920. Her case was of widespread interest in France and had significant national implications, unlike most cases where alleged visionaries lived and were investigated in rural and politically neutral settings.

The Reformation churches and exorcism

The sixteenth-century Reformation brought about a reaction against what were considered the superstitious practices of the medieval church, with exorcism regarded with suspicion, though initially part of the baptism ritual. Luther, in his *Taufbuechlein*, spoke of the seriousness of acting against the devil by the celebration of the baptismal rite, but said that the traditional ancillary ceremonies, such as insufflation, placing salt in the mouth, and the like were of little importance (*minimi momenti*).[29] He extolled baptism as 'the only consolation and entry to all God's blessings' and required the minister to say: 'Go out, you unclean spirit!, and give space to the Holy Spirit.' Before the reading of the Gospel, the minister was to say: 'I adjure you, you unclean spirit, by the name of the Father + and the Son + and the Holy Spirit +, to go out and depart from this servant of Jesus Christ. Amen.'

Not all Lutheran churches were in favour of the use of exorcism in baptism, some considering it an *adiaphoron* or optional rite, while others in South Western Germany simply excluded it; it was never used in four of the principalities and four cities. Philip Melanchthon 'had mixed feelings about the rite. He would have preferred to see it done away with, but tolerated it where it had been retained'.[30] A controversy developed in various principalities as many Lutherans viewed its abolition as 'an indication of crypto- or outright Calvinism'.[31] Interference by secular authorities complicated the matter as various princes or electors began to favour the Calvinist view of exorcism as a relic of 'papal superstition'. Pastors who insisted on its inclusion were removed from their parishes and in some cases imprisoned. In 1590, a new *Tauchbuechlein*, produced in Anhalt, eliminated exorcism. A displaced pastor, along with others, wrote a protest:

> Now they are eliminating exorcism from baptism, then the altars will have to go, thereafter pictures and paintings, and finally all organs and singing.[32]

29. J. T. Müller, *Die symbolischen Bücher der evangelisch-lutherischen Kirche* (Stuttgart: Verlag von Samuel Gottlieb Liesching, 1860), 835–7.

30. Bodo Nischan, 'The exorcist controversy and baptism in the later reformation', *The Sixteenth-Century Journal*, vol. 18, no. 1 (1987): 31–52 at 33.

31. Ibid., 34.

32. Ibid., 42; R. Po-Chia Hsia, *Social Discipline in the Reformation: Central Europe 1550–1750* (London: Routledge, 1989), 27: 'According to [Calvinists in Germany] Lutheranism had not gone far enough in eradicating all vestiges of "papal superstition". Where Calvinist

These events were signs of the gradual encroachment of Calvinist doctrine into Lutheran (and Catholic) Germany, a process enhanced by the publication of the Calvinist *Heidelberg Catechism* (1563).[33] Calvin believed that the addition of ceremonies came about because the 'boldness of men' considered that simply to be baptised with water was a 'contemptable thing'.[34] Elsewhere, he spoke of the seriousness of using God's name: the tongue should take account of the 'loftiness of the sacred name' and he condemned the 'abominable abuse of God's name' in 'unlawful exorcisms and other wicked incantations'.[35]

The history of exorcism in the churches of the Reformation since then is marked by the divergence of views arising from the theological differences between the Lutheran and Calvinist traditions. Calvin's reserve about the use of God's name made him (in addition to basic Reformation principles) reluctant to speak of the saints traditionally honoured. Protestant tradition further developed his attitude by eschewing invocation of saints in prayer, a further abuse they believed of the worship due to God. In what was a paradoxical consequence there came a refusal also to address demons directly in exorcisms.[36]

The question arises as to whether a reductionist approach to ritual, especially if there is radical emphasis on the Word to the neglect of sacramental rites as happens in some forms of Protestant worship, has had over centuries an adverse effect on the psychological well-being of worshipers. The comparison with the more ritualistic and colourful liturgies of the Catholic and Orthodox traditions is well known. Irrespective of the use of exorcism among the various groups, it may be that ritual in the performance of worship has a healing effect in relation to the dark side of people's experiences, and staves off threats to mental health. Émile Durkheim's sociological study of suicide in the nineteenth century included a chapter on suicide statistics for various religious groups:

> If one casts a glance at the map of European suicide, it is at once clear that in purely Catholic countries like Spain, Portugal, Italy, suicide is very little developed, while it is at its maximum in Protestant countries, in Prussia, Saxony, Denmark.[37]

worship was proclaimed, the churches were "purified": the High Altar, clerical vestments, paintings and sculptures disappeared; bread replaced wafers at communion, to be broken and not consecrated; exorcism vanished from infant baptism.'

33. See Robert Kolb and Carl R. Trueman, *Between Wittenberg and Geneva: Lutheran and Reformed Theology in Conversation* (Grand Rapids, MI: Baker Academic, 2017), 147–74.

34. John Calvin, *Institutes of the Christian Religion* IV.xv.19, F. L. Battles, trans. (Philadelphia, PA: Westminster Press, 1960), 151.

35. Ibid., II.viii.22, 388.

36. Francis Young, *A History of Anglican Exorcism: Deliverance and Demonology in Church Ritual* (London: Bloomsbury, 2018), 4.

37. Émile Durkheim, *Suicide: A Study in Sociology*, John A. Spaulding and George Simpson, trans. (London: Routledge, 1952), 105.

He did speculate that the minority status of Jews and Catholics in the countries surveyed could be a factor explaining the relative rarity of voluntary deaths in those two confessions.

> Obviously, the less numerous confessions, facing the hostility of the surrounding populations, in order to maintain themselves are obliged to exercise severe control over themselves and subject themselves to an especially rigorous discipline.[38]

But after further analysis, he concluded that 'the only essential difference between Catholicism and Protestantism is that the second permits free enquiry to a far greater degree than the first'.[39] This was a sociological study and did not take account of an 'essential' difference such as ritual, which would seem of greater psychological and religious importance in relation to coping with fundamental evil.[40]

History of the Catholic Rite of Exorcism

In part because of the repudiation of the use of exorcisms by some of the emerging Reformation churches, the Catholic Church reasserted its belief at the Council of Trent and created a *Rite of Exorcism* in 1614. This included a solemn form of exorcism more developed than those used in the baptismal ceremony. It recognised that in cases where certain phenomena, such as blasphemous utterances or speaking in languages not known by the person, the devil had taken over control of the person's thoughts and action, though official belief was that the devil could not have total control over the person's will and so cause him/her to sin.[41] This restriction of the devil's powers, asserted for example by Augustine, fell short of the popular medieval belief in possession in the form of the inhabiting of the body by a demon while the soul was in *Inferno*, as recorded by Dante. Such a belief showed evidence of an extreme dualistic anthropology, while tradition continued

---

38. Ibid., 110.
39. Ibid., 112.
40. Ben Ryan, 'Christianity and Mental Health: Theology, Activities, Potential', *Theos*, July 2017, 56: 'When it comes to mental health there is now an evidence base from which to claim that Christianity makes a positive difference. The Theos Report, Religion and Wellbeing, ... demonstrates a particularly strong correlation between good mental health and participation in group religious activities (e.g. attending church), and between good mental health and high levels of subjective religiosity.' https://ctbi.org.uk/christianity-and-mental-health-theos-report/.
41. Cardinal Estévez, 'Prefect of the Congregation for the Divine Cult and Discipline of the Sacraments', Press Conference, 26 January 1999.

to consider demons as consisting of 'some kind of aerial substance', forces capable of affecting the body, as Augustine held.[42]

The nuns of Loudun

The notorious case of the alleged demonic possession of some Ursuline nuns of Loudun, France, in September 1632 comes to mind in this regard. As in that of Jeanne d'Arc, the case involves quite non-religious aspects such as personal enmity between clergy, political calculation (by Cardinal Richelieu) and the unjustified torture and execution of a priest, Urbain Grandier, who was considered the devil's agent. All these put a question mark against the authenticity of any diabolical involvement with the nuns. Of interest here, however, is the record of the exorcism of the nuns by a priest, Pierre Barré, at the order of the archbishop of Bordeaux and following the procedure laid down in the *Rituale Romanum* of 1614. One of the tests approved was the language test. Barré therefore questioned the afflicted in Latin to establish whether they could speak in a language of which an allegedly possessed nun had no knowledge, and seemed to get replies in inaccurate Latin. According to Michel de Certeau in his *La Possession de Loudun*, 'Barré made several attempts to make the demons speak Irish (*lingua Scotica*) and Hebrew but was accused of excessive curiosity by the demons (a fault specifically condemned in the Rituale).'[43]

Aldous Huxley, in his *The Devils of Loudun*, gave a more credible account of the event. He explained the odd reference to the *lingua Scotica* by referring to a visit to the scene of the exorcisms by a James Maitland from Scotland, who challenged the exorcist by offering to confound both the credulous friars in attendance and the alleged possessed by speaking in Scots Gaelic. His offer was not taken up, but the friars countered by saying that some devils were not well educated. With regard to those who believed the nuns were possessed, Huxley, who 'saw nothing self-contradictory in the idea of possession', concluded: 'How such an opinion can be held by anyone who has read the relevant documents, and who has even the slightest knowledge of abnormal psychology, I confess myself unable to understand.'[44]

---

42. Augustine, *City of God*, XV, 23 (Washington, DC: Catholic University of America, 1951), 471.

43. Michel Certeau, *La Possession de Loudun* (Paris: Archives Gallimard Juliard, 1980²), 65–7; See also Wade Baskin, 'The devils of Loudun', in *Exorcism through the Ages* (New York: Philosophical Library, 1974), 22–7. According to Baskin's account, two exorcists, not Barré, died insane and a Br Surin brought the exorcisms to an end.

44. Aldous Huxley, *The Devils of Loudun: A Study in the Psychology of Power Politics and Mystical Religion in the France of Cardinal Richelieu* (New York: Harper Torchbooks, 1952), 176. But see also D. P. Walker, *Unclean Spirits: Possession and Exorcism in France and England in the Late Sixteenth and Early Seventeenth Centuries* (London: Scolar Press, 1981), 1, referring to 'Aldous Huxley's well-informed but vulgar and fictionalised, account in his

The veracity of the nuns was questioned by a contemporary, Marc Duncan, a school principal, who recorded his impressions in *Discours de la Possession de Religieuses Ursulines de Lodun* (1634). The exorcist told one of the nuns to release her hold on the arm of another and she replied that she could not because a demon held it fast: 'it must be that he is stronger than I.'[45]

The Miracle of Laon

This concerns the case of a girl of fifteen or sixteen, Nicole Obry, of Vervins near Laon in Picardy, who was exorcised in public in the Cathedral of Laon many times in 1566, in ceremonies involving the administration of the Eucharist. It was a novel approach for an exorcism and came about because of the larger context of the dispute between Catholics and Huguenots on the nature of the Eucharist, which in turn had powerful political connotations.[46] Another unusual aspect of the case was that the possessing devil, identified early on as Beelzebub, seemed to engage verbally in the dispute centring on what was referred to as the Real Presence of the body and blood of Christ in the consecrated host, and, oddly, not in support of the Huguenots. The girl at the centre of the dramatic events, Nicole, had a far from normal history: recently married in her teens, she had been reared and educated in a convent where she had learned to read, but was not very intelligent. She had had two bad head injuries in previous years, one because of a dog-bite, and the other through being hit on the head by a falling tile.[47] She suffered from constant headaches and convulsive fits. Clearly, such a history introduced further difficulties for exorcists endeavouring to get to the bottom of an affair which began when she claimed to have been possessed by the soul of her maternal grandfather, seeking suffrages in order to be released from Purgatory. The clergy intervened, relying on the official teaching that the deceased faithful do not return for such purposes, and the visitor was induced to admit he was a devil. Following procedures in the various manuals available at the time, the Dominican exorcist Pierre de la Motte established that the possessing devil was Beelzebub. 'From this point onwards', according to D. P. Walker's account, 'Beelzebub takes over the management of the whole affair'.[48]

Devils of Loudun'; See also Alexandre Dumas, *Demons! The Possession and Exorcism of the Nuns of Loudun, and the Execution of Urbain Grandier* (Durham, NC: Lulu.com, 2019).

45. Marc Duncan, *Discours de la Possession des Religieuses Ursulines de Lodun*, 1634, 44: 'Laissez lui le bras: car comment se feront les contortions si vous le tenez: à qui le dit sieur repondit à haute voix: Si c'est un demon qui le fait, il doit ester plus fort que muy.'

46. See Lyndal Roper, *Oedipus and the Devil: Witchcraft, Sexuality and Religion in Early Modern Europe* (London: Routledge, 1994), 172: 'The 1560s and 1570s ... saw the emergence of a revitalized Catholicism. Under the influence of the Jesuit Peter Canisius, Catholicism began to win new and powerful converts.'

47. Walker, *Unclean Spirits*, 21.

48. Ibid., 22.

Great interest was aroused among the people by the revelation that this traditionally high-profile devil was involved and public exorcisms began to take place on a stage in the church in Vervins, allegedly after demands by Beelzebub for a public contest, and later transferred to the Cathedral in Laon, again because of the demand of Beelzebub that a devil of his rank could only be expelled by a bishop. It was at this stage that the Eucharist began to be administered to Nicole, an unusual stratagem at that time. It is likely that the controversy with the Huguenots made this move seem appropriate; a successful exorcism would vindicate the Catholic teaching. This proved to be the case but only after the Eucharist had been administered many times, and opportunity afforded for Beelzebub to intervene:

> When Jean de Bours, Bishop of Laon, was exorcising Nicole in the Cathedral, he threatened the devil with the consecrated host. 'Who?' asked Beelzebub, 'your Jack the White (*Ton Jean le Blanc*)?' The bishop then asked him who had taught him to call it thus, to which the reply was: 'But it was I who taught my Huguenots to call it that.' To the question: Why has the host such power over you? Beelzebub answered: 'Aha, you haven't told the whole story; there is HOC, ... referring of course to the words of consecration, *hoc est corpus meum*.'[49]

Repossessions of Nicole continued after this encounter and were dealt with in private and in public by the administration of the host. When possessed, she was able to answer questions in Latin, French, German and Flemish and reveal the secret sons of bystanders, according to contemporary chroniclers.[50] It is a fact that large numbers of the faithful had recourse to the Sacrament of Penance because of her claims. She lived on at least until 1577, when she went temporarily blind and on this occasion was cured, not by the administration of the host but by a relic of John the Baptist. The religious and political context in which these events took place make it difficult to conclude whether a real diabolic possession took place in a girl of delicate health and elementary education, but who showed an ability to adopt a public role by going with an entourage, after the events had ceased, to visit the Prince of Condé, the Huguenot leader, Louis de Bourbon (who detained her for some months). That the devil, Beelzebub, appeared to adopt a role in vindicating the Catholic doctrine is also a bizarre element in the story, and today the basic story would seem to so be overlaid with political and religious factors that it is difficult to conclude that an authentic exorcism took place, even though at the level of the general population, it is known that many people returned to the practice of the Catholic faith, and many accounts were written of the Miracle of Laon at the time and in the following century. But the gap between today and the ethos of that time leaves judgement about authenticity uncertain.

The practice of exorcism, after the introduction of the official *Rite* in 1614, had a rather chequered history in subsequent centuries. The eighteenth-century

---

49. Ibid., 23.
50. Young, *A History of Exorcism in Catholic Christianity*, 105–6.

Enlightenment was not confined to the *philosophes*, but had an influence on the life of the Catholic Church in its worship, which in France, for example, meant reduced rituals and the adoption of a more moralistic tone in preaching. The eighteenth century has been described by Francis Young as a battle between three views of exorcism: a magical tradition, which drew on charismatic resources, the moderate and restrictive position of the *Rituale Romanum*, and outright scepticism.[51]

Seventeenth-century Ireland

In Ireland, a tension existed between the regular and the diocesan clergy (seen earlier in continental Europe) as the mendicant friars carried out a missionary apostolate involving exorcisms, while bishops endeavoured to eliminate irregularities such as quasi-religious rituals performed by laymen, and implement a programme of parochial consolidation in accord with the decrees of the Council of Trent.[52] Both groups were endeavouring to show the superior powers of the Catholic Church compared with Protestantism. 'When in the early 1630s the Discalced Carmelite Steven Browne performed an exorcism in Dublin, a large number of people gathered to see him drive out a devil which a Protestant clergyman had failed to do.'[53] The best known of these exorcists was, however, a diocesan priest, James Finaghty, who gained a reputation as a healer and an exorcist in 1662, though he did not distinguish between physical infirmity and possession and used rather forceful physical methods in dealing with clients.[54] He was equally lauded by a big following of supporters as he travelled through Ireland and dismissed by both Catholic and Protestant clergy as a mountebank, yet was favoured by some of the aristocracy and even sent for by the ailing Queen Henrietta, mother of Charles II. His efforts to cure her developing blindness were unsuccessful.[55] The point that most clearly emerges is that the medical profession of the day seems to have played no role in discerning possible fraudulent aspects of the situation, perhaps indicating that in the late seventeenth century that profession did not have the prestige it had elsewhere.

The use of the charismatic or magical type of exorcism persisted in Spain in the eighteenth century at a time when the Roman authorities were endeavouring to suppress exorcism manuals that went beyond the ceremonies of the *Rituale Romanum*. This was because in Spanish territories the king had the right not to promulgate the new regulations, but by 1710 several Italian popular rites were

---

51. Ibid., 155.

52. Samantha A. Meigs, *The Reformation in Ireland: Tradition and Confessionalism, 1400–1600* (Dublin: Gill and Macmillan, 1997), 131.

53. Raymond Gillespie, *Devoted People: Belief and Religion in Early Modern Ireland* (Manchester: Manchester University Press, 1997), 67.

54. Anselm Faulkner O.F.M., 'Father O'Finaghty's Miracles', *The Irish Ecclesiastical Record*, vol. 103, 1965 (Dublin: Browne and Nolan, 1965), 352.

55. Ibid., 361.

suppressed. From around 1740 onwards the practice of exorcism came under sustained pressure from the church, the civil authorities of most Catholic countries and the medical profession.

The eighteenth-century progress in science and medicine led to more restrained language in the official *Rituale Romanum*. For example, the original text spoke of the need to distinguish between possession and the medical condition 'black bile' (i.e. melancholy) or 'some disease'. In 1752 this was changed to 'who suffer from some disease, especially those caused by psychic factors'. The 1614 text also had 'the signs of a possessing demon are'; this became 'the signs of a possessing demon can be'.[56] In his *A History of Exorcism in Catholic Christianity*, Francis Young reports that a *Rituale* was printed in Paris in 1738 specifically for use in Ireland and Scotland.[57] Bearing in mind the shorter history of Christianity in the United States, it is worth noting that the earliest recorded example of an exorcism there occurred in 1928, when a Capuchin friar, Theophilus Reisinger, on the bishop's authority, exorcised a young woman over a period of twenty-three days before achieving success.[58]

Eighteenth-century Germany

Sensational cases of exorcism occurred in late eighteenth-century Germany, at first in the Diocese of Constanz and later in the Franconian town of Ellwangen, which, as it happens, had been the location for witchcraft trials two centuries previously. This new phenomenon came about because of the activities of Johann Joseph Gassner, who had acquired the reputation of being a healer and an exorcist, two roles not always easily distinguished. He was a priest, and his healing rituals were religious ones, so it was not simply a case of natural healing powers, especially as his sessions often went on to become exorcisms. This was a time when Catholic theologians and authorities were affected, like their Lutheran counterparts, by Enlightenment thinking, and sceptical in relation to such rituals in consequence. So his activities were surrounded by controversy, while hugely popular.

His career has been chronicled in comprehensive detail in H. C. Midelfort, *Exorcism and Enlightenment: Johann Joseph Gassner and the Demons of Eighteenth-Century Germany* (2005).[59] Johann Gassner was born at Braz in Austria in 1727. He was ordained a diocesan priest in 1750 and after some temporary postings took up duty in 1758 as parish priest of Klösterle in Vorarlberg, Austria. From

---

56. Henry Ansgar Kelly, *Towards the Death of Satan: The Growth and Decline of Christian Demonology* (London: Geoffrey Chapman, 1968), 84.

57. Young, *A History of Exorcism in Catholic Christianity*, 169.

58. Carl Vogl, *Begone Satan*, Celestine Kapsner O.S.B., trans. (Collegeville, MN: St John's Abbey, 1935), 6–46.

59. H. C. Erik Midelfort, *Exorcism and Enlightenment: Johann Joseph Gassner and the Demons of Eighteenth-Century Germany* (New Haven, CT: Yale University Press, 2005), 12.

early in his ministry he had health problems and sought relief from doctors, but their ministrations proved unsuccessful. The 'headaches, fainting spells and sudden weakness he experienced, especially whenever he was to preach or say Mass',[60] caused him to speculate that his problems, especially noticeable when he was preparing for his religious duties, were of diabolical origin. He invoked the name of Jesus and experienced relief, convinced that this was the cause of his problems. From the perspective of modern clinical psychology, this linking of symptoms with religious duties would be seen as a case of 'ecclesiogenic neurosis'.[61] Acting on his conviction, he began to minister to others, praying at first simply for a healing of an illness, before going on to exorcise the patient, if no healing had taken place. When he moved on to the exorcism phase of his ritual, he did not use the *Roman Rite of Exorcism* of 1614, but his own formulas, relying on the fact that he was under the protection of the prince-bishop of Regensburg.

The preliminary rite of praying for healing became his standard approach. It was a probing exercise, as the cases presented to him were often ones in which there seemed to be demonic influence. It was said by some that he believed all illnesses were from the devil, a common medieval perception, but this he specifically denied. This should have gained him credibility within the Enlightenment culture by then dominant in Germany, but the enormous success he began to enjoy, not only in his own area but also in Germany when he moved to upper Swabia in 1774, brought with it a corresponding level of suspicion. A prominent member of the Bavarian Academy of Sciences, Don Ferdinand Sterzinger, a priest who had been active in the attack on witchcraft in the 1760s, was among his critics, having read a short book Gassner had written to explain his ministry.[62] Through his influence the book was banned in Bavaria.[63] From his perspective, now that the phenomenon of diabolical activity – a reflection of pre-Enlightenment superstition – belonged to the past, news of this priest's exorcising activity was not welcome. However, Gassner was receiving support from some secular rulers in the diverse principalities of the Holy Roman Empire.[64] But divided opinions among them led to an order

60. Ibid.

61. Burkhard Peter, 'Gassner's Exorcism – not Mesmer's Magnetism – is the real predecessor of modern hypnosis', *International Journal of Clinical and Experimental Hypnosis*, vol. 53, no. 1 (2005): 1–12: 'Today, we would probably diagnose this as an ecclesiogenic neurosis with migraine as the primary symptom.'

62. Ferdinand Sterzinger, *Die aufgedeckten Gassnerschen Wunderkuren: Aus authentischen Urkunden beleuchtet, und durch Augenzeuen bewiesen* (Augsburg: C. H. Stage, 1775).

63. Midelfort, *Exorcism and Enlightenment*, 43.

64. Ibid., 15; Norman Hampson, *The Enlightenment: An Evaluation of Its Assumptions, Attitudes and Values* (London: Penguin Books, 1990), 144: 'In the Habsburg dominions, the pious Maria Theresa (1740–1780) and her son Joseph II (co-regent from 1765 and sole ruler 1780–1790) had no sympathy with the scepticism of the Enlightenment.'

from the emperor Joseph II requiring Gassner to leave Regensburg, while two archbishops issued pastoral letters warning against the misuse of exorcism. His opponents secured a condemnation of his ministry by Pope Pius VI, and he retired to the tiny parish of Pondorf, where he died in 1779.[65]

His move to Germany had come about because of a summons he received from the Provost Anton Ignaz von Fugger-Glött, whose seat was in Ellwangen and who suffered from serious eye problems. The provost became prince-bishop of Regensburg in 1769, but held property in Ellwangen, in his diocese. Gassner went there with the permission of his own bishop, and decided that the provost's illness was natural and incurable. Bishop von Fugger remained his patron and protected him until the Papal edict left him with no choice and he moved him to Pondorf. A number of his exorcism ceremonies were held in Ellwangen in 1774. One of them has been described in detail in Midelfort's work, a summary of which follows.

On 21 December 1774, according to a 1775 account by Ferdinand Sterzinger, Gassner conducted a ritual for a man who suffered from St Vitus Dance, an illness which may have been common in the area, as the fact that the local church was dedicated to St Vitus would suggest – people who sought cures would be likely to appeal to the local patron saint. The disease itself is caused by streptococcal infection, producing involuntary movements of limbs in various parts of the body. A crowd had gathered, including noblemen and visitors from distant Munich:

> Astonishingly, the priest did not immediately summon forth the demons afflicting the man; instead, with solemn imprecations he bade demons do their worst. At his command the demons responded. The farmer began suddenly dancing and snapping his fingers. He hopped around the room three times, making some of the assembled observers giggle. … When this had gone on for a time, however, the priest ordered the demons to give the poor man an attack of epilepsy. Suddenly the fellow collapsed on the floor, flailing and thrashing, hurling himself about and 'bellowing like an ox'. Then with one Latin word – *cesset*, 'let it cease' – the exorcist made it all stop. Only then did the priest proceed to a full exorcism.[66]

There are many accounts by Gassner himself in his *Diarium*, indicating that he claimed to have healed over two hundred people in the period 1767–9, from purely physical disorders to psychosomatic to mental illness. From detailed reports relating to the final years of his healing ministry, and the images which circulated in households, the procedure he followed can be established with some accuracy.

---

65. Midelfort, *Exorcism and Enlightenment*, 16.
66. Ibid., 3–4.

In 1820, an account of Gassner's method was published in *Archiv für den thierischen Magnetismus* by C. A. von Eschenmayer of Tübingen University, an editor of the journal:

> Gassner is seated on a small chair with a *stola* around his shoulders, a cross around his neck, a table at his side on which there is a crucifix and around the table there is a row of chairs for the high persons of authority attending the treatments and witnessing them. A secretary has to take the minutes of the curious procedures. The patient brought to the priest kneels in front of him and is asked about the nature and the particulars of his or her illness. On having gained sufficient information on the condition, Gassner gives a few words of reassurance to inspire confidence and urges the person to inwardly consent that all that he would command would happen. When everything is prepared, he then says: 'If there is something unnatural in this illness, then I command in the name of Jesus that it show itself again immediately.' ... This procedure, called the *Exorcism Probativum*, is to discover if the illness is unnatural or natural, and at the same time is to raise the patient's trust, by achieving the concurrence of the symptoms with his commands and to make the power of the holy name of Jesus known and manifest to all present. If the evil did not show itself on the first command, he then repeats it over again up to 10 times. If it is still to no effect, he then postpones the patient to the next day or even later, or he sends him or her away altogether with the comment that either the illness is a natural one or that the person lacks sufficient confidence.
>
> When the priest by means of exorcism commands the illness to come out the first time, he usually allows the symptoms to prevail for several minutes; he then causes them to disappear and to reappear using the same commands. When the patient is convinced of the cause of the illness and the power of the method, the priest instructs him how to help himself in the future and requires him to try it out in the priest's presence. For this purpose, he commands the illness to reappear, and now the patient, by means of a counter-command that he inwardly gives in the name of Jesus, has to prevent the outbreak or, should the attack have already appeared, to cure it.
>
> Such I have seen and the patients agree with it. It is to be noted that not all patients are conscious of the same effect, ... that many are not completely cured, as they lack the vitality of confidence, even though their illness is not natural. It takes no more, according to Gassner, than that you believe in your illness being natural for the effect of exorcism to be prevented. Finally, he maintains that many illnesses are just natural *and* therefore only to be cured by means of the natural methods of doctors.[67]

---

67. C. A. Eschenmayer, 'Über Gassners Heilmethoden', *Archiv für den thierischen Magnetismus*, vol. 8, Brochure 1, 1820, 86–92.

Eschenmayer made no reference to demons; as a scientist he may well not have believed in their existence and the journal was a scientific one – still tied to the idea of the mysterious powers of magnets. He noticed that Gassner made the sickness come and go and that he instructed the patient to reproduce this effect by his own effort, invoking the name of Jesus. Similarly, an Abbot Bourgeois noticed this at Ellwangen and wrote a description of other oscillations such as cramps felt and dispelled, contradictory emotions, uncontrolled laughter followed by weeping. Midelfort remarks that some symptoms, such as different pulses in the two arms, would be hard to replicate clinically.[68]

Nevertheless, Gassner is of interest to modern clinical psychology, precisely because of his unusual practices. An article by Burkhard Peter analysed Gassner's method from the perspective of modern hypnosis research:

> It is most interesting to learn what Gassner did during his exorcisms, for the detailed description demonstrates that at least his therapeutic practice was in no way a simple religious rite – a conjuring of the devil – but included principles of modern cognitive therapy and hypnotherapy.[69]

Peter's article relied on Eschenmayer's 1820 description of Gassner's rite given above, and both represent a modern scientific viewpoint, prescinding from the religious dimension that was obviously at the heart of Gassner's efforts. But Peter's summary of Gassner's ritual led to the conclusion that Gassner's method was in accord with today's therapeutic task, namely, to help the patient to re-establish contact and communication with his or her own body and reality. His method of provoking symptoms and teaching the client to control them provided evidence of this.

From the modern scientific perspective, Gassner wins favour as the pioneer of psychotherapeutic treatment over his contemporary and rival Anton Mesmer and his 'animal magnetism' therapy. Gassner was not seen in that light in his own day. The two men were representatives of contrasting world views that had come into conflict with the emergence of the Enlightenment. Gassner could hardly have been aware of this role, but Mesmer was a partisan, 'who called Gassner a certain honest, albeit far too eager clergyman and said his therapeutic success in healing was due to the help of the animal magnetism that Mesmer had just discovered'.[70] The conflict between two world views would continue into the next century, and perhaps much longer, as the Catholic Church continued to uphold belief in the need for the *Rite of Exorcism*, to be used, however, exactly as the text indicated, and only by priests authorised to do so.

68. Midelfort, *Exorcism and Enlightenment*, 92.
69. Burkhard Peter, 'Gassner's Exorcism – not Mesmer's Magnetism – is the Real Predecessor of Modern Hypnosis', *International Journal of Clinical and Experimental Hypnosis*, vol. 53, no. 1 (February 2005): 1–12.
70. Ibid.

Anglicanism

The English Reformation, based on Lutheran theology of justification by faith, was marked by suspicion regarding ceremonies that seemed to reflect Catholic superstition. Consequently, the *Sarum Rite*, which was extensively used in England, was abandoned in favour of liturgical texts authored by Archbishop Cranmer, the 1549 *Book of Common Prayer* and the revised version of 1552 (influenced by Bucer). While these involved significant liturgical changes, especially in relation to understanding how Christ was present in the Eucharistic celebration, the rejection of perceived Catholic superstition in the old rite did not affect traditional belief in the existence of the devil:

> In the 1552 litany and suffrages, radically different to the Kyries of the Sarum missal, God was asked to spare man 'from all evyl and mischief, from sinne, from the craftes and assaults of the deuyll, from thy wrath and from eternal damnation'.[71]

Demonology was not in focus in the writings of the English Reformers; they were more concerned with instructional material for Christian living based on the Scriptures, and in particular, with regulations concerning lifestyle, for example, new rules regarding food and clothing introduced in the Sumptuary Laws.[72]

> There was no attempt to alter the fundamentals of belief in the devil or to deny him the power he had previously been accorded. Indeed the major writers of the early (English) Reformation produced no dedicated works of demonology, and with the exception of discussion of witchcraft, such works remained rare throughout the sixteenth and seventeenth centuries. But mainstream Protestant writing was pervaded by a profound sense of the devil's power.[73]

The issue of real or alleged witchcraft in early modern England tends to complicate discussion of demonic possession. According to Nathan Johnstone, 'English cases were unusual in Europe in tending to attribute possession to the agency of a witch, rather than directly to the Devil'.[74] He stated further that

> social historians have understood the demonisation of witches, with its lethal consequences, to be the most significant expression of demonological beliefs,

---

71. Nathan Johnstone, *The Devil and Demonism in Early Modern England* (Cambridge: Cambridge University Press, 2009), 62.
72. Fintan Lyons, O.S.B., *Food, Feast and Fast: From Ancient World to Environmental Crisis* (Dublin: Columba Press, 2020), 219–20.
73. Johnstone, *The Devil and Demonism in Early Modern England*, 29.
74. Nathan Johnstone, 'The Protestant Devil: The Experience of Temptation in Early Modern England', *Journal of British Studies*, vol. 43, no. 2 (April 2004): 173.

and so have concentrated on a small number of theoretical witch tracts and pamphlet narratives. However, while these studies present an accurate picture of the Devil within witch-beliefs, their assumption that it is representative of a more general demonism in early modern England is not borne out by the study of a wider source base. The Devil pervaded the written culture of early modern England, in tracts, sermons, devotional and conduct literature, plays and ballads, as well as in diaries and commonplace books.[75]

It seems that as in the Calvinist and Puritan tradition, concern with the devil's activities centred more on temptation. According to a Puritan writer, William Prynne, in 1624,

> Dancing is the pomp of the devil and he that danceth maintains his pomp and singeth his mass ... The woman that singeth in the dance is the prioress of the devil and those that answereth are clerks, and beholders are parishioners, and the music are the bells and the fiddlers, the ministers of the devil.[76]

The attitude in the Anglican tradition today towards the use of exorcism varies widely according to the spread of that tradition over the worldwide cultures where it is found. The African cultures, for example, differ from the typically English, and the use of exorcism differs accordingly. A recent study of the practice in the Church of England by Francis Young notes that the history of exorcism has not been well documented, especially because Canon 72 of 1604[77] prohibited exorcism without episcopal licence, thus creating an assumption among historians that the clergy of the established church were opposed to exorcism. 'The Canon ensured that an anti-exorcistic tradition would dominate the Church of England until the twentieth-century'.[78] The study, which covers the period from 1549 to the present, sums up the current situation comprehensively:

> The Church of England's approach to exorcism is shaped by a number of factors, only one of which is confident belief in an unseen world of malevolent spirits. Although some Anglican exorcists are completely committed to the traditional belief that evil spirits take possession of people's bodies, there is a wide and colourful range of demonological views among exorcists, with some believing someone can be literally possessed by Satan himself, others arguing that only lesser demons can possess a person, and still others choosing to speak more generally of a 'spirit of evil' dominating rather than literally possessing a person.

---

75. Ibid., 175.
76. P. G. Maxwell Stuart, *Satan: A Biography* (Stroud: Amberley, 2011), 165.
77. The Article was plainly directed against the Puritans. See D. P. Walker, *Unclean Spirits: Possession and Exorcism in France and England in the Late Sixteenth and Early Seventeenth Centuries* (London: Scolar Press, 1981), 77.
78. Young, *A History of Anglican Exorcism*, 17.

Others may be entirely agnostic about the possibility of possession, and even the existence of a personal devil, yet believe the rite of exorcism has psychological benefits.[79]

Young's study compares the current Roman Catholic use of exorcism with Anglican practice, saying, inaccurately, that the *Revised Roman Rite* 'withdrew from imperative exorcism, recommending deprecative forms'.[80] In fact, the imperative form remains, to be used in appropriate circumstances, but the *Rite* does now emphasise the usefulness of a deprecative form in other circumstances, as will be seen below in the description of such use in Portland, Oregon, and San Rafael, California, in 2020. The author adds:

> This trend has not been followed by the Church of England, whose approach to exorcism is now more 'traditional' than that of the Roman Catholic Church.[81]

Contemporary theological perspectives and exorcism

In the aftermath of the Second World War, Western Europe engaged in a phase of re-building, in many situations physical re-building of houses, cities, infrastructure and pre-eminently of the economies. To some extent, there was a resurgence of religious practice associated with the restoration of normality, but concentration on material recovery, the need and opportunity to turn technological advance towards peaceful purposes, including leisure, with a corresponding need for technical education, were priorities. A similar phase of development took place in the United States. All this created a Western society more inclined than before towards secularism and more oblivious to negative elements in a materialist lifestyle. There were notable examples of reaction against this in the decades after the second war; for example, the 'founding fathers', Robert Schuman, Alcide de Gasperi, Konrad Adenauer, Jean Monnet, who were theologically informed, were determined to create a new Europe that would put 'an end to war and guarantee peace'.[82] Nonetheless, the secularising process proceeded apace in Europe and the United States.

---

79. Ibid., 10. See also Brendan C. Walsh, 'Book review: *A History of Anglican Exorcism. Deliverance and Demonology in Church Ritual*', Preternature: Critical and Historical Studies on the Preternatural, vol. 8, no. 1 (2019): 163: 'Young convincingly argues that the re-emergence of exorcism in the Church of England was largely driven by Pentecostal spirituality and a concerted effort to evangelise the laity, rather than by a desire to return to the "exorcistic tradition" of early modern Anglicanism.'

80. Young, *A History of Anglican Exorcism*, 193.

81. Ibid.

82. Robert Schuman, speaking in Strasbourg, 16 May 1949, announcing the founding of the new European community.

In the United States, according to Pew Research Center telephone surveys conducted in 2018 and 2019, the decline of Christianity is continuing at a rapid pace. Around two-thirds of US adults (65 per cent) describe themselves as Christian (43 per cent Protestant and 20 per cent Catholic), down 12 percentage points since 2009. There is a decrease within the denominations themselves due to the number of people of denominational origin who now describe themselves as non-denominational Christians:

> At the same time, the share of 'nones' – religiously unaffiliated adults who describe their religion as atheist, agnostic or 'nothing in particular' – has reached 26%, up from 17% a decade ago.[83]

The various churches have obviously endeavoured to react to the increasing secularisation. Jürgen Moltmann, an ex-prisoner of war with personal experience of evil, pioneered the re-formulation of the Christian faith within Lutheran theology. He sought to put the crucified Christ, who had suffered the greatest evil imaginable, at the centre of theology, as he explained in his *The Crucified Christ*. Christ by his sufferings defeated evil and restored hope to humanity. There was need to state the Gospel message in a way that confronted evil. Both he and the Anglican theologian N. T. Wright wrote books on hope.[84] As already described, the Reformed theologian Karl Barth, who experienced the hardships and challenges brought about by the war, wrote his well-known *Church Dogmatics*, with a long section devoted to the question of evil.

Catholic theological reflection preceded the Second Vatican Council (1962–5) by at least a generation and was the motivational force that enabled it to take place – following Pope John XXIII's inspired decision to call a Council. The concern here was the need to re-formulate theology in a way that would enable the church to cope with the challenge of an increasingly secular milieu.[85] There was a twofold drive employed by this programme, both an *aggiornamento*, or bringing up to date, a forward movement, and also a look back for inspiration to the early hard-won formulations of Christian doctrine, the sources from which later development grew, a *ressourcement*. Inevitably, these two drives could pull in opposite directions, becoming antiquarianism on the one hand, or an embracing of theological ideas subtly influenced by secularism's dismissal of the transcendent, and sometimes,

---

83. https://www.pewresearch.org/fact-tank/2019/12/13/19-striking-findings-from-2019/.

84. Jürgen Moltmann, *Theology of Hope* (London: S.C.M Press, 1967); N. T. Wright, *Surprised by Hope* (London: S.P.C.K., 2007).

85. The need for reform of pre-Vatican II theology was spelled out forcefully by Dermot Lane in 'Fifty Years of Theology', *The Furrow*, vol. 60, no. 7/8 (2009): 399: 'It was manualistic, scholastic, dogmatic, unbiblical, deductive and *a priori*, non-historical, supersessionist, dualistic, otherworldly and predominantly un-ecumenical. This was the background against which Vatican II took place.'

though not often in Catholic circles, an embracing of demythologisation that destroyed the truth in the attempt to strip away mythical layers on the other.

An interesting example of an attempt to free theology from the restrictions imposed by the Jewish world view at the time of the Gospel narratives was identified and critiqued by the then professor Joseph Ratzinger, when a fellow academic, Herbert Haag, an Old Testament scholar, published a booklet, *Abschied von Teufel* (*Farewell to the Devil*), in 1969. Ratzinger's response, using the same title, though with a question mark added, challenged Haag in many areas, the first being that as an exegete Haag could not assert that in the N. T. 'devil' and 'sin' were far from equivalents. It was not as an exegete that he considered the existence of the devil untenable but on the basis of his contemporary world view. Ratzinger admitted that 'by no means is it always obvious how far the doctrinal message of the bible extends and what may be only the temporally contingent vehicle for its real theme'.[86] To find the core of the message it was important to consider the relation between the two Testaments as the Church Fathers did:

> The notion of demonic powers enters only hesitantly into the Old Testament, whereas in the life of Jesus it acquires unprecedented weight, which is undiminished in Paul's letters and continues into the New Testament writings, the captivity letters and the Gospel of John.[87]

The notion was hesitant in the Old Testament because any ambiguity about faith in the one and only God in an environment saturated with belief in idols made it necessary that there should first be an unshakable faith in the one God, before reference to the devil could become prominent. As noted in Chapter 3, by the time of the Book of Wisdom (2.24), the last book of the Old Testament 100–50 BC, the devil has become the adversary against God's plan for humankind because of envy, and this perception was unquestioned from the beginning of New Testament times. The continuing presence of the adversary was evident, for example, in the exorcism rites of the baptismal ceremony in the time of Tertullian and these remained in the liturgy throughout the Middle Ages and beyond.

The revision of the rites of the Catholic Church in the period after the Second Vatican Council (1962–5) was a result of the message of hope in the Council documents. Some criticism did emerge from those who felt that *aggiornamento*, coming to terms with the modern world, reflected unjustified optimism. As summarised by the then theologian, Joseph Ratzinger, some draft versions of the Constitution on the Church in the Modern World were thought to be committed to an optimistic view of human nature, which was opposed by 'theologians from the German-speaking countries'. He denied Lutheran influence, but at the same

---

86. Joseph Ratzinger, 'Farewell to the Devil?' in Pope Benedict XVI, *Dogma and Preaching: Applying Christian Doctrine to Daily Life* (San Francisco: Ignatius Press, 2011), 198.

87. Ibid., 200.

time Lutheran theology of the person was closer to German minds compared with, as he noted also, the French understanding.[88]

The revision of the rites of the church did show a more positive theological anthropology than previously. The Baptismal Rite from the time of the Council of Trent had retained exorcisms indicative of a strong belief in Satan's existence and grip on the unbaptised. The ceremony began at the entrance to the church and included the exorcism: 'Go forth from him/her, unclean spirit, and give place to the Holy Spirit, the Paraclete.' Two further exorcisms followed, the second, imperative, one described as a 'Solemn Exorcism':

> I exorcise thee, every unclean spirit, in the name of God the Father +Almighty, in the name of Jesus + Christ, His Son, our Lord and Judge, and in the power of the Holy + Spirit, that thou depart from this creature of God N, which our Lord has deigned to call unto His holy temple ...

The rite, therefore, included three exorcisms similar in form to those in the 1614 *Rite of Exorcism*. There followed a Renunciation of Satan and anointing with the Oil of Catechumens. Only then did the party move to the baptismal font and the priest change from a violet to a white stole. The ceremony also implied that the unbaptised could be in thrall to multiple 'unclean spirits'.

In the postconciliar revised rite, the emphasis in this and all the sacramental rites has been on participation in Christ's Paschal Mystery through the action of the Holy Spirit. After a celebration of the Word, the celebrant prays:

> By the mystery of your death and resurrection, bathe this child in light, give him/her the new life of baptism and welcome him/her into your Church.

From the beginning, the atmosphere is one of welcome: 'The Christian community welcomes you with great joy, in its name I claim you for Christ our Saviour by the sign of the cross.' There is an invocative exorcism towards the end of the preliminary ceremonies, when in a prayer that acknowledges Christ's victory over Satan, the priest says: 'We pray for this child, set him/her free from original sin, make him/her a temple of your glory and send your Holy Spirit to dwell in him/her.'

Trust in Christ's victory over sin and death justifiably creates an optimistic view of life, but the danger that the temptations of a secular world presents needs also to be taken into account. Even though the rite refers to freeing from original sin, tradition holds that a tendency to sin and temptation by the devil remain in the baptised. In contrast, where both belief in God and belief in the existence of the devil are lacking, intuitions about good and evil are confined to psychological

---

88. Joseph Ratzinger, *Commentary on the Documents of Vatican II*, vol. 5 (London: Burns & Oates, 1969), 119–23.

perceptions, unrelated to transcendent values, as Jeffrey Burton Russell noted.[89] The Vatican Council's Constitution on the Church in the Modern World included many references to evil, sometimes, not only in relation to humankind's inclination towards evil or the evil present in relations between nations (no. 83), but also on account of the existence of the devil.

Personified evil and the Fall

There was in the text of the Constitution a notable reference to 'personified evil', when it said that Christ 'was crucified and rose again to break the strangle hold of personified evil, so that the world might be fashioned anew according to God's design and reach its fulfilment' (no. 2), with 'personified evil' translating a capitalised *Malignus*, 'the evil One'. This accords with the later reference (no. 13) to Christ casting out the 'prince of this world' (Jn 12.31). Clearly, the text was relying on the way the New Testament presents Satan as a personalised evil force, as Jesus seems to have done in various encounters with people described as 'having' demons. While the Constitution acknowledged 'humankind's inclination towards evil', there was no comment on its origin as a fall from an original state of justice.

The issue of the Fall of humanity has been studied in modern times by theologians of all churches, especially those conscious of the weight of evidence provided by biological evolutionary theory, and the typical conclusion is that evil just 'is'. (See John Hick's discussion in Chapter 1.) As Stephen J. Duffy put it, 'Evil is the corruption that occurs within a creation that is already complete and good'.[90] Paul Ricoeur spoke for many when he concluded that there never was a time of primal innocence. According to Ricoeur, the function of the Adamic myth

> is to posit a 'beginning' of evil distinct from the 'beginning' of creation, to posit an event by which sin entered the world and, by sin, death. The myth of the fall is thus the myth of the first appearance of evil in a creation already completed and good. By thus dividing the Origin into an origin of the goodness of the created and an origin of the wickedness in history, the myth tends to satisfy the twofold confession of the Jewish believer, who acknowledges, on the one hand, the absolute perfection of God and, on the other hand, the radical wickedness of man.[91]
>
> In the Instant I am created, in the Instant I fall. ... [The] 'event' of sin terminates innocence in the Instant; it is, in the Instant, the discontinuity, the breach, between my having been created and my becoming evil. The myth puts in succession that which is contemporaneous and cannot not be contemporaneous.

---

89. Jeffrey Burton Russell, *Mephistopheles: The Devil in the Modern World* (Ithaca, NY: Cornell University Press, 1986), 252.

90. Stephen J. Duffy, 'Our Heart of Darkness: Original Sin Revisited', *Theological Studies*, vol. 49 (1988): 598.

91. Paul Ricoeur, *The Symbolism of Evil* (New York: Harper and Row, 1967), 243.

... Thereby the myth proclaims the purely 'historical' character of radical evil; it prevents it from being regarded as primordial evil.[92]

Dietrich Bonhoeffer had similarly commented on the origin of evil in a series of lectures in Berlin University in 1932/3, published in 1937 as *Shöpfung und Fall*. Though he refrained from outright description of the doctrine of the Fall as a myth, 'he fully embraced the Darwinian account of human origins. Indeed, it could be argued that Darwinism and Christian theology were thoroughly integrated in that work'.[93]

Bonhoeffer stated:

> The serpent, one creature of God among others, itself becomes an instrument of evil. How does this happen? The Bible does not give an answer, at any rate not a direct or an unequivocal one; characteristically it answers indirectly. We would be simplifying and completely distorting the biblical narrative if we were simply to involve the devil, who, as God's enemy caused all this. This is just what the bible does not say. ... It is not the purpose of the Bible to give information about the origin of evil, but to witness to its character as guilt and as the infinite burden of man. ... It will never be possible to blame the devil who has led us astray. The devil will always be in the place where I ought to have lived and did not wish to live as God's creature in God's world. It is of course just as impossible to blame the creation for being imperfect and make it responsible for my evil.[94]

Bonhoeffer relied on the fact, as contemporary theologians do, that there is no account in the Bible of the fall of Lucifer, making Adam (or Eve) Lucifer's first victim, and he is thus 'in principle relieved of his burden'.

Ecumenical perspectives

As Roman Catholic theologians held views similar to those of Ricoeur and Bonhoeffer prior to the Vatican Council, it is not surprising that there is no direct command in the renewed Baptismal Rite driving out Satan. Comparing the old and the new rites, three exorcisms in the old rite compared to one rather 'indirect' one in the new, puts a very different emphasis on what the rite is about.

Many churches share this approach to baptism. The Faith and Order Commission of the World Council of Churches developed a statement, *Baptism,*

---

92. Ibid., 251.

93. Rodney Holder, *The Heavens Declare: Natural Theology and the Legacy of Karl Barth* (West Conshohocken, PA: Templeton Press, 2011), 55.

94. Dietrich Bonhoeffer, *Creation and Fall: Temptation: Two Biblical Studies* (New York: Macmillan, 1959), 64.

Eucharist and Ministry,[95] in 1982 articulating a convergence if not consensus on the theology of baptism among very many of the member churches of the Council. *Baptism, Eucharist and Ministry 1982–1990: Report on the Process and Responses*, published by the World Council, concluded thus in relation to baptism:

> The most remarkable fact emerging from the responses of churches to the baptism section is the degree of convergence that exists in areas of previous dissension.[96]

This is a positive development, but there is no mention of exorcism in the document, most likely because there would be little evidence of convergence in this regard.

The current growth of exorcisms

During the twentieth century, there had been a rise in occult movements and Satanic cults in Europe and the United States, while various long-established pagan cults in South America and Africa also reacted against secularism's denial of all reality other than the material. In the Western world, dissatisfaction with the culture created by scientism manifested itself especially in the literary, musical and cinematic productions of the postmodern culture with their highlighting of evil and even of exorcism.

Another contrasting development was the charismatic movement, of fundamentally Pentecostal origin, but also taking root in the Catholic Church in the 1960s and linked to the post-Vatican Council renewal. The significance of the charismatic movement in the context of exorcism is that the use of 'deliverance' rituals by the predominantly lay membership of the movement meant that the churches' restriction of the exorcism rite to clergy officially mandated could be compromised. There could be misunderstanding of the difference between the kinds of rituals, and even the illicit use of a church's rite by people not authorised to do so.

Belgian Cardinal Léon-Joseph Suenens, who was a proponent of the charismatic movement, was also aware that the freedom and gifts of the Spirit being emphasised within the movement could give opportunity for the cultivation of interest in malign spiritual forces. He wrote a book identifying the danger; the English translation, *Renewal and the Power of Darkness*, appeared in 1983.[97] In his book, Suenens declared:

---

95. 'The Meaning of Baptism', *Faith and Order Paper No. 111* (Geneva: WCC Publications, 1982), 2–3.
96. *Faith and Order Paper No. 149* (Geneva: WCC Publications, 1990), 54.
97. Cardinal L.-J. Suenens, *Renewal and the Power of Darkness* (London: Darton, Longman and Todd, 1983).

It is essential to establish a consistent and commonly accepted terminology and to draw a firm distinction between the prayer of deliverance and the exorcism of deliverance effected by a direct summons to the devil.[98]

A provocative work by a critic of the Vatican Council, an ex-Jesuit, Malachi Martin, claimed that many thousands of exorcisms were carried out by laity in the United States. *Hostage to the Devil* (1976) attracted a large readership. This was perhaps one reason why the Vatican Congregation for Divine Worship expressed a cautious note in 1975, in a document, 'Christian Faith and Demonology', issued in the context of the suppression of traditional Minor Orders:

> The special ministry of the exorcist, though not totally abolished, has in our time been reduced to a remotely possible service, which may be rendered only at the request of the bishop; in fact there is now no rite for the conferring of this ministry. ... (The church) no longer attributes to exorcisms the important role they had in the early centuries of its life.[99]

The Catholic *Rite of Exorcism* remained unchanged until the overall renewal of the church's liturgy after the Second Vatican Council, when it took on a new form, not as a sacrament like the Rite of Reconciliation but clearly as a sacramental (a ceremony with sanctifying power, not one of the sacraments). There was renewed emphasis on the qualifications and permission needed by an exorcist, who had to be a priest. It still involved the imperative and the invocative forms of exorcism. The revision was completed in January 1999, with the declared purpose of casting out demons or freeing from demonic influence.[100] As in the 1614 rite, the revised rite contains two forms of exorcism: the imperative form in which Satan is directly addressed and ordered to leave the afflicted person and the invocative form in which the exorcist prays that God will not permit the afflicted to be possessed by the 'father of lies' or held in captivity by the devil.[101] The Latin version of the *Rite of Exorcism* was promulgated in 2004. Translations into various languages were made and approved in the years leading up to 2004; the Italian version (to be commented on here) was approved in March 2002. Its introduction was clearly a result of widespread calls expressing the need for such a ritual. The English translation in use in the United States, *Exorcisms and Related Supplications*, was only approved by the bishops in June 2017. Extensive use of the rite has been made in both jurisdictions, Italy and the United States, since then. In the United States, the concluding section, 'Related Supplications', exorcism of an invocatory rather

---

98. Ibid., 96.
99. 'Christian Faith and Demonology', in *Vatican Council II*, vol. 2, *More Post-Conciliar Documents*, Austin Flannery, ed. (Dublin: Dominican, 1982), 47.
100. Cardinal Estévez, 'Prefect of the Congregation for the Divine Cult and Discipline of the Sacraments'.
101. Conferenza Episcopale Italiana, *Grande Rito degli Esorcismi*, no. 61.

than an imperative kind designed for more widespread use, was employed in a very public environment in 2020 by two archbishops:

> In Portland, Oregon, Archbishop Alexander Sample led a procession of more than 200 people to a city park on Oct. 17, offered a prayer, and then conducted a Latin exorcism rite intended to purge the community of evil. The event followed more than four months of racial justice protests in Portland, mostly peaceful but sometimes fuelling violence and riots.[102]

On the same day, after a protest demonstration in San Rafael, California, in which a statue of Blessed Junipero Serra was knocked over, Archbishop Salvatore Cordileone conducted a similar exorcism, praying that 'God might purify this place of evil spirits, and might purify the hearts of those who perpetrated this blasphemy'.[103]

Presumably, this was a coordinated action, an attempt to draw attention, on the one hand to the secularisation of culture in which the non-existence of the devil is taken for granted and, on the other, the official use of exorcism in the United States by Catholic clergy. Prior to the introduction of the revised rite, some employed formulas in English or Latin, improvised or derived from the old *Rituale*. Micheal Cuneo, a sociologist, produced in the 1990s evidence of exorcisms of various degrees of dramatic kind performed throughout the country by Protestant as well as Catholic clergy. This was especially true of the Pentecostal communities, a phenomenon, he noted, which had grown significantly after the publication of William Blatty's book, *The Exorcist*, in 1971, the subsequent movie, and also Malachi Martin's *Hostage to the Devil*.[104]

The environment, of both unbelief and superstition, also obtains in some Central and South American countries such as Mexico, Argentina and Brazil, with the result that the use of the official Catholic rite is also extensive in these countries, having in fact a longer history there than in European countries. It seems a historical irony that in parts of South America, seventeenth-century missionaries introduced belief in the existence of the devil to tribes unaware of such a being. Jesuit missionaries in Central and South America were sympathetic in many ways to the cultures they encountered but 'were convinced that wherever they went they were seeing evidence of Satan's rule over the indigenous peoples, in spite of the fact that ... the inhabitants had no conception of a personal expression of evil who sought the down fall of mankind'.[105] The arrival of Pentecostal denominations in Africa in the twentieth century also brought the practice of exorcism with it.

102. David Crary, 'Exorcisms: Increasingly Frequent, Including after U. S. Protests', *Crux*, 31 October 2017.

103. Ibid.

104. Michael Cuneo, *American Exorcism: Expelling Demons in the Land of Plenty* (London: Bantam, 2002), 13.

105. Stuart, *Satan: A Biography*, 174. According to Daniel T. Reff, *Plagues, Priests, Demons: Sacred Narratives and the Rise of Christianity in the Old World and the New* (Cambridge: Cambridge University Press, 2005), 178-9:

Official exorcism occurs today in circumstances very different from those recorded in the Gospels. Jesus performed exorcisms on his own authority; today individuals mandated by the church perform exorcisms on behalf of the church and in that respect there is continuity with the ministry of Jesus. The circumstances differ in that Jesus had at that time not completed his work of defeating the devil and death, though that was certainly to come: 'the ruler of this world has been condemned' (Jn 16.11). The individual Christian who presents or is presented for exorcism in the post-Resurrection era can, in principle, be regarded as differing in some fundamental way from those whom Jesus in the Gospel accounts exorcised by ordering demons to leave them. These latter afflicted may be thought of as in the power of the prince of this world in a way which baptised Christians are not. Nonetheless, the church continues to recognise not only the evils that are so prevalent in the world, but also the continuing presence and activity of the 'prince of this world'.

Officially sanctioned exorcisms did increase in some countries especially in Italy. The noted exorcist for the diocese of Rome, Fr Gabriele Amorth (1925–2016), in his book published originally in Italian in 1994 and in English in 1999, with the title, *An Exorcist Tells His Story*, claimed that in nine years he had exorcised over 30,000 people, and that he had exorcised people from Austria, France, Switzerland, England and Spain.[106] In the decade 1960–70 in France there were six or seven official exorcists, while by the 1990s there were close to one hundred.[107] There has been less interest in, or enthusiasm for, the use of the rite in some other countries because of diverse attitudes on the part of bishops and clergy.[108] As noted above, the US Conference of Catholic Bishops sanctioned the use of the *Rite* in 2017.

> From an Indian perspective, what was particularly attractive about the Jesuit worldview was that it shifted the burden of guilt from the Indians to Satan. At the outset of an epidemic, the Indians naturally questioned themselves on how they may have offended the spirit world. The offence was not really theirs; they were simply caught up in a cosmic struggle between God and Satan. So argued the Jesuits.

106. Ibid., 172; Beppe Amico, *A colloquio con Padre Gabriele Amorth – L'opera di Satana, la sua azione ordinaria e straordinaria* (Trento: Reverdito, 2022): e-book loc. 442 'I diavoli sono un'enormità, più volte hanno detto in tanti esorcismi: "Se fossimo visibili, oscureremmo il sole", aggiungo anche che sono un numero grandissimo'; Gabriele Amorth, *The Devil Is Afraid of Me* (Bedford, NH: Sophia Press, 1998); Gabriele Amoth, *An Exorcist: More Stories* (San Francisco: Ignatius Press, 2002).

107. Dominique Cerbelaud O.P., *Le Diable* (Paris: Éditions de l'Atelier, 1997), 74.

108. See Marcel Hampf, *Exorcismus: Ein Vergleich der Praxis in der katholischen Kirche in Deutschland und Polen* (München: Grin Verlag, 2015); Willem C. van Dam, *Satan Existiert: Erfahrungen eines Exorzisten* (Augsburg: Pattloch, 1994), 127: 'Natürlich weiß ich daß.viele Seelsorger an dieser Stelle äußerst skeptisch sind.'

Chapter 11

TOWARDS A THEOLOGICAL ASSESSMENT OF EXORCISM*

The current Catholic Rite of Exorcism

The presentation of the *Rite* by the Italian Episcopal Conference in 2001[1] stressed that it was being introduced in a cultural milieu marked by deviant cultic or openly superstitious nature. The bishops were acknowledging that in Italy there were widely varying cultural attitudes in relation to the invisible world, from the industrialised North to the rural South. It called for Christian vigilance, while pointing out that Christ had conquered Satan and shattered the dominion of the 'malign spirit'. While diabolical phenomena such as 'tormenting and possession' – the terms highlighted by the *Rite* – are possible, they are also rare. It added pastoral recommendations regarding credulous approaches that would see diabolical interventions in anomalous events, emphasised the need to be on guard in relation to books, TV programmes and the social media, and stressed the importance of catechesis.

The US Conference of Catholic Bishops issued an explanatory document, 'Exorcisms', in connection with the introduction of *Exorcisms and Related Supplications* in 2017, explaining the nature of and need for exorcisms. It drew attention to the classification of exorcisms into major and minor, the latter being exemplified by the exorcisms used in the baptismal *Rite* and in the second part of the new document, the *Related Supplications*. It stressed that the minor forms in the document may be used by the faithful, but that only a priest delegated by the bishop of the diocese may perform the major *Rite*. It included a useful note on the moral certainty the exorcist requires regarding the state of the afflicted person as possessed.

---

* For a psychological assessment, see Appendix p. 327.

1. The Latin Typical Edition of the *Rite*, first issued in 1998, was slightly emended in 2004. The English translation by the International Commission for English in the Liturgy (ICEL) was issued in 2013, approved by the Holy See in 2016 and adopted in the United States in 2017, as in other English speaking countries, around that time.

Moral certainty is classically understood as falling between the two poles of absolute certainty and probability. Bearing that in mind, moral certitude is achieved through the examination of proofs, which are weighed in accordance with the conscience of the one passing judgment. Therefore, the exorcist must utilise whatever resources are available to him when investigating a claim of demonic possession, along with input from medical and mental health professionals.[2]

The document also includes an important note on whether an exorcism may be performed without the recipient's permission:

> Given the nature of the devil's workings and the afflicted person's possible complicity in the resulting demonic possession, the exorcist should ascertain the person's consent, if at all possible, before proceeding with the Rite of Major Exorcism.

The sections of the *Rite*[3] consist of: Initial Greeting – sprinkling with Blessed Water may be included; Litany of the Saints; Recitation of a Psalm; Proclamation of a Gospel passage; Imposition of Hands; Profession of Faith; The Lord's Prayer; the Sign of the Cross; Insufflation (if considered appropriate); Exorcism Formula in the Invocative Form, followed by the Imperative Form, if judged opportune; Thanksgiving, including the Canticle of Zachary; Concluding Rite.

Possession, its extent and theological meaning

It is very difficult to establish how extensive instances of possession are in any country, and more importantly, what they are. The analysis is complicated by the fact that in the exorcisms performed by Jesus – where he casts out a demon as distinct from a healing – possession is taken for granted as a real factor in the life of the population without any awareness of what is today known as a psychiatric illness. In relation to possession, the *Rite*, today as in 1614, takes the meaning of the term as self-evident, simply referring to a brief of Benedict XIV of 1745 and Canon 1151.2 of the *Code of Canon Law*, 1917, in which the afflicted is referred to as *obsessus* (oppressed).[4] Benedict asserted the importance of assessing whether the claims of those who declared themselves oppressed by demons were genuine. His brief was occasioned by the case of a German Third Order Franciscan nun and mystic, Crescentia Höss (+1744), who claimed to be regularly tormented by

---

2. https://www.usccb.org/prayer-and-worship/sacraments-and-sacramentals/sacramentals-blessings/exorcism.

3. The text of the *Rite* is not publicly accessible; in the various translations it is a confidential document for national Catholic Bishops' Conferences.

4. The *Commentary on the Code of Canon Law* 1917 by T. L Bouscaren and A. C. Ellis S.J. (Milwaukee: Bruce Publishing, 151) 647 makes no comment on the nature of possession.

demons and made prophetic pronouncements.[5] She was declared Venerable after her death.

There is no authoritative doctrinal statement about the nature of possession. (Descriptions by two specialists involved in the ministry of exorcism will be given below.) Insofar as it is defined, this results from the compilation of the many scriptural texts referring to it. Lk. 8.27 refers to the man who 'has' the demon; in Mk 5.6 the afflicted identifies himself with the demon; Eph. 4.27 talks of the danger of 'making room for the devil'. In a sense broader than personal, political and social institutions are permeated with demonic influence according to Revelation 13.[6]

Personal relations in theological perspective

As the performance of the *Rite* centres on interaction between the priest, the afflicted person and the putatively present demon, some principles with regard to encounters in the form of personal relations need to be established at the outset. This is with a view to clarifying what kind of relation there can be between the exorcist and the demon and between the afflicted and the demon; it can be assumed that the relation between the exorcist and the afflicted will emulate that of Jesus. These will also be the concern of the psychological assessment of personal relations in the appendix.

Martin Buber

The personalist philosophy of Martin Buber (1878–1935) is relevant here. The requirement of a 'positive relation' for personal interaction is in accord with his philosophy formulated in his *I and Thou*[7] study. Buber maintained that in the I–Thou relationship people are aware of each other as having a unity of being; they engage in a dialogue involving each other's whole being, while in an I–It relationship they view themselves as parts of a world that consists of things. I–It is a relationship of separation and detachment.

> The I of the basic word I–It, the I that is not bodily confronted by a You, but surrounded by a multitude of contents has only a past and no present, In other words, insofar as a human being makes do with the things that he experiences and uses, he lives in the past, and his moment has no presence. He has nothing but objects that consist in having been.[8]

---

5. Young, *A History of Exorcism in Catholic Christianity*, 165.
6. Karl F. Trublar, 'Possession, Diabolical', in *Sacramentum Mundi*, vol. 5 (London: Burns & Oates, 1970), 63–4.
7. Martin Buber, *I and Thou*, Walter Kaufmann, trans. (Edinburgh: T&T Clark, 1975).
8. Ibid., 65–6.

In contrast, for Buber, the You confronts the person and leads to a relationship that is at once one of being chosen and choosing,

> The You encounters me. But I enter into a direct relationship to it. Thus the relationship is election and electing, passive and active at once. ...The basic word I–You can be spoken only with one's whole being... I require a You to become; becoming I, I say You. All actual life is encounter.[9]

The two kinds of relationships arise for Buber from the double aspect of man as 'from above' and 'from below'. Only the I-You, 'which establishes essential immediacy between me and an existing being, brings me precisely thereby not to an aspect of it, but to that being itself'.[10]

In the third part of the book, the You becomes the eternal You and the I–You becomes a presence, a revelation of the eternal God.[11] According to Emil Brunner,

> the heart of the creaturely existence of man is freedom, selfhood, to be an 'I', a person. Only an 'I' can answer to a 'Thou', only a self which is freely determining can fully answer God.[12]

This makes Buber's and Brunner's thought relevant to the present discussion.

Joseph Ratzinger

In his post-war student days, the young Joseph Ratzinger and his fellow seminarians were impressed by the moral personalism in Theodor Steinbüchel's *Umbruch des Denkens*, but then they discovered Buber and saw in his thought a foundation for a theology of the person:

> We ... found philosophy of personalism reiterated with renewed conviction in the great Jewish thinker, Martin Buber. This encounter with personalism was for me a spiritual experience.[13]

However, as Cardinal Ratzinger he subsequently had reservations about personal relations and spoke of the 'abyss of loneliness of man in general, of man who is alone in his innermost being'.[14]

---

9. Ibid., 62.

10. Martin Buber, 'God and the Spirit of Man', in *The Writings of Martin Buber* (New York: New American Library, 1956), 111.

11. Buber, *I and Thou*, 160.

12. Emil Brunner, *The Christian Doctrine of Creation and Redemption*, Dogmatics. Vol. II, Olive Wyon, trans. (Eugene, OR: Wipf and Stock, 2014), 56.

13. Joseph Ratzinger, *Milestones. 1927–1977* (San Francisco: Ignatius Press, 1978), 44.

14. Joseph Cardinal Ratzinger, 'Descent into Hell – Ascension – Resurrection', in *Credo for Today: What Christians Believe* (San Francisco: Ignatius Press, 2009), 87.

As Pope Benedict XVI in 2005, in his essay, 'Farewell to the Devil', he maintained that

> one cannot possibly explain all of reality with the categories of I and Thou – that precisely the 'in between' that connects the two poles with each other is a reality of its own, having its own force. The 'in between' is a fateful power, which our 'I' can by no means completely control.[15]

This 'fateful power' in a true I–You situation would be for Buber simply the Eternal You, the presence of God. Ratzinger, however, seemed to think of 'fateful power' in impersonal and potentially threatening terms; he claimed that the idea of an in-between is one that comes from Asian thought but gave no sources. This in-between may be disordered, frustrated, dysfunctional, and that is why, he claimed, in psychological illness the I is out of joint too.

> Here, it seems to me, modern thought places at our disposal a category that can help us to understand more exactly the power of demons, whose existence is of course independent of such categories. They are a power of the 'in between', which man encounters at every turn without being able to apprehend it.[16]

This is at odds with Buber's thought. For Buber, the 'between' was in fact the realm of the Eternal, the locus of revelation. His view was analysed by a researcher Alex Pole in the following terms:

> The realm of the 'between' was classified as a form of the archetype of the coincidence of opposites. The 'between' was understood by Buber as the ontological ground of all relations. This study identified the meeting of an I with a Thou, the realm of the 'between', with the reality of the Spirit. The Spirit as realm of the 'between' was for Buber the ground of the experience of religiosity.[17]

There is a contradiction between the two thinkers, but it is due to a confusion of terms. What Ratzinger called an I–Thou is clearly for Buber an I–It. But Ratzinger's insight was helpful in that a pathological I–It relationship is really prevented from becoming an I–Thou relationship with another person by the disordered condition of the I.

---

15. Pope Benedict XVI (Joseph Ratzinger), 'Farewell to the Devil', in *Dogma and Preaching: Applying Christian Doctrine to Daily Life* (San Francisco: Ignatius Press, 2005), 204.
16. Ibid.
17. Alex Polo, 'The Realm of the between in Martin Buber's Writings and Its Implications for the History of Religions' (1986). *ETD Collection for Fordham University*. https://research.library.fordham.edu/dissertations/AAI8615689.

Following Ratzinger's line of thought, the idea of an in-between can be a help towards understanding more exactly the power of demons, whose existence, if accepted, is in a different category from psychological illness. In fact, psychiatric studies describe personality disorders as 'in-between kinds of things'[18] affecting the 'I – Thou' relationship, so there is a commonality that can cause confusion when what is described as demonic possession in the Gospels seems more likely to be a pathological state such as epilepsy. As noted in Chapter 3, apparent demonic possession is in fact translated thus in some versions of the Gospels reporting the incidence of the curing of the boy in Mt. 17.21.

The demonic forces of the in-between category against which, according to Eph. 6.11, Christians struggle, 'the cosmic powers of this present darkness ... the spiritual forces of evil in the heavenly places', are characterised by facelessness and anonymity, according to Pope Benedict in the article quoted above.

> If someone asks whether the devil is a person, we would probably have to answer more accurately that he [sic] is the un-Person, the disintegration and collapse of personhood and that is why he characteristically appears without a face and why his being unrecognisable is his real strength.[19]

In his *Introduction to Christianity*, he spoke of the 'Hydra of evil', which keeps growing new heads.[20] The limitations of syntax are evident when an attempt is made to say something about an 'un-Person', as it is hardly possible to avoid attributing reality to the subject of a sentence. This was not a problem for theology as long as it was strongly based on Scripture, as the role of the power of evil was identified with a named individual, Satan or the devil.

As mentioned in the introductory chapter, the text of the Constitution on the Church in the Modern World of the Second Vatican Council implied personification of Satan. The *Catechism of the Catholic Church*, in the context of enlarging on the petition of the Lord's Prayer, 'But deliver us from evil', is explicit in this regard:

> In this petition, evil is not an abstraction but refers to a person, Satan, the Evil One, the angel who opposes God. (No. 2851).[21]

---

18. Peter Zachar, 'Epistemic Iteration or Paradigm Shift', in *Philosophical Issues in Psychiatry* IV, Kenneth Kendler and Josef Parnas, eds (Oxford: Oxford University Press, 2017), 298.

19. Pope Benedict XVI, '"Farewell to the Devil" 204; Karl Lehman, "Der Teufel – Eine personales Wesen?"' in *Teufel, Dämonen, Bessenenheit*, Walter Kasper und Karl Lehman, eds (Mainz: Matthias-Grünewald-Verlag, 1978), 75: 'W. Beinert schliesst sich J. Ratzinger an und sieht eine gewisse Austauschbarkeit und eine Art von unaufhebbarem Übergang zwischen dem Bösen als einem anonymen "ES" und als personaler Wirklichkeit.'

20. Joseph Ratzinger, *Introduction to Christianity* (San Francisco: Ignatius Press, 2004²), 18.

21. Commenting on this paragraph, Christoph Schönbörn (the editorial secretary of the Catechism project) simply repeated this text in a series of commentaries on the Catechism;

In addition to Ratzinger's assertion that the devil is 'the un-person, the disintegration and collapse of personhood', some insight on the issue of personhood in the case of a satanic being radically opposed to God may be gained from John Zizioulas's study of the personhood to which humanity aspires (which for him will only be found in communion with the Trinity). The choices of radical freedom over against God on the part of a fallen angel or a human being reflect each other and suffer the same constraints because of createdness.

John Zizioulas

Considering the human situation, Zizioulas (1931–) says:

> The moral sense of freedom to which Western philosophy has accustomed us is satisfied with the simple power of choice: a man is free who is able to choose one of the possibilities set before him. But this 'freedom' is already bound by the 'necessity' of these possibilities, and the ultimate and most binding of these 'necessities' for man is his existence itself: how can a man be considered absolutely free when he cannot do other than accept his existence? Dostoevsky poses this great problem in a startling manner in *The Possessed*. There Kirilov says: 'Every man who desires to attain total freedom must be bold enough to put an end to his life. ... This is the ultimate limit of freedom; this is all; there is nothing beyond this. Whoever dares to commit suicide becomes God. Everyone can do this and so bring the existence of God to an end, and then there will be absolutely nothing.'[22]

Zizioulas expanded on Kirilov's expression of the tragic side of the person's quest, the desire to transcend the 'necessity' of existence so that man's existence comes not from recognition of a given fact but as the product of free consent and affirmation. But this quest comes into conflict with createdness: 'As a creature he cannot escape the "necessity" of his existence.'[23] Zizizoulas's concern was with the process formulated by the Greek Fathers, in which humanity achieves true personhood through participation in the communion of the Trinity, but the quotation from the character Kirilov is a shocking illustration of, or testimony to, what must be the fate of an angelic spirit seeking ultimate freedom, but destined for final destruction or the eternal isolation of some kind of non-being or *Nichtige* existence.

Christoph Schonbörn, *Living the Catechism of the Catholic Church*, vol. 1, The Creed (San Francisco: Ignatius Press, 1995), 69; *The Compendium of the Catechism of the Catholic Church* (Dublin: Veritas Publications, 2006), 49: 'Satan and the other demons ... were transformed into evil because with a free and irrevocable choice they rejected God and his Kingdom, thus giving rise to the existence of hell.'

22. John D. Zizioulas, *Being as Communion: Studies in Personhood and the Church* (Crestwood, NY: Saint Vladimir's Seminary, 1993), 42.

23. Ibid., 43.

Relationships in exorcism: Theological perspective

As will be seen later, in the context of the pastoral use of the *Rite of Exorcism*, exorcists' accounts seem to take it for granted that the devil (or demons) can – in person, so to speak – enter into dialogue of a responsive and confrontational nature with the exorcist. Exorcists do recognise that the voice is in a physical sense that of the afflicted person. The issue then is whether the voice is *more* than that of the afflicted, whether possession means that a non-person, a non-relational being, can acquire a human voice. The dynamics of the various interchanges will now be analysed theologically, and in the Appendix psychologically.

Jesus' exorcisms

At the level of the Gospel story, there are both friendly and hostile encounters in the course of Jesus' exorcisms, and real relations are assumed: between Jesus and the person afflicted, between Jesus and the demon and, importantly, between the afflicted and the demon. These relationships need to be assessed, both in the case of Jesus' exorcisms and those of the church.

Between Jesus and the afflicted

First, there is a positive relation between Jesus and the afflicted person and it is obviously one of great empathy. In the case of modern exorcisms, the status of the minister, personally or as representative of the church, is clearly important. The necessary qualifications, both canonical and spiritual, are stated in the *Rite of Exorcism* no. 11 and underlined in a recent publication, *Linee guida per il ministero dell'esorcismo*, produced by the International Association of Exorcists, which has the approval of the Vatican authorities.[24]

Between Jesus and the demon

Second, in the case of anyone's interaction with a demon including that of the human Jesus – demon being identified as a fallen angel – what is required for such interaction needs to be clarified. According to Hans Urs von Balthasar, in his discussion of the extent to which the concept of 'person' can be applied to the satanic being of the fallen angels,

> Being a person always presupposes a positive relation to some fellow person, a form of sympathy or at least natural inclination and involvement. Precisely this,

---

24. International Association of Exorcists, *Linee guida per il ministero dell'esorcismo* (Padova: Edizioni Messagero, 2020).

however, would be no longer predicable of a being that had, in its entirety, made a radical decision against God, or absolute love.[25]

Von Balthasar's criterion for a relationship could not be satisfied by such a being, and there is no reason to assume that this would not apply in the case of the encounters recorded about the life of the historical Jesus. A being that had made a radical decision against God would be incapable of a personal relationship and therefore the voice responding to Jesus – or an exorcist – must be that of the possessed person, with possession establishing only an indirect relationship. What that implies about the Church's *Rite of Exorcism* will have to be considered later, as guidelines for exchanges between the exorcist and the demon are laid down in detail in the Vatican-approved document of the International Association of Exorcists.

The Church's exorcism today

Between exorcist and demon

Even though the *Rite* involves words (not questions) addressed to the demon, clearly there is no relationship between the exorcist and the demon that could be described as personal; the implications of this need to be taken into account in light of the publication *Linee guida* of the International Association of Exorcists, which includes chapter 18 on 'Questions to the Demon'. The *Rite* itself does not include such a rubric, though no. 38 does allow an Episcopal Conference to produce its own Pastoral Directory to assist exorcists by the use of additional documents regarding, for example, interrogations during the *Rite*. The Association's text (no. 392) warns that it is never licit to ask a question of the demon that is not relevant to the purpose of the exorcism. The tone of voice used must be of authority and command 'directed to an enemy' (no. 393). It warns the exorcist that loquacity will give the demon opportunity to engage in a dialogue that distracts from the purpose of the exercise (no. 394) and lists sins the exorcist may commit by, for example, asking questions about hidden or future events (no. 397). It asserts that asking the demon how many there are in possession is an approved tradition (no. 403), as is asking the cause that brought it about.

The *Linee* concludes by assuring the exorcist that the 'principle of continuity' between the *Rite* of 1952 and the current one, which does not mention interrogation, gives the exorcist freedom to use this procedure (no. 410). It is a matter of concern that some exorcists in the United States, according to the exorcist Vincent Lampert, find the prayers of the older *Rite* 'richer in content and expression'[26] and prefer to

---

25. Hans Urs von Balthasar, *Dare We Hope 'That All Men Be Saved?'* (San Francisco: Ignatius Press, 1999), 114.
26. Vincent Lampert, *Exorcism: The Battle against Satan and His Demons* (Steubenville: Emmaus Road Publishing, 2020), 46.

use it. The late Fr Gabriele Amorth, the second president of the Association, held the controversial view that the newer ritual's lesser stress on commands was less effective than the more traditional approach to exorcism.[27] In response to this, the Congregation for Divine Worship gave permission in 2011 to 'priests who are stably appointed exorcists to use whichever of the *Rites* they find beneficial'.[28] There is a disturbing implication here that the current official *Rite* is in some way less effective than the original.

What all this apparent exchange between exorcist and demon implies is that there is sufficient analogy between demonic knowing and willing and that of humans for communication to be possible to the extent that the exorcist can issue a command to a demon, but that does not imply that a dialogue is possible between them, as the *Linee guida* assumes. Quite an assumption is involved in the idea of dialogue with a demon; it assumes that a non-person can interact in some way with the exorcist as well as that the demon has in fact control of the will of the afflicted, despite the statement of Cardinal Estevéz to the effect that it cannot take it captive. In the *Rite* itself it is stated that the devil cannot go beyond (*Italian oltrepassare*) the limits set by God.[29] The traditional teaching could do with some elaboration.

Between afflicted and demon

If belief in the existence of demons is accepted, the question remains as to what kind of 'relation' there can be, short of true possession, between the afflicted and the demon, the 'un-person', or philosophical theology's *privatio boni* (absence of good) and Barth's *das Nichtige*, all of which indicate the absence of a necessary pole in a relationship, to use Ratzinger's term. Buber's words about I–It can help here: 'The I of the basic word I–It, the I that is not bodily confronted by a You, but surrounded by a multitude of contents has only a past and no present.'[30] The multitude of contents in this kind of relationship, which includes *no present*, can include objects that 'consist in having been'. In other words, memories or associations and experiences an afflicted person may have had. The afflicted person may be drawing on a store of memories while it appears that a demon is engaged in dialogue with the exorcist. In that way, a psychotic person can believe in a 'presence' of a demon in his/her life, even though this is the consequence of a pathological condition and personal history.

---

27. Richard Gallagher, *Demonic Foes: My Twenty-five Years as a Psychiatrist Investigating Possessions, Diabolic Attacks and the Paranormal* (New York: HarperOne, 2020), 141.

28. Lampert, *Exorcism*, 46.

29. Cardinal Estévez, Press Conference, 26 January 1999. *Rito degli Esorcismi*, no. 10. A footnote refers to Pope John Paul's Apostolic Exhortation, *Reconciliatio et paenitentia* 14-22, *AAS* 77 (1985).

30. Martin Buber, *I and Thou*, Walter Kaufmann, trans. (Edinburgh: T&T Clark, 1975), 65-6.

In a corresponding way, in true possession the reality must be that a demon is communicating information to the afflicted through having taken control of the person's intellect. Empirical evidence would be needed to decide, for example, whether there is knowledge of things the afflicted person cannot possibly know, and not just languages, indicating a complete takeover of the knowing faculty. Exorcists do report such evidence as will be seen below.

Ratzinger's 'collapse of personhood' must imply, from the perspective of Buber's system, the impossibility of an I–You relationship between the afflicted and a demon. So, what other relationship can exist? It is clear that in a case that is simply one of psychological or psychiatric illness, a disordered I, the I-Eternal You relationship can still exist, because of the ontological state of a baptised person, though pathological symptoms may make it difficult to recognise it.

But as long as the person can be considered to possess free will there can also be the situation of radical yielding to the allurement of evil, to the devil's temptation and, paradoxically, this can be envisaged even in the situation of unbelief in the existence of the devil. The issue of experimenting with satanic *rituals* and gradually, not fully consciously, handing over control to a demon which the person believes to exist, has to be considered relevant here, as there is evidence that people do adhere to such cults, causing the use of the *Rite* to be appropriate.

It is difficult to envisage a situation in which someone manifestly rational and obviously not suffering from psychiatric symptoms will present seeking an exorcism to be freed from demonic possession, though cases do seem to be reported. If truly possessed, in the sense of having knowingly allowed a takeover by the devil in some Faustian pact, would an act of free will repenting of the decision be likely, as in some versions of the Faustian legend? Some case histories to be considered below indicate that once a person has accepted demonic control it is very difficult to be freed from that connection, the will to be freed apparently insufficiently strong. The issue will be considered below in connection with actual cases.

If full control is indeed a fact, it will be a case of the demon using the faculties of the afflicted to communicate with and challenge someone who has an exorcist's role. Cases where a person has been cursed may be of that kind, but are an anomaly difficult to explain. Paradoxically, the influence of a demon in the case where will and judgement are impaired by psychiatric illness has in principle to be less than what traditional teaching holds about the reality and power of temptation by the devil of a healthy person.

Whether an allegedly possessed person has, from the evidence of phenomena listed earlier, chosen to give control of his/her whole life to a demon is what has to be assessed. According to the *Rite* (16), the exorcist may only use the imperative form in a situation of 'moral certainty' that the person is 'truly possessed' by a demon, and in all cases must use the invocative first. Without a clear concept of what possession means, it seems virtually impossible for an exorcist to reach certainty other than the moral, that is, by relying on external phenomena. How is anyone to know the secret history of another's moral life?

It is possible that someone being exorcised today may have repudiated the divine grace conferred in baptism and allowed the devil to take possession, though there is the issue of whether a baptised Christian can so alter the ontological state conferred in baptism. In any case, such a repudiation differs fundamentally from the case of the pre-Christian afflicted person, who may or may not have repudiated connection with God, but would not be in the same position as a baptised person of today. This puts possession by the devil, which the church holds to be possible, into an extremely serious category and the phenomena associated with it un-surprising, but, as was stated above, phenomena such as alleged exchanges between the exorcist and a demon present considerable difficulty of authentication. Another possible situation, then, is that the strange phenomena encountered in exorcism cases today are for the most part bizarre results of extreme psychiatric illness, leaving only a very small number for which demonic possession is the genuine cause.

Current pastoral practice

The interpretation given above of what happens in an exorcism event puts emphasis on the non-personal nature of the devil (or demon). The accounts of exorcism by exorcists, however, all seem to accept some kind of personification, as will be seen below. Nonetheless, it is important to take their experiences and interpretations into account while bearing in mind a degree of subjectivity in their interpretations. Accounts of exorcism in the United States are extensive, unlike in other Western countries, and it can be speculated as to whether this is a case of under-reporting in some countries or quite dramatic reports in others, as sometimes in the United States.

Gabriele Amorth

Fr Gabriele Amorth (d. 2016), for many years the official exorcist of the diocese of Rome, and perhaps the best-known exorcist internationally, was quite outspoken about the presence of the devil. In an interview with a Marco Tossati (who had co-authored books with him), the following questions and answers featured:

> Is the devil also in the Vatican? Yes, there are many members of Satanic sects also in the Vatican.
> Who are they? Are they priests or simple laymen? There are priests, monsignors, and also cardinals.
> Excuse me, Father Gabriele, but how do you know? I know it from people who have referred [reported?] them to me, because they have a direct way of knowing it. And it is also often 'confessed' by the demon that is under obedience in the exorcism.[31]

---

31. Gabriele Amorth and Marcello Stanzione, *The Devil Is Afraid of Me: The Life and Work of the World's Most Famous Exorcist*, Charlotte J. Fasi, trans. (Manchester, NH: Sophia Institute Press, 2019), 18.

The first of Amorth's several books about exorcism, *An Exorcist Tells His Story* (1994 in Italian), was a record of his career up to that time and a defence of the ministry. He presented the devil or demons in a strongly personified form (always male), with human-like characteristics. In the following passage, he was evidently referring to the 1952 *Ritual*, which was the version then in use of the 1614 original.

> Demons are very reluctant to speak. The *Ritual*, very rightly, admonishes the exorcist not to ask questions out of curiosity but to ask only what is useful for liberation. The first thing that must be asked is the name. For the demon, who is so reluctant to reveal himself, revealing himself is a defeat; even when he has revealed his name, he is reluctant to repeat it. ... There can be many or few [demons], but there is always one chief, and he is always the first to be named. When the demon has a biblical name or one given in tradition (for example, Satan, Beelzebub, Lucifer, Zebulun, Meridian, Asmodeus) we are dealing with 'heavyweights' tougher to defeat.[32]

Amorth was engaged in the pastoral work of exorcism, before the revised *Rite* was issued in 1999. He referred to that *Rite* in his later works, but did not mention the fact that it does not include 'questioning' the demon. He seemed to ally himself with the approach of the International Association of Exorcists, of which he was a founder member. In his approach, names from Scripture or tradition were considered to be appropriately and properly ascribed to demons, which Ratzinger earlier in this text described as 'characteristically without a face'; here personal characteristics were clearly implied.[33]

In the chapter 'The "Cinderella" of the Ritual' of his *An Exorcist Tells His Story*, he said he had 'noted the names of everyone who was possessed, ninety-three people, and that all had been possessed for approximately ten years'.[34] His experience was very extensive and well recorded. The chapter consists of a passionate defence of his exorcist ministry and a critique of the attitudes of contemporary Italian theologians and bishops, who seemed to him (in 1994) to be in denial with regard to the extent and seriousness of diabolical influence in the population. He was critical of exorcists who did not even own a *Ritual*, and commented on the controversial case of Annelise Michel of Klingenberg, Germany, whose death in 1976 after many exorcisms led to the trial of the two exorcists involved. 'The data published in the newspapers ... hinted that the two priests involved were all too

---

32. Gabriele Amorth, *An Exorcist Tells His Story* (San Francisco: Ignatius Press, 1999), 93.

33. Vincent Lampert, in his *Satan: The Battle against Satan and His Demons* (Steubenville: Emmaus Road Publishing, 2020), 55, described an exorcism in which he identified the demon he called Leviathan. Leviathan was the fleeing serpent that would be destroyed by God according to Isa. 27.1.

34. Amorth, *An Exorcist Tells His Story*, 169.

eager to suspect the presence of diabolical possession.'[35] Amorth reported that a later book, *Annelise Michel*, by Kasper Bullinger, substantially exonerated the two exorcists. Having commented unfavourably on the attitudes of bishops in Italy, he added, 'I reiterate my statement: the conditions abroad are worse than in Italy.'[36] He was presumably thinking about European countries.

In the United States, as noted in the previous chapter, much publicity has been given to exorcism as a prevalent phenomenon. In recent years, books recording exorcists' experiences have been published with official permission.

Vincent Lampert

Fr Vincent Lampert's *Exorcism: The Battle against Satan and His Demons* is a practical manual for the use of those called to be exorcists in the various dioceses. He pointed out both the low rate of Christian belief in the country (as noted in the previous chapter) and a corresponding scepticism about the existence of the devil:

> For some people today, including those in the Church, to even talk about the existence of the devil is an embarrassment. ... Interestingly, the Second Vatican Council references the devil more than any other Council. There are references to the devil in the great documents of *Lumen gentium*, *Gaudium et spes*, *Ad gentes*, and *Sacrosanctum concilium*. Indeed, in the Catholic tradition, Sacred Scripture and the Magisterium of the Church consistently confirm the truth of the existence of angels and demons.[37]

In a Protocol for the use of exorcism in his own diocese, he lists the questions asked of the person who seeks an exorcism, in order to establish whether a psychiatric condition is the explanation or whether involvement in occult or even Satanic rituals has resulted in serious diabolical influence or even possession. The emphasis is on questioning the afflicted person rather than a concealed demon, but Lampert does imply dialogue with the demon:

> Once during an exorcism, the manifesting demon gave the impression that it had been cast out. It remarked to me, 'You can stop praying now. Thank you so much for what you have done here today. Stop praying. I feel so much better now. Stop praying. You have been so helpful. Stop praying.' Knowing that the

---

35. Ibid., 170. Johannes Mischo, 'Dämonische Besessenheit', in Walter Kasper und Karl Lehman (Hg), *Teufel, Dämonen, Bessenenheit* (Mainz: Matthias Grünewald Verlag,1978), 116, held that the revelations of the *naiv-gutgläubige* Fr Renz, one of the two exorcists, in a television interview, were as damaging as the half-truths published by certain sections of the press in creating a bias among readers before the truths of a complex situation were established.

36. Amorth, *An Exorcist Tells His Story*, 172.

37. Lampert, *Satan*, 15.

demon was trying to deceive me, I blessed the person again with holy water and the demon screamed at me, 'I said you can stop praying!'[38]

He reports an extraordinary case of possession:

> On another occasion a lady said she believed one of her friends was possessed, and in a misguided act of charity looked her friend in the face and said, 'Whatever is in you I freely invite to come into me.' No sooner did the words come out of her mouth than she felt a presence overtake her. She did want the help of the Church, and during the exorcism seven demons identified themselves in her. Leviathan was the dominant demon and the last of the seven to be cast out.[39]

Lampert's book resulted from television interviews and from his talks to seminarians to prepare them for future contact with this aspect of pastoral ministry and possible involvement with it. The book is then pastorally oriented and a sober account of what is involved in this ministry. In the introduction to the book, he says:

> In this ministry, I submit myself to God so he may use me to help people, who are up against the forces of evil, to experience the immense and unconditional love that God has for each and every person.[40]

Gary Thomas

A similarly balanced, unsensational approach to the exorcist ministry is evident in the account of one priest's personal journey in preparation for his work as an exorcist. The book by Matt Baglio, *The Rite: The Making of a Modern Exorcist* concerns the unanticipated appointment to, and preparation for, the role of exorcist of Fr Gary Thomas of the diocese of San Jose, California. His situation is interesting in that he came to this ministry with no previous interest but with only a short preparatory course and reservations about the need and effectiveness of such a ministry. His initial exorcism sessions for people who came expressing fears that they were possessed were uneventful. He used a selection of prayers from the *Rite* and other sources, and repeated sessions on request until the clients were satisfied and ceased to attend. One case, however, turned out to be quite different. A couple originally from Honolulu came with their twenty-seven-year-old daughter, who claimed that since the age of seventeen 'she had been hearing voices and seeing demons, which would always tell her "You belong to us"'.[41] Her

---

38. Ibid., 45–6.
39. Ibid., 55.
40. Ibid., 9.
41. Matt Baglio, *The Rite: The Making of a Modern Exorcist* (London: Simon & Schuster, 2009), 215.

parents told him that a witch doctor, who had performed an exorcism on her in Honolulu, told them that her troubles most likely related to a curse. With the family now living in the United States, her troubles had recently returned.

Fr Gary prayed from his selection of prayers and noticed that almost immediately her body began to twitch, her legs rocking back and forth. As he continued,

> Maria suddenly screamed. She began thrashing violently on the couch. Then, much to Fr Gary's amazement, her facial muscles tensed in such a way that her appearance completely changed, and she took on the visage of an adder. Even her mannerisms seemed to become snakelike. Her eyes, which had become dead black discs, bored into him, while her tongue shot in and out like a snake's. ... He threw some holy water on to Maria, and she lunged at him, but was grabbed at the last minute by her parents, who were sitting on each side of her. Deep hatred poured out at him through her black eyes.[42]

When the prayers were over, the girl calmed down and her face returned to normal, leaving Fr Gary convinced that she needed a solemn exorcism, not a simple blessing. The book does not record the further outcome, but does include his reflection on the case.

> Beyond the sensational, a profound element to it gave him hope. He was finally able to set aside his doubts once and for all about whether the *Ritual* would work for him. 'These prayers do have power,' he thought.[43]

Fr Gary Thomas exemplifies the type of exorcist – an official of a diocese with the requisite training and no previous inclination to that kind of ministry – on

---

42. Ibid., 216. The symptoms of possession, which took Fr Gary by surprise, were recorded many times in history. A typical example comes in the catechetical lectures of Cyril of Jerusalem (313–386 CE):

> Everything which has not a gross body is in a general way called spirit. Since, therefore, the devils have not such bodies, they are called spirits: but great is the difference; for the unclean devil, when he comes upon the soul of a man, ... he comes like a wolf upon a sheep, ravening for blood, and ready to devour. His presence is most cruel; the sense of it most oppressive; the mind is darkened: his attack is an injustice also, and the usurpation of another's possession. For he tyrannically uses another's body, another's instruments as his own property. ... Foam comes instead of words; the man is filled with darkness; his eye is open, yet the soul sees not through it; and the miserable man quivers convulsively before his death.

Cyril of Jerusalem, *Catechetical Lectures* XVI (Oxford: Henry Parker, 1838), 210–11. One has to note that Cyril's description could also apply to an epileptic attack.

43. Baglio, *The Rite*, 217–18.

whom the church everywhere should be able to rely. Training in psychology could be an asset, though the simple requirement that clients should have had psychiatric assessment should be adequate. Up to recent times, exorcists have tended to emerge because of special qualities of character and personality and with ministries marked by some dramatic phenomena.

Stephen Rossetti

A 2021 book, *Diary of an American Exorcist: Demons, Possession, and the Modern-Day Battle*,[44] by Stephen J. Rossetti, includes some dramatic details connected with exorcisms and are difficult to harmonise with objective theological analysis. The book is significant, however, because the author, Monsignor Rossetti, is a clinical psychologist and research professor at the Catholic University of America, and was the chief exorcist of the Archdiocese of Washington for more than thirteen years. It is clearly an honest account of his experiences. His interpretation of events may, however, be marked by subjective factors, and his book does contain more dramatic elements than accounts by such authoritative exorcists as the late Gabriele Amorth or Vincent Lampert. In the introduction, he recounts a powerful experience he had as a seminarian.

> I had just gone to bed but hadn't fallen asleep yet. Suddenly I was invisibly attacked. It was unbelievably powerful and incredibly fast. With a graced insight, I instantly knew what it was. Satan was attacking me. And I was going to be quickly overwhelmed. My rosary beads were on the table at the foot of my bed. The moment the attack started, I instantly thought of these beads. I lunged out of bed and thrust out my hand to grab my rosary. The instant I touched the beads, the attack stopped. So I went back to bed and fell quickly asleep. In those two seconds, I learned about 80 percent of what an exorcist needs to know. Satan is very powerful and moves at lightning speed. Angels, and demons, travel at the speed of thought.[45]

This observation sets the tone for the remainder of the book. The author does not discuss what interpretations of his experience other psychologists might give. He records an incident from later life in which cellphone (mobile) calls between him and another priest repeatedly failed once connected until they said a prayer and then communication continued uninterrupted. This led him to remark:

> I've heard from many of the people I have helped over the years that they often cannot get through to me on the phone. We see a clear pattern of demonic interference in trying to stop these troubled people from getting help.[46]

---

44. Stephen J. Rossetti, *Diary of an American Exorcist: Demons, Possession, and the Modern-Day Battle against Ancient Evil* (Manchester, NH: Sophia Institute Press, 2021).
45. Ibid., 10–11.
46. Ibid., 10.

His theology of the nature of a demon and of possession is more clearly in accord with tradition and is insightful regarding relationships:

> Demons are fallen angels. And, like all angels [and humans too], they were created to be in a loving unity with creation, with one another, and with God. We were all built for relationships. Unfortunately, the fallen angels, or demons, as they are called, rejected God and thus rejected all that God is. God is first and foremost a loving Trinitarian relationship of Father, Son, and Holy Spirit. … Because of their radical sin, demons cannot build and enter into such loving relationships. There are no friendships in Hell. The demons' primal urge for union remains, but it is now distorted, and instead of engaging in free, loving relationships, demons try to control, dominate, and possess. … When given an opening, demons will therefore try to enter and possess. They can possess an object, such as a cursed occult artefact. They can also possess a place, especially if sinful or occult behaviour has occurred there. A house, an apartment, or another building can be 'infested' with demons if someone invites them in, even unknowingly.[47]

Rossetti intersperses his 'diary' of actual exorcisms – which he says are not exaggerated in any way – with theological observations, one of which lists the signs of demonic possession.

> If a person is possessed, the demons are able to take over the person's body for a period of time and manifest, or reveal, their presence. The exorcist looks for signs of a demonic manifestation to make the diagnosis of a true possession. A possessed person can manifest a demonic presence anytime. A demonic manifestation is more likely to happen when the person is engaged in holy, religious activities such as going to a church service, praying, or, especially, undergoing exorcism. … There are many typical signs of a demonic manifestation, and these can vary from person to person. Some of the classic signs include writhing and showing an aversion to holy objects. In more serious cases, the demonic presence will temporarily take over the personality of the afflicted person, and the person's consciousness will recede into the background. Then the demons can speak through the person's voice and the look on the person's face will often reflect a demonic rage. In such instances, the demons are fully manifesting, and it is clear that the person is possessed.[48]

These remarks relate to possession; however, there seems to be another category of 'demonic manifestation' noted in the Introduction to the original (1998) and in the current 2014 version of the *Rite of Exorcism*, no. 10:

---

47. Ibid., 15.
48. Ibid., 19.

With God's permission, sometimes there occur cases of particular torment or possession (*peculiaris vexationis seu obsessionis*) on the part of the devil of some human being who is a member of the People of God, and has been enlightened by Christ so as to walk as a child of light towards eternal life.

There is an issue here as to whether a distinction is being made between 'torment' and 'possession', as in a later paragraph, no. 14, the text says that the exorcist

> absolutely should not believe that possession is present when for the first time someone claims to be tempted in a special way by the Devil, to be desolate, and finally to be tormented (*vexatum*) for one can be deceived by one's own imagination.

Rossetti does appear to make a distinction between what the *Rite* calls torment (*vexatio*) – more commonly, 'oppression', – and full possession, when he records in Diary 42 the case of Jason, whom he does not describe as possessed, but nonetheless one on whom Satan was 'laying a claim', after he had some years previously asked Satan for financial success, though he had subsequently repented and returned to the church.

> Jason woke up with a very ugly four-inch upside-down cross burned deeply into his shoulder. Strangely, he said he didn't feel it; he just felt a little tingling. Four days later it rapidly disappeared.[49]

The upside-down cross Rossetti describes as a Satanic symbol. He returns to Jason's case in Diary 71:

> Jason woke up with several long, ugly, eighteen-inch gouges on his back. It looked as if a beast had raked its claws down his back. In fact, that's exactly what happened. The demons' attacks against him have intensified. He is aggressively assaulted and abused. At night, and even during the day, his bed shakes violently when he lies on it. Jason is terrified. Friends freak out when they see it.[50]

In neither case does he say that Jason felt physical pain. The implication of these references is that Jason was being 'tormented' in a way that manifested itself physically outside of exorcism sessions, though that is not made clear.

---

49. Ibid., 81.
50. Ibid., 123. One might well ask if Jason was familiar with Ps. 129.3: 'The ploughers ploughed on my back, they made their furrows long', and what might be the significance of such knowledge.

When one would expect that Rossetti, a clinical psychologist, would comment on the effects on the imagination of an afflicted person, he simply reports what one said to him.

> One possessed person had a direct vision of demons that he described to me. He said, 'The demons were horrific to look at. They were distorted and misshapen ... Some had claws instead of hands ... If they had two eyes or any recognizable limbs, they were malformed ... These demons were all like naked, ugly, vicious animals.'[51]

One of his theological observations defends the idea that demons can cause physical injury to possessed people:

> Possessed people ... are not uncommonly the subject of extraordinary demonic attacks. Demons are allowed to attack possessed people in a variety of ways. For example, possessed people sometimes have unexplained scratches and bruises. In fact, we have seen such scratches and bruises appear on the body of a possessed person in the midst of a session.[52]

In these cases, he is referring to physical injury sustained by a possessed person. However, in accordance with tradition, he holds that demons 'cannot kill or maim us', but also that many saints reported being beaten up by demons. He relies on reports of the type already recounted in this work (Antony and other desert fathers; John of the Cross), where natural explanations have been suggested. Gabriele Amorth also claimed that Satan could inflict physical harm and named several saints thus afflicted.[53]

Rossetti calls these cases examples of Satan's 'extraordinary activity' as opposed to his ordinary activity of tempting us. In support of this view, he quotes Aquinas' *Summa Theologiae* I, q114, a1, a text in which Aquinas made no mention of physical attacks, but spoke of wicked angels assaulting people in two ways, the first by instigating them to sin and the second as a punishment allowed by God, but in the same spiritual category. Augustine, and Aquinas following him, did not regard demons capable of inflicting physical harm on people, but did not discuss the case of possessed people, on whom Rossetti is mainly focused.

It is important to reach a conclusion in relation to the credibility of claims regarding 'demonic manifestation' causing physical or apparent physical injury in the case of those *not* possessed, but in some way under satanic influence – 'Satan laying a claim'.

---

51. Ibid., 119.
52. Ibid., 26.
53. Amorth, *An Exorcist Tells His Story*, 33: 'We know that Saint Paul of the Cross, the Curé of Ars (John Vianney), Padro Pio and many others were beaten, flogged and pummelled by demons.'

Richard Gallagher

The testimony of Richard Gallagher in his book, *Demonic Foes*, is relevant here.[54] For many years, exorcists seeking a psychiatrist's opinion on the state of oppressed people have consulted him. The book relates what he describes as 'unmistakable cases of demonic possession and other diabolic attacks that I directly encountered over the past twenty-five years'.[55] At the same time he shows scientific detachment when he stresses the need to recognise the rarity of possession. 'Most doctors will never see such a case; even the vast majority of clergy are unlikely ever to encounter a genuine case of possession.'[56] He gives a useful definition of possession:

> The essence of a possession is the actual control of the body [never the 'soul' or will] of a person by one or more evil spirits. At its full manifestation, victims no longer are acting on their own accord; the demon has taken charge of their functioning and, periodically at least, their consciousness. The evil spirit tends to manifest openly only intermittently; that is, the spirit seems to come and go as it pleases in most serious possessions, though it apparently never really 'leaves'. In this 'complete' type of possession, subjects do not remember at times when the full 'takeover' by the evil spirit occurs; it is outside their awareness, and they have no later recollection of the demon's activity.[57]

Oppression or vexation is then a state short of full possession, but he holds that there is a continuum between them as oppression shows many similar symptoms. Oppression exists in two forms, internal and external; the internal is typically in the form of voices a person hears, while the external results in physical wounds or symptoms like those of an illness. In his clinical practice, he has found that

> frequently individuals who are externally oppressed may report scratches, bruises, or other marks on their skin. Many such individuals have shown me their lesions or provided pictures of them ... When no common medical

---

54. He studied classics at Princeton University, and then lived in France for a number of years teaching English, before returning to study psychiatry at Yale University and psychoanalysis at Columbia University. Since the 1990s, he has been an active member of the International Association of Exorcists, as well as serving as a scientific advisor on its governing board.

55. Richard Gallagher, *Demonic Foes: My Twenty-five Years as a Psychiatrist Investigating Possessions, Diabolic Attacks and the Paranormal* (New York: HarperOne, 2020), 2. On pages 177–8, he tells the story of a shaman from Siberia who was arrested in September 2019 after walking about seventeen hundred miles towards Moscow to exorcise Vladimir Putin and drive demonic forces out of the Kremlin. The man had intended to have a public bonfire with pagan rituals in Red Square to make Putin come to his senses and quietly resign.

56. Ibid., 6–7.

57. Ibid., 80.

explanation for these sorts of cases can be found, one may entertain the more remote possibility that a paranormal or preternatural factor is involved.[58]

Some of the cases he dealt with enabled him to come to a conclusion about the origin of the oppressed person's state. In one case, he was faced with a man who showed scratches to his neck and face, and brought photos of past cuts that crisscrossed his legs and torso, while he and his wife insisted it was not self-mutilation. The doctor engaged in long sessions with him and the man eventually admitted that he had in his youth 'spent a few weeks worshipping Satan and even "promised his soul" to that figure if he received favours and experiences in return'. Gallagher had already learned that 'oppressive phenomena of beatings and other sorts of physical attacks had been reported throughout history in surprisingly sound documents'.[59] It is rather unsatisfactory that in his book he does not see the need to discuss the exact nature of the reported scratches, whether, for example, they were painful or located on a part of the body the afflicted could reach, but accepts their demonic origin, as Rossetti did in the case of Jason (above) with the eighteen-inch gouges on his back.

He approves of the fact that exorcists with whom he has worked favour the practice of admitting possessed clients (Catholics) to reception of the Eucharist, even though 'oppressed individuals may ... experience an unexplained pain upon entering a church or waiting in line to receive Communion'.[60]

Overall, the testimony of Gallagher, the psychiatrist, in this and the other more dramatic cases on which he has been consulted over twenty-five years has to be taken seriously.

One of Rossetti's observations, supported by Gallagher in his account,[61] is that in the more serious cases 'the demonic presence will temporarily take over the personality of the afflicted person, and the person's consciousness will recede into the background'.[62] Note, though, that in Gallagher's definition of possession above, he excludes control of the will. This raises the issue of possession and free will

---

58. Ibid., 99.

59. Ibid., 35–7.

60. Ibid., 99; T. K. Oesterreich, *Possession Demoniacal and Other: Among Primitive Races, in Antiquity, the Middle Ages and Modern* (Abingdon: Routledge, 1930), 164, noted that 'a Father of the Church, the Syrian Rabbulas, writes that "priests should not give the Host to possessed persons lest the Most Holy Thing be profaned by contact with demons." Cassian, on the contrary, was of the opinion that they should receive communion every day if possible as a spiritual remedy. It would be unjust to withhold it from them on the strength of the saying that pearls should not be cast before swine, that the communion should not become the devil's food.'

61. Gallagher, *Demonic Foes*, 144: 'In the dazed state, a person exhibits diminished control of his or her faculties, though not as much as during the full trance when a person's consciousness completely submerges beneath the presence of the possessing entity.'

62. Rossetti, *Diary of an American Exorcist*, 19.

The relevance of free will

There has been theoretical speculation in recent times on the extent to which human freedom can choose definitively for or against God. The issue has arisen especially in the context of revisiting the early Christian theory of apocatastasis, the subject of speculation by Origen and others.[63] It 'maintained that the entire creation, including sinners, the damned and the devil, would finally be restored to a condition of eternal happiness and salvation'.[64] The discussion includes the focus on whether a person can choose definitively to reject all relationship with God and it has therefore relevance for the present issue. The issue is to what extent a person can irrevocably choose Satan rather than God and thus give the idea of possession an inherent credibility.

Karl Rahner

Discussing the possible final state, that is after death, of the person enjoying human freedom, Karl Rahner held that presumptuous knowledge of a universal apocatastasis and of the certainty of salvation of the individual before death, as well as certain knowledge of a damnation that has actually occurred, must be excluded, but, because the grace of Christ must be acclaimed triumphant, the church can claim that martyrs and some others who have died in Christ have attained salvation.

> But [the church] cannot allow itself a corresponding affirmation of the certain and actual damnation of other men. Thus Christian eschatology is not the *parallel* prolongation of a 'doctrine of the two ways'[65] [which is rather Old Testament than Christian] to reach the termini of these two ways. Its central affirmation is concerned only with the victorious grace of Christ, which brings the world to its

---

63. Henri Crouzel, *Origen*, A. S. Worrall, trans. (Edinburgh: T&T Clark, 1989), 264: '(It) would be wrong to see in the texts expressing the non-eternity of Gehenna a firm statement of conviction. Origen hesitates, not seeing how to reconcile all the statements of Scripture: sometimes he makes no pronouncement, sometimes he ventures an opinion in one direction, sometimes in the other.'

64. John R. Sachs, S.J., 'Current Eschatology: Universal salvation and the problem of evil', *Theological Studies*, vol. 52 (1991): 227–54.

65. Referring, for example, to texts such as Mt. 7.13: 'Enter through the narrow gate; for the gate is wide and the road is easy that leads to destruction, and there are many who take it.'

fulfilment, though couched indeed in terms which safeguard God's mystery with regard to individual men.[66]

For Rahner, God's mystery is the triumph of grace, which prevents the possibilities of salvation and damnation being seen in the same light or equally balanced in 'living in the boldness of freedom'. In a similar way, Hans Urs von Balthasar spoke of the symmetrical doctrine of the Old Testament concerning final reward and punishment giving way to a fundamental 'asymmetry' between the reality and possibilities of human sin and the ever-greater grace of God, which always already accompanies it.[67] Similarly, rather than accepting St Bernard's idea of justice and mercy being the two feet of God, which makes the divine qualities seem more to stand alongside each other than be integrated, Balthasar held that between the misdeeds of the creature and the goodness of God, there is no equilibrium; 'justice with respect to the former is subordinated to divine mercy, indeed must be a mode of this mercy'.[68] These authors effectively hold that human freedom must be seen in the wider context of God's mystery of justice and mercy continually involved in the individual's exercise of freedom.

What this intrinsic involvement of God's judgment, which is one of love and mercy, in acts of human freedom implies is that no single act or even all acts taken together can constitute a final decision before God, as all acts are in principle revisable, during one's lifetime at least. What Rahner called an *option fondamentale* 'takes shape in and through the individual concrete decisions made during the course of a lifetime as a whole and becomes definitive and finally manifest in the process of death'.[69] Nevertheless, 'the total decision in which man finally disposes of the whole of his reality in its freely determined finality is, according to revelation subject to the sole judgment of God'.[70]

According to John R. Sachs S.J.:

> The point Rahner wishes to make seems to be that while we do make real choices vis-à-vis God in our concrete actions, we cannot know with absolute certitude the real depth and implications of anything we do. ... Nothing makes this clearer than human mortality itself. ... Precisely because of death, the human person does not and cannot come to finality by a radically (one-sided) autonomous decision but only by God's final act of judgment.[71]

---

66. Karl Rahner S.J., *Theological Investigations*, vol. 4 (Baltimore, MD: Helicon Press, 1966), 340.
67. Hans Urs von Balthasar, *Theodramatik* 4. 46–53, cited by Sachs, 'Current Eschatology', 240.
68. Balthasar, *Dare We Hope 'That All Men Be Saved'*, 121.
69. Sachs, 'Current Eschatology', 250.
70. Rahner, *Theological Investigations*, 204.
71. Sachs, 'Current Eschatology', 251.

It is one thing then for an afflicted person to believe that he or she is possessed, and another for an exorcist to decide that an afflicted person is possessed, and yet another to establish theologically as distinct from medically what possession means. All of these involve some ambiguities.

In applying all these to the putative situation of the person who now seems to be possessed by the devil, the issue of the person's freedom is central: the extent to which he/she has freely chosen to succumb to temptation by the devil. Cases where exorcism is being considered differ considerably, but usually an exorcism is requested by a person who believes that he/she is possessed and gives no explanation how this came about. It may be a case of a person having chosen against God 'without knowing the real depth and implications' of the decision, but is gradually moving towards an *option fondamentale*

Perhaps this can be regarded as the devil *taking* possession, especially if the signs indicative of possession listed by the *Rite* are present:

> Speaking freely languages unknown or not understood by the person; revealing things hidden and distant; demonstrating force greater than the age or the physical condition (no. 16)

These are signs which, however, according to the *Rite*, need not necessarily be considered as coming from the devil and there is need to attend to other signs, especially those of a moral and spiritual nature.

> These can be strong aversion towards God, against the person of Jesus, the Virgin Mary, the saints, the church, the Word of God, against things sacred, especially the sacraments, against sacred images. (no. 16)

The afflicted person may accept that symptoms of mental illness have been experienced, but if he/she seems to have freely engaged in dangerous rituals, the issue of whether this has been an example of *option fondamentale* becomes relevant. In pastoral practice, exorcists speak of the need in many cases for repeated exorcisms. This indicates that whatever possession actually means, it is deep-seated. For the medical profession, this may simply mean a profound dissociative identity disorder, requiring repeated treatment, while for the exorcist it means that the devil resists the exorcism process to such an extent that repeated exorcisms are needed. It is difficult to understand what can be lacking in the use of the imperative formula by the exorcist on behalf of the church, though the regulations do warn against expecting 'automatic efficacy'. 'The liberation of the afflicted person occurs if and when God wills it' (no. 13). There may be something lacking on the part of the exorcist, who is required to be of exemplary moral character, as an exorcism is a rite the effect of which is not *ipso facto* guaranteed. A film about Fr Amorth released in 2018, included an interview between William Friedkin (director of the film *The Exorcist*) and Bishop Robert Barron, in which the bishop expressed fear about being an exorcist, stating that he was 'not spiritual enough'.[72] In fact the regulations governing exorcism do require that only a priest, and one noted for his piety, knowledge, prudence and integrity of life, be considered suitable by the bishop and expressly mandated by him (no. 11).

Similarly, in the psychiatric profession, only an appropriately qualified and trained specialist can undertake treatment of a patient with a deep-seated identity disorder. In effect, the treatment of the afflicted follows parallel lines with regard to spiritual and medical processes, and this means that in the end, the case of such an afflicted person can be understood in radically different ways depending on whether there is belief in the existence of the devil or not. Some of the ambiguity already mentioned may be removed by saying that the church has always accepted that diabolical possession is possible, if rare, while the medical profession can acknowledge a personality disorder called 'possession' without attaching any transcendent meaning to the term.

And there is no reason to deny that possession can be permanent, when no successful exorcism has taken place. It will be helpful at this point to note Ratzinger's assertion:

> [Christ] does not ... treat man as an immature being, deprived in the last analysis of any responsibility for his own destiny. Heaven reposes upon freedom and so leaves the damned the right to will their own destruction. The specificity of Christianity is shown in this conviction of the greatness of man. Human life is fully serious. ... The irrevocable takes place, and that includes, then, irrevocable destruction.[73]

Christian reassurance

From the perspective of the Christian ethos, both the Gospels and the New Testament continually testify to the intimate relationship of Christ with the Christian, while also warning how this relationship can be lost. Those who fall away are described in Eph. 5.6 as the 'disobedient'. But the obedient Christian comes within the sphere of Christ's victory.[74] The implication of what Jesus says in Jn 14.23: 'Those who love me will keep my word. And my Father will love them, and we will come to them and make our home with them', is a very powerful reassurance of the secure existence of Christians against the danger of evil forces taking possession of their lives. There is also the reassurance offered by Jesus of the coming of the Spirit to teach the apostles (Jn 14.26). Texts like these formed

---

72. https://www.ncronline.org/news/media/new-film-documents-famous-exorcist-fr-gabriele-amorth.

73. Joseph Ratzinger, *Eschatology: Death and Eternal Life*, Michael Waldstein, trans. (Washington, DC: Catholic University of America Press, 1988), 216–17.

74. Trublar, 'Possession, diabolical', 64.

the basis of Paul's many references to the Holy Spirit in the life of the Christian, for example, Rom. 8.9; 2 Cor. 3.16 and Gal. 4.6. There is the incident, too, in Acts 19.11-16 regarding the 'extraordinary miracles' God did through Paul and the hapless seven sons of a Jewish high priest who tried to emulate Paul's success, only to be overpowered by the man 'with the evil spirit' and made to flee naked and wounded.

Ultimately, there are two possible approaches to the issue of possession and exorcism. Where there is belief in the devil's existence, the use of exorcism is vindicated on the basis of pastoral need and there is success in some cases at least, however little is understood about the nature of the *Rite* – what is actually happening. Where there is no belief in the devil's existence, exorcism will be seen as perhaps having some curative power for psychiatric disorders, as 'a therapeutic technique that could work'.[75]

---

75. Professor Michael B. First, in conversation with William Friedkin in *The Devil and Father Amorth*, October 2016. https://www.vanityfair.com/hollywood/2016/10/father-amorth-the-vatican-exorcist.

Chapter 12

CONCLUSION

Evil: Polarised views

This work set out to investigate the phenomenon of evil, the ever-present reality in the world that shows itself in wars, in ethnic cleansing, in human trafficking, in crime and in corruption, as well as in the natural disasters and pandemics that have their own evil effects on humanity and degrade the physical environment. If an understanding of all these is to be sought, rather than saying that evil 'just is', as materialism logically implies, it seems reasonable, even compelling, to predicate the existence of a *nameless but real force* operating unpredictably in the world. In physical phenomena described traditionally as natural evils, it is within the scope of empirical science to look for a complete explanation, even though the 'theory of everything' remains elusive. In human affairs, only materialists can be content with no need of explanation. The history of intellectual enquiry described so far seems to have arrived at the conclusion that this nameless, real force exists, but that the devil does not. It is true, however, that awareness of this real force is only sporadically prominent in public consciousness – obviously at times when major evils strike, as happened in Ukraine on 24 February 2022. Then the realisation that great evil exists comes as a shock. In past centuries, in contrast, belief in the devil's existence lessened the sense of surprise and shock at the irruption of evil.

For many centuries, this belief seemed to supply the explanation of all moral and even natural evil. As this is no longer the case, there is need for a synthesis between the real but unnamed and an unreal (in the ordinary sense) but named force, if harm to society is to be avoided by reversion to primitive beliefs, on the one hand, or by failing to recognise the dangers that threaten it, on the other. The role of religion, especially the Christian religion, is at stake here, but has the potential to create a cultural stance needed for a healthy psychological situation to obtain in society.

It is interesting that Barth's huge work contains some forty references in a scriptural context to the devil, as well as a comprehensive account of *das Nichtige* – which is somehow not part of creation – without his seeing it necessary to try to achieve a synthesis. If anything, he moves towards attributing reality to the devil and unreality to *das Nichtige*, though at one point, in *Church Dogmatics* III.3. c.49, he spoke of an actuality that exists 'only under the mighty No of God, but does have and is actuality in that sense. To this sphere there belongs the devil, the father of lies.'

This lack of synthesis is at the heart of the problem of polarised views on evil and its explanation, though for the Christian this is not in the end an insoluble problem, because Christ's life, death and resurrection brought reassurance of the final victory over evil. As 2 Cor. 5.17 puts it, 'if anyone one is in Christ, there is a new creation, everything old has passed away, see, everything has become new!'

Fundamental theology

Nevertheless, a conundrum exists because of this polarisation, and it affects the very foundations of theology. Fundamental Theology (and the pastoral theology and practice derived from it) has its foundation in Divine revelation, which takes place through symbolic events and words, and above all through the person of Christ. Divine revelation takes the form of an experience for its recipients, and this experience was from the beginning recorded in the writings of the Old Testament and in the events of salvation history.[1] Fundamental Theology draws therefore on human experience both in the past and in the ongoing life of the Christian community. In some forms, it relies more on the written records and the reflections of theologians past and present, while in other forms it draws on the situations the Christian community encounters in the present.[2] In both cases, Fundamental Theology has to perform an interpretative exercise in order to establish its principles and there is always the danger of selectivity in relation to both received tradition and present experience. There may be a problem in this regard today, in that among some theologians the tradition in relation to the existence of the devil has little influence on theological foundations and on the pastoral theology that must take account of the experiences of the faithful. Superficiality can result from not recognising the depths of reality, with the result that pastoral theology may fail to convince those whom it addresses.

---

1. As the Constitution on Divine Revelation of the Second Vatican Council stated: 'It was (God's) strategy that Israel might learn by experience God's ways with humanity' (no. 14).

2. Gerald O'Connell S. J., *Retrieving Fundamental Theology. The Three Styles of Contemporary Theology* (London: Geoffrey Chapman, 1993), 9–11. O'Connell adopts a position contrasting with Barth, and perhaps Catholic tradition, in asserting: 'There can be no such things as purely negative experiences or symbols. ... [The] Jewish-Christian faith and classical metaphysics assure me that there neither is nor can be *pure* unadulterated evil, or in equivalent terms, the absolutely negative. Everything has come from the hands of the infinitely good God. Not even the ultimate in human or diabolic perversion can totally undo that fact.' Ibid., 112–13.

Hence, the practical issue of how to understand the many exorcism practices that exist today. It has to be asked whether pastoral practice should lean towards recognising diabolical possession in some cases or give greater weight to advances in psychiatric knowledge to resolve the issue. There is the further issue of how to understand the connection between society and evil, to what extent society itself can be, or needs to be, exorcised.

The suggestion of this work is that a malevolent quasi-personality, or as some contemporary theologians put it, a non-person, remains to be reckoned with. In Western culture's present climate, this view is not likely to be much favoured. As Jürgen Moltmann stated,

> Though hardly anyone today believes in a personal devil, many people speak, in a variety of spheres of life, of vicious circles, of the vicious circles of poverty, of violence and alienation, of industrial pollution, of the vicious circles of the black, the immigrant worker, the prisoner, the mentally ill.[3]

Here, Moltmann was referring to the traditional figure, the devil, as Milton, for example, portrayed this being, or indeed as the Scriptures and Christian tradition prefers to put it, a personal being, rather than, as today's theology endeavours to state it, an existing being but not a person – to recall Ratzinger's enigmatic sentence: 'he is a non-person'. Moltmann looks for a source of evil elsewhere, in the many categories of life where evil flourishes.

The devil: Contrasting conclusions

In recent times, when on the theodicy issue much theological ink was spilled in favour of the existence of evil and the non-existence of God, adherence to belief in God made the issue of the devil's existence a major concern for two prominent American theologians, Henry Ansgar Kelly (1934–) and Jeffrey Burton Russell (1934–). They reached contrasting conclusions in their final publications.

Henry Ansgar Kelly

Writing in 1968, he concluded:

---

3. Jürgen Moltmann, *The Crucified God, The Cross of Christ as the Foundation and Criticism of Christian Theology* (London: S.C.M. Press, 1973²), 293. Note, however, the comment regarding the attitudes to the demonology of the desert fathers of Columba. Stewart O.S.B., in *The World of the Desert Fathers* (Oxford: S.L.G. Press, 1986), 24: 'The two great stumbling blocks for modern readers of desert literature are the harsh ascetical regimen practised by the monks and their apparent obsession with demons. … [B]ecause this is an age that prides itself on having given up superstitions of all sorts – a pride with little actual foundation – demons are distasteful if not plain silly.'

> Although it is possible that evil spirits exist, at the present time it does not seem probable, but whether or not they exist, it does not appear necessary to believe in them in order to cope with the problems of human life.[4]

He expressed doubt about their existence and, what ultimately seems more significant, came to the conclusion that the doctrinal tradition asserting the opposite did not have a binding force for believers.

Jeffrey Burton Russell

In his final work (1986), Russell set out two conflicting positions, clearly espousing one of them (as he had done throughout his books):

> Whether it is meaningful to believe that the devil exists depends upon one's world view. It is clearly meaningful in a Christian world view, and just as clearly meaningless in a materialist one. But the question must be put in the context of the larger question of whether any spiritual entity exists. God is as unscientific a concept as the Devil.[5]

His own position was that evidence for or against must be considered in light of other world views than that of materialistic science. His analysis of the prevalence of evil in the world led him to conclude that the cause of evil does not lie in human nature alone but can only have some transpersonal origin in some kind of collective unconscious, or even beyond the transpersonal as something truly transcendent, 'an entity that would exist even if there were no human race to imagine it'.[6] His position was rather like that of Barth, though he held that the idea of a 'transcendent Devil' was difficult to defend philosophically. But for him diabology based on Revelation is on much firmer ground. This approach accords with that of Karl Rahner, who agreed there was the need to correct 'popular' demonology of medieval or even patristic origin. In contrast with Kelly's view, Rahner held:

> The official teaching of the (Catholic) Church is confined to what is strictly necessary, and to what is possible; that is, to the existence of finite created powers of a personal kind which are, because of their own fault, evil, and have been rejected, and which cannot be restored to a state of perfection, apocatastasis.[7]

---

4. Kelly, *Toward the Death of Satan*, 131.
5. Russell, *Mephistopheles: The Devil in the Modern World*, 297.
6. Ibid., 299.
7. Karl Rahner S.J., 'Demonology', in *Encyclopedia of Theology*, Karl Rahner, ed. (London: Burns & Oates, 1975), 334.

Of particular note here is that Rahner's demonology included the term 'powers of a personal kind'. This usage can be explained as arising from his earlier treatment of angels as personal beings, which formed the basis, as he stated, for his treatment of demons: 'For the history of demonology as a theological treatise, see *Angels*.'[8] The same linking of the two types of spirits had been noted earlier in the writing of Aquinas (Chapter 3) and is surely the reason why writers of such ability continued to accept the idea of personality for the devil.

If, instead, the synthetic view is attempted, bringing together the current acceptance of a nameless but real force operating unpredictably in the world with the concept of the formerly named real force, previously simply called the devil, a fruitful analysis of the persistence of evil may be possible.

Christian tradition has always held the Scripture-based belief that a malevolent agent is at work in the world influencing people and events. This belief is probably more widespread than either scepticism or denial and ultimately does tend to vindicate the pastoral practice of exorcism where a right understanding of what is occurring obtains. The previous chapter was concerned with establishing this right understanding, based on a real, though non-personal, agent of evil clashing with the exorcist.

That is a 'localised' encounter. It is rather more difficult to present a rationale of such an agent being at work in all the spheres to which Moltmann referred and in the world generally, in society's cultural framework, in the functioning of the economy, and in the platforms and operations of the media of communication.

Where secularism reigns there is an assumption that there is no other world than the one amenable to sensory experience and empirical experiment. While the sickness of society may be accepted as real, a materialistic approach will see it in terms of a summing up of individual psychological pathologies. There is a belief that mental states exist as part of a mind/body composite, and are in the end part of the material foundation. Psychological disorders are routinely treated with pharmacological products, on the basis that mental states can be accessed, altered and cured by material means, without acknowledging any transcendent reality.

Social sin

Yet there is a widespread conviction that, in a way that is more than the sum of individuals' actions, the various spheres of activity in society are not morally neutral. The idea of social sin is distinct from personal sin; 'it is not necessarily formal sin in the sense of being deliberate; it is precisely social sin'.

> The sinful aspect of social involvement can be drawn out by a consideration of the phenomenon of social guilt, not guilt for the society of the past of which it was not a part, but responsibility for the present and future sin of society.

---

8. Ibid., 333.

> ... [One] should be clear at the outset about certain qualifications. First and foremost, social guilt is not individual guilt, but precisely an analogous reality that is social. The sameness and difference that constitute this analogy are crucial. We do not control society in the same way that we control ourselves. Yet we participate in society and contribute to its functioning. As prior to individual guilt, social guilt is part of the complex of prior sin. Second, it is impossible to quantify this social guilt, because it exists at so many levels and in so many different degrees. Within the framework of these qualifications, however, social guilt remains inescapable. [9]

The concept of social sin is often linked with Original Sin, but that concept is itself so complex and intrinsic to human nature, that it makes more sense, when beyond the scope of individual responsibility, a further agency is believed to be at work influencing corporate action. There are of course influencers in the spheres of politics, finance, commerce and media production, but Paul Tillich spoke of the demonic (his formulation) affecting institutions such as the state itself, institutions such as political parties, even the churches. Yet, care is needed lest 'what is in man' (cf. Jn 2.35), personal inclination to evil, not be taken into account and society simply 'demonised'.

Paul Tillich (1886–1965)

In a 1926 essay, reproduced in his *Interpretation of History* (1936), Paul Tillich (1886–1965) made some cogent observations about the demonic aspects of culture.[10] Beginning with the art of primitive peoples, he spoke of a peculiar tension, which sculptures and masks reveal.

> There is something positively contrary to form that is capable of fitting into an artistic form. There exists not only a lack of form but also a contradiction of form. ... Only by denying, on principle, the aesthetic qualities of a negro [*sic*] sculpture or a Shiva picture, could one escape this conclusion, that is, by making classical aesthetics absolute. Whoever cannot assent to this conclusion, must admit that human art reveals to us the actuality of that which is positively contrary to form, the demonic. [11]

In a succinct statement, he spoke of the distinction between the demonic and the satanic:

---

9. Roger Haight, 'Sin and Grace', in *Systematic Theology. Roman Catholic Perspectives*, Francis Schüssler Fiorenza and John P. Galvin, eds (Dublin: Gill and Macmillan, 1992), 423.
10. Paul Tillich, *The Interpretation of History* (New York: Charles Scribner's Sons, 1936).
11. Ibid., 79. See George Tavard, *Paul Tillich and the Christian Message* (London: Burns & Oates, 1962), on the 'Protestant principle' and the demonic, 102-3.

Mythologically speaking, Satan is the foremost of the demons; ontologically speaking he is the negative principle contained in the demonic.[12]

This statement is in effect a synthetic approach to evil, a recognition that Satan underpins the reality of the demonic aspects of society he will identify as 'demonries'. He saw 'holy demonries' even in the 'religions of grace', asserting that the final depth of holy demonry was the Grand Inquisitor as Dostoevsky visualised him and placed him opposite Christ:

> The religion which makes itself absolute and therefore must destroy the saint in whose name it is established – the demonic will to power of the sacred institution.[13]
>
> In cultures influenced by Humanism there is a tendency to place the demonic in close connection with form, and trace back destiny and creation to the demon, in the long run emptying the concept. In contrast, in deeply religious times the demonic is brought so close to the Satanic, which has no actual existence, that the creative potency disappears and the concept becomes unreal. The depth of the demonic is the dialectical quality in it.[14]

Saying that the Satanic has no actual existence restricts Tillich's synthetic approach, but the context is that of 'deeply religious times', in effect, times when Satan was given an exaggerated role in the life of the Christian community. He knew that in the early Christian centuries the focus was on Christ and his identity. When discussing the battle against the demonic in the history of religion, he asserted that the way of overcoming it depended on a 'manifestation of the unconditional', a manifestation of God in the soul, and he considered that the Christological work of the old church had the aim of warding off demonic distortions of every kind. The Christological and Trinitarian dogma was the powerful evidence of the victorious anti-demonic battle of early Christianity.

But he said that the church has again and again succumbed to demonry.

> This is true of the sacramental hierarchy of the Catholic Church with its reconstruction of numerus demonries once overcome in earliest Christianity.
> It is true, despite its fundamentally anti-demonic tendency, of the Protestant

---

12. Ibid., 81. His more extended comment: 'The tension between form-creation and form-destruction upon which rests the demonic, comprises the boundary between the latter and the Satanic, in which destruction is symbolized without creation – is only symbolized – because the Satanic has no actual existence, unlike the demonic. In order to have existence, it would have to be able to take on form' (80). This seems to go further than Barth's saying 'No' to what he called *das Nichtige*. It seems a denial of the existence of Satan/the devil, while Barth accepted the biblical teaching on the devil.

13. Ibid., 81.

14. Ibid., 82.

orthodoxy with its demonry of pure doctrine. ... And yet the Christian confession contains the certainty that the demonic has been overcome.[15]

Tillich would not have been surprised by the revelations that were to come concerning sexual abuse and other evils in the life of the churches, but in the end, he recognised the importance of religion in the combat with the unnamed but real, evil force in the world. When treating of the demonries 'of the present', he concluded that in the practical sphere two demonries surpassed all others in significance and symbolic force, capitalism and nationalism, with the second in part a counter-movement against the first.[16]

He assessed demonries in relation to his concept of 'ultimate concern', which he articulated in discussions at the University of California in 1963.

> Finding or losing the meaning of one's life as Jesus expressed quite clearly when he said 'He who will lose his life will find it and he who will seek his life shall lose it' (Mt. 10.39), this is not life in the sense of survival, but life in the sense of finding the precious jewel, something that carried ultimate concern. ... Every concrete concern is probably conditional.[17]

In that perspective, the Nazis making people believe that Hitler was the voice of God was a 'misplaced ultimate concern'. 'This was a bad cause, a demonic cause.'[18]

He wrote the original essay in 1926 in Germany, when he was beginning to discern the signs of the time, and would soon emigrate to the United States. He believed that it was probably possible, in accordance with the prophetic spirit, to see some signs of redeeming fate, but there was no certainty that a finite reality, even if it be a Christian culture, was indestructible – in the thirties the Western world had not reached the state of secularisation obtaining today.

Moltmann circles

Much has changed in the world order since then, and pop culture was, for example, a dominant feature of life during his later years in the United States but was not

---

15. Ibid., 107.
16. Ibid., 119.
17. D. Mackenzie Brown, ed., *Ultimate Concern: Tillich in Dialogue* (New York: Harper & Row, 1965), 21.
18. Ibid. In a comment on Tillich's California dialogue, John E. Smith wrote: 'Tillich might have been clearer in distinguishing among misplaced concerns; all are to be sure idolatrous, but it is not clear that all are necessarily demonic. Some false ultimates may merely deceive us in the promise they hold out, and, tragic though this is, the failure falls short of the destructiveness and horror manifest in the truly demonic.' 'The Impact of Tillich's Interpretation', in *The Thought of Paul Tillich,* James Luther Adams, Wilhelm Pauck, Roger Lincoln Shinn, eds (San Francisco, CA: Harper & Row, 1985), 245.

the focus of his attention. What follows will consider the various areas of life, the Moltmann 'circles', in which the synthesis of evil is to some degree at work, in combat with whatever graces God bestows on the world. Account has to be taken also of the work of the Holy Spirit guiding believers.

War

War is an obvious theatre for such engagements. In the aftermath of the Second World War, just as after the First World War, there was widespread conviction that war itself is an evil. The traditional just war theory held that the use of arms must not create evils and disorders graver than the evil to be eliminated. This could be true of modern war, because the destruction of human life and property, and the financial losses incurred, put an enormous burden on both victor and vanquished. This realisation led to the founding of the United Nations Organisation in 1945, with the aim of maintaining peace and security by upholding international law in the International Court of Justice. Its mission includes protecting human rights, delivering humanitarian aid and promoting sustainable development. All of these functions bear directly on the issue of evil, both natural and moral, and the UN today finds it necessary to focus on both of these evils in addition to guarding and endeavouring to restore peace. The conflicts which continue to break out in the world today cause very great displacement of populations[19] – perhaps the greatest evil in today's world – while sustainable development has become a great challenge because of the evils the prosperous economies' concentration on their own advancement have inflicted on developing countries, economic and climatic. The UN climate reports make it clear that just as there is a growing understanding that war is evil, so too the undeclared but real international economic war must be declared evil.

Protests against the evils of war by the 'War Poets' in Britain were recorded in a previous chapter, though as noted there, their vocabulary made little reference to transcendent reality, and it was largely the contents and language of the poems that conveyed the awareness of evil. During the recovery period after the Second World War, the United States' anti-Communist policy led to its being involved in two major wars, the Korean War from 1950 to 1956 and the Vietnam War from the mid-1960s to 1974 and continuing as the Cold War. During that period, it was involved in an arms race with the principal Communist regime, Soviet Russia, through the development of nuclear weapons by both sides. By the late 1950s, protests against these developments were growing steadily.

Daniel Berrigan

Fr Daniel Berrigan S.J. (1921–2016) was probably the most prominent of the protesters, a spokesperson for what now seems an enlightened culture, though not

---

19. While this was being written, the 24 February 2022 invasion of Ukraine by Russian forces led to the displacement of millions of people, in addition to all the death and destruction involved.

so perceived then. Of an Irish-German family,[20] he was educated by Jesuits and joined the Order. He progressed from writing books, articles and letters to the papers, protesting against US involvement in Vietnam, to destroying with others hundreds of military draft files. He is largely remembered for these activities and the jail sentences he received, but he was also a professional theologian, an author and an award-winning poet. Charged with his brother Philip and others with burning 378 military draft files in the car park of Catonsville, Maryland, Draft Board on 17 May 1968, he went on the run and became the first priest to be put on the Wanted Persons list during Edgar Hoover's tenure in the FBI. After the burning, he read the following statement on behalf of the group –which included his brother, Philip:

> We confront the Roman Catholic Church, other Christian bodies, and the synagogues of America with their silence and cowardice in face of our country's crimes. We are convinced that the religious bureaucracy in this country is racist, is an accomplice in this [Vietnam] war.[21]

This brief statement was highly significant. Though he would remain a Catholic and a member of the Jesuit Order, he effectively charged the religious establishment in general with connivance with what he considered evil activity, not only war, but the racism endemic in American society. It amounted to tacit approval of Tillich's concept of 'holy demonries'. They had met once.

While on trial for the Catonsville offence, he made a statement:

> The great sinfulness of modern war it that it renders concrete things abstract. … My intention on that day [of the burning] was to save the innocent from death by fire. I was trying to save the poor who are mainly charged with dying in this war. … I was trying to be concrete about death, because death is a concrete fact, as I have tried throughout my life to be concrete about the existence of God, who is not an abstraction but is someone before me, for whom I am responsible. [22]

In a country where support for, or membership of, the armed forces was linked in the popular mind with patriotism, and pacifism generally not held in high regard, as Albert Einstein had discovered in 1950,[23] attitudes to the Berrigan brothers varied and support would always be from a minority. Citizens who placed great value on being law-abiding were shocked by the civil disobedience that included damage to government property. Dorothy Day, an initial supporter, disapproved of their draft-burning action. But Naom Chomsky, the influential philosopher, strongly supported their view on the immorality of the Vietnam war in a 1971 essay.

20. Daniel Berrigan S.J., *Portraits of Those I Love* (New York: Crossroad, 1952), 107.
21. Quoted by Stephen Zunes, *National Catholic Reporter*, 9 May 2016.
22. Daniel Berrigan S.J., *The Trial of the Catonsville Nine* (Boston, MA: Beacon Press, 1970), 82–3.
23. Walter Isaacson, *Einstein: His Life and Universe* (London: Simon and Schuster, 2007), 501.

> I believe we must conclude that the American war in Indochina is criminal, in both the technical legal and general moral sense. The belief that the war is legitimate, though perhaps unwise, is, in my opinion, scandalous by strictly intellectual as well as decent moral standards. And it is deeply disturbing that this view is dominant. [24]

War is never simply a military exercise; there were repercussions for civil society as the war dragged on:

> Growing casualties, indications that more troops might be needed, and LBJ's belated request for a tax increase, combined in 1967 to produce unmistakable signs of war weariness. ... By the end of the year, for many observers, the war had become the most visible symbol of a malaise that afflicted American society. Rioting in the cities, a spiralling crime rate, and noisy street demonstrations suggested that violence abroad set off violence at home.[25]

Berrigan's pessimistic view of the American establishment was still there in 1986. In an interview to mark his eighty-fifth birthday, he said:

> This is the worst time of my long life, really. I have never seen such a base and cowardly violation of any kind of human bond that I can respect. [26]

In a mordant comment on American life, he wrote in 1967:

> Satan's works are always epiphanies; it is only Christ who dares to disappear in the world. [27]

He died at ninety-five in 2016.

Culture wars

In addition to war as commonly understood, there is also the phenomenon of 'culture wars', where opposing sides imply that the other's cause promotes evil or embraces it. The term has its origin in the *Kulturkampf* of the 1870s, where the issue was ultimately a religious one, while today, under the broad umbrella of politics,

---

24. Naom Chomsky, 'On the Limits of Civil Disobedience', in *The Berrigans*, William Van Etten Casey, S. J. and Philip Nobile, eds (New York: Praeger, 1971), 42.

25. George C. Herring, *From Colony to Superpower. U.S. Foreign Relations since 1776* (Oxford: Oxford University Press, 2011), 741.

26. Amy Goodman, interview with Dan Berrigan on *Democracy Now!* https://www.democracynow.org/2016/5/2.

27. Daniel Berrigan S.J., *Consequences, Truth and Justice ...* (New York: Macmillan, 1967), 33.

conflict flares up regarding economic, social, gender and life issues, all of which have religious implications. Popular or 'pop' culture in the late twentieth century, especially in the United States, was an expression of protest against mainstream society with its conservative values and its prejudices against the less educated, marginalised sectors of society. Of interest in the present context of evidence for the persistence of evil and belief in the devil's existence is that part of pop culture that focuses on entertainment – movies and music in particular. The significance of pop culture in this regard would merit extensive study; here, reference can be made only to some notable events. The release by Mick Jagger – the lead singer of the pop group, The Rolling Stones, of the record *Sympathy for the Devil* in 1968 – was a significant factor in the introduction of demonic themes in the world of popular entertainment. The song was unique in that the lyrics included an apparent and unprecedented address by the devil to listeners. Other popular songs of the Heavy Metal or Punk Rock kind at that time could contain anarchic lyrics promoting violence, though often having garbled words.[28]

Artistic performance has always produced examples of the virtuoso musician in a high state of concentration, moving towards a state transcending ordinary awareness, yet not ecstasy in the deeper sense of being 'outside oneself'. This phenomenon tends to be associated with very difficult classical music, but singers and musicians of the pop culture can perhaps also reach such a state. However, if the personal culture is one of violent protest or anti-religious bias, a spiritually transcendent dimension cannot obtain. In Tillich's language, there could be something of the demonic about it. That does not imply that such performers actually believe in the existence of the devil. Proponents of pop culture were from mixed social backgrounds. Jagger, for example, was middle-class English, grammar school educated, of a background less likely to be marked by belief in the devil's existence, while having to work at integrating into the culture he met in the United States. Many with whom he performed (or competed with) were African Americans with belief systems going back to the teaching of Puritan colonists and their Evangelical successors. For them it was often the case that the devil was real and was the influencer of the cultural 'other', the mainstream culture.

> In 1990, John Cardinal O'Connor of New York announced his belief in the devil and his works in demonic possession, Satanism and heavy metal music in modern American culture. His comments caused a brief stir. Ozzy Osbourne, former lead singer of Black Sabbath and godfather of the metal movement

---

28. The background to this release is that the lead singer, Mick Jagger, had read the novel by Mikhail Bulgakov, *The Master and Margarita*, chronicling the devil and his entourage from the time of Christ through the Soviet Russia of Bulgakov's time. (See Chapter 9 of this work.) Jagger had apparently dabbled in the occult and the song was really about him, as he knew he was demonised in social circles. See Marc Spitz, *Jagger. Rebel, Rock Star, Rambler, Rogue* (New York: Gotham Books, 2012), 113.

responded with an open letter that insisted that the Cardinal had 'insulted the intelligence' of heavy metal fans throughout the nation.[29]

In 1996, an album by Marilyn Manson, *Antichrist Superstar*, featured a 'supernatural' being intent on destroying the world. The album was an expression of social protest, as many of the songs of the time were, but the style of music could easily entice young fans to engage in violent action.

At the time of *Sympathy for the Devil* there were many movies in circulation in which the devil featured, such as *Rosemary's Baby* of the same year, but these tended to be horror movies with diabolical overtones rather than appearances by the devil. Ken Russell's *The Devils* turned to history to create a realistic picture of evil with a 1971 movie on witches and burnings at the stake. The movie, *The Exorcist*, based on a William Blatty's novel, followed in 1973, featuring a contemporary contest between an exorcist and the devil. It was very influential at a time when interest in exorcism was growing, and bolstered a new widespread tendency towards belief in the existence of the devil. Its legacy remains powerful in today's US culture. Other movies, such as *The Omen* (1976), followed – in this one the evil action involved a changeling. Similar movies were *The Exorcist II: The Heretic* (1977), *Damien: Omen II* (1978) and *Final Conflict* (1981). Many of the movies of the time featured well-known actors, giving them a certain respectability.

How influential the pop culture of this kind may have been on boosting belief in the devil's existence or, for that matter, on belief in diabolical activity in real-life events, cannot be established, but it is true that an outbreak of massacres and mass-suicides took place in various cults and in school shootings around the same time. The school shooters in the United States and elsewhere were of an age that could indicate an influence from the more harmful music and movies. Analysis after the event tended to identify school shooters as loners with psychiatric problems, and universally, it seems, does not mention religious faith or Christian rearing. It is well established that in the notorious Columbine school massacre of 1999, at least one victim was asked if she believed in God and replied affirmatively before being killed.

In general, the cults that resulted in mass suicides were established by older individuals who held apocalyptic views and saw themselves as messianic figures destined to bring about an apocalypse. In effect, they showed antichrist characteristics and employed distorted religious terminology. It is noticeable that post-tragedy analyses in many cases show that these individuals did not belong to any mainstream Christian tradition, but often created cults of their own with satanic content, as a protest against the presumed religious orthodoxy of mainstream culture. Jesus Constanzo, of Cuban origin but born in Florida, a drug-dealer and would-be guru, created a voodoo-type cult involving a devil's cauldron, torture and human sacrifice, resulting in the murder of thirteen people between

---

29. W. Scott Poole, *Satan in America: The Devil We Know* (New York: Rowman and Littlefield, 2009), 118; Patella OSB, *Angels and Demons*, 121–2.

1986 and 1989. He may be taken as an example of those individuals who established cults that ended in mass suicides or shoot-outs with police.[30] They generally had a dysfunctional family background, a seriously deprived childhood, a history of petty or serious crimes, drug addiction, social isolation, depression and hostility to society, all of which are conducive to the extreme reaction of dabbling in evil-oriented, even satanic, cults. Søren Kierkegaard's study, *The Sickness unto Death*, dealt with the isolated, despairing individual who, determined to be himself, directed his whole energy to passionate, demoniacal rage.[31]

Bringing attention to the real-life horror stories, as well as all aspects of the entertainment industry, depended in the 1970s on the newspapers, radio, record companies and television industry. The development of new means of communication, the social media, which came to dominate the culture afterwards, made a very big difference to the dissemination of popular culture and still does. In 2004, the social network Facebook was created, significantly in the isolation of a bedroom. Other platforms have followed, up to the recent Twitter and TikTok.

Social networks

Concerns have been raised in relation to the possible harmful effects the use of these media can have on users, because of their worldwide spread, difficulty in controlling the content of their messages, and, more insidiously, the extent to which they influence users' attitudes and values. Johann Hari published a major study of the influence of the social media in 2022, *Stolen Focus: Why You Can't Pay Attention*. Apart from the finding implied by the title, that people's attention span is affected by the use of the social media, he reported on various experiments done to gather information about users and how this information could be used to influence their behaviour.

> In 2002, students on a special course in the Persuasive Technological Laboratories at Stanford University came up with the idea of tracking all the information people offer on social media to come up with a detailed profile of them, not just gender, age etc., but a psychological profile – figuring how their personality works, and the best way to persuade them. It would know if the user was an optimist or a pessimist, if they were open to new experiences. … It would figure out dozens of characteristics they have.[32]

Using this information, a social media company could be employed to target a cohort of users with an advertisement likely to be of interest to them, or of course,

---

30. Ingrid Carlander, 'Rise of "Satanic" Violence in the United States', *Le Monde Diplomatique*, 28 February 1991.
31. Søren Kierkegaard, *The Sickness unto Death* (Princeton, NJ: Princeton University Press, 1941), 115.
32. Johann Hari, *Why You Can't Pay Attention* (New York: Bloomsbury, 2022), 106–7.

to bombard them with publicity likely to influence them, as in fact occurred during the election campaign of Donald Trump in 2016.

What should cause a great deal of concern is that an algorithm can be designed to make the user to see things sad or happy and spend longer time on the screen.

> On average, we will stare at something negative and outrageous for a lot longer than we will stare at something positive and calm. …A major study at New York University found that for every word of moral outrage you add to your tweet, your retweet rate will go up by 20% on average, and the words that increased your retweet rate most were 'attack', 'bad' and 'blame'. … If enough people are spending enough of their time being angered, that starts to change the culture.[33]

There was a reaction in October 2021 on the part of Facebook by Mark Zuckerberg, its founder, to claims of this sort. In response to an allegation by a whistleblower, Frances Haugen, he said it was deeply illogical to argue that Facebook deliberately pushed content that made people angry. A statement from the company in the same month said: 'We've always had the commercial incentive to remove harmful content from our sites. People don't want to see it when they use our apps and advertisers don't want their ads next to it.'[34]

Business

The business world is prone to the invasion of evil influences because in the end its function is to enable the survival and prospering of human beings, who need to be fed, clothed and housed. In the right ordering of things the economy is embedded in the social order, and things go awry when the social order is embedded in the economic system, instead.[35] In all three areas of life, forces employed by the few can manipulate the market for their personal gain and at the cost of deprivation and suffering on the part of many. This is true on a global level as well as national and local levels. To an extent, the blame for this situation can be laid at the door of the few – identified individuals – but as the scale is enlarged to transnational and then global levels, it becomes more and more difficult to establish where evils come from. The idea of social sin, from the Christian perspective, or the demonic from a philosophical perspective, becomes more relevant. Its presence is indicated by the discontent many experience with their lives, discontent arising in the first place from being economically deprived, and socially disadvantaged as a consequence. But even those not economically disadvantaged feel their lives

---

33. Ibid., 125–6.
34. John Karefa-Smart, 'Doctors, Development and Demons in Africa', *Irish Times* Report, 22 February 2022.
35. See the discussion of Karl Polyanyi's *The Great Transformation* (1944) in Kevin Hargaden, *Theological Ethics in a Neoliberal Age. Confronting the Christian Problem with Wealth* (Eugene, OR: Cascade Books, 2018), 6–10.

are not under their own control because of the power of big business. A 2021 study claimed:

> Despite the ongoing successes of capitalist development, we see a lot of discontent in continental Europe, the United Kingdom, and the United States. Underlying this discontent is a sense of *unfairness*. This has several dimensions. One dimension concerns people's personal experiences of losses – of jobs, incomes and opportunities – caused by adverse developments outside of their control. Another dimension concerns the observation that, for some other people, the past few decades have provided extraordinary opportunities for personal enrichment. A third dimension concerns the perception that political processes have been distorted so that the concerns of ordinary people have been shoved aside.[36]

Corporate business comes in for much criticism for its 'maximisation of profit' policy, caused by greed and resulting in ruthlessness, in injustice towards employees, in corrupt practices and in some cases in financial fraud. The policy also has consequences for the earth itself. According to Pope Francis,

> we need to reject a magical conception of the market, which would suggest that problems can be solved simply by an increase in the profits of companies or individuals. Is it realistic to hope that those who are obsessed with maximising profits will stop to reflect on the environmental damage they will leave behind for future generations? Where profits alone count, there can be no thinking about the rhythms of nature, its phases of decay and regeneration, or the complexity of ecosystems which may be gravely upset by human intervention.[37]

Not all multinationals deserve such strictures, but often it is a case of purchasing environmental credits rather than scaling back or investing in cleaner technologies. To its critics, corporate business does not seem to have a conscience. Yet many, perhaps most, people engaged in business are upright, conscientious people. It may be that individual persons succumb in small ways to ethically objectionable

---

36. Martin Hellwig, 'Capitalism: What Has Gone Wrong?: Who Went Wrong? Capitalism? The Market Economy? Government? Neoliberal Economics?', in *Oxford Review of Economic Policy*, vol. 37, no. 4 (Winter 2021): 66. Emphasis added by Hellwig. A 1975 study of development in the former colonial countries of Africa saw demonic influence in the rich nations' encouragement to aspire to their standards of wealth: 'In our preoccupation with development, (the devil) has found a very useful disguise. This disguise is a false notion of development held out to us by powerful agents of his demonic power.' John Karefa-Smart, 'Doctors, Development and Demons in Africa', in *Disguises of the Demonic: Contemporary Perspectives on the Power of Evil*, Alan M. Olson, ed. (New York: Association Press, 1975), 151.

37. Pope Francis, *Laudato Si'* (Vatican State: Vatican Press, 2015), no. 190.

actions, and that these when summed up over a large corporation bring about a grossly unethical situation, a moral profile that would not be recognised by the individuals themselves. In such a situation it is appropriate to ask whether the 'summing up' produces more than the sum of its parts, whether an opportunity has been provided for an evil force to create something new, whether from a Christian point of view this is the origin of social sin. While individual ambition and covetousness may be minor flaws, the corporation itself at boardroom level may have what Tillich called a 'demonic will to power', a desire not just to compete, but to crush competitors. There can be an incrementing of malpractice when diverse interlocking spheres, financial, political, the influencer sphere, symbiotically combine to create a new entity yet one more removed from considerations of transparency, accountability and honesty.[38]

Psychological considerations

By James Dixon

Even in cases of harmful corporate action and decision-making, where many lives are negatively impacted by mass layoffs or 'downsizing', some psychological distancing is necessary before the average human can act in ways so catastrophic to many others lives.[39] Under the right settings, with enough personal motivation and/or social or cultural support, even the average human mind is open to such corruption.[40] Psychological findings offer some insight into both the perspective of an evil actor (be they demon or human), and also the vulnerabilities to corruption existent within the human species itself.

The majority of the population develops the skills necessary to negotiate a safe path through these influences but often with a firm preference for the tangible reality of the material world as a result. In this case, those who nonetheless claim to be religious are likely to have a superficial grasp of traditional beliefs. Superficiality appears to be a characteristic of much of Western Christianity, in the sense of religious terms lacking conceptual content and having little influence in daily living, and hence allowing acceptance in daily life of standards of conduct that appear to be indifferent morally but are in fact to a degree evil in nature. A whole population can become desensitised to the evil cultivated by a political regime and come to live by its norms. In that way people who do not reflect, or allow themselves to reflect, on the evil endemic to the regime, are complicit in evil.

38. Hargaden, *Theological Ethics in a Neoliberal Age*, 105.

39. R. D. Hare, *Without Conscience. The Disturbing World of the Psychopaths among Us* (New York: Guilford Press, 1999).

40. S. Hitlin, *Moral Selves, Evil Selves. The Social Psychology of Conscience* (London: Palgrave MacMillan/Springer, 2008), 167.

Acts of omission and inaction can also be central to evil emerging. 'Learned helplessness'[41] is a state of apathy emerging from a series of failures to escape distress or discomfort over time, leading to acceptance of the conditions and passive acceptance of the ill that befalls one and those around. Such states may occur along a continuum that might include other forms of passivity to others, such as cases described as 'Stockholm Syndrome' (in the case of cults or kidnappings) where people take up the cause of their kidnappers and detach from previously existing relationships and values. They transition to psychotic states where people experience themselves as controlled by forces outside of themselves (delusions of passivity).[42] Often the intention of the other forces or influences are malevolent and so acts of harm can follow which otherwise would not be carried out. The person who chooses to forgo their choice to act differently may be complicit through omission or may initiate harmful acts. In such cases the person remains responsible for their actions, given that they maintain the capacity to act independently. However, in many cases it is argued that a person's capacity is reduced. In cases of psychosis, Mental Health Acts and assessments of capacity are used, because the person is seen as less culpable, though it can be hard to gauge how much control they maintained over the sequence of actions that led to harm being caused.

In cases where societies and cultures allow setting events to develop, or even promote the setting events (e.g. dictatorships), the society as a whole is required to take some portion of responsibility for the evil acts that occur during such times and conditions (e.g. war, extreme social deprivation, extreme political conditions such as fascism).[43]

In much more common daily examples of evil emerging, evil follows from acts of omission (not choosing to halt an evil action). The Bystander Effect is an often-quoted phenomenon (though prone to misrepresentation), occurring where people divorce themselves from the responsibility of acting to reduce pain or suffering in the belief another person will act in their place.[44] In such cases there is often a need for specific setting events to be present, such as the recognition that many others are present and aware of the harm being done. Nonetheless, people can choose to believe it is not their place to act even if they know that is the right thing to do, and in so doing choose to believe and perceive their sense of culpability as diminished. Much if not all of the world's population is likely to be guilty of this attitude in relation to issues such as hunger, global warming, injustices and social deprivation.

---

41. M. F. Seligman, 'Learned Helplessness', *Annual Review of Medicine*, vol. 23, no. 1 (1972): 407–12.

42. American Psychiatric Association, *Diagnostic and Statistical Manual of Mental Disorders* (Arlington, VA: 2013).

43. R. Cesur and J. J. Sabia, 'When War Comes Home: The Effect of Combat Service on Domestic Violence', *Review of Economics and Statistics*, vol. 98, no. 2 (2016).

44. Colin Fraser Burchell, Colin Hay, F. Dale and Gerald Duveen, eds, *Introducing Social Psychology* (London: Wiley On-line Library, 2001).

C. G. Jung (1875–1961)

With so much psychological analysis available to explain behaviour that leads to evil, it is appropriate to ask whether retaining belief in the devil as a source of evil is useful or merely atavistic; that is, whether the proposed synthesis of the understanding of evil makes sense intellectually or morally. If 'hardly anyone today believes in a personal devil' such a synthesis is problematic, given the general conviction psychological factors create in a population, unless an understanding of the devil compatible with psychological mechanisms is reached. Belief in the existence of such a being is easily discarded. Psychology itself, however, can help, if C. G. Jung's analytic psychology is taken into account.

In addition to types of personality with dominant attitudes either extraverted or introverted, Jung identified four function types: thinking, feeling, sensation and intuition. One has either a conscious dominant thinking or feeling function (not both) and either a sensation or intuition function. The first two could be said to characterise the process involved in the historical development described in this work, with the conclusion arising from thought or a judgemental feeling that a nameless real force exists, but that the devil does not. A thinking or feeling process has in many cases arrived at that conclusion.

Turning to the other pair, of sensation and intuition, where sensation indicates that something is, and intuition what it might be, Jung's technical language is as follows:

> Both [the intuitive and sensation types] have the mechanism of introversion and extraversion in common with the rational types, but they do not – like the thinking type – differentiate the perception and contemplation into thought nor – like the feeling type – differentiate the affective experience of instinct and sensation into feeling. On the contrary, the intuitive raises unconscious perception to the level of a differentiated function, by which he also achieves his adaptation to the world. He adapts by means of unconscious directives, which he receives through an especially sensitive and sharpened perception of dimly conscious stimuli. To describe such a function is naturally very difficult on account of its irrational and quasi-unconscious character. In a sense one might compare it to the daemon of Socrates – with the qualification, however, that the strongly rationalistic attitude of Socrates repressed the intuitive function as far as possible, so that it had to make itself felt in the form of concrete hallucinations, since it had no direct access to consciousness, But this not the case with the intuitive type.[45]

---

45. C. G. Jung, *The Collected Works of C. G. Jung*, vol. 6, Psychological Types, Bollingen Series XX, Herbert Read et al., eds (Princeton, NJ: Princeton University Press, 1971), 145–6.

Intuition and sensation seem an appropriate way to characterise a perception and contemplation of the devil that is not differentiated into thought, basically because it is a case of a non-person, making syntax impossible. The intuitive person with sharpened perception – sensation without judgement – receives unconscious stimuli to allow him/her to be aware of the reality traditionally called the devil, and will be wise in not rationalising the intuition to the extent of enabling 'concrete hallucinations' consisting of visual images to occupy consciousness.[46]

What then of the traditional concept of temptation by the devil? Temptation can be understood to mean that a malicious force constantly exerts a fascination for fallen human beings, and, inevitably, there are occasions when it presents itself in more attractive guise than usual or the person's receptiveness is greater for a variety of reasons, from the physical to the mental. Jesus said in Mk 7.21, 'For it is from within, from the human heart, that evil intentions come', and the Letter of James spoke of 'two wisdoms'. Bitter envy and selfish ambition indicates a wisdom that does not 'come down from above, but is earthly, unspiritual, devilish' (Jas 3.15). There is in human nature a tendency to go along with evil, but thinking and judgement are involved. From the synthetic perspective, here the intuition is that the devil is at work while thinking may give way to feeling, a judgement of rejection or acceptance.

Is there a future, then, for the familiar figure of artistic tradition? The images from earlier centuries presented Satan in human, though rather distorted form; in the Middle Ages the tendency was to use animal imagery – the devil seen as a winged dragon, for example,[47] while during the Reformation the pope was often depicted with a donkey's head, as a man possessed by the devil. That return to the grotesque itself fell victim to the disenchantment cultural phase, which reached its peak in the Enlightenment dismissal of the devil. However, the renewed struggle between traditional Christian teaching and Enlightenment attitudes in Europe and in the United States in the twentieth century brought a significant return of interest in the devil; catechisms for children in Belgium and the Netherlands included dramatic illustrations of the adversary.

Anthropomorphic rather than animal representations are a problem, because they are symbols of personal beings. Non-human figurative presentation is less so, but it is a distortion of the intuition, which can only be kept authentic if neither described nor pictured. To fall back on naming the 'devil' is an instinctive

---

46. Dostoevsky presents Stavogrin in his interview with Bishop Tikhon as a man who has allowed the hallucinations arising from his sense of guilt to take the form of 'some kind of malignant creature, mocking and rational, in all sorts of guises and in different characters, but it is the same, and it always makes me angry'. Fyodor Dostoevsky, *The Devils (The Possessed)*, David Magarshack, trans. (Harmondsworth: Penguin Books, 1971), 676.

47. Robert Muchembled, *A History of the Devil. From the Middle Ages to the Present*, Jean Birrell, trans. (Cambridge: Polity Press, 2003), 27: 'Gothic sculptors had imagined the Evil One as a deformed human being.'

but not intuitive way of knowing reality, and has its roots in a primitive world view. It has always been a way of avoiding the denial of reality. But the intuition, and even the sensation, of the persistent presence of this malevolent force is what is really necessary, if the world is not to be caught unawares by its sudden 'appearance'.

APPENDIX: TOWARDS A PSYCHOLOGICAL ANALYSIS OF POSSESSION AND EXORCISM

James Dixon

Possession understood psychologically

From the psychological point of view, there can be a very different understanding from the theological of these cases of alleged possession. The human mind has the capacity to alter reality to the point that one person's perspective and understanding of the surrounding world can no longer be shared with those around it, even people very close, such as family or those who share the same culture or background. This ability of the mind can leave a person living a reality – for that is what it is to the individual – divorced from anything others can see or experience through their own senses. In psychological terms this is often called psychosis, but there are often other forms of experience which allow altered states of perception and thinking, such as those triggered by direct physical causes (delirium), other states often considered direct consequences of traumatic events (dissociation or post-traumatic stress disorder – PTSD) or states triggered by substance use (prescribed or other forms).

Such clinical conditions of the mind can often be used to explain experiences that manifest within an individual that would previously have been misunderstood as something else. The growing understanding of the capacity of mind and how it generates our 'reality' can be used to offer an alternative explanation for some of the behaviours and expressions described within the Bible, especially as many of these behaviours and beliefs are still exhibited today within the current manifestations of mental health problems people are experiencing. It is not uncommon for people to perceive themselves as possessed, hearing or seeing what they believe to be demons or devils working within them, who can often be heard saying things to them that they would never consider themselves to think or say.

Horrible or frightening visions of demons or religious persecutors are also relatively common as are the positive perceptions of angels or other religiously important figures, which can be perceived as positive and supportive. In many cases when people have received the right support or changes have occurred in the environment, which has alleviated the stress placed upon their mind, they can later reflect that the mind generated these experiences as representations of the conflict or trauma they were experiencing. Or in the case of positive experiences, their mind had created the resources they needed at the time to find comfort and hope. These psychological explanations for many individuals, such as those experiencing psychosis, are sufficient and allow individuals to accept the concept of stress impacting on their mind to produce such experiences. For others it remains important to leave open the possibility that there were some greater forces working within them. This need is acknowledged even within the most mainstream of clinical reference material.

For example, in the section 1.2.8 'Dissociative Disorders' of the *Diagnostic and Statistical Manual of Mental Disorders*, fifth edition,[1] published by the American Psychiatric Association, there is a category of Dissociative Identity Disorder, called 'Possession', a particular disorder which may or may not be associated with 'hyper-religiosity'. Empirical psychiatric research is required in order to make the consistent observation, within mental health settings, that religion and religious beliefs are often closely related to mental health. Such beliefs and understanding about the world can manifest in either a constructive or detrimental way depending on the impact it has on what we generically call well-being.

This last point is important to emphasise because there are many who have experiences or make interpretations of the world by drawing meaning from experience in a way that others cannot experience or make sense of. That is not a problem in and of itself if people and those around them do not experience a negative impact on functioning and well-being. Many such people who experience life in this way are happy, and in functioning do not require clinical support or services, and therefore should not have their experiences categorised in clinical terms in a way that diminishes their experiences or seeks to limit the understanding or acceptance of them. We have yet to understand our world fully through a scientific or clinical lens and therefore there will inevitably be a limit to what we can understand or explain using clinical or scientific language in every case. In many such examples, there must be a recognition that every human culture has within it a role for some form of religious or spiritual understanding. Therefore, the argument can be made that at times religion or spirituality is not just being used to paper over the cracks of human ignorance, but rather to serve a purpose and function that cannot be completely substituted by science or clinical terminology. This will not be accepted by many, so it will be necessary to build an integrated understanding of experience that seeks to know where psychology, religion and spirituality can work together to understanding meaning in life. One example of where this interaction may be happening is the experience of possession and the rite of exorcism.

---

1. American Psychiatric Association, *Diagnostic and Statistical Manual of Mental Disorders*, 5th edn (Washington, DC: American Psychiatric Association, 2013).

Relationships in exorcism: A hybrid perspective incorporating the psychological

What can be said about the relational components explicit within exorcisms from a psychological perspective? What psychological concepts can be drawn upon to provide an understanding of how an evil force, such as a devil, could effectively act upon a separate individual, one considered to have capacity for autonomous action and intention, the capacity for free will? The conceptualisation of 'subjectivity' is needed as this concept will be central to framing interactions purported to be part of an exorcism.

To infer subjectivity, one needs to infer an organism has the capacity for internal experience and that the organism can reflect on those internal experiences.[2] As humans, we draw upon our inner world of thoughts and feelings and see evidence of these phenomena in 'subjective' beings like our fellow humans. Subjectivity is therefore composed of characteristics of the personal, private, mental and affective phenomena that make us consider ourselves as 'I' while seeing the collection of these phenomena in others as 'Thou'.

How does this help when understanding the interaction between Exorcist-Afflicted and Demon? Inferences can be drawn from exploring human behaviour and how humans can act psychologically in evil ways upon other human beings. First, a psychological definition provided within psychological literature is offered by Philip Zimbardo from his book: 'Evil consists in intentionally behaving in ways that harm, abuse, demean, dehumanise, or destroy innocent others – or using one's own authority and systemic poorer to encourage or permit others to do so on your behalf.'[3]

This idea of evil has been investigated empirically by Zimbardo and others to discover what factors explain how humans as a species can harm one another and what factors increase or decrease our ability to act in this way. From their conclusions we can draw inferences as to the perspective of a demon focused solely on carrying our evil. For we as a species can be demons too.

Human acts of evil and the enablers for such behaviour

The majority of people are prevented from acting against others in cruel or hurtful ways because of the consequences we face when doing so. Another social psychologist Steven Hitlin summarises how 'conscience' makes it difficult for people to act in evil way. Most humans will face social and personal consequences for acting in an evil way. Social rejection and isolation (i.e. imprisonment or being

---

2. A. S. Reber, and E. Reber, *The Penguin Dictionary of Psychology* (London: Penguin, 2001³).

3. P. Zimbardo, *The Lucifer Effect: How Good People Turn Evil* (London: Random House, 2007).

exiled), internal punishments in the form of unpleasant emotional states such as shame, guilt and self-blame or other forms of unpleasant experiences, such as unwanted intrusive images, dreams or memories associated with previous harmful actions, all act to promote a path towards positive social and moral behaviour. Therefore, to act in an intentionally harmful or cruel way, especially towards another human being, requires most people to overcome these powerful barriers. Unfortunately, this can be done in various ways, either via the individual's own distortional processes or by societal or cultural (systemic) processes.

One way to evil is through the individual's dispositional state. Distortions of one's perception of another's subjectivity to a point where subjectivity is removed are often necessary so that intentional acts of harm can be carried out. In such a relationship, negating subjectivity via the elimination of affective connection between both parties – to the point that what happens to 'Thou' holds no resonance for 'I' – allows perception to move from subjectivity to objectivity (the 'Thou' becomes an 'It'). In these cases, the will to act against others in a harmful way can be released without fear of the consequences normally expected.[4]

Attempting to merge the psychological with the theological

The relationship between demon and exorcist and with afflicted

The above summary now allows us to imagine the mind of a demon and its relation to the exorcist, the demon–afflicted–exorcist relationship. One can begin to imagine there would be no 'I–You' relation from demon *to* Exorcist or from demon to the afflicted party. Given the assumed intention of the demon to act with evil intent (corrupt or deny God's will), there will need to be a lack of acknowledgement of subjectivity by such a creature because to act in consistently evil ways requires one to deny relationship with that being acted upon. Functionally, subjectivity or the awareness of the characteristics of subjectivity needs to be denied, through objectification or de-individuated. A truly evil actor, who desires only to harm, would need to take a position of negation only when it comes to subjectivity. It is impossible for a human being to imagine being in a position of non-subjectivity, given we can only experience as a subjective being ourselves. One analogy perhaps that might help consider such a relationship is to imagine a person walking outside on a perfectly calm day. As he or she walks, they impact upon the surrounding air, moving through it, but remain blind to their effect on it and it on them (unless it happens to be a strong breeze). In this example, the focus remains purely on his or her internal world, their intentions and what other stimuli they are focused on. Similarly, for a demon possessing a human, another analogy might be one of a human driving a car down the road with the windshield, killing insects. Calling on

---

4. S. Hitlin, *Moral Selves, Evil Selves: The Social Psychology of Conscience* (Springer 2008).

the demon to leave the human alone would be akin to stopping someone driving in a hurry by asking them to consider the flies.

The direction of influence

With possession, there is a two-way relationship from the perspective of the human. The individual would need to forego their own subjectivity – denying their own agency and capacity to act against the evil influence. Therefore the only hope relationally an exorcist has when attempting to offset evil intent of a demon is to focus on the afflicted person–demon relationship by reigniting the afflicted person's subjectivity – in exorcism by reigniting the relationship the afflicted has with a higher power, which in spiritual terms would be God. This is because the concept of free will offers a challenge to the idea that a human subject of God can have their free will taken over completely. If free will is a gift conferred by God, it cannot be taken back by any power other than God's. Nor can it be refused other than by God's will. It follows therefore that possession of a human being with free will must mean the human is required to readily deny their own free will or freely choose to forego free will so as to enable evil forces to work through them. Again, the capacity of the human mind to alter self-perception so as to allow such a context to develop is fathomable. One such hypothetical example is that of cases where an individual comes to believe themselves as so corrupted, vile or valueless that resistance to malevolent forces is pointless. Thus, evil actions are allowed because there is no point resisting as the person believes themselves or the world to be so bad there is nothing they can do to prevent it (namely a complete loss of faith in God, themselves and hope in general) such as might be found in psychotic depression. Such a state of mind can be developed through persistent abuse or neglect of the individual (themselves evil actions) to the point that evil is all they can perceive and experience. Chronic states of hopelessness, pain and distress without support and meaningful connection to others could lead to people giving up on acting according to their previously held values (e.g. to live a caring and kind life towards self and others).

Either the explicit example of someone choosing to believe that they are a lost cause, or their choice to forego their free will for another's, or the more implicit and often more insidious creep towards a belief one's responsibility to act is diminished could all be relational positions that could be adopted by one who perceives themselves to be 'possessed'. In this way their perception of their free will could be diminished sufficiently for the perception that evil forces have taken over, they are no longer responsible or capable of control and so can be misled into acting in ways they would otherwise, in other settings, or in other states simply refuse to act in. In each of these examples, however, the capacity to act in accordance with one's own free will is never completely lost and the assumption therefore is that it is the exorcist's responsibility to help the individual to find their capacity to reconnect with their subjectivity, perhaps retriggering the 'I–Thou' relationship with other subjective beings through the power of belief in God, a power above and beyond themselves, and re-instigating their capacity and motivation to make more benevolent choices independent of negative forces, impulses or desires.

BIBLIOGRAPHY

Abelard, Peter, *Petri Abelardi Omnia Opera, Expositio de Symbolo Apost. Patrologia Latina* (Paris: Migne, 1854), 178.

Ackermann, Josef, *Heinrich Himmler Als Ideologe* (Göttingen: Musterschmidt, 1970).

Adams, James Luther, Wilhelm Pauck and Roger Lincoln Shinn, eds, *The Thought of Paul Tillich* (San Francisco, CA: Harper & Row, 1985).

Alighieri, Dante, *The Divine Comedy 1. Hell*, Dorothy L. Sayers, trans. (Harmondsworth: Penguin Books, 1949).

Alighieri, Dante, Letter to the Cardinals of the Church after the death of Clement V in 1314.

Althaus, Paul, *The Theology of Martin Luther*, Robert C. Schultz, trans. (Philadelphia, PA: Fortress Press, 1966).

American Psychiatric Association, *Diagnostic and Statistical Manual of Mental Disorders*, Fifth Edition (Washington, DC: American Psychiatric Association, 2013).

Amico, Beppe, *A colloquio con Padre Gabriele Amorth – L'opera di Satana, la sua azione ordinaria e straordinaria* (Trento: Reverdito, 2022).

Amorth, Gabriele, *An Exorcist Tells His Story* (San Francisco, CA: Ignatius Press, 1999).

Amorth, Gabriele, and Marcello Stanzione, *The Devil Is Afraid of Me: The Life and Work of the World's Most Famous Exorcist*, Charlotte J. Fasi, trans. (Manchester, NH: Sophia Institute Press, 2019).

Anon., *Satan* (London: Sheed and Ward, 1951).

Applebaum, David, *The Vision of Hume* (Rockport, MA: Element Books, 1996).

Aquinas, Thomas, *Questiones Disputatae De Potentia Dei*. English Dominican Fathers trans. (Westminster, MD: Newman Press, 1952).

Aquinas, Thomas, *Summa Contra Gentiles* III. lxxi. 10.

Aquinas, Thomas, *Summa Theologiae* Ia. (London: Burns, Oates & Washbourne, 1912).

Arendt, Hannah, *Eichmann in Jerusalem: A Report on the Banality of Evil* (London: Penguin Books, 1965).

Arendt, Hannah, *The Origins of Totalitarianism* (Cleveland, OH: Meridian Books, 1958).

Ariel, David S., *Kabbalah: The Mystic Quest in Judaism* (Lanham, MD: Rowman and Littlefield, 2006).

Athanasius, St, *The Life of Saint Antony*. Ancient Christian Writers No. 10 (New York: Newman Press, 1978).

Augustine, *City of God* (Washington, DC: Catholic University of America, 1951).

Augustine, *Confessions* (London: Sheed and Ward, 1944).

Augustine, *Contra Julianum*. Fathers of the Church, Vol. 35 (New York: Catholic University of America, 1957).

Augustine, *De doctrina Christiana* III. *Sancti Augustini Opera Omnia*, Tomus V (Paris: Paul Mellier, 1842).

Augustine, *De Genesi ad Litteram*. *Sancti Augustini Opera Omnia*, Tomus V (Paris: Paul Mellier, 1842).

Augustine, *De libero arbitrio* III. The Fathers of the Church 59 (Washington, DC: Catholic University of America, 1968).

Augustine, *De natura boni* XXXVI. *S. Augustini Opera Omnia* 29 (Paris: Paul Mellier, 1842).
Augustine, *On Marriage and Concupiscence*, https://www.newadvent.org/fathers/15071.htm.
Augustine, *Sermons on the Liturgical Seasons*, Vol. 38 (New York: Fathers of the Church, 1959).
Augustine, *The Letters of Saint Augustine*, Vols 1, 2 (Washington, DC: Catholic University of America, 1953).
Augustine, *Tractates on the Gospel of John*. Fathers of the Church (Washington, DC: Catholic University of America, 1993).
Baglio, Matt, *The Rite: The Making of a Modern Exorcist* (London: Simon & Schuster, 2009).
Bainton, Roland, *Erasmus of Christendom* (Tring, Herts: Lion Publishing, 1988).
Bainton, Roland, *Here I Stand* (Oxford: Lion Publishing, 1978).
Bainton, Roland, *The Reformation of the Sixteenth-Century* (Boston, MA: Bacon Press, 1985).
Barclay, William, *The Gospel of Mark* (Edinburgh: Saint Andrew Press, 1956²).
Barrow, John D., and Frank J. Tipler, *The Anthropic Cosmological Principle* (Oxford: Oxford University Press, 1986).
Bartels, *Spectacles of Strangeness: Imperialism, Alienation, and Marlowe* (Philadelphia: University of Pennsylvania Press, 1993).
Barth, Karl, *Ad Limina Apostolorum* (Richmond, VA: John Knox Press, 1968).
Barth, Karl, *Church Dogmatics* II.1, *The Dogma of Creation* (Edinburgh: T&T Clark, 1960).
Barth, Karl, *Church Dogmatics* III.3, *The Dogma of Creation* (Edinburgh: T&T Clark, 1960).
Barth, Karl, *Dogmatics in Outline* (London: S.C.M., 1966).
Barth, Karl, *The Faith of the Church: A Commentary on the Apostles' Creed* (London: Fontana Books, 1960).
Baskin, Wade, 'The Devils of Loudun', in *Exorcism Through the Ages* (New York: Library, 1974).
Baudelaire, Charles, *Baudelaire: His Prose and Poetry*, T. R. Smith, trans. (New York: Boni and Liveright, 1919).
Baudelaire, Charles, *Oeuvres Complètes de Charles Baudelaire* (Paris: Éditions de la Revue Française, 1918).
Becker, Ernest, *Escape from Evil* (New York: Free Press, 1975).
Becker, Ernest, *The Denial of Death* (New York: Free Press, 1973).
Berrigan S.J., Daniel, *Consequences, Truth and ...* (New York: Macmillan, 1967).
Berrigan S.J., Daniel, *Portraits of Those I Love* (New York: Crossroad, 1982).
Berrigan S.J., Daniel, *The Trial of the Catonsville Nine* (Boston, MA: Beacon Press, 1970).
Beze, Theodore, *Vie de Calvin*. Publié et annotteé par Alfred Franklin (Paris: Cherbuliez Libraire, 1859).
Birrell, T. A., 'The Figure of Satan in Milton and Blake', in Anon. *Satan* (London: Sheed and Ward, 1950), 379.
Blake, William, *The Marriage of Heaven and Hell: In Full Color* (New York: Dover Publications, 1994).
Boccaccio, Giovanni, *Decameron* (Oxford: Oxford University Press, 1998).
Bonhoeffer, Dietrich, *Creation and Fall: Temptation: Two Biblical Studies* (New York: Macmillan, 1959).

Bornkamm, Heinrich, *Luther in Mid-Career, 1521–1530*, E. Theodore Bachmann, trans. (Philadelphia, PA: Fortress Press, 1983).
Boswell, Charles Stuart, *An Irish Precursor of Dante: A Study of the Vision of Heaven and Hell Ascribed to the Eighth Century Irish Saint Adomnán* (London: AMS Press, 1972).
Bossy, John, *Christianity in the West: 1400–1700* (Oxford: Oxford University Press, 1985).
Botte O.S.B., Bernard, *La Tradition Apostolique* (Paris: Les Éditions du Cerf, 1946).
Bouscaren S.J., T. L. and A. C. Ellis S.J., *Commentary on the Code of Canon Law 1917* (Milwaukee, WI: Bruce Publishing, 1951).
Bovey, Alixe, 'Medieval Monsters', *The Middle Ages* (British Library, London, 2015). https://www.bl.uk/the-middle-ages/articles/medieval-monsters-from-the-mystical-to-the-demonic.
Boyle, Nicholas, *Goethe. The Poet and the Age*, Vol. 1, *The Poetry of Desire (1749–1790)* (Oxford: Oxford University Press, 1991).
Brakke, David, *Demons and the Making of the Monk: Spiritual Combat in Early Chistianity* (Cambridge, MA: Harvard University Press, 2006).
Bredero, Adriaan H., *Christendum and Christianity in the Middle Ages*, Reinder Bruinsma, trans. (Grand Rapids, MI: William B. Eerdman, 1994).
Brenan, Gerald, *San Juan de la Cruz* (Barcelona: Editorial Laia, 1980).
Broderick, S.J., James, *St Ignatius Loyola: The Pilgrim Years* (London: Burns & Oates, 1956).
Brooke, Rupert, *The Letters of Rupert Brooke*, Geoffrey Keynes, ed. (New York: Harcourt, Brace and York, 1968).
Brown, D. Mackenzie, ed., *Ultimate Concern: Tillich in Dialogue* (New York: Harper & Row, 1965).
Brown, Peter, *Augustine of Hippo: A Biography* (London: Faber and Faber, 1969).
Brown, Peter, *The Body and Society: Men, Women and Sexual Renunciation in Early Christianity* (New York: Columbia University Press, 1988).
Brown, Peter, *The Making of Late Antiquity* (Cambridge, MA: Harvard University Press, 1978).
Brown, Raymond, *New Testament Essays* (London: Geoffrey Chapman, 1963).
Brunner, Emil, *The Christian Doctrine of Creation and Redemption*, Dogmatics: Vol. II, Olive Wyon, trans. (Eugene, OR: Wipf and Stock, 2014).
Buber, Martin, 'God and the Spirit of Man', in *The Writings of Martin Buber* (New York: New American Library, 1956), 111.
Buber, Martin, *I and Thou*, Walter Kaufmann, trans. (Edinburgh: T&T Clark, 1975).
Bulgakov, Mikhail, *The Master and Margarita*, Michael Glenny, trans. (London: Fontana, 1984).
Burchell, Colin Fraser, Colin Hay, F. Dale and Gerald Duven, eds, *Introducing Social Psychology* (London: Wiley, 2001).
Burleigh, Michael, *The Third Reich: A New History* (London: Macmillan, 2000).
Cahill, Thomas, *The Mysteries of the Middle Ages: The Rise of Feminism, Science and Art from the Cults of Catholic Europe* (New York: Nan A. Talase, 2006).
Calvin, John, *A Harmony of the Gospels: Matthew, Mark, Luke, and the Epistles of James and Jude*, A. W. Morrison, trans. (Edinburgh: Saint Andrew Press, 1972).
Calvin, John, *Commentary on the First Book of Moses*, Vol. 1, J. King, trans. (Edinburgh: Calvin Translation Society, 1847).
Calvin, John, *Commentaries on the Book of the Prophet Jeremiah and the Lamentations*, Vol. 4 (44:8), John Owen, trans. (Edinburgh: Calvin Translation Society, 1854).

Calvin, John, *Institutes of the Christian Religion*, John T. Neill, ed., F. L. Battles, trans. (Philadelphia, PA: Westminster Press, 1960).

Calvin, John, *Joannis Calvini opera quae supersunt omnia*, Tome 12 (Brunswige: C.A. Schwetschke et Filium, 1864).

Calvin, John, *John Calvin's Sermons on Ephesians* (Edinburgh: Banner of Truth Trust, 1973).

Campagne, Fabián Alejandro, 'Ignacio de Loyola y Teresa de Ávila Inspectores de Espíritus: Institución y Carisma en los albores da la Era confesional', in Letras de Universidade do Porto, *Via Spiritus: Revista de História da Espiritualidade e do Sentimento Religioso* 01/2014, Vol. 21. 83. Letras de Universidade do Porto.

Cantor, Petrus, *Summa de Sacramentis et Consiliis*, Vol. 3 (Beauvechain: Nauwelaerts, 1952).

Caraman, S. J., *Ignatius Loyola: A Biography of the Founder of the Jesuits* (San Francisco, CA: Harper & Row, 1991).

Carey, John, Emma Nic Cárthhaigh and Catríona Ó Dochartaigh, eds, *The End and Beyond: Medieval Irish Eschatology*, Vol. 1 (Aberystwyth: Celtic Studies Publications, 2014).

Carlander, Ingrid, 'Rise of "Satanic" Violence in the United States', *Le Monde Diplomatique*, 28 February 1991.

Casartelli, Louis C., *The Popes in the Divina Commedia of Dante* (London: Sands, 1921).

Casartelli, Louis C., *Catechism of the Catholic Church* (Dublin: Veritas, 1994).

Cawley, A. C., ed., *Everyman and Medieval Miracle Plays* (London: Dent, 1957^2).

Cerbelaud O. P., Dominique, *Le Diable* (Paris: Éditions de l'Atelier, 1997).

Certeau, Michel, *La Possession de Loudun* (Paris: Archives Gallimard Juliard, 1980^2).

Cesur R., and J. J. Sabia, 'When War Comes Home: The Effect of Combat Service on Domestic Violence', *Review of Economics and Statistics*, vol. 98, no. 2 (2016): 209.

Chadwick, Owen, *The Reformation* (Harmondsworth: Penguin Books, 1972).

Charles, R. H., *The Book of Enoch* (London: S.P.C.K., 1917).

Chomsky, Naom, 'On the Limits of Civil Disobedience', in *The Berrigans*, William Van Etten Casey, S.J. and Philip Nobile, eds (New York: Praeger Publishers, 1971), 42.

Christian, Jr, William A., *Apparitions in late Medieval and Renaissance Spain* (Princeton, NJ: Princeton University Press, 1981).

Clagett, Marshall, ed., 'The Role of Art', in *Critical Problems in the History of Science* (Madison: Wisconsin University Press, 1969).

Clayton, Philip, 'God and the World', in *The Cambridge Guide to Postmodern Theology*, Kevin J. Vanhoozer, ed. (Cambridge: Cambridge University Press, 2003).

Cohen, Joseph, *Journey to the Trenches: The Life of Isaac Rosenberg 1890–1918* (London: Robson Books, 1975).

The Collected Works of St John of the Cross, Kieran Kavanagh OCD and Otilio Rodriguez OCD, trans. (Washington, DC: ICS Publications, Institute of Carmelite Studies, 1979).

Conferenza Episcopale Italiana, *Grande Rito degli Esorcismi*, 28 November 1999.

Cornman, J. W., and Keith Lehrer, *Philosophical Problems and Arguments: An Introduction* (New York: Macmillan, 1968).

The Coptic Narratives of the Ministry in *The Apocryphal New Testament, Being the Apocryphal Gospels, Acts, Epistles and Apocalypses*, Montague Rhodes James, trans. (Oxford: Clarendon Press, 1924).

Coulton, George G., *Life in the Middle Ages: Selected, Translated Annotated by G.G. Coulton* (Cambridge: Cambridge University Press, 1967).

Courtenay, William J., 'Spirituality and Late Scholasticism', in *Christian Spirtiualty: High Middle Ages and Reformation*, Jill Rait, ed. (London: S.C.M. Press, 1988).
Craig, William Lane, 'In Defense of Theistic Arguments', in *The Future of Atheism: Alister McGrath and Daniel Dennett in Dialogue*, Robert B. Stewart, ed. (London: S.P.C.K., 2008).
Crary, David, 'Exorcisms: Increasingly Frequent, Including after U. S. Protests', *Crux*, 31 October 2017.
Crouzel, Henri, *Origen*, A. S. Worrall, trans. (Edinburgh: T&T Clark, 1989).
Cuneo, Michael, *American Exorcism: Expelling Demons in the Land of Plenty* (London: Bantam, 2002).
Cyril of Jerusalem, *Catechetical Lectures* XVI (Oxford: Henry Parker, 1838).
Daniel-Rops, Henri, *The Catholic Reformation*, Vol. 1, John Warrington, trans. (New York: Image Books, 1962).
Davies, Brian, *The Thought of Thomas Aquinas* (Oxford: Clarendon Press, 1992).
Davies, Jeremy, *Exorcism: From Catholic Perspective* (London: C.T.S., 2009).
Dawkins, Richard, *Outgrowing God: A Beginner's Guide* (London: Bantam Press, 2019).
Dawkins, Richard, *River out of Eden: A Darwinian View of Life* (London: Weidenfeld and Nicholson, 1995).
Dawkins, Richard, *The Blind Watchmaker: Why the Evidence of Evolution Reveals a World without Design* (New York: W.W. Norton, 1986).
de Jesús O.C.D., Crisógóno, *The Life of St John of the Cross*, Kathleen Pond, trans. (New York: Harper Brothers, 1958).
Delatte O.S.B, L., ed., *Un Office byzantin de l'Esorcisme* (Bruxelles: Académie royale Belgique, 1957).
de Nicolás, Antonio T., *St John of the Cross: Alchemist of the Soul* (New York: Paragon House, 1989).
Denzinger, H., and A. Schönmetzer, *Enchiridion Symbolorum* (Herder: Barcinone, 1965).
de Santillana, 'The Role of Art', in Marshall Clagett, ed., *Critical Problems in the History of Science* (Madison: Wisconsin University Press, 1969), 41–2.
de Vogüé, 'Les Mentions des oeuvres de Cassien chez Saint Benoît et ses contemporains', in *De Saint Pachôme à Jean Cassien* (Roma: Studia Anselmiana, 1996).
Dillenger, John, *Martin Luther: Selections from His Writings* (New York: Anchor Books, 1961).
Dombrowski, Daniel A., *St John of the Cross: An Appreciation* (Albany: State University of New York Press, 1992).
Dostoevsky, Fyodor, *The Devils (The Possessed)*, David Magarshack, trans. (Harmondsworth: Penguin Books, 1971).
Driscoll O.S.B., Jeremy, *The 'Ad Monachos' of Evagrius Ponticus: Its Structure and a Select Commentary* (Roma: Studia Anselmiana, 1991).
Drob, Sanford L., *Symbols of the Kabbalah: Philosophical and Psychological Perspectives* (Northvale, NJ: Jason Aronson, 2000).
Duffy, Eamon, *A People's Tragedy* (London: Bloomsbury Continuum, 2020).
Duffy, Eamon, *The Stripping of the Altars: Traditional Religion in England 1400-1580* (New Haven, CT: Yale University Press, 1992).
Duffy, Stephen J., 'Our Heart of Darkness: Original Sin Revisited', *Theological Studies*, Vol. 49 (1988): 598.
Dumas, Alexandre, *Demons! The Possession and Exorcism of the Nuns of Loudun, and the Execution of Urbain* (Durham, NC: Lulu.com, 2019).

Duncan, Marc, *Discours de la Possession des Religieuses Ursulines de Lodun*, 1634.
Durkheim, Émile, *Suicide: A Study in Sociology*, John A. Spaulding and George Simpson, trans. (London: Routledge, 1952).
Edwards, Mark, Jr, *Luther's Last Battles: Politics and Polemkcs 1531–1546* (Minneapolis, MN: Fortress Press, 1989).
Egremont, Max, *Some Desperate Glory: The First World War the Poets Knew* (New York: Farrar, Strauss and Giroux, 2014).
Eire, Carlos M. N., '"Bite This, Satan"! The Devil in Luther's *Table Talk*', in *Piety and Family in Early Modern Europe: Essays in Honour of Steven Ozment*, Marc R. Forster and Benjamin J. Kaplan, eds (Aldershot: Ashgate Publishing, 2005).
Eire, Carlos M. N., *Reformations: The Early Modern World 1450–1650* (New Haven, CT: Yale University Press, 2016).
Eire, Carlos M. N., *War against the Idols: The Reformation of Worship from Erasmus to Calvin* (Cambridge: Cambridge University Press, 1986).
Eisenmann Robert, and Michael Wise, *The Dead Seas Scrolls Uncovered* (Rockford, MA: Element, 1992).
Elert, *The Structure of Lutheranism*, Vol. 1, Walter Hansen, trans. (Saint Louis, MO: Concordia Publishing, 1962).
Elliott, Dyan, 'Raptus/Rapture', in *The Cambridge Companion to Christian Mysticism*, Amy Hollywood and Patricia Beckman, eds (New York: Cambridge University Press, 2012).
Emmerson, Richard Kenneth, and Ronald B. Herzman, 'Antichrist, Simon Magus, and Dante's *Inferno XIX*'. Traditio, 29 July 2016.
Encyclopedia of the Enlightenment, Vol. 1, Michel Delon, ed. (Abingdon: Routledge, 2001).
Engammare, Max, 'John Calvin's Use of Erasmus', *Erasmus Studies*, vol. 37 (2017): 196.
Erasmus, Desiderius, *The Handbook of the Militant Christian* I.2, in John P. Dolan, ed. *The Essential Erasmus* (New York: Mentor-Omega Books, 1964).
Erikson, Erik H., *Young Man Luther: A Study in Psychoanalysis and History* (London: Faber and Faber, 1959).
Eschenmayer, C. A., 'Über Gassners Heilmethoden', in *Archiv für den thierischen Magnetismus*, Vol. 8, Brochure 1, 1820.
Estévez, Cardinal, 'Prefect of the Congregation for the Divine Cult and Discipline of the Sacraments', Press Conference, 26 January 1999.
Euchologion to Mega, Nicholas Papadopolous, ed. (Athens: Michael Salivou Press, 1927).
Evagrius Ponticus, *Praktike and Chapters on Prayer*, John Eudes Bamberger, trans. and introduction (Kalamazoo: Cistercian Publications, 1981).
Evans, G. R., 'Evil', in *Augustine through the Ages: An Encyclopedia*, Allan D. Fitzgerald O.S.A., ed. (Grand Rapids, MI: Eerdmans, 1999).
Faith and Order Paper No. 111 (Geneva: WCC Publications, 1982).
Faith and Order Paper No. 149 (Geneva: WCC Publications, 1990).
Farrer, Austin, *Love Almighty and Ills Unlimited* (London: Collins, 1962).
Faulkner O. F. M., Anselm, 'Father O'Finaghty's Miracles', in *The Irish Ecclesiastical Record*, Vol. 103 (Dublin: Browne and Nolan, 1965).
Fiddes, Paul S., 'Christianity, Atonement and Evil', in *The Cambridge Companion to the Problem of Evil*, Chad Meister and Paul K. Moser, eds (Cambridge: Cambridge University Press, 2017).
Fischer, Klaus P., *Nazi Germany: A New History* (London: Constable, 1995).
Flew, Anthony, 'Divine Omnipotence and Human Freedom', *Hibbert Journal*, vol. 53, no. 135 (1954): 135.
Flick, A. C., *The Decline of the Medieval Church*, Vol. I (London: Kegan Paul, 1930).

Ford, David, 'Barth, Karl', in *The Blackwell Encyclopedia of Modern Christian Thought*, Alister E. McGrath, ed. (Oxford: Blackwell Publishing, 1993).

Ford, J. Massynberde, *Revelation*. Introduction, translation and commentary (New York: Doubleday, 1975).

Forde, *On Being a Theologian of the Cross: Reflections on Luther's Heidelberg Disputation, 1518* (Grand Rapids, MI: William B. Eerdman, 1997).

Forest, Jim, *At Play in the Lions' Den: A Biography and Memoir of Dan Berrigan* (New York: Orbis Books, 2017).

Fox, Robin Lane, *Pagans and Christians* (London: Penguin Books, 1988).

Francis, Pope, *Laudato Si'* (Vatican State: Vatican Press, 2015).

Frankopan, Peter, *The Silk Roads: A New History of the World* (London: Bloomsbury, 2015).

Fussell, Paul, *The Great War and Modern Memory* (Oxford: Oxford University Press, 1975).

Gallagher, Richard, *Demonic Foes: My Twenty-five Years as a Psychiatrist Investigating Possessions, Diabolic Attacks and The Paranormal* (New York: HarperOne, 2020).

Ganss S.J., George E., ed., *Ignatius of Loyola: The Spiritual Exercises and Selected Works* (Mahwah NY: Paulist Press, 1991).

George, Timothy, *Theology of the Reformers* (Nashville: Broadman and Holman Publishers, 1988).

Gerson, Joannes, *De Theologia Mystica: Tractatus Secundus Practicus*, André Combes, ed. (Lugano: Thesaurus Mundi, 1958)

Gingerich, Owen, 'Did the Reformers reject Copernicus?', *Christianity Today*, no. 76 (2002): 20.

Glynn O.C.D., Joseph, *The Eternal Mystic: St Teresa of Avila, The First Woman Doctor of the Church* (New York: Vantage Press, 1987).

Gillespie, Raymond, *Devoted People: Belief and Religion in Early Modern Ireland* (Manchester: Manchester University Press, 1997).

Goddu, André, 'The Failure of Exorcisms in the Middle Ages', in *Witchcraft, Magic and Demonology: A Twelve Volume Anthology of Scholarly Articles*, Brian Levack, ed., Vol. 9, *Possession and Exorcism* (New York: Garland, 1992).

Goethe, *Faust: A Dramatic Poem*, A. Hayward, trans. (London: Edward Moxon, 1834).

Goetz, Hans-Werner, *Life in the Middle Ages: From the Seventh to the Thirteenth Century*, Albert Wimmer, trans. (Notre Dame: Notre Dame University Press, 1993).

Goldhagen, Daniel J., *Hitler's Willing Executioners: Ordinary Germans and the Holocaust* (London: Little, Brown, 1996).

The Gospel (Questions) of St Bartholomew in the Apocryphal New Testament (Oxford: Clarendon Press, 1924).

Gould, Graham, *The Desert Fathers on Monastic Community* (Oxford: Clarendon Press, 1993).

Graf, E. C., 'The Devil's Perspective in El Greco's "Alegoria de la Liga Santa", San Juan de la Cruz's "Cántico Espiritual" and Cervantes's "La Numancia"', *Romance Notes*, vol. 53, no. 1 (2013): 54.

Grant, Robert M., *Irenaeus of Lyons* (London: Routledge, 1997).

Hageman, 'Reformed Spirituality', in *Protestant Spiritual Traditions*, Frank. C. Senn, ed. (New York: Paulist Press, 1986).

Haight, Roger, 'Sin and Grace', in *Systematic Theology: Roman Catholic Perspectives*, Francis Schüssler Fiorenza and John P. Galvin, eds (Dublin: Gill and Macmillan, 1992).

Hampf, Marcel, *Exorcismus: Ein Vergleich der Praxis in der katholischen Kirche in Deutschland und Polen* (München: Grin Verlag, 2015).

Hargaden, Kevin, *Theological Ethics in a Neoliberal Age: Confronting the Christian Problem with Wealth* (Eugene, OR: Cascade Books, 2018).

Haritos-Fatouros, M., *The Psychological Origins of Institutionalized Torture* (London: Routledge, 2012).

Hari, Johann, *Why You Can't Pay Attention* (New York: Bloomsbury, 2022).

Harnack, Adolf von, *The Mission and Expansion of Christianity in the First Three Centuries* (London: Williams and Norgate, 1908).

Hasel, Frank M., 'Karl Barth's *Church Dogmatics* on the Atonement: Some Translational Problems', in *Andrews University Seminary Studies*, vol. 29, no. 3 (Autumn 1991): 208.

Hauw, Andreas, *The Function of Exorcism Stories in Mark's Gospel* (Eugene, OR: Wipf and Stock, 2019).

Hawthorne, Nathaniel, *The Scarlet Letter* (Ware: Wordsworth Editions, 1992).

Healy, Thomas, 'Marlowe's Biography', in *Marlowe's Biography in Context*, Emily Bartels and Emma Smith, eds (Cambridge: Cambridge University Press, 2013).

Hellwig, Martin, 'Capitalism: What Has Gone Wrong?': Who Went Wrong? Capitalism? The Market Economy? Governments? "Neoliberal" Economics?' in *Oxford Review of Economic Policy*, vol. 37, no. 4 (Winter 2021): 66.

Herring, George C., *From Colony to Superpower: U.S. Foreign Relations Since 1776* (Oxford: Oxford University Press, 2011).

Herzman, Ronald B., and Richard Kenneth Emmerson, 'Antichrist, Simon Magus, and Dante's *Inferno* XIX', *Traditio*, 29 July 2016.

Hibberd, Dominic, *Wilfred Owen: A New Biography* (Chicago: Ivan R. Dee, 2003).

Hick, John, *Evil and the God of Love* (Glasgow: Collins. Fontana Paperbacks, 1968).

Hick, John, 'Incarnation and Atonement. Evil and the Incarnation', in *Incarnation and Myth: The Debate Continued*, Michael Goulder, ed. (Grand Rapids, MI: Eerdmans, 1979).

Hick, John, 'Religious Statements as Factually Significant', in *The Existence of God: Readings Selected, Edited and Furnished with an Introductory Essay* (New York: Macmillan, 1964).

Hillerbrand, Hans J., *The Division of Christendom* (Louisville: Westminster John Knox Press, 2007).

Hills, Julian, 'Who Saw Satan Fall? Luke 10:18', in *The Journal for the Study of the New Testament* vol. 14, issue 46 (Sage Publications, 1992): 20.

Himma, Kenneth, 'I Can't Help What I Believe: The Moral Case Against Religious Exclusivist Doctrines', *Think: Philosophy for Everyone*, vol. 17, no. 48 (Spring 2018), 65.

Himma, Kenneth, 'Plantinga's Version of the Free-Will Argument: The Good and Evil That Free Beings Do', *Religious Studies*, vol. 46, no. 1 (March 2010), 21.

Hitlin, S., *Moral Selves, Evil Selves: The Social Psychology of Conscience* (London: Palgrave Macmillan/ Springer, 2008), 167.

Holder, Rodney, *The Heavens Declare: Natural Theology and the Legacy of Karl Barth* (West Conshohocken, PA: Templeton Press, 2011).

Howard, Virgil, and David B. Peabody, 'Mark' in *The International Bible Commentary*, W. Farmer, ed. (Collegeville: Liturgical Press, 1998).

Howard-Snyder, Daniel, and Paul K. Moser, eds, *Divine Hiddennness: New Essays* (Cambridge: Cambridge University Press, 2001), 17.

Hsia, R. Po-Chia, *Social Discipline in the Reformation: Central Europe 1550–1750* (London: Routledge, 1989).

Hume, David, *Dialogues Concerning Natural Religion* (Buffalo, NY: Prometheus Books, 1989).
Huxley, Aldous, *The Devils of Loudun: A Study in the Psychology of Power Politics and Mystical Religion in the France of Cardinal Richelieu* (New York: Harper Torchbooks, 1952).
Idel, Moshe, *Kabbalah: New Perspectives* (New Haven, CT: Yale University Press, 1988).
International Association of Exorcists, *Linee guida per il ministero dell'esorcismo* (Padova: Edizioni Messagero, 2020).
Irenaeus, *Five Books of S. Irenaeus, Bishop of Lyons, Against Heresies*, John Keble M. A., trans. (Oxford: James Parker, 1872).
Isaacson, Walter, *Einstein: His Life and Universe* (London: Simon and Schuster, 2007).
Jackson, Robert Louis, 'Criticism', in *One Day in the Life of Ivan Denisovich: A Critical Companion*, Alexis Klimoff, ed. (Evanston: Northwestern University Press, 1997).
Jackson, W. T. H., *The Literature of the Middle Ages* (New York: Columbia University Press, 1960).
James, William, *The Varieties of Religious Experience* (Harmondsworth: Penguin Books, 1982).
Jedin, Hubert, 'Catholic Reformation or Counter-Reformation', in *The Counter-Reformation*, David M. Luebke, ed. (Oxford: Blackwell Publishers, 1999), 14.
Jeremias, *New Testament Theology*, Vol. 1. *The Proclamation of Jesus*, John Bowden, trans. (London: SCM Press, 1971), 93.
John Paul II, Pope, 'Apostolic Exhortation', *Reconciliatio et paenitentia*, Acta Apostolicae Sedis 77 (1985): 14–22.
Johnson, Samuel, *Lives of the English Poets* (Oxford: Oxford University Press, 1961).
Johnson, Samuel, *Life of Milton* (London: George Bell, 1894).
Johnstone, Nathan, *The Devil and Demonism in Early Modern England* (Cambridge: Cambridge University Press, 2009).
Johnstone, Nathan, 'The Protestant Devil: The Experience of Temptation in Early Modern England', *Journal of British Studies*, vol. 43, no. 2 (April 2004): 174.
Jones, Dan, *Crusaders: An Epic History of the Wars for the Holy Land* (London: Head of Zeus, 2019).
Josephson-Storm, Jason Ā., *The Myth of Magic, Modernity, and the Birth of the Human Sciences* (Chicago: University of Chicago, 2017).
Jung, C. G., *Aion Disenchantment: Researches into the Phenomenon of the Self*, R. F. C. Hall, trans. (Princeton, NJ: Princeton University Press, 1959^2).
Jung, C. G., *The Collected Works of C. G. Jung*, Vol. 6, Psychological Types, Bollingen Series XX, Herbert Read et al., eds (Princeton NJ: Princeton University Press, 1971).
Justin Martyr, *The Works of S. Justin the Martyr, Dialogue with Trypho*, LXXVI (Oxford: J. H. and J. S. Parker, 1861).
Kane, G. Stanley, 'The Failure of Soul-Making Theodicy', *International Journal for Philosophy of Religion*, vol. 6 (1975): 1–22.
Karefa–Smart, John, 'Doctors, Development and Demons in Africa', in *Disguises of the Demonic: Contemporary Perspectives on the Power of Evil*, Alan M. Olson, ed. (New York: Association Press, 1975).
Kasper, Walter, and Karl Lehman, Hg, *Teufel, Dämonen, Bessenenheit* (Mainz: Matthias Grünewald Verlag, 1978).
Keegan, John, *The First World War* (London: Pimlico, 1999).
Kelly, Henry Ansgar, *Satan: A Biography* (Cambridge: Cambridge University Press, 2006).

Kelly, Henry Ansgar, *Satan in the Bible: God's Minister of Justice* (Eugene, OR: Cascade, 2017).
Kelly, Henry Ansgar, *Towards the Death of Satan: The Growth and Decline of Christian Demonology* (London: Geoffrey Chapman, 1968).
Kelly, J. N. D., *Early Christian Doctrines* (London: A. & C. Black, 1977⁵).
Kelly, J. N. D., *Jerome: His Life, Writings and Controversies* (London: Duckworth, 1975).
Kertelge, Karl, 'Teufel, Dämonen, Exorzismen in biblischer Sicht', in *Teufel, Dämonen, Bessenheit*, Walter Kasper and Karl Lehman, Hg (Mainz: Matthias Grünewald Verlag, 1978).
Kidd, H. J., *Documents of the Continental Reformation* (Oxford: Oxford University Press, 1911).
King, Peter, *Western Monasticism: A History of the Monastic Movement in the Latin Church* (Kalamazoo: Cistercian Publications, 1999).
King, Martin Luther, *Strength to Love* (New York: Harper & Row, 1963).
King, Martin Luther, *Stride Toward Freedom* (Eastford, CT: Martino Fine Books, 2015).
King, Martin Luther, *The Papers of Martin Luther King, Jr*, Vol. 1, *Called to Serve*, Clayborne Carson et al., eds (Berkeley: University of California Press, 1991).
Kirkegaard, Søren, *The Sickness unto Death* (Princeton, NJ: Princeton University Press, 1941).
Kline Coen, Samuel, *Hate and Compassion: From the Plague of Athens to Aids* (Oxford: Oxford University Press, 2018).
Knasas, John F. X., *Aquinas and the Cry of Rachel: Thomistic Reflections on the Problem of Evil* (Washington, DC: Catholic University Press, 2013).
Kocher, Paul H., 'Viewpoints', in *Twentieth Century Interpretations of Doctor Faustus*, William Farnham, ed. (Englewood Cliffs, NJ: Prentice Hall, 1969).
Kolb, Robert, and Carl R. Trueman, *Between Wittenberg and Geneva: Lutheran and Reformed Theology in Conversation* (Grand Rapids, MI: Baker Academic, 2017).
Kontos, Pavlos, 'Radical Evil in Aristotle's Ethics and Politics', in *Evil in Aristotle*, P. Kontos, ed. (Cambridge: Cambridge University Press, 2018).
Kroeker, Greta G., 'Calvin, Erasmus, and Humanist Theology', in *Calvin and the Early Reformation*, Brian C. Brewer and David M. Whitford, eds (Leiden: Brill, 2019).
Krötke, Wolf, *Sin and Nothingness in the Theology of Karl Barth*, Philip G. Ziegler and Christina-Maria Bammel, ed. and trans. (Princeton, NJ: Princeton Theological Seminary, 2005).
Kulik, Alexander, 'How the Devil Got His Hooves and Horns: The Origin of the Motif and the Implied Demonology of 3 Baruch', *Numen,* vol. 60, no. 2/3 (2013).
Kyper, Albert, *Institutiones physicae* (Lugduni Batavorum: apud Adrianum Wyngaerden et Franciscum Moiardum, 1745).
Lactantius, *On the Anger of God*, Ante Nicene Fathers, Vol. 22 (Edinburgh: T&T Clark: 1871).
Lampert, Vincent, *Exorcism: The Battle Against Satan and His Demons* (Steubenville: Emmaus Road Publishing, 2020).
Lane, Dermot, 'Fifty Years of Theology' in *The Furrow*, vol. 60, no. 7/8 (2009): 399.
Langland, William, *The Vision of Piers Plowman*, translation into Modern English Verse with introduction by Terence Tiller (London: British Broadcasting Corporation, 1981).
Latimer, Hugh, *Sermons by Hugh Latimer, Martyr 1555*. Parker Society, G. Corrie, ed. (Cambridge: Cambridge University Press, 1844).
Le Gal, Frédéric, 'L'Exorcisme. La Dépossession du Corps Surmontée', *Stress et Trauma*, vol. 8, no. 2 (2008): 108.

Le Goff, Jacques, *Medieval Civilization: 400–1500*, Julia Barrow, trans. (Oxford: Basil Blackwell, 1988), 108.
Le Goff, Jacques, *San Francesco d'Assisi* (Roma-Bari: Editori Laterza, 2000).
Levi, Primo, *If This Is a Man: The Truce* (London: Abacus, 1987).
Levi, Primo, *Moments of Reprieve* (London: Abacus, 1987).
Lewis, C. S., *A Preface to Paradise Lost* (London: Oxford Paperbacks, 1960).
Lewis, C. S., *Essay Collection and Other Short Pieces* (London: HarperCollins, 2010).
Lewis, C. S., *The Screwtape Letters* (New York: Macmillan, 1948).
Lofstedt, Torsten, 'Paul, Sin and Satan: The Root of Evil according to Romans', *Svensk Exegetisk Årsbok*, vol. 75 (2010): 109.
Lossky, Vladimir, *Orthodox Theology: An Introduction*, Ian and Ihita Kesarcodi-Watson, trans. (Crestwood, NY: St Vladimir's Seminary, 1978).
Louth, *The Origins of the Christian Mystical Tradition: From Plato to Denys* (Oxford: Clarendon Press, 1981).
Luther, Martin, *Commentary on Genesis*, Vol. 1, John L. Lenker, trans. (Project Gutenberg: E Book #$8193, 2015).
Luther, Martin, *D. Martin Luthers Werke, Briefwechsel* I, 391 (Weimar, 1930).
Luther, Martin, *D. Martin Luthers Werke Tischreden* II n. 1557 (Weimar, 1930).
Luther, Martin, *Luther's Works, Vol. 40; Vol. 53*: Church and Ministry II, Jaroslav Pelikan et al., eds (Philadelphia, PA: Fortress Press, 1999).
Luther, Martin, *Table Talk*, William Hazlett, trans. (London: Fount Paperbacks, 1995).
Luther, Martin, *The Theologia Germanica of Martin Luther*, translation and introduction by Bengt Hoffman (New York: Paulist Press, 1980)
Lynch, Joseph H., *The Medieval Church: A Brief History* (London: Longman 1992).
Lyons O. S. B., Fintan, 'Luther's Last Sermon. In Commemoration of the 450th Anniversary of Martin Luther's Death', *Pro Ecclesia*, vol. 5, no. 3 (1996).
Lyons O. S. B., Fintan, *Martin Luther: His Challenge Then and Now* (Dublin: Columba Press, 2017).
MacCulloch, Diarmaid, *A History of Christianity: The First Three Thousand Years* (London: Allen Lane, 2009).
Macnab, David, 'Augustine's Trope of the Crucifixion as a Trap for the Devil and Its Survival in English Middle Ages', https://core.ac.uk/download/pdf/54198127.pdf.
Macdonald, 'Calvinist Theology and "Country Divinity" in Marlowe's "Doctor Faustus"', *Studies in Philology*, vol. 111, no. 4 (Fall 2014): 824.
Mackie, J. L., 'Evil and Omnipotence', *Mind*, vol. 64 (1955): 200–12.
Mackie, J. L., *The Miracle of Theism: Arguments for and against the Existence of God* (Oxford: Oxford University Press, 1982).
Mahoney, Daniel J., *The Other Solzhenitsyn* (South Bend: St Augustine's Press, 2014).
Mahoney, Jack, *Christianity in Evolution: An Exploration* (Washington, DC: Georgetown University Press, 2011).
Malone, Edward E., *The Monk and the Martyr: The Monk as the Successor of the Martyr*, Johannes Quasten, ed. (Washington, DC: Catholic University of America, 2011).
Markides, Kyriakos S., *The Mountain of Silence: A Search for Orthodox Spirituality* (New York: Doubleday, 2001).
Marlowe, Christopher, *Dr Faustus* (The A Text), David Ormerod and Christopher Wortham, eds (Nedlands: University of Western Australia Press, 1985).
Matheson, Peter, *The Rhetoric of the Reformation* (Edinburgh: T&T Clark, 1998).
Maxwell Stuart, P. G., *Satan: A Biography* (Stroud: Amberly Publishing, 2011).

May, John R., 'American Literary Variations on the Demonic', in *Disguises of the Demonic: Contemporary Perspectives on the Power of Evil*, Alan M. Olson, ed. (New York: Association Press, 1975).
Mazzotta, Giuseppe, *Dante, the Poet of the Desert: History and Allegory in the Divine Comedy* (Princeton, NJ: Princeton University Press, 1979).
McCabe O. P., Herbert, *God and Evil in the Theology of St Thomas Aquinas* (London: Continuum, 2010).
McCann, Hugh J., 'Getting Scientific about Religion', in *The Future of Atheism: Alister McGrath and Daniel Dennett in Dialogue*, Robert B. Stewart, ed. (London: S.P.C.K., 2008).
McColley, Grant, 'The Book of Enoch and Paradise Lost', *The Harvard Theological Review*, vol. 31, no. 1 (January 1938).
McGinn, Bernard, *Antichrist: Two Thousand Years of Human Fascination with Evil* (New York: Columbia University Press, 2000).
McGovern, J. B., 'The Popes of Dante's *Divina Commedia*', *The Antiquary*, vol. 9 (December 1913).
McGrath, Alister E., *Reformation Thought: An Introduction* (Oxford: Blackwell, 1993²).
McKim, Donald K., ed., *The Westminster Handbook to Reformed Theology* (Louisville: Westminster John Knox Press, 2001).
Meigs, Samantha A., *The Reformation in Ireland: Tradition and Confessionalism, 1400–1600* (Dublin: Gill and Macmillan, 1997).
Meir, John P., *A Marginal Jew: Rethinking the Historical Jesus*, Vol 2: Mentor, Message and Miracles (New York: Doubleday, 1994).
Meier, Samuel A., 'Evil', in *The Oxford Companion to the Bible*, Bruce M. Metzger and Michael D. Coogan, eds (Oxford: Oxford University Press, 1993).
Meissner S. J., M. D., *Ignatius of Loyola: The Psychology of a Saint* (New Haven, CT: Yale University Press, 1992).
Meister, Chad V., *Evil: A Guide for the Perplexed* (New York: Bloomsbury Academic, 2018²).
Merrill, Jessica E., 'The Stalinist Subject and Mikhail Bulgakov's "The Master and Margarita"', *Russian Review*, vol. 74, no. 2 (April 2015): 293.
Midelfort, H. C. Erik, *Exorcism and Enlightenment: Johann Joseph Gassner and the Demons of Eighteenth-Century Germany* (New Haven, CT: Yale University Press, 2005).
Mill, John Stuart, *Nature and Utility of Religion and Theism* (London: Longmans, Green, Reader and Dyer, 1874).
Milton, John, *Poetical Works*, Douglas Bush, ed. (London: Oxford University Press, 1966).
Minnis, A. J., and A. B. Scott, *Medieval Literary Theory and Criticism, c. 1100– c. 1375: The Commentary Tradition* (Oxford: Clarendon Press, 1988).
Mischo, Johannes, 'Dämonische Besessenheit', in *Teufel, Dämonen, Bessessenheit*, Walter Kasper und Karl Lehman, Hg (Mainz: Matthias Grünewald Verlag, 1978).
Moehn, Wilffred H. Th., *The Relation between God and his Audience in Calvin's Sermons on Acts*, Lydia Verburg, trans. (Genève: Librairie Droz, 2001).
Moltmann, Jürgen, *The Crucified Christ: The Cross of Christ as the Foundation and Criticism of Christian Theology* (London: S.C.M. Press, 1973²).
Moltmann, Jürgen, *Theology of Hope* (London: S.C.M. Press, 1967).
Muchembled, Robert, *A History of the Devil: From the Middle Ages to the Present*, Jean Birrell, trans. (Cambridge: Polity Press, 2003).
Müller, J. T., *Die symbolischen Bücher der evangelisch-lutherischen Kirche* (Stuttgart: Verlag von Samuel Gottlieb Liesching, 1860).

Mullett, Michael, *The Counter-Reformation and the Catholic Reformation in Early Modern Europe* (London: Methuen, 1984).

Murphy, Nancey, 'Natural Science', in *The Oxford Handbook of Systematic Theology*, John Webster et al., eds (Oxford: Oxford University Press, 2007).

Murphy, Roland and O. Carm., 'Psalms', in *The Jerome Biblical Commentary*, Raymond Brown, S. S. et al., eds (London: Geoffrey Chapman, 1969).

Necker, Gerold, 'Circle, Point and Line', in *Creation and Recreation in Jewish Thought: Festschrift in Honor of Joseph Dan*, Rachel Elior and Peter Schäfer, eds (Tübingen: Mohr and Siebeck, 2005).

Nicholl, Charles, '"Faithful Dealing": Marlowe and the Elizabethan Intelligence Service', in *Marlowe, History, and Sexuality: New Essays on the Life and Writings of Christopher Marlowe*, Paul Whitfield White, ed., Studies in the Renaissance, Vol. 35 (New York: AMS Press, 1998).

Nichols O. P., Aidan, *The Shape of Catholic Theology* (Edinburgh: T&T Clark, 1991).

Nicola, John, *Diabolical Possession and Exorcism* (Rockford, IL: Tan Books, 1974).

Niebuhr, H. Richard, *The Kingdom of God in America* (Nottingham: Shoe String Press, 1956).

Niesel, Wilhelm, *Reformed Symbolics: A Comparison of Catholicism, Orthodoxy, and Protestantism* (Edinburgh: Oliver and Boyd, 1962).

Nietzsche, Friedrich, *Beyond Good and Evil*, Helen Zimmern, trans. (New York: Modern Library, 1917).

Nischan, Bodo, 'The Exorcist Controversy and Baptism in the Later Reformation', *Sixteenth-Century Journal*, vol. 18, no. 1 (Spring 1987): 33.

Noakes, K. W., 'From New Testament Times until St Cyprian', in *The Study of the Liturgy*, Cheslyn Jones et al., eds (London: S.P.C.K., 1992).

Novak, Jr., Frank G., 'The Satanic Personality in Updike's *Roger's Version*', *Christianity and Literature*, vol. 55, no. 1 (Autumn 2005): 4.

Oberman, Heiko A., *Luther: Man between God and the Devil* (New Haven, CT: Yale University Press, 1989).

Oberman, Heiko A., *The Dawn of the Reformation: Essays in Late Medieval and Early Reformation Thought* (Edinburgh: T&T Clark, 1986).

O'Brien, Kate, *Teresa of Avila* (Cork: Mercier Press, 1951).

O'Connell S. J., Gerald, *Retrieving Fundamental Theology: The Three Styles of Contemporary Theology* (London: Geoffrey Chapman, 1993).

Oengus the Culdee, *Félire Oengusso Céili Dé*, Whitley Stokes, ed. (London: Henry Bradshaw Society, 1905).

Oesterreich, T. K., *Possession Demoniacal and Other: Among Primitive Races, in Antiquity, the Middle Ages and Modern* (Abingdon: Routledge, 1930).

Olin, John C., *Catholic Reform: From Cardinal Ximénes to the Council of Trent 1495–1563* (New York: Fordham University Press, 1990).

O'Meara, O. P., Thomas F., *Thomas Aquinas Theologian* (Notre Dame: Notre Dame Press, 1997).

O'Neill, John, 'Intrinsic Evil, Truth and Authority', *Religious Studies*, vol. 31, no. 2 (June 1995): 209.

Oppy, 'Logical Arguments from Evil and Free-Will Defences', in *The Cambridge Companion to the Problem of Evil*, Chad Meister and Paul K. Moser, eds (New York: Cambridge University Press, 2017).

O'Reilly, Terence, *Humanism and Religion in Early Modern Spain: John of the Cross, Francisco de Aldana, Luis de Leon* (London: Routledge, 2022).

Origen, *De Principiis*, The Ante-Nicene Fathers Vol. 4, Alexander Roberts, James Donaldson, eds (Buffalo, NY: Christian Literature Publishing, 1885).
Otto, Rudolf, *The Idea of the Holy: An Inquiry into the Non-rational Factor in the Idea of the Divine and Its Relation to the Rational,* John W. Harvey, trans. (Oxford: Oxford University Press, 1958).
Pagels, Elaine, 'The Social History of Satan, Part II: Satan in the New Testament Gospels', *Journal of the American Academy of Religion*, vol. 62, no. 1 (Spring, 1994): 17.
Papademetriou, George C., 'Exorcism and the Greek Orthodox Church', in *Exorcism Through the Ages* (New York: Philosophical Library, 1974).
Patella, Michael, *Angels and Demons: A Christian Primer of the Spiritual World* (Collegeville, Liturgical Press, 2012).
Peter, Burkhard, 'Gassner's Exorcism – not Mesmer's Magnetism – Is the Real Predecessor of Modern Hypnosis', *International Journal of Clinical and Experimental Hypnosis*, vol. 53, no. 1 (February 2005).
Peters, Greg, *The Monkhood of All Believers: The Monastic Foundation of Christian Spirituality* (Grand Rapids, MI: Baker Academic, 2018).
Peterson, Michael L., 'Recent Work on the Problem of Evil', *American Philosophical Quarterly*, vol. 20, no. 4 (1983): 22.
Peterson, Michael L., ed., *The Problem of Evil: Selected Readings: Second Edition* (Notre Dame: Notre Dame Press, 2017²).
Pettazoni, Raffaele, 'The Supreme Being: Phenomenological Structure and Historical Development', in *The History of Religions: Essays in Methodology,* Mircea Eliade et al., eds (Chicago: University of Chicago Press, 1959).
Pickthall, Muhammad M., *The Meaning of the Glorious Qur'an: An Explanatory Translation* (Birmingham: Islamic Dawah Centre International, 2000).
Plantinga, Alvin, *God, Freedom and Evil* (Grand Rapids, MI: Eerdmans, 1977).
Plantinga, Alvin, 'The Probabilistic Argument from Evil', *Philosophical Studies: An International Journal for Philosophy in the Analytic Tradition*, vol. 35, no. 1 (January 1979): 6.
Plato, *The Cratylus, Phaedo, Parmenides, and Timaeus* (London: J. & W. White, 1793).
Polkinghorne, John, *Belief in God in an Age of Science* (New Haven, CT: Yale University Press, 1998).
Polkinghorne, John, *Science and Christian Belief: Theological Reflections of a Bottom-Up Thinker* (London: S.P.C.K., 1994).
Polkinghorne, John, *The Polkinghorne Reader: Science, Faith and the Search for Meaning,* Thomas J. Oord, ed. (West Conshohocken, PA: Templeton Press, 2010).
Pollok, Jan, 'The Present State of Studies on the *Apophthegmata Patrum*: An Outline of Samuel Rubenson's and Graham Gould's Perspectives', in *The Spirituality of Ancient Monasticism*. Acts of the International Colloquium, Cracow-Tyniec 1994, Marek Staroewieyski, ed. (Cracow: Wydawnictwo Benedyktnów, 1995).
Polo, Alex, 'The Realm of the between in Martin Buber's Writings and Its Implications for the History of Religions'. ETD Collection for Fordham University, 1986.
Polgar, Nenad, and Joseph A. Selling, *The Concept of Intrinsic Evil and Catholic Theological Ethics* (Lanham, MD: Fortress Academic, 2019).
Poole, W. Scott, *Satan in America: The Devil We Know* (New York: Rowman and Littlefield, 2009).
Rahner S. J., Karl, 'Demonology', in *Encyclopedia of Theology*, Karl Rahner, ed. (London: Burns & Oates, 1975), 334.

Rahner S. J., Karl, *Theological Investigations*, Vol. 4 (Baltimore, MD: Helicon Press, 1966).
Rahner S. J., Karl, *Theological Investigations*, Vol. 6 (Baltimore, MD: Helicon Press, 1966).
Rahner S. J., Karl, *Theological Investigations*, Vol. 19 (London: Darton, Longman and Todd, 1984).
Ratzinger, Joseph, *Commentary on the Documents of Vatican II*, Vol. 5 (London: Burns & Oates, 1969).
Ratzinger, Joseph, 'Descent into Hell – Ascension – Resurrection', in *Credo for Today: What Christians Believe* (San Francisco, CA: Ignatius Press, 2009).
Ratzinger, Joseph, *Echatology: Death and Eternal Life*, Michael Waldstein, trans. (Washington, DC: Catholic University of America Press, 1988).
Ratzinger, Joseph, 'Farewell to the Devil?', in Pope Benedict XVI, *Dogma and Preaching: Applying Christian Doctrine to Daily Life* (San Francisco, CA: Ignatius Press, 2011).
Ratzinger, Joseph, *Introduction to Christianity* (San Francisco, CA: Ignatius Press, 2004²).
Ratzinger, Joseph, *Milestones: 1927–1977* (San Francisco, CA: Ignatius Press, 1997).
Read, Mike, *Forever England: The Life of Rupert Brooke* (Edinburgh: Mainstream Publishing, 1997).
Reber, A. S., and E. Reber, *The Penguin Dictionary of Psychology* (2001³).
The Reformation in Medieval Perspective, introduction and edited by Steven T. Ozment (New York: Quadrangle Press, 1971).
Reff, Daniel T., *Plagues, Priests, Demons: Sacred Narratives and the Rise of Christianity in the Old World and the New* (Cambridge: Cambridge University Press, 2005).
Renna, Thomas, 'Avignon vs. Rome: Dante, Petrarch, Catherine of Siena', *Expositions*, vol. 4, nos. 1&2 (2010): 49.
Ribera, Francisco de, *La Vida de la Madre Teresa de Jesús, fundadora de las Descalças y Descalços*, Jaime Pons, ed. and introduction (Barcelona: Gustavo Gili, 1908).
Ricoeur, Paul, 'Evil, a Challenge to Philosophy and Theology', in *Figuring the Sacred: Religion, Narrative and Imagination*, David Pellauer, trans. (Minneapolis, MN: Fortress Press, 1995).
Ricoeur, Paul, *The Symbolism of Evil* (New York: Harper & Row, 1967).
Rifkin, Jeremy, with Ted Howard, *Entropy: A New World View* (Toronto: Bantam Books, 1981).
Riggs, David, 'Marlowe's Quarrel with God', in *Marlowe, History, and Sexuality: New Essays on the Life and Writings of Christopher Marlowe*, Paul Whitfield White, ed. (New York: AMS Press, 1998).
Robert, Colb, and Robert R. Trueman, *Between Wittenberg and Geneva: Lutheran and Reformed Theology in Conversation* (Grand Rapids, MI: Baker Academic, 2017).
Roberts, John Stuart, *Siegfried Sassoon* (London: Richard Cohen, 1999).
Roest, Bert, 'Demonic Possession and the Practice of Exorcism: An Explanation of the Franciscan Heritage', *Franciscan Studies*, vol. 76 (2018): 301.
Roper, Lyndal, *Martin Luther: Renegade and Prophet* (London: Bodley Head, 2016).
Roper, Lyndal, *Oedipus and the Devil: Witchcraft, Sexuality and Religion in Early Modern Europe* (London: Routledge, 1994).
Rossetti, Stephen, *Diary of an American Exorcist: Demons, Possession, and the Modern-Day Battle Against Ancient Evil* (Manchester, NH: Sophia Institute Press, 2021).
Rudwin, Maximilian, *The Devil in Legend and Literature* (Chicago: Open Court Publishing, 1931).
Rubenson, Samuel, *The Letters of St. Antony: Monasticism and the Making of a Saint* (Lund: Lund University Press, 1990).

Runciman, Steven, *The Medieval Manichee: A Study of the Christian Dualist Heresy* (Cambridge: Cambridge University Press, 1988).
Rupp, Gordon, *The Righteousness of God* (London: Hodder and Stoughton, 1953).
Ruse, Michael and Edward O. Wilson, 'The Evolution of Ethics', in *Philosophy of Biology*, Michael Ruse, ed. (New York: Macmillan, 1986).
Russell, Jeffrey Burton, *Lucifer: The Devil in the Middle Ages* (Ithaca, NY: Cornell University Press, 1984).
Russell, Jeffrey Burton, *Mephistopheles: The Devil in the Modern World* (Ithaca, NY: Cornell University Press, 1986).
Russell, Robert John, *Cosmology from Alpha to Omega* (Minneapolis, MN: Fortress Press, 2008).
Russell, Robert John, 'Entropy and Evil', *Zygon*, vol. 19, no. 4 (December 1984): 449.
Ryan, Ben, 'Christianity and Mental Health: Theology, Activities, Potential', *Theos*, July 2017.
Sachs, S.J., John R., 'Current Eschatology: Universal Salvation and the Problem of Evil', *Theological Studies*, vol. 52 (1991): 251.
Sacks, Jonathan, *To Heal a Fractured World: The Ethics of Responsibility* (London: Continuum, 2005).
Saperstein, Marc and Joshua Trachtenberg, *The Devil and the Jews: The Medieval Conception of the Jew and Its Relation to Modern Anti-Semitism* (New Haven, CT: Yale University Press, 1943).
Searle, G. W., *The Counter Reformation* (London: University of London Press, 1974).
Sassoon, Siegfried, *Collected Poems* (London: Faber and Faber, 1949).
Sassoon, Siegfried, *Memories of a Fox-Hunting Man* (London: Faber and Faber, 1967).
Sassoon, Siegfried, *Siegfried's Journey (1916–1920)* (London: Faber and Faber, 1946).
Schaeffer, Claude F., *Ugaritica II: Nouvelles Études Relatives aux Découvertes de Ras Shamra* (Paris: Librairie Orientaliste Paul Geuthier, 1949).
Schlier, Heinrich, *Principalities and Powers in the New Testament* (New York: Herder and Herder, 1961).
Schonbörn, Christoph, *Living the Catechism of the Catholic Church*, Vol. 1, The Creed (San Francisco, CA: Ignatius Press, 1995).
Schulweis, Harold M., 'Karl Barth's Job', *The Jewish Quarterly Review*, New Series, Vol. 65, No. 3 (January 1975): 156.
Scott, A. B. and A. J. Minnis, *Medieval Literary Theory and Criticism, c. 1100 – c. 1375: The Commentary Tradition* (Oxford: Clarendon Press, 1988).
Searle, G. W., *The Counter Reformation* (London: London University Press, 1974).
Seligman, M. F., 'Learned Helplessness', *Annual Review of Medicine*, vol. 23, no. 1 (1972): 407.
Shaw, G. B., 'Why for Puritans?', in *Three Plays for Puritans* (Harmondsworth: Penguin Books, 1946).
Shawcross, John T., 'An Early View of Satan as Hero of Paradise Lost', *Milton Quarterly*, vol. 32, no. 3 (Baltimore, MD: Johns Hopkins University Press, 1998), 104.
Shelley, Percy Bysshe, *A Defence of Poetry* (Indianapolis, IN: Bobbs Merrill, 1904).
Smith, John E., 'The Impact of Tillich's Interpretation', in *The Thought of Paul Tillich*, James Luther Adams, Wilhelm Pauck, Roger Lincoln Shinn, eds (San Francisco, CA: Harper & Row, 1985).
Solzhenitsyn, Aleksandr, *A Day in the Life of Ivan Denisovich* (London: Victor Gollancz, 1970).

Solzhenitsyn, Aleksandr, *The Gulag Archipelago*, Vol. 2, Part IV, 'The Soul and the Barbed Wire' (London: Collins/Fontana, 1976).
Spitz, Marc, *Jagger: Rebel, Rock Star, Rambler, Rogue* (New York: Gotham Books, 2012).
Stallworthy, Jon, *Wilfred Owen: A Biography* (London: Chatto and Windus, 1974).
Starr, Mirabai, *Teresa of Avila: The Book of My Life* (Boston, MA: New Seeds, 2008).
Stendhal, Krister, ed., *The Scrolls and the New Testament* (New York: Crossroad, 1992).
Sterzinger, Ferdinand, *Die aufgedeckten Gassnerschen Wunderkuren: Aus authentischen Urkunden beleuchtet, und durch Augenzeuen bewiesen* (Augsburg: C. H. Stage, 1775).
Stevenson, David, *The History of the First World War: 1914–1918* (London: Penguin Books, 2004).
Stewart, Charles, *Demons and the Devil: Moral Imagination in Modern Greek Culture* (Princeton, NJ: Princeton University Press, 2016).
Stewart, Columba O.S.B., *The World of the Desert Fathers* (Oxford: SLG Press, 1986).
Stuart, P. G. Maxwell, *Satan: A Biography* (Stroud: Amberly Publishing, 2011).
Suenens, Cardinal L.-J., *Renewal and the Power of Darkness* (London: Darton, Longman and Todd, 1983).
Sundberg, Walter, 'A Primer on the Devil', *First Things*, January 1993.
Surin, Kenneth, 'Evil, Problem of', in *The Blackwell Encyclopedia of Modern Christian Thought*, Alister E. McGrath, ed. (Oxford: Blackwell Publishing, 1993).
Surin, Kenneth, 'Theodicy?', *The Harvard Theological Review*, vol. 76, no. 2 (April, 1983).
Tavard, George, *Paul Tillich and the Christian Message* (London: Burns & Oates, 1962).
Taylor, Charles, *A Secular Age* (Cambridge MA: Harvard University Press, 2007).
Teresa of Ávila, *The Book of my Life*, Mirabai Starr, trans. (Boston, MA: New Seeds, 2008).
Tertullian, Quintus Septimius, *Apologetic and Practical Rreatises*, C. Dodgson M.A., trans. (Oxford: John Henry Parker, 1842).
Thomas, *Religion and the Decline of Magic* (New York: Scribner, 1971).
Thompson, Colin, *St John of the Cross: Songs in the Night* (London: S.P.C.K., 2002).
Thomson, Ian, 'Dante's Debt to Islam', *The Tablet*, 24 July 2021.
Thorpe, Michael, *Siegfried Sassoon: A Critical Study* (London: Oxford University Press, 1966).
Tipler, Frank, *The Physics of Immortality: Modern Cosmology, God and the Resurrection of the Dead* (London: Pan Books, 1994).
Todd, John M., *Martin Luther: A Biographical Study* (London: Burns & Oates, 1964).
Trakakis, N. N., 'Anti-Theodicy', in *The Cambridge Companion to the Problem of Evil*, Chad Meister and Paul K. Moser, eds (Cambridge: Cambridge University Press, 2017).
Trethowan, Illytd, 'Dr Hick and the Problem of Evil', *Journal of Theological Studies*, vol. 18, 1967: 407.
Trigg, Joseph, *Origen* (London: Routledge, 1998).
Trublar, Karl F., 'Possession, Diabolical', in *Sacramentum Mundi*, Vol. 5 (London: Burns & Oates, 1970).
Twain, Mark, *The Mysterious Stranger Manuscripts*, Vol. 7, edited with introduction by William Gibson (Berkeley: University of California Press, 1969).
Underhill, Evelyn, *Mysticism: The Development of Humankind's Spiritual Consciousness* (London: Bracken Books, 1995[14]).
Urban, David V., 'C. S. Lewis and Satan: *A Preface to Paradise Lost* and Its Respondents, 1942–1952', *Connotations*, vol. 28 (2019): 95.
Valensin S. J., Auguste, 'The Devil in the Divine Comedy', in Anon., *Satan* (London: Sheed and Ward, 1951).

van Dam, Willem C., *Satan Existiert: Erfahrungen eines Exorzisten* (Augsburg: Pattloch, 1994).
Van Fleteren, Frederick, 'Demons', in *Augustine through the Ages: An Encyclopedia,* Alan D. Fitzpatrick O.S.A., ed. (Grand Rapids, MI: William D. Eerdmans, 1991).
Van Fleteren, Frederick, 'Devil', in *Augustine through the Ages: An Encyclopedia*, Alan D. Fitzpatrick O.S.A., ed. (Grand Rapids, MI: William D. Eerdmans, 1991).
Vanhoozer, Kevin J., *Remythologizing Theology: Divine Action, Passion and Authorship* (Cambridge: Cambridge University Press, 2010).
Varazze, Jacopo da, *Legenda Aurea* (Tavarnazze Firenze: SISMEL Edizioni del Galluzzo, 1998).
Vatican Council II, 'Christian Faith and Demonology', in *Vatican Council II*, Austin Flannery, ed. (Dublin, Dominican Publications, 1982).
Vatican Council II, *Gaudium et Spes*, in *Vatican Council II: The Conciliar and Post Conciliar Documents,* Austin Flannery, ed. (New York: Costello., 1975).
Vogl, Carl, *Begone Satan*, Celestine Kapsner O.S.B., trans. (Collegeville: St John's Abbey, 1935).
von Balthasar, Hans Urs, *Dare We Hope 'That All Men Be Saved?'* (San Francisco, CA: Ignatius Press, 1999).
von Balthasar, Hans Urs, *Origen, Spirit and Fire: A Thematic Anthology of His Writings*, Robert J. Daly S. J., trans. (Washington, DC: Catholic University of America Press, 1984).
von Balthasar, Hans Urs, *The Glory of the Lord* 4 (Edinburgh: T&T Clark, 1989).
Waddell, Mark A., *Jesuit Science and the End of Nature's Secrets* (Farnham: Ashgate, 2015).
Walker, D. P., *Unclean Spirits: Possession and Exorcism in France and England in the Late Sixteenth and Early Seventeenth Centuries* (London: Scolar Press, 1981).
Walker, E. V., 'Demons and Disenchantment', in *Disguises of the Demonic: Contemporary Perspectives on the Power of Evil*, Alan M. Olson, ed. (New York: Association Press, 1975).
Warner, Michael, Jonathan Vanantwerpen and Craig Calhoun, eds, *Varieties of Secularism in a Secular Age* (Cambridge, MA: Harvard University Press, 2010).
Wayne, Viney Donald and George W. Shields, 'Charles Hartshorne: Dipolar Theism', in *Internet Encyclopedia of Philosophy ISSN 2161-0002,* https://iep.utm.edu/29/01/22.
Weber, Alison, 'Saint Teresa, Demonologist', in *Culture and Control in Counter-Reformation Spain,* Anne J. Cruz and Mary Elizabeth Perry, eds (Minneapolis: University of Minnesota Press, 1992).
Webster, John, 'Introducing Barth', in *The Cambridge Companion to Karl Barth,* John Webster, ed. (Cambridge: Cambridge University Press, 2000).
Webster, John, *The Displaying of Supposed Witchcraft Wherein It Is Affirmed That There Are Many Deceivers and Impostors* (London: Printed by J.M., 1677).
Wendel, François, *Calvin: The Origin and Development of His Religious Thought*, Philip Mairet, trans. (London: Collins, 1969).
Whelan, Ruth, 'Biodegradable Calvin', *Doctrine and Life*, vol. 60, no. 1 (January 2010): 36.
Wiesel, Elie, *All Rivers Run to the Sea* (New York: Knopf Doubleday, 2010).
Wilde, Oscar, *The Picture of Dorian Gray* (Harmondsworth: Penguin Books, 1962).
Wiley, Irena, *Around the Globe in Twenty Years* (New York: David McKay, 1962).
Wilkinson, David, *Christian Eschatology and the Physical Universe* (London: T&T Clark International, 2010).
Wright, N. T., *Surprised by Hope* (London: S.P.C.K., 2007).

Young, Francis, *A History of Exorcism in Catholic Christianity* (Switzerland: Palgrave Macmillan, 2016).

Young, Francis, *A History of Anglican Exorcism: Deliverance and Demonology in Church Ritual* (London: Bloomsbury Publishing, 2018).

Zachar, Peter, 'Epistemic Iteration or Paradigm Shift', in *Philosophical Issues in Psychiatry IV*, Kenneth Kendler and Josef Parnas, eds (Oxford: Oxford University Press, 2017).

Zeeden, Ernst Walter, *Das Zeitalter der Gegenreformation* (Basel: Herder-Bücherei, 1967).

Ziegler, Philip, *The Black Death* (London: Guild Publishing, 1992).

Zimbardo, P., *The Lucifer effect: How good people turn evil* (London: Random House, 2007).

Zizioulas, John D., *Being as Communion: Studies in Personhood and the Church* (Crestwood NY: Saint Vladimir's Seminary, 1993).

Zumther, Paul, 'The Turning-Point of Romanticism', in Anon., *Satan* (London: Sheed and Ward, 1951).

INDEX OF NAMES

Abraham, Abba 95
Abraham, Patriarch 70, 183, 221
Adam 14, 75–6, 80, 120–1, 130, 274
Adenauer, Konrad 279
Ahab 63
Alighieri, Dante 73, 111–12, 117
Álvarez, Catalina 175
Ambrose 16, 140
Aminadab 182–3
Amorth, Gabriele 211, 217, 278, 288–92, 295, 298, 303
Ananias 70
Anderson, Anthony 206–7
Anselm of Canterbury 20, 32, 104
Antony of Egypt 78–81, 83
Aquinas, Thomas 10, 14, 19, 22–3, 26, 27–30, 32–4, 51, 55, 100, 104–7
Aránzazu 150
Arendt, Hannah 241–2
Ariel, David 41
Aristotle 19, 100, 104, 112
Arius 98
Asmodeus 291
Augustine 5, 11, 13, 15–19, 20, 22, 30, 34, 55–6, 90–107, 112, 112, 127–9, 142, 144, 178, 257–8, 298
Augustus 117
Avicenna 112
Azazello 235

Baglio, Matt 293
Barré, Pierre 258
Barron, Robert 303
Barrow, John D. 57
Barth, Karl 42–5, 48–51, 270, 288, 306, 309, 312
Basil, Saint 91, 253
Batteux, Charles 195
Baudelaire, Charles 200–1
Beatrice 116
Becker, Ernest 56

Beelzebub 69, 144, 196, 259–60, 291
Belloc, Hilaire 224
Beltrán, Don 153
Berlioz, Mikhail 232, 234
Bernard of Clairvaux 123
Berrigan, Daniel 314–16
Blatty, William 211, 277, 318
Boccaccio 118–19
Boethius 19
Bonaventure, Saint 250
Bonhoeffer, Dietrich 274
Bornkamm, Heinrich 130, 132
Borromeo, Carlo 119
Bossy, John 185
Boswell, Charles Stuart 113
Bourgeois, Abbot 266
Brakke, David 83
Branca d'Oria 116
Brandt, Karl 240
Brenan, Gerald 182
Brightman, Edgar 226
Brooke, Rupert 213, 216
Brown, Peter 16, 85–6
Brown, Raymond 65
Browne, Steven 261
Brunner, Emil 282
Bruno, Giordano 50
Brutus 115
Buber, Martin 281–3, 288–9
Bucer, Martin 147, 267
Bulgakov, Mikhail 231–6
Bullinger, Kasper 292
Bunyan, John 192

Cajetan, Cardinal 130
Calvin, John
    Calvin and Barth 37–41
    Calvin and Erasmus 139
    Calvin and Plantinga 32
    early life and conversion 137–8
    Elizabeth I, Queen 184

exile to Basel 140
Institutes (1541) 138–40
references to devil 141–5
Cangrande della Scala 111
Cassian, John 79, 96–9
Cassius 115
Catherine von Bora 134
Cauchon, Pierre 254
Chadwick, Owen 152
Charles II, King 193, 261
Charles V, Emperor 154
Charles VII, King 254–5
Chillingworth, Roger 202–3
Chomsky, Naom 315
Christian, William A. 170
Chrysostom, Saint 96, 253
Coleridge, Samuel Taylor 199
Columbus, Christopher 127
Constanzo, Jésus 318
Cop, Nicolas 138
Copernicus, Nicolaus 137, 141, 143
Cordileone, Archbishop 277
Cornman, J. W. 23, 32
Coulton, George C. 110
Courtenay, William 124
Cranmer, Archbishop 267
Cromwell, Oliver 192
Cuneo, Michael 277

Daniel-Rops, Henri 154
Dawkins, Richard 36–7
Day, Dorothy 316
de Bourbon 260
de Bours, Jean 260
de Celano, Thomas 249–50
de Cepeda y Ahumada, Rodrigo 163
de Certeau, Michel 258
de Cisneros, Francisco 153
de Gaspari, Alcide 269
de Jesús, Aña 183
de Jesús, Crisógonó 176
de la Motte, Pierre 259
de Peñalosa, Aña 183
de Soto, Francisco 163
de Toledo, Garcia 162
de Voragine, Jacob 154
Demogenes 48, 78
Dibelius, Otto 238

Dimmesdale, Arthur 202, 205
Dominic, Saint 154
Dostoevsky, Fyodor 285, 312
Dryden, John 195
Dudgeon, Dick 206–8
Duffy, Eamon 185
Duncan, Marc 259
Durkheim, Émile 256

Eichmann, Adolf 241
El Greco 172
Elert, Werner 132
Elizabeth I, Queen 184
Elohim 43
Elymas Magos 71
Epicurus 2
Erasmus, Desiderius 39–40, 153
Eunomius 98

Farel, Guillaume 138
Fiddes, Paul 48
Finaghty, James 261
Flew, Anthony 26–7
Foch, Ferdinand 22–3
Ford, David 44
Forgione, Padre Pio 298
Francis of Assisi 247–50
Franklin, Benjamin 201
Franz Ferdinand, Archduke 222
Friedkin, William 211, 303
Froben, Hironymous 140

Gallagher, Richard 299–300
Gassner, Johann Joseph 262–3
Gerbel, Nicholas 132
Germanus 96
Gerson, Jean 123
Goddu, André 248–9
Godwin, William 195
Goethe, Johann Wolfgang 188, 197–8, 200
Gonzalo de Yepes 175
Gorky, Maxim 228
Grandier, Urbain 258
Gregg, Robert C. 85
Gregory Nazianzen 91
Guardini, Romano 54
Guido da Montefeltro 116
Gutenberg, Johannes 126

Haag, Herbert 271
Haig, Douglas 221–2
Hapsburgs 222
Hari, Johan 319
Harnack, Adolf 44
Hartshorne, Charles 10
Haugen, Frances 320
Hawthorne, Nathaniel 202–3
Hegel, G. W. F. 44
Henrietta, Queen 261
Hick, John 2, 10–11, 13, 19, 23–9
Hilary of Poitier 5
Himma, Kenneth 31–2
Hitler, Adolf 239–41
Höss, Crescentia 280
Hugo, Victor 199–200
Hume, David 2, 38
Huxley, Aldous 258

Ignatius of Loyola
  death 1556 160
  early life 153–4
  new vocation at Monserrat 156
  references to the devil, 157
  Society of Jesus, Rome (1539) 160
  Spiritual Exercises 157
  wounded at Pamplona 155
Irenaeus 10–14
Isabella, Queen 153

Jagger, Mick 317
James, William 205
Jeanne d'Arc 254
Joffre, Joseph 222
John of the Cross
  assaults by devil 178
  early life 175–6
  first exorcism 177
  imprisonment and escapes 179
  met Teresa of Ávila 176
  references to devil in his
    writings 179–82
John the Baptist 66, 260
Johnson, Samuel 195
Johnstone, Nathan 267
Joseph II, Emperor 264
Joshua, prophet 137
Journet, Charles 23
Judas Iscariot 65

Jung, C. G. 324–5
Justin Martyr 64, 76, 248

Keats, John 219
Keegan, John 212
Kelly, Henry Ansgar 308
Kierkegaard, Søren 319
King, Martin Luther 224–7
Knasas, John 26–9
Kornfeld, Boris 228–9
Koroviev 233, 235
Kramer 190
Kyd, Thomas 189
Kyper, Albert 191

Lactantius 1–3
Lainez, Diego 153, 160
Langland, William 121–2
Latimer, Hugh 184
Lauria, Isaac 42
Léfevre d'Etaples, Jacques 138
Leibniz, G. W. 3
Levi, Primo 224, 226, 232
Leviathan 62, 293
Lewis, C. S. 133, 208
Lewis, David 176
Lombard, Peter 19, 104, 114–18, 120, 122
Lucifer 104, 112
Ludolph 154, 157
Luther, Martin
  Anfechtungen 127
  the antichrist and the papacy 131
  apocalypticism 136
  early life 126–7
  exorcism 129
  Ninety-Five Theses 130
  Tischreden 133
  Wartburg experiences 132–3

Macarius 191
Mackie, J. L. 11, 26–7, 31, 33
Magdalena of the Cross 168
Maitland, James 258
Manson, Marilyn 318
Marguerite of Navarre 138
Maritain, Jacques 23
Marlowe, Christopher 184–7
  Faustus 187–9

Marot, Clément 138
Martin, Malachi 276-7
Martinez, Inés 170
Mazzotta, Giuseppe 117
McCabe O.P., Herbert 21-2, 28
McCann, Hugh J. 36
McCrae, John 214
Meissner S.J., W. W. 155-6
Meister, Chad 35-7
Melanchthon, Philip 130
Mephistopheles 188-9, 197-8, 233
Mesmer, Anton 266
Michael, Archangel 73, 79, 254
Michel, Annelise 291-2
Midelfort, H. C. 262, 264, 266
Milton, John 64, 117, 136, 188, 191-5
Moltmann, Jürgen 10, 270, 308-14
Monnet, Jean 269
Moser, Paul 39
Moses 79, 105
Muhammad 111
Müntzer, Thomas 139

Nájera, Duke of 153
Niebuhr, Helmut Richard 211
Nietzsche, Friedrich 35, 208

O'Connor, Cardinal John 312
Oberman, Heiko A. 124, 135
Obry, Nicole 259
Oppy, Graham 33, 35
Origen 78-80
Ormaneteo, Papal Nuncio 178
Osbourne, Ozzy 117
Otto, Rudolf 38-9
Owen, Wilfred 214, 218-21

Pachomius 79, 87-91
Palamon 88
Pannwitz, Dr 237
Pazuzu 62
Peter the Chanter 251
Peter, Burkhard 266
Peterson, Michael 11, 33
Philip the Fair 115
Plantinga, Alvin 9, 10, 11, 23
Plato 79, 101, 190
Poemon 95
Polanco 153

Pole, Alex 283
Poniryov, Ivan 232
Pontius Pilate 234
Pot, Pol 224
Prynne, Hester 202
Prynne, William 268
Pseudo-Dionysius 20, 104
Ptolemy 72, 100
Putin, Vladimir n55 299

Rahner S.J., Karl 51-4
Raphael, Archangel 74
Ratzinger, Joseph 271, 282-5, 288-9, 291, 304, 308
Reisenger, 262
Reni, Guido 205
Richelieu, Cardinal 258
Roest, Bert 248
Rosenberg, Isaac 214-16, 223
Rossetti, Stephen 295-8
Rubenson, Samuel 81
Rudwin, Maximilian 195
Ruse, Michael 14
Russell, Jeffrey Burton 273, 308-9
Russell, Ken 318
Russell, Robert J. 54

Sachs S.J., John R. 302
Sacks, Jonathan 41-2
Sample, Archbishop 277
Sassoon, Siegfried 214-16
Satan
    immobile, frustrated 44
    intelligent and cunning 114
    Satan's works, epiphanies 316
    Sathan 146
    shadowless 215
Schellenberg, J. L. 37-8
Schelling, F. W. 50
Serenus, Abbot 98
Serra, Junipero 277
Shakespeare, William 184, 186
Shaw, George Bernard 206, 208
Shawcross, John D. 195
Shelley, Percy Bysshe 194-5
Silas 70
Solzhenitsyn, Aleksandr 224, 227-9, 231
Southey, Robert 200, 203

Index of Names

Spalatin, George 131, 133
Sprenger 190
Steinbüchel, Theodor 282
Sterzinger, Ferdinand 243, 264
Stewart, Charles 253
Strauss, Johann 234
Suenens, Léon Joseph 275
Sundberg, Walter 10
Surin, Kenneth 9–10

Tauler, Joannes 124
Taylor, Charles 148
Teresa of Avila
  devil's appearances 171
  early life 159–63
  founded Monastery of St Joseph (1562) 170–3
  founded others until her death in 1582 179
  mystical visions 162
  near death experience 165
Tertullian 77–8, 105, 248, 271
Theodore, 89–90
Thomas, Gary 293–4
Tillich, Paul 311, 312–13, 317
Tipler, Frank 57
Tnugdalus 113
Tossati, Marco 290
Traum, Philip 188, 204
Trump, Donald 320
Twain, Mark 188, 202–3, 205

Underhill, Evelyn 124
Updike, John 202–3

Valentinian 11
Van Inwagen, Peter 11
Vanhoozer, Kevin J. 40
Velásquez, Don Juan 153
Viret, Pierre 141
Virgil 14, 116, 117
Voltaire 198, 200
von Balthasar, Hans Urs 286–7, 302
von Bora, Catherine 134
von Eschenmayer, C. A. 265
von Fugger-Glött, Anton 264
Von Galen, Clemens 240
Von Hindenberg, Paul 222
von Rheineck, Elias 110
Von Stauffenberg, Count Claus 241
Von Staupitz, Johann 127

Walker, D. P. 259
Webster, John 191
Wiesel, Elie 236
Wilde, Oscar 186–7
Wilhelm II, Kaiser 222
Woland, Professor 233–5
Wordsworth, William 199
Wormwood 209–11
Wotton, Lord Henry 186
Wycliffe, John 122

Young, Francis 262

Zebulun 291
Zechariah, Prophet 6
Zizioulas, John 295
Zuckerberg, Mark 320

INDEX OF SUBJECTS

abba 94–6
abdomen 193
abode, subterranean 72–3, 200
Abschied von Tuefel 271
absurdity 196, 200
abyss 52–4, 73
   of God 124, 138
   of hell 209, 235
   of loneliness 282
Act of Pardon 193
Acta Sanctorum 249
Adamic myth 273
Adiaphoron 255
adolescent 164
affections, perverse 140–2
African cultures 268, 317
Against the Execrable Bull 131
Against the Papacy at Rome 131
aggiornamento 271
agnostic 23, 38–9, 55, 209, 269–70
Aktion T4 240
algorithm 320
allegory 111, 196
allurement 132
Almagest 72
altercation 135
alumbrado 154
Amadís de Gaula 153, 163
ambition 91, 153, 189, 32, 325
ambivalence 51, 158
analogy 26, 48–9, 65, 239, 288, 311
anarchic lyrics 238
Anfechtungen 127, 132, 311
angels
   good 6, 16, 54, 64–5, 70, 75, 99, 100,
      108, 120, 147, 155
   fallen 22, 24, 52, 74, 76, 78, 100–3, 114,
      116–17, 121
Anglican(ism) 3, 185, 187, 189, 192,
   194–5, 209, 218, 220, 223, 268–70
Anhalt 255

animal magnetism 266
'Anthem for Doomed Youth' 219
Anthropic Cosmological Principle, The 57
anthropodicy 44
anthropology, theological 12, 32, 258, 272
anthropomorphic 63–4, 109, 196, 325
Antichrist 72, 115–16, 130, 133,
   136, 317–18
Antichrist Superstar 318
antiquarianism 270
antisemitism 236
anxiety 73, 83, 127–8
apatheia 91
apocatastasis 30, 301, 309
Apostolic Tradition 248
apparitions 85, 10–11, 173, 253
aquarium 237
Arabic culture 112
Aristotelianism 190
arms race 314
Aryan Cleansing 240
Ascent of Mount Carmel 176, 179
assault (by devil) 82, 84, 87, 91–3, 127–8,
   132, 139, 144–5, 178, 182, 250,
   267, 297–9
astronomers 100, 137
astronomy 127
atheism 37, 39, 61, 185, 232
atheists 11, 30, 33, 35, 37–8, 270
Auschwitz 27, 52, 236, 240, 242
Austrian village 204
autonomy, human 25
averah 42
aversion 195, 290, 304

Baal worship 61–2
baptism 5, 30, 79, 95, 102, 129, 148,
   250–2, 255–6, 271–2, 275
*Baptism, Eucharist and Ministry
1982-1990* 275
baroque 172

360　　　　　　　　　　　　　*Index of Subjects*

Bastille 200
Bavarian Academy of Sciences 263
beauty 11, 186, 199, 215
bedclothes 178
beer 134
beggar(s) 156, 220
behafft 128
belly 83, 86, 196
besessen 128
Big Bang 56
bitterness 201, 225
black bile (melancholy) 262
black boy 83
Black Death 118
Black Sabbath 317
blasphemy, blasphemies 92, 158, 197
Blind Watchmaker, The 36
boardroom 322
Body and Society, The 86
bogey, half 133
Bolshevik Revolution 227
Book of Common Prayer 267
Book of Hours 109
Book of Job 197
Book of Jubilees 74
Book of Wisdom 6, 272
bowels 133–4, 215–16
bread 70, 84, 88, 147, 256
'Break of Day in the Trenches' 214–15
brokenness of thought, theology 50
Buddhism 247
Buna concentration camp 236
bureaucracy 241, 315
Bystander Effect 323
Byzantine Church 252

Cacodemon 191
capitalism 313
career 127, 129, 132, 137, 140, 153, 155, 161, 188, 224, 232, 255, 262, 291
Carthusian Order 159, 176
casualties 217, 317
Catechism of the Catholic Church 284
Catharist 252
cauldron, devil's 318
cenobitic 88–9, 97, 100
censorship 231
certainty, moral 279, 281, 289
charismatic movement 275

Chester Pageant, the 121
chimera 213, 237
Christian life 81–2, 87, 95, 127, 140, 157, 162, 210
Church Dogmatics 43–6, 50, 270, 306
City of God 102, 105–6
Civil Rights Movement 225
cleaner technologies 322
climate reports 314
cloister 128
Code of Canon Law 280
Cold War 314
Commentary on Galatians 130
Commentary on Psalm 145 145
Commentary on the Psalms 137
Commonwealth, Cromwellian 192
Communist 224
Complutensian Polyglot Bible 152
concentration camps 237–8, 240
Concerning the Jews 205
conciliarism 123
Confessions 17, 113
conflict, internecine 212
conflict
　erotic, phallic 156
conscience 147, 222, 228, 237
consciousness 71, 84, 123, 205, 37, 296, 299–300, 306, 324–5
consent 265, 280, 295
Constitution on Divine Revelation 123
continuum 299, 323
Contra Arianos 81
Contra Julianum 129
controversy 96, 130, 139, 255, 260, 262
conundrum 4, 307
Convent of St Joseph 170
Convent of the Incarnation 164
converso 161
Convocation of Clergy 184
corporate 30, 311
corporate business 321–2
corruption 17–19, 21, 102, 115, 206, 273, 306, 322
cosmos, cosmology 72, 160, 109, 199
Councils
　Constance 123
　Fourth Lateran 248
　Fifth Lateran 152
　Trent 152

Vatican II 6
Counter-Reformation 151–2
countries
   Argentina 277
   Austria 203
   Belgium 213
   Brazil 277
   Cambodia 224
   Denmark 256
   Egypt 78
   England 109
   France 109
   Germany 110
   Hungary 236
   Ireland 261
   Italy 115
   Japan 230
   Kazakhstan 227
   Korea 224
   Mexico 277
   Netherlands 222
   Poland 226
   Portugal 222
   Romania 236
   Russia 236
   Spain 152
   Taiwan 230
   USA 99
   Vietnam 224
covenant 192
Coventry Passion Play 120
covetousness 322
Craiglockhart Military Hospital 218
credulity 107, 189
crime 28, 196, 240
critique 10, 19, 27, 35, 116, 137, 197, 230–1, 291
Crucified Christ, The 270
crucifix 265
Crystal Palace Exhibition 212
culture 64, 99, 185, 198, 313
culture wars 316
curandera 164
curiosity
   demonic 291
   excessive 258
   natural 195
   personal 237
   theoretical 53

Dachau 239
damnation 142, 185, 267, 301–2
Damnation of Faust, The 232
Dark Night of the Soul, The 176, 180
Darwinian perspective 35
Das Nichtige 45–6, 51, 288, 307, 312
Das Volk 238
De Civitate Dei 18
De Genesi ad Litteram 18
De Incarnatione 81
De libero arbitrio 18
De Monarchia 112
De Mystica Theologia 123
De natura boni 18
De Oratione 79
De Principiis 79
Dead Sea Scrolls, The 61
'Dead, The' 213
Decameron 118
Decapolis 68
defamation 180
defeat, of evil, Satan 5, 50–1, 64, 66, 73, 77, 83, 97, 109, 115, 117, 169, 194, 196, 243
Defence of Poetry 194
deist(ic) 2, 26, 197
delation 161
deliverance 49, 167, 275–6
demonic
   activities 93, 98, 106, 118, 243
   attacks 95
   dream 95
   forces 4, 42, 284–5
   influence 248, 276
   manifestation 296
   offspring 74
   possession 6, 49, 248, 251, 267, 280, 284–5, 289–90, 299
   presence 300
Demonic Foes 299
demonology 73, 77, 79, 82, 83–6, 98–9, 102, 105, 108, 122, 190–1, 233, 267, 276, 309–10
demonries 312
demon(s) 94, 98–9, 312–13, 315
Demons and the Devil 253
Demons and the Making of the Monk 83
demythologisation 271

depravity 196, 212
deprivation 54, 86, 320, 323
derangement, mental 2
de-sacralisation 136–7, 148, 192
desolation 158–9
despair, bouts of 93, 133, 172, 177, 198, 226
Deus absconditus 37, 43
development, sustainable 314
devil(s). *See also* Satan
   cauldron 318
   contrasting conclusions 308
   envy 65
   father of lies 117, 276, 307
   half buffoon 133
   hominization of 192
   illusions of 135
   incurable 225
   Malignus 273
   mighty No of God 307
   quasi-personality 308
Devils of Loudon 258
Devil's Disciple, The 206
diabology 130, 133, 139, 187, 309
dialectical method 43
Dialogue of the Body and the Soul, The 113
Diarium 267
Diary of an American Exorcist 295
dictatorship 323
Dido 185
Die Leiden des jungen Werthers 198
Din 42
dinosaurs 27
disadvantaged economically 320
disasters, natural 1, 306
Discalced Orders 174, 176, 178, 261
discernment 4, 154–5, 157
discipline, personal 84, 127, 238, 257
discontent 174, 320–1
Discours de la Possession de Religieuses 259
disease(s) 27, 62, 69, 77, 93, 118–19, 129, 190–1, 240, 262, 264
disenchantment 148
Dissociative Identity Disorder 328
Divina Commedia 111–12, 115, 117, 122
Divine Hiddenness 37–9
Document Q 65
'Does It Matter?' 217
Dogmatics in Outline 45

dream
   angelic 95
   demonic 95
dualistic
   doctrine 75
   tendencies 150
   train of thought 28
'Dulce Et Decorum Est' 219

earthquake 18, 70, 120
Easter 49, 123
ecclesiopolitical issues 123
ecological crisis 230
ecosystems 322
Edward II 185
Eichmann in Jerusalem 241
Einsatzgruppen 240
Eisleben 126
Elizabethan Age 184
emanation 41–2
emigration, forced 239
Empire, Holy Roman 263
empirical science 36, 54–6, 57–8, 148, 190
enchantment 51, 108, 149
Enchiridion 139
endosomatic, exosomatic 155
English Faust Book, The 188
Enlightenment, the 194, 197
entropy 5, 54–5, 56–7
environmental credits 321
epistemic, distance 25, 39
epistemology 39
eschatological 26, 39, 66, 73
Eschaton 57
Essay on Man 223
ethnic cleansing 242, 306
eugenics, euthanasia 239–40
evil
   absence of good 10, 20
   forces 5
   foul and misshapen 16
   hypothesis 199
   metaphysical 56
   moral 3
   mystery 226
   natural 18–19, 55
   negation 22
   origin 27

pervading 224
privation of good 20, 288
evolution 25, 36, 54–5
execution 65, 184, 232, 258
exile 42, 96, 112, 123, 138, 227–30, 243
exorcism 66, 67–78, 129, 144, 172, 177–8, 191, 243, 247–78, 279–305
Exorcism and Related Supplications 276
Exsurge Domine 131
Eyn Sof 41

Facebook 319–20
facsimiles 179
Faith of the Church, The 45
Fall, historical 120, 130
fantasies 111, 132, 164, 188
'Farewell to the Devil' 283
fascism 323
fasting 83, 97
feather, demon's 199
fertiliser, pit of 56
fever 69, 144–5
fig tree 90–1
Final Conflict 318
Final Solution 10, 239, 240
financial
    fraud 321
    losses 314
    success 291
'Finished with War. A Soldier's Declaration' 218
firmament 16
flagellants 119
flames 114–15, 17, 158
flesh 5, 14, 115, 117, 158
Fonteviros 175
fornication, spirit of 61, 74, 94
free will 18–19, 27, 31, 33, 226, 289, 30
fugitive 193

Gadara 68
galaxies 54
gallows 207
gambling 153
gargoyles, grotesques 108
gas masks 220
Gascons, covetous 116
gene pool 36, 240
Geneva Catechism 45

global level 320
Gnostics 11–13
God's existence 25, 30, 32–3, 37, 40, 41, 43, 46, 126, 315
Golden Legend, The 113
gouges 297
Grand Inquisitor 312
Great Depression 234
Great Purge 243
Greek Orthodox Church 252
Guide for the Perplexed, A 35
guilt(y) 46, 72, 198, 202, 225, 227–8, 230–1, 236–9, 274, 278, 310–11, 323, 330
Gulag Archipelago, The 228–9, 231, 236

hagiographical genre 86
hallucinations 174, 324–5
harassment 135, 178
hardship 53, 133, 166, 180, 219, 239, 290
Harmony of the Gospels 144
Harrowing of Hell, The 120–1
Harz Mountains 198
hatred 3, 32, 102, 184, 206, 211, 225, 294
headaches 165, 259, 263
heaven 16, 43, 63, 72–4, 76, 80, 80, 82–3, 87–8, 105, 109, 112–13, 115, 119, 121–2, 136–7, 158, 187, 189, 193, 195, 199, 209, 304
Heavy Metal 317
Heidelberg Catechism 256
Heidelberg Disputation 129
hell 6, 45, 111–12, 116–17, 120–2, 164–5, 169, 172–3, 186, 189–90, 194, 209, 227, 285, 296
heresy 111, 124, 252, 254
hermit 83, 97, 254
Hesed 42
hidalgo 161
Hinduism 247
Hitler Youth 239
Holocaust 28, 202, 212, 236
homoerotic style 219
hospital 67, 156, 175, 179, 218, 220, 228
Hostage to the Devil 276
Huguenots 259
human race, computer simulation 56, 58
human trafficking 306
humanism 137–9, 312
Hyalou 253

hypnotherapy 266
hypocrisy 99, 166, 203

I and Thou 281, 283
idolatry 39, 105
imperative exorcism 269, 272, 276, 280, 289, 303
imperialism 185
imprisonment 179, 242, 339
'In Flanders Field' 214
incantations 67, 249, 256
inconsistencies 9, 85
incubi 101, 106
Indulgences 130
industrialisation 198
Inferno 112–13, 115, 117, 257
infestation 132
influencers 311
injury, permanent 55–6, 222, 298
Inquisition 154, 161, 162–3, 190, 254–5
insufflation 255, 280
intelligence 162, 315
Interior Castle 170
International Association of Exorcists 286–7, 291
International Court of Justice 314
Interpretation of History 311
Introduction to Christianity 28
invalided 219
invisible 73, 147
invocative exorcism 272, 276, 280
Irish Precursor of Dante, An 113
Islam(ic) 1, 77, 111, 175

Jewish ancestry 216
Jewish population 223, 239–40
Judaism 42, 67, 228, 247
Judenrein 242
Just War Theory 242, 314

Kabbalah 41–2
keys, three musical 160
Khmer Rouge 224
Kingdom of God in America, The 231
Klingenberg 291
Krystallnacht 239
Kulturkampf 316
Kyoto Protocol 44

La Fin de Satan 199
La Possession de Loudun 59
La Storta 160
landscape, devastated 219
Laon 260
laughter 50, 193
laws, natural 18–20, 32, 89, 91
laxity, moral 183
Le Figaro 200
Le Jouer Généreux 201, 260
Learned Helplessness 323
'Les Litanies de Satan' 201
Letter from Birmingham City Jail 225
Letters to Satan 205
Libertines 143
libido 156
life as information processing 57
Life of Christ 154, 157
Linee guida per il ministero dell'esorcismo 286
'Live Not by Lies' 229
Living Flame of Love 176
locusts 62
locutions 168–9, 179
logismoi 92–3
Lollards 122
Lodun 258–9
Luther: Man between God and the Devil 135
Lyrical Ballads 199

magic 71
magician 76, 118, 148
magnetism 190, 266
Making of Late Antiquity, The 85
Malleus Malificarum 190
malum culpae 21
malum poenae 21
Manichees 15–16
martyrdom 13, 113, 163, 166, 227
Martyrology of Oengus the Culdee 113
Massacre, The 185
massacres, mass suicides 318
Master and Margarita, The 231
materialism 306
measuring rod 44
meat, computers made of 57
media 310–11, 319
melancholy 113, 199, 262

Index of Subjects

Mental Health Acts 323
mentality, scientific 141
Messianic figures 43, 318
miracle of Laon 260
mire 116, 138
'Misconception of Nothingness' 46–7
modernity 77, 141, 149, 190
Moments of Reprieve 236
Montgomery Bus Boycott 225
moon 69, 80, 137, 204, 35
Moors 153
mountains 155, 164, 198, 235
mousetrap 104
mule ridden by God or devil 136
multinational 321
mutilation 300
Mysterious Stranger, The 188
Mystery Plays 108, 119
mysticism 79, 123–4, 162

napalm bombs 53
narcissistic, phallic 156
National Socialists 238, 240
Nazi regime 228, 224
neck 90, 134, 205, 207, 300
networks, social 319
neurosis 263
newspaper 232, 291, 319
Noah, Book of 74
noetic structure 33
Nominalism 126
non-believers 34
non-corporeal 64
non-theists 35
nothingness 40, 45, 46–9, 50, 52, 54–5, 199
numinous 39

oath 206, 241
Observant Augustinians 127
obsessed 128, 133, 183, 203, 275, 396
occult 190, 203, 275, 296
odour, offensive 173
oil of exorcism 248
'Old Vicarage, Grantchester, The' 213
Omega point 57
Omen, The 318
On the Jews and Their Lies 238
On the Wrath of God 1
One Day in the Life of Ivan Denisovich 227

ontological argument 20, 31
oppression 124–5, 297
optimism, evolutionary 57
option fondamentale 302–3
Original Sin 30, 102, 272, 311
Orthodox Book of Prayers 253
orthodoxy, Anglican 185

pacifist 210, 218–19
pandemics 306
papacy 113, 115–17, 130–1, 134–5, 143, 145, 152
Paphos 71
'Parable of the Old Men and the Young, The' 219
Parable of the Prodigal Son 48
Paradise Regained 193
Paradiso 115
paranormal 6, 300
parental relationship 25
passions 92
pathologies, psychological 311
Patillas (devil) 162
Peace Pledge Union 218
pentagram 197
persecution 13, 113, 239, 243
personality functions 324
personification 6, 194, 284, 290
Persuasive Technological Laboratories 319
perturbations 143
Pew Research Center 270
philosophes 200
philosophy 15–16, 92, 104, 113, 281, 286
Physics of Immortality 57
Picture of Dorian Gray, The 186
Pilgrim's Progress 192
plastic arts 108
polarised views 306
polemical 143
poltergeists 132
Pondorf 264
pop culture 313, 327
popes
  Adrian V 116
  Benedict XIV 280
  Benedict XVI 283
  Boniface VIII 115
  Clement V 112
  Francis 321

Innocent III 116
John XXIII 270
Leo X 131
Nicholas III 115
Paul III 160
Pius VI 264
Portland 269, 277
Possessed, The 285
possession 6, 66, 68, 94, 116, 200, 248–9, 251, 253, 258, 260, 263, 267–8, 293–4, 296, 297, 299–300, 303–5, 318, 328
postmodern culture 275
post-traumatic stress disorder 327
powers, prodigious 201
predestined 143
Preface to Paradise Lost, A 196
pre-modern 126
preternatural 109, 190–1
preternatural order 108
Primitz 135
principalities and powers 72–3, 75, 255
professionals, medical, 240, 270, 280
progress, technological 126, 199
protest, social 318
Providence, Divine 19, 21, 47–8, 53, 56, 142, 149, 153, 179, 204
Prussianism 219
psychiatric illness 290
psychoanalysis 155
psychology 258, 263, 266, 295, 324, 328
psychosis 323, 327–8
Punk Rock 317
Purgatorio 115–16
Purgatory 111
Puritanism 187, 191, 195

quarantining 119
Qumram 74
Qur'an 76

rage, demoniacal 319
raptures 181
reassurance, Christian 309
rebellion 46, 76, 81, 99, 200
Red Army 238
reductio ad absurdum 57
reformatio 57
relics 254
religious conviction lacking 223

religious practice, resurgence 269
Renewal and the Power of Darkness 275
resentment 228, 239
ressourcement 270
Resurrection 5, 24, 49, 56, 109, 117
revelation 39–41, 43–4
revenge 177, 196, 202, 217, 237
rhetoric 6, 159, 214
Rhétoriquers 138
rider, skilled *v.* wanton 142
Rite of Exorcism 4, 257, 267, 272, 276, 279, 282, 296
Rite, the Making of a Modern Exorcist, The 293
Rituale Romanum 258, 261–2
Roger's Version 202
Romantic Movement 194, 199, 203
Rosemary's Baby 318
ruthlessness 321

salt, spilling superstition 136
samizdat 232
San Gimignano 250
San Jose diocese 293
San Juan de la Cruz 176
San Rafael 269
Sarum Rite 267
Satan. *See also* devil 90, 132, 196, 202, 235, 275, 285–6, 289–90, 292, 297–8, 312, 318, 320
Satanic cults 275
Satanic School 200, 20
satyrs 132
Scarlet Letter 202–3
school shootings 318
Schöpfung und Fall 274
Screwtape Letters, The 208
Sea of Galilee 68
Second Temple 62–3
secularisation 192, 270, 277, 313
segregation, racial 224–6
selection, natural 55
sensuous particulars 219–20
sensuousness 206
Sequences 224
sexualised culture 162
Shaddai 43
shadowside 47, 54
Sherston Trilogy 216

shevirat 41
Sickness unto Death, The 319
Siegfried's Journey 223
sins 29, 48, 80, 95, 115, 118, 173, 180, 186, 287
Slade School 214
social networks 318
Society of Jesus 152
soul-making 26–7, 29–30
Spirit, Holy 71, 97, 141, 145, 168–9, 191, 255, 272, 305, 314
Spiritual Canticle 176, 181
Spiritual Exercises 155, 157, 181
Spring Festival 234
St Vitus Dance 264
sterilisation 240
starvation 225, 236, 240
stigma, social 202
Stockholm Syndrome 323
'Strange Meeting' 219
Strength to Love 225
suicide 186, 198, 228, 234, 256, 228, 318–19
Summma de Sacramentis 251
Sumptuary Laws 267
superstitions 127, 138, 145, 147
Supputatio Annorum Mundi 136
sustainable development 314
Sympathy for the Devil 317–18
synthesis 306–8, 314, 324

taboos 149
Taoism 50
Taufbuechlein 256
tectonic plates 18
terror 172, 188
Thebaid 87
Theologica Germanica 128
theology, fundamental 307
theory of everything 306
thermodynamics 36
Tikkum olam 42
TikTok 319
Timaeus 190
Tischreden 128
'To Victory' 217
tragedy 133, 175, 23, 216, 242, 318
transcendence 41, 145, 149
transparency 322
transverberation 169

Treatise on the Miracles of Blessed Francis 250
trench warfare 23–4
Truce, The 236
Tübingen 285
Twitter 319
tyranny 145, 241
tzimtzum 40

ultimate concern 313
Umbruch des Denkens 282
Un Office byzantin d'Esorcisme 252
United Nations 314
Urania 193
urbanisation 198
Ursuline nuns 259

vanity 164, 181
Varieties of Religious Experience, The 205
vaskania 252
Vervins 259
via antiqua 126
via moderna 126
Vida de San Juan de la Cruz 176
violence 28, 77, 225, 277, 308, 316–17
Visio Tnugdali 173
Vision of Piers Plowman, The 121–3
Vita Secunda 250
volcano 19, 27

war
　First World 212
　incessant 142
　Second World 227
　Vietnam 224
Wartburg 132
Washington diocese 295
whistleblower 320
why does God allow us to suffer? 52
Why You Can't Pay Attention 319
witchcraft 110
witches' coven 198
witch hunt 136
Wittenberg 127, 128
world view 15, 108, 117–18, 135–6, 190, 192, 267, 271, 309, 326
'Worm Fed on the Heart of Corinth, A' 215
Worms, Synod of 131